THE BIRTH OF MODERN BELIEF

The Birth of
Modern Belief

FAITH AND JUDGMENT
FROM THE MIDDLE AGES
TO THE ENLIGHTENMENT

Ethan H. Shagan

PRINCETON UNIVERSITY PRESS
PRINCETON & OXFORD

Published by Princeton University Press
41 William Street, Princeton, New Jersey 08540
6 Oxford Street, Woodstock, Oxfordshire OX20 1TR

press.princeton.edu

Library of Congress Control Number: 2018937605
First paperback printing, 2021
Paperback ISBN 978-0-691-21737-6
Cloth ISBN 978-0-691-17474-7

British Library Cataloging-in-Publication Data is available

Editorial: Brigitta van Rheinberg, Eric Crahan, and Pamela Weidman
Production Editorial: Karen Carter
Cover Design: Lorraine Doneker
Jacket/Cover Credit: Hieronymus Bosch (c. 1450–1516),
Ascent of the Blessed, c. 1500, oil on panel, 86.5 cm × 39.5 cm
Production: Jacquie Poirier
Publicity: Tayler Lord
Copyeditor: Karen Verde

This book has been composed in Miller

For Jonathan Sheehan

CONTENTS

Ret.

Sat: Intro
Sun: Ch 1-2
Mon: Ch 3-4
Tue: Ch 5-6
Wed: Ch 7 + Con.

LEO TOLSTOY once likened historians to deaf people who go on answering questions no one has asked. That is a fair description of what it has felt like to write this book. People often ask me about religious beliefs, but no one ever asked me about the history of belief itself, and colleagues give me strange looks when I tell them about it anyway. I have tried to dispel their perplexity by describing my project as "Shapin for religion": that is, like Steven Shapin's classic *A Social History of Truth*, but with religious rather than scientific knowledge as its focus. But in the end that is only partially accurate, both because I cannot live up to such a high standard, and because Shapin focused like a laser on a particular moment, while I range over centuries to trace the origins of what I argue is a peculiarly modern credulity. My effort to write a history of modern belief is therefore (at least in part, and with due deference to my predecessors) an attempt to create a subject. Is Tolstoy's historian more or less pitiable if, rather than being deaf, he merely insists that people have not been asking him the right questions?

My inspirations to attempt such sweeping folly are two of my many mentors: Ted Rabb and the late Lawrence Stone. I admit Stone's influence only with hesitation, because he was so often accused of exceeding the bounds of his expertise. In what remains one of the most acerbic academic reviews of all time, Edward Thompson wrote, "Where other historians might spend weeks in covering up their own sensitive areas of ignorance, Stone shouts, 'Don't know!' and walks blithely into them." My excuse for following Stone into those sensitive areas is that, having tried with inevitably limited success (but for much more than weeks!) to cover my own boundless ignorance, I nonetheless continue to believe that the real point of cobbling together learning is to be able to write books about forests rather than trees. Rabb's influence is less fraught and more practical. In his landmark 1975 book, *The Struggle for Stability in Early Modern Europe*, he explained that the era was defined by a crisis of epistemic authority: political, economic, artistic, and religious debates all reduced to the fundamental question, "Can one rely on anything?" As a mentor, he impressed upon me that early modernity is the most fascinating era in European history because it was an epistemic watershed between past and present. If this book contributes anything to our understanding of that epochal transformation, it is because of his influence.

But those were early inspirations; more proximately, I owe thanks to many scholars, both at Berkeley and elsewhere, who have helped me to make sense of this vast, sprawling subject. My greatest intellectual debt by far is to Jonathan Sheehan. For a long time, he and I intended to write this book together; during our regular morning coffees over several years, we bounced ideas off of one another and honed our sense of the problem. It is my deepest regret that, on the heels of another collaboration, he felt obliged to go in his own direction. But his fingerprints are everywhere in these pages. This would have been a very different book, and a far better one, if he had written it with me, but nonetheless it is much better for his influence. I dedicate this book to him with profound gratitude.

I have also been blessed to have at Berkeley a lively community of fellow scholars who have been barking up similar trees. Barbara Shapiro, Vicky Kahn, and Albert Ascoli have all written about the history of belief/faith from their different disciplinary perspectives, and I have benefited enormously from my conversations with them. In particular, in 2012 Albert and I co-convened a Collaborative Research Seminar entitled "Problems of Faith: Belief and Promise in Medieval and Early Modern Europe," generously funded by the Townsend Center for the Humanities, in which an interdisciplinary community of students and faculty met for weekly discussions; I owe profound thanks to the participants, especially the students who offered such original and compelling insights. Then in 2013, building on those discussions, we convened a large international conference, and I owe thanks to the participants for all that I learned from their presentations and engagement: Albert Ascoli, Lorna Hutson, Craig Muldrew, Walter Stephens, Joanna Picciotto, Edward Muir, Alex Dubilet, Robert Harkins, Jess Herdman, Lili Loofbourow, Steven Justice, Niklaus Largier, Nick Popper, Giovanna Ceserani, Jane Tylus, Diego Pirillo, Claire McEachern, David Marno, and Jonathan Sheehan.

Earlier versions of this book, or of individual chapters, were read by Jonathan Sheehan, Carla Hesse, Tom Laqueur, Mark Peterson, Alec Ryrie, Vicky Kahn, Steve Justice, Ed Muir, Bruce Gordon, Kinch Hoekstra, Susanna Elm, Geoff Koziol, Maureen Miller, and Tony Grafton. I owe them all enormous thanks, both for their comments and for their patience in slogging through what were sometimes very primitive versions. I have also benefited from conversations with many scholars with overlapping interests, including James Simpson, Kathryn Murphy, Alastair Bellany, Subha Mukherji, Peter Lake, George Hoffmann, Helena Skorovsky, Jane Shaw, Brad Gregory, Randall Zachman, Craig Harline, Debora Shuger, Regina Schwartz, David Sacks, Chris Ocker, Erik Midelfort, Remi Alie, Diarmaid MacCulloch, John Morrill, and many others whom I fear I am forgetting. At the "Crossroads of Knowledge" conference at Cambridge in 2012, I was privileged to engage with many fine scholars working at the intersection of religion and epistemology whom I would not otherwise have met, of whom I would like to thank particularly Sophie Read, Tim Stuart-Buttle, Tobias Gregory, and the indomitable Rowan Williams.

Material from this project has been presented at numerous scholarly venues: the Centre for Research in the Arts, Social Sciences and Humanities, Cambridge University; the Sixteenth Century Studies Conference (twice); the joint conference of the American Society for Church History and the American Catholic Historical Association; a conference entitled "Rethinking Early Modernity" at the University of Toronto; Clio Taiwan; Brigham Young University; Columbia University; Baylor University; the North American Conference on British Studies; and multiple times at different venues at the University of California, Berkeley. I owe thanks to all of the audiences for their constructive criticisms, without which this would be a much weaker book.

A confession about languages is in order: I am a terrible linguist. I have good French, mediocre Latin (I have been a second-year Latin student for the past twenty-two years), and bad German left over from university. With those languages as guides, I can and do hack my way through other romance languages—Spanish is much easier than Italian. To a much more limited degree, and if I can locate the relevant paragraph, I also hack my way through Dutch, especially early modern dialects that look German if you squint your eyes. But that is the extent of my ability, and I make no false claims of fluency. About half of the foreign-language works cited in these pages I read initially in English translation and then checked the relevant passages against the original; in those cases I have generally quoted the translation that I read, making occasional changes as noted. The other half of foreign-language works I read in their original languages and so the translations are my own. I hope it will be clear in the notes which translations are mine; but in any case, I have included many key words and occasionally whole passages from the original sources in brackets or in the notes. I owe thanks to many of the colleagues mentioned in these acknowledgments, especially Tony Grafton, for helping to save me from translation errors (although undoubtedly errors remain, for which I take full responsibility), and I owe thanks to my research assistant Jason Rozumalski for tracking down some of the original language sources. Richard Kagan encouraged me to have the confidence to read sources in Spanish despite my lack of training, and I will always be grateful for how much he liked my first readings of Juan de la Cruz.

I owe thanks to many people at Princeton University Press who have played a role in getting this book into the hands of readers: Brigitta van Rheinberg, Amanda Peery, Stephanie Rojas, Lorraine Doneker, Karen Verde, and Karen Carter. I also owe thanks to the Humanities Research Fellowship at Berkeley for funding a year of leave to write the rough draft. A small amount of material has appeared previously, in Ethan Shagan, "Taking Belief Seriously? An Early Modern Catholic Perspective," in Mark Jurdjevic and Rolf Strøm-Olsen, eds., *Rituals of Politics and Culture in Early Modern Europe: Essays in Honour of Edward Muir* (Toronto, 2016); and Ethan Shagan, "Towards a Modern Regime of Believing," *Archiv für Reformationsgeschichte* 108 (2017): 33–41.

Personal thanks are always the hardest part of academic acknowledgments. Is it enough to say that I owe thanks to everyone who has kept me sane during the years when I was simultaneously writing this book, chairing my department, and trying to raise two children? Rather than listing all of my family and friends individually, let me thank them collectively: it is because of you that I remain a human being first and a scholar second. But I could not possibly finish without acknowledging the love and support of my beloved New York family, Rena, Diana, Jillian, and Henry. Most important, I owe everything to my wife, Dr. Sarah Paul (it's a thing), and my children, Hannah and Noah. Thank you for believing in me.

THE BIRTH OF MODERN BELIEF

Introduction

BELIEF HAS A HISTORY: it changes over time. Countless historians have studied the content of religious belief, but the category itself—what it meant to believe—has stubbornly resisted historical analysis, even as it has been pondered by philosophers and theologians, and even as related categories like "truth" and "fact" have become robust objects of historical study. This resistance is not an accident. Secular historians of Christianity have needed a stable object called "belief" whose decline could be measured, while pious historians of Christianity have needed a stable object called "belief" to certify the identity of believers across time and space. They have thus conspired to treat belief as a default condition, indivisible and irreducible, with iterations rather than history. This book argues, by contrast, that belief changed. Between the Middle Ages and the Enlightenment, successive revolutions in religious knowledge refashioned what it meant to believe, dissolving old certainties and producing a distinctively modern space of belief. The transformation of belief, rather than the rise of unbelief, propelled Western thought into modernity.

MAIN
ARG.

The resulting configuration has shaped the conditions of religion in a secular age.

An illustrative example, suggesting that belief itself rather than its supposed eclipse might be worthy of investigation, can be found in a remarkable debate that occurred on the banks of the Rhine River in the summer of 1538. The instigator was a Dutchman named David Joris, a glass painter by profession but by vocation an Anabaptist preacher, a scion of the most radical branch of the Reformation. Three years earlier, the Anabaptists had suffered a devastating defeat when their stronghold at Münster was sacked and the mangled bodies of their leaders were exhibited in iron cages. In response to this debacle, Joris declared himself a prophet, the "Third David," whose divine visions would lead the scattered Anabaptists into a spiritual age. After recruiting the Anabaptists at Oldenburg, Joris traveled to Strasbourg to appeal to the followers of the imprisoned Anabaptist leader Melchior Hoffman. In a three-day conference, transcribed so that the manuscript could be smuggled to Hoffman in jail, Joris attempted to win their allegiance.[1] But remarkably, rather than offering examples of his prophecies or other reasons why they ought to believe him, Joris repeatedly told the Melchiorites, "If you will first believe me, then I will speak to you."[2] That is, he refused to give them any account of his revelations until *after* they had agreed to believe him, because without belief there can be no understanding.

Not so fast, said the Melchiorite spokesman Jan Pont: "All faith stands on truth and reason. Therefore prove your pretensions, then we will believe." Joris responded angrily: "You know that a child never understands his elders. For this reason, how can I give the judgment, of those things about which I must speak, to you?"[3] The next day, Pont's uncertainty had grown into blunt skepticism: "We must become convinced by you with reasonable proofs, or otherwise we would make useless disciples for you. Surely you do not desire that we believe you without reasonable proofs, for that belief has no endurance."[4] But Joris would not budge: "If you will now believe me and give yourselves to fulfill it, then you could understand the spirit, without which you cannot understand me. But how can you understand me, when you refuse to believe me?"[5] Or again, Joris told them, "You do not hear or believe me, instead you desire to understand everything, as if you had the wisdom." To which Peter van Geyen responded, "Should I believe that you have more wisdom simply because you say so? This is an amazing faith to me, that we should believe such. If so, we should previously also have believed others who spoke in this way from the spirit's inspiration. We had as little proof."[6]

From a modern perspective, Joris comes across as a carnival con man, appealing to the hearts of people whose minds he cannot win. The notion that one can believe first and understand later, without even knowing what one is believing, violates our whole sense of what belief is. But Joris actually speaks for a long tradition: belief belongs to humble vessels who accept God's truth from authorized sources, not to the proud who think that they can judge for themselves. Belief, in this model, is not judgment based upon evidence but rather trust that your own reason and experience are wrong. So, the position of the Melchiorites in this debate, while so natural and normal to modern sensibilities, was actually a powerful solvent. Their demand for "proof," and their awkward realization that they needed some reason to believe one revelation over another, were steps down a slippery slope from inspired belief to the belief of the world.

As this story suggests, the explosion of religious conflict in the sixteenth century made belief an urgent problem in the Christian West. But a central argument of this book is that the Reformation was *not* an engine of modernity; on the contrary, modern belief developed in reaction against the religion of Luther and Calvin as much as against the Council of Trent. As we shall see, despite their theological differences, Protestants, Catholics, and Anabaptists in the sixteenth century participated in a common project to make belief *hard*. Facing unprecedented religious competition, and desperate to preserve for Christian belief a special epistemic prestige, the rival churches redefined belief as a privileged condition, a rarefied status unavailable to many or even most people. This was the first revolution in religious knowledge, a project of exclusion and discipline that arrayed communities of believers against a world now understood to be saturated with unbelief. But this revolution soon generated a powerful backlash as dissidents on both sides of the Reformation rejected its stark logic. To do so, they loosened belief, shattering the partition wall between Christian belief and secular ways of knowing. This was the second revolution in religious knowledge, the birth of modern belief, perhaps no less important a rupture in Western thought than the scientific revolution with which it occasionally intersected.

So, then, what is this thing called "modern belief" whose emergence requires a history? The question at first appears misguided. An uncharitable reader might respond with the very assumption this book is intended to refute: belief does not have a history, belief is just belief, so its modernity is beside the point. But even a sympathetic reader, willing to grant belief a history, might respond that no single version of belief can possibly represent modernity: just as belief changes over time, so it means different things to different people. This is a reasonable concern, which presents an opportunity to explain some of the stakes of this book.

Rather than approaching the question with analytical rigor, let me begin by way of familiar experience. In modern, Western society, we are routinely asked if we believe in God. A June 2016 Gallup poll found that some 89 percent of Americans do.[7] Is it even remotely possible that all those people who tell the pollster they believe in God mean the same thing by that claim? Not at all. Belief can mean absolute certainty, or vague probability. Belief can subsist wholly in the mind, or it can require stirrings of the heart or actions of the body. Belief can rely on reason, or belief can reject reason. So, given that even a moment's reflection reveals that "believing" can mean many different things, when the pollster asks, "Do you believe in God?" why does no one ever respond, "What do you mean, *believe*?" In mosques, synagogues, and churches, people think a great deal about the precise nature of their religious belief; in more secular contexts, people labor to locate themselves in the no man's land between agnosticism and atheism. Yet, despite this complexity, people tend to treat different species of belief as commensurate with one another. A characteristic of Western modernity is to act as if belief were simple.

Just as routinely, we are asked whether we believe in global warming, and whether we believe in ghosts, just to name two examples of the myriad propositions placed before the judgment of modern, liberal subjects. Every day, in ordinary conversation, we are asked whether we believe things seen and unseen, banal and extraordinary, scientific, social, religious, ethical, and political, without differentiation or any sense that these might be qualitatively different operations. "Belief" can signify the unassailable heart of the zealot, the concerned participation of the citizen, or the fickle passions of the consumer. Vastly different and sometimes contradictory sorts of claims hide within the thick folds of this little word. So, is believing in God the same kind of thing as believing in ghosts or global warming? Well, maybe or maybe not. But once again, why does no one ask, "What do you mean, *believe*?"

My answer, in brief, is that in the modern West belief has effectively become a synonym for opinion or judgment: a space of autonomy rather than a prescription for its exercise. And because opinion or judgment is so essential to modern societies, to ask "What do you mean, *believe*?" would abdicate the sovereignty of liberal subjects to decide for themselves what their belief is. In a society of autonomous, deracinated individuals, our beliefs locate us in the world. Beliefs identify us as consumers, voters, and voluntary participants in civil society, making us legible in a vast, multidimensional matrix of free choice. To demand criteria for belief, to challenge the notion that all kinds of judgment or opinion are basically commensurate, would threaten an important mechanism by which post-Enlightenment subjects engage with the world. And this, in a nutshell, is what I mean by "modern belief": the sense that belief is synonymous with private judgment, and therefore modern subjects believe or disbelieve according to their own conception of whether a given proposition is credible. I shall refer to this condition with the shorthand "sovereign judgment."[8]

Now, as a matter of practice, some version of "rationalism" is at the heart of how many people would claim to make their judgments, about religion as well as other things: they consider the evidence for and against a claim. And yet, while "reason" may be a conventional component of modern belief, modern subjects are sovereign over the criteria of judgment as well as judgment itself, and their reasons are answerable to no one. People who believe whatever a charismatic leader tells them, for instance, or who refuse to listen to new evidence that might change their minds, are not acting in accordance with most understandings of rationalism; but they would still claim to be using their judgment as sovereign finders of fact.[9]

The point is that modern belief is not a particular epistemic regime, it is rather a space in which epistemic controversy is managed. In modern belief, people do not all believe the same way—far from it!—but acting as if they do becomes a way of defending their own right of judgment. The willingness not to interrogate the belief-talk of others underwrites the formation and functioning of a modern society which is in some sense the sum of all our divergent beliefs. Hence, when the pollster asks if they believe in God, global warming, and ghosts, modern subjects respond with their own private judgment based upon whatever criteria they find most probative. Their commonality lies in agreeing to the nature of the space itself: anyone is free to disagree with them, and to present what they regard as better evidence, but no one may deny belief-status to other people, or tell them their subjectivity does not rise to the level of believing.[10]

Whether this formation is better understood as a structural consensus or the soft domination of liberalism is, of course, a matter of perspective: modern belief enables some sorts of freedoms while precluding others. Much has been written about how the modern category of "religion" asserts the rationality of Christian and particularly Protestant values against the alleged backwardness of Islam and other non-Christian "religions."[11] This book is in one sense a deep history of that configuration, showing how the Enlightenment authorized religion by limiting its claims. But, as we shall see, modern belief emerged in the seventeenth century as a critique of sectarian exclusivity, an emancipation rather than a limitation; that it has produced intolerance in the centuries since is not the least of its ironies and represents only one small part of its cultural work.

I hope this understanding of modern belief corresponds to the intuitions of my readers. It also happens to accord with one of the first philosophers of the modern condition, G.W.F. Hegel, who wrote, "The principle of the modern world at large is freedom of subjectivity."[12] As Hegel explained it, "The right of the subject's particularity to find satisfaction, or—to put it differently—the right of subjective freedom, is the pivotal and focal point in the difference between antiquity and the modern age."[13] This conception of modern subjective right—"The right to recognize nothing that I do not perceive as rational is the highest right of the subject"—maps closely onto modern belief, and Hegel praised its ability to actualize our highest moral selves.[14] But he also feared that, at its worst and when misapprehended, freedom of subjectivity meant that "the concepts of truth and the laws of ethics are reduced to mere opinions and subjective conditions, and the most criminal principles—since they, too, are convictions—are accorded the same status as those laws."[15]

Hegel's worry about relativism, although not his celebration of freedom, is echoed by the historian Brad Gregory, whose 2012 book *The Unintended Reformation* blamed Protestantism for the emergence of what he called "hyperpluralism": the descent of the world into a cacophony of competing truth-claims with no criteria to choose between them.[16] According to Gregory, hyperpluralism developed from the medieval philosophy of "univocity," the notion that God shares characteristics with creation and therefore might be interpreted using the tools of the world.[17] But, according to Gregory, hyperpluralism proliferated with Protestantism's doctrine of *sola scriptura*, the notion that the Bible authenticates itself through the Holy Spirit rather than being authenticated or interpreted by any ultimate religious authority on earth. Having thus concluded that there is no final arbiter of meaning in the world, Gregory writes, the Reformation inevitably fragmented, and it is still fragmenting, to the point that today every individual, with authority over their own ethical system and understanding of the world, is a Reformation unto themselves.

Quite apart from the fact that Catholics have been making versions of this argument since before the ink was dry on
Luther's Ninety-Five Theses, there is considerable irony in
Gregory's agreement with Hegel and the secular academic tradition. Far from being a new discovery, hyperpluralism—with
or without the pejorative tone—is a commonplace of scholarship on the effects of the Reformation. As early as 1959, for instance, Reinhart Koselleck noted, "The Reformation and the
subsequent split in religious authority had thrown man back
upon his conscience, and a conscience lacking outside support
degenerates into the idol of self-righteousness . . . Instead of
being a *causa pacis*, the authority of conscience in its subjective plurality is a downright *causa belli civilis*."[18] The literary
historian Joanna Picciotto has described it more recently:

> We are all familiar with the story: by putting so much pres-
> sure on the category of belief, reformers turned articles of
> faith into objects of critical reflection and debate, setting
> into motion a tortuous, bloody, and still unfinished his-
> torical process enabling the emergence of a secular sphere
> of toleration . . . As a consequence of these developments,
> Western civilization is now characterized by a degree of
> ideological diversity and social atomization that would be
> considered intolerable by the generations that lived before
> secularism's triumph.[19]

From the perspective of the history of belief, however,
a different picture emerges. What is most decisively new in
modernity is not diversity of judgment—unanimity is always
a rare bird—but rather that all the different judgments people make should be accounted beliefs at all. The category of
belief itself has evolved into a new kind of epistemological
space that properly admits plurality and competition, so that
diversity, which in the old dispensation represented a crisis or

absence of belief, in the new dispensation signifies belief itself. In modernity, belief is the space in which rival claims subsist as commensurate alternatives, rather than the space in which one claim triumphs over others.

Gregory's lament that the modern world lacks "any shared or even convergent view about what 'we' think is true or right or good" thus fails to take into account a second-order agreement about the condition of belief itself.[20] Modern belief represents a new form of order rather than simply a descent into chaos, because while of course people today believe vastly different things, they generally accept the epistemic status of one another's beliefs *as* beliefs. They argue about whether given beliefs are justified, warranted, true, or good, whereas premodern Christians routinely denied that other people's claims were beliefs at all. This is not merely a semantic shift, it is about access to a fundamental marker of sovereign personhood, creating the conditions for peace in a diverse society.[21]

The Reformation did not inaugurate this change. As we shall see, the Protestant doctrine of interpretation did not open belief to private judgment; instead it introduced an alternative authoritarianism based upon the supremacy of a believing minority over an unbelieving world. The Reformation and Counter-Reformation thus participated in parallel projects of religious discipline: while Catholics disciplined populations to believe, Protestants disciplined populations of unbelievers. Modern belief did not emerge from either of these models, but rather in reaction against the stark regime they jointly created.

There are a few excellent histories of belief upon which the present study builds. Perhaps the greatest is *Did the Greeks*

Believe in Their Myths? by Paul Veyne, who argued that normal epistemic belief did not apply to Greek mythology because "the content of myth was situated in a noble and platonic temporality": myths were "accepted as true in the sense that they were not doubted, but they were not accepted the way that everyday reality is."[22] Malcolm Ruel briefly outlined six stages of historical development of Christian belief: from a form of trust, to a factual conviction, to an initiatory doctrine, to a corporately declared orthodoxy, to an inwardly organized experience, to a common value.[23] Paul Ricoeur identified three modalities of belief in the history of philosophy: the Platonic idea of belief as opinion, the Cartesian idea of belief as judgment or consent, and the Christian idea of belief as faith.[24] Jean Wirth explored what he called the "birth of the concept of belief," especially the differentiation of cognitive assent from faith.[25] More recently, Susan Schreiner's *Are You Alone Wise?* identified many of the pathologies that attached to the early modern insistence that true belief was by definition certain.[26] Glenn Most's *Doubting Thomas* explored the problem that religious belief ought not to rely on the evidence of the senses.[27] Steven Justice and George Hoffman both explored, in different ways, how unbelief was at times constitutive of, or implicated in, the construction of belief.[28]

These and other fine studies are dwarfed by the enormous scholarship on the alleged decline of belief in the West. The literature on atheism, skepticism, and doubt is truly vast, and quite apart from its size, it sits at the center of the project of modern history, tacitly denying that belief can have a history beyond its fall. Against this emphasis on unbelief, there are, of course, innumerable histories of particular beliefs and belief systems. But to a remarkable extent, these, too, are written as if belief were an empty vessel waiting to be filled with content, stubbornly denying that the category itself has a history.

↳ His contribution to the field.

This is not, I think, because belief appears so natural and self-evident that scholars have not felt the need to provide it with a history. Recent decades have seen an explosion of fascinating histories of related (and no less seemingly natural) categories. Just to recommend a few examples, Steven Shapin's *A Social History of Truth* and Richard Green's *A Crisis of Truth* historicize one epistemological category, while Mary Poovey's *A History of the Modern Fact* and Barbara Shapiro's *A Culture of Fact* historicize another; Stuart Clark's *Vanities of the Eye* explores the early modern crisis in the reliability of sensory knowledge; Craig Muldrew's *The Economy of Obligation* explores the evolving concept of credit; Valentin Groebner's *Who Are You?* explores the emergence of reliable knowledge of individual personhood.[29] More broadly, historicizing supposedly natural categories, sometimes under the heading *Begriffsgeschichte* or "conceptual history," has been at the heart of our discipline since the 1980s.[30] So why is there so little history of belief?

One answer must surely involve the privileged status of religion: within the "knowledge problem," belief remains the most sacred of cows. Most historians of Christianity are practitioners of Christianity, if only because, just as so many historians of science have advanced degrees in science, the ability to make sense of highly technical subjects requires special training. Scholars who are not already invested in these recondite fields typically seek specialties with lower entry barriers than theology or physics. But while historians of science are not also running laboratories, many historians of Christianity are, if no longer typically members of the clergy, then at least still concerned about their Christian identity and spiritual estate. Perhaps it should not be surprising, then, that while historians of science have systematically challenged the foundational categories and transcendent presumptions of science, historians of Christianity have not followed suit. While most historians of science do not still believe in early modern science, many historians of Christianity still believe in early modern Christianity.

Moreover, writing a history of belief necessarily challenges any notion that belief itself is ineffable or timeless. It therefore presents at least an implicit challenge to certain versions of Christian orthodoxy—perhaps not orthodoxies to which most historians would adhere, but ones that they may be concerned about offending. Yet this should be no impediment. When Christian belief appears in the historical record, it collapses onto the mundane: there is no separate language with which to describe the inexpressible, hence it emerges from our sources in terms historians can comprehend, like any other human category. Ever since the Epistle to the Hebrews defined faith as "the substance of things hoped for, the evidence of things not seen," Christianity has been haunted by its reliance upon material signifiers—substance, evidence—to explain the spiritual. Thus, what makes the historical study of belief possible also makes it potentially unsettling to Christian presumptions. To "take belief seriously," that clarion call of historians of religion, requires confronting all the surprising ways that the purportedly transcendent changes over time. Even the very assertion that Christian belief is categorically different from other kinds of knowledge has evolved as a result of its paradoxical intersection with profane ways of knowing. No wonder "belief" has so little history.

⟨⟨⟩⟩

An excursus may be useful here concerning the word "belief," especially in relation to another word, "faith."

I want to stress from the outset that this is not a book about a word, it is a book about a *problem*. My central concern is

Question 3 [margin annotation]

with what we might call "religious knowledge," particularly the problem of what sort of knowledge that might be. When I ask, "What did it mean to believe?" I am asking about the changing relationship between religion and epistemology: what was religious knowledge, and how did it relate to other things people thought? My attention to this configuration is not intended to foreclose other articulations of the problem.[31] But what interests me are the complexities that emerged whenever the epistemic qualities of belief were activated. The prominence of doctrinal content is often described as one of Christianity's distinctive features among world religions; this book studies the challenges posed by that peculiar emphasis and suggests that they were central to the intellectual development of the modern West.

But, of course, the word belief is ineluctably tied to another word, faith. Faith can certainly refer to epistemic claims, so it is of interest here, but while in English belief almost always involves the problem of knowledge, faith only sometimes does.[32] Faith can also refer to the spiritual state in which knowledge is received, as when Augustine distinguished *fides quae creditur* from *fides qua creditur*—the faith which is believed, and the faith *by* which it is believed.[33] In the Middle Ages, furthermore, faith could mean loyally commending oneself to the protection of another person; this sociopolitical meaning bled into the religious, in the sense that a faithful Christian was someone loyal to the Church.[34] Faith could also refer more broadly to social trust, like the fidelity of a spouse. And while belief usually made claims about the present, faith often implied a trust in some future outcome. To historicize belief, then, is not the same thing as historicizing faith, even if there is significant overlap between them—indeed their relationship, and the question of when faith did indeed imply knowledge, is part of what must be historicized.[35]

Different contexts pose different challenges. In ancient Greek, where there were not separate words for belief and faith, the most famous description of the semantic field I am considering occurs in Plato's *Republic*, when Socrates asks Glaucon to imagine an unequally divided line: the smaller segment represents *doxa*, usually translated as opinion, while the larger segment represents *episteme*, or knowledge. Doxa is then further divided into *eikasia*, or imagination, and *pistis*, or belief. So pistis functioned as a subset of opinion concerning the lower world of sensible things. Elsewhere, in the dialogue *Theaetetus* and more famously in the *Meno*, Plato proposed that knowledge is *orthos doxa*—right opinion—when *logos* can be provided to justify it, suggesting the famous axiom that knowledge is justified true belief; unlike mere belief, which can so easily be misled, knowledge is constitutively bound to the truth.[36] But this epistemological framework, with its more or less derogatory view of pistis, was not the end of the story. A different framework could be found in the Greek rhetorical tradition, where pistis could mean evidence or proof, but it could also mean an argument using proof (in this sense there were three species of *pisteis*: arguments from *ethos*, *pathos*, and *logos*), and it could mean the state of mind induced by proof, in other words, belief.[37]

Despite its importance to philosophy and rhetoric, pistis was not a central term in classical Greek religion, nor in the Greek Septuagint translation of the Hebrew Bible.[38] Christians thus invented, as Teresa Morgan shows, employing all their practical knowledge of social trust, distinguishing between salutary pistis in a master or friend, and perilous pistis in hearsay or discourse.[39] Some have argued that the Christian concept of faith developed from the Greek rhetorical concept of persuasion (*peithō*), etymologically linked to pistis; but the "persuasion" of the New Testament is usually

persuasion *without* evidence and argument, rather than persuasion *from* evidence and argument, making it more of a
response to the classical concept than an elaboration of it.[40]
Only in Acts 17:31, when Paul submits Christ's resurrection
as "assurance" [pistis] of Christian doctrine, does the word
function as evidence; here, as David Marno has argued, Paul
had just arrived in Greece and was offering the Greeks a bit
of their own rhetoric.[41] Elsewhere, the New Testament radically distinguished pistis from proof. The classic definition
in Hebrews 11:1—"*Pistis* is the substance [*hypostasis*] of
things hoped for, the evidence [*elenchus*] of things not seen"—
ironically suggests that in the invisible realm pistis must function without proof at all. As Jesus said to Doubting Thomas,
"Blessed are they that have not seen and yet have believed
[*pisteusantes*]."

In German, as in Greek, the words belief and faith are not
ordinarily distinguished: the noun *der Glaube* is both belief
and faith, while the verb *sie glaubt* is usually translated "she believes" simply because we have no term "she faiths." So, for instance, when in 1534 the radical spiritualist Sebastian Franck offered the paradox *Der Glauben glaubt im Unglauben*—belief
believes in unbelief—should we understand this as a statement about knowledge or fidelity? We cannot know for certain; but the ambiguity itself was often productive of the very
problem we are pondering. Consider translations of Martin
Luther's *Small Catechism* from German into Latin. One key
passage was, in English translation, "I believe that by my own
understanding or strength I cannot believe in Jesus Christ."[42]
In the original German, both iterations of "believe" are forms
of the verb *glaube*. When two translations into Latin appeared
almost simultaneously in 1529, one of them, by an unknown
translator, used *credere* for both iterations of "believe"; this
version quickly passed into oblivion. But the other translation

by Johann Sauermann, which was approved by Luther himself and saw more than sixty editions before the end of the century, translated the first "believe" with credere and the second with *fidere*. Luther and his translator chose this alternative, which means "to trust" or "to rely," to make a theological point: what is missing from human assent to divine propositions is trust.[43]

Latin has its own problems. As in English, the verb credere (to believe) has a different root than the noun *fides* (faith). This maps more or less neatly onto French, Spanish, and other romance languages. The problem, however, is that classical Latin did not quite use a noun corresponding directly to the verb credere: that is, it had the verb "to believe" but not really the nouns "belief" and "beliefs." I say "not really" because there were important partial exceptions. Of course, rough synonyms were employed—*assensus, opinio, persuasio*—whose different roots suggested different connotations. More importantly, there was the noun *credulitas*. But while its antonym, *incredulitas*, corresponds closely to our word "unbelief," credulitas was not usually used to mean belief. In the Vulgate Bible, the word incredulitas appears more than thirty times, but the noun credulitas is absent: the Greek pistis is instead translated mechanically by fides, much to the aggravation of the early sixteenth-century translator Erasmus, who thought credulitas or *fiducia* was often better suited.[44] The closest the Vulgate comes to using credulitas is the adjectival variant *credulus*, which appears only once and does not refer to religious belief at all: in Genesis 39:19, Potiphar is too *credulus* to his wife's malicious accusation against Joseph. More generally, in the Christian tradition, credulitas usually means "credulity" in the negative sense, often applied to superstition. Even when used in a positive sense, it typically connotes simplicity; it is not the positive content of Christian belief so much as the guileless condition of the humble Christian before God.

Another Latin candidate for belief is *credendum*, or its plural *credenda*, a gerundive form of the verb credere which we might translate as "a thing to be believed." Credenda is sometimes used to mean doctrine, the positive content or "beliefs" of Christianity. But beliefs is not a very good translation, because the gerundive in Latin carries connotations of requirement or necessity: credenda are things that *ought* to be believed or *must* be believed. The word corresponds grammatically to *agenda*, things to be done, and as every department chair knows, what is on the agenda is not necessarily what happens. A better translation would be dogma, or rules of faith. No one would use credenda for things that they happened to believe as individuals, or to distinguish one set of beliefs from another; credenda were instead the intellective requirements of Christianity upon Christians.[45]

The things we call beliefs could be organized under the medieval Latin *credentia*, a twelfth-century neologism which could mean doctrine, but also meant letters of commercial credit or safe conduct. But much more often, as in the Vulgate Bible, beliefs were simply represented in Latin by the term fides: what Augustine termed *fides quae creditur*, the faith which is believed. The trick, then, is figuring out when fides particularly concerned knowledge. Luckily, it was common for Christian writers to authorize us to hear belief-talk by using the verb credere to describe what they meant. So, just to give one example, the Italian Jesuit Roberto Bellarmino argued that the phrase "one faith, one baptism" in Ephesians 4:5 refers to the "object of faith," that is, "what we all believe," rather than to trust; here Bellarmino was self-consciously repudiating the theological interpretation that had led Martin Luther's authorized translator to replace credere with fidere in his *Small Catechism*.[46]

I do not describe these lexical problems because I have solved them. Rather, the problems themselves demonstrate my fundamental point that belief is not the natural or simple category it is usually presumed to be. It is instead a constantly changing space where the nature of religious knowledge is contested and constructed.

{≈≈≈⟩ⲱ⟨≈≈≈}

If historians have not much contemplated the meaning of belief, other academic disciplines have. Considering two of those disciplines—anthropology and philosophy—suggests what might be gained by a properly historical account.

Anthropology, like history, "includes countless descriptions of the content of people's beliefs, but . . . only a handful of critical examinations of the concept." But more so than in history, those critical examinations have had significant impact.[47] Rodney Needham's foundational *Belief, Language, and Experience* (1972) urged banishing the term belief from ethnography altogether, on the grounds that it is an untranslatable Christian construct which ipso facto judges other cultures according to Western norms. Needham's work proved influential, especially forcing open the alleged dichotomy between propositional belief and embodied practice.[48] Thus, a lively debate in recent years has considered whether and how anthropologists might legitimately re-deploy the concept of belief, given both its lexical unavoidability and a postcolonial modernity in which ethnographic subjects all over the world apply the exogenous European concept of belief to themselves.[49]

One unintended consequence of this debate is a tendency among anthropologists to carefully define what belief *is* in order to avoid using it insensitively, with the perverse effect of naturalizing the very thing they seek to problematize. Either anthropologists declare that belief *is* a cognitive commitment to a clear set of doctrinal propositions, so they can avoid foisting it upon cultures with other priorities; or they declare that belief *is* a nonliteral social or ethical commitment embodied in symbolism and practice, so they can transport it across boundaries; or they reject both these alternatives and invent sui generis versions of belief that authorize their own cross-cultural comparisons.[50] From an historian's perspective, these various interpretive gambits are generally plausible, in that each could find support in the Christian tradition where the Western concept of belief developed. Yet each would also encounter opposition in that tradition, and to take any of them for granted creates normativity rather than challenging it.[51]

The most influential contributor to this debate is Talal Asad, whose *Genealogies of Religion* extended Needham's critique of belief to the concept of religion more broadly. Asad argued that there can be no transcultural definition of religion, because the project to create one, the desire to design an abstract category of religion that transcends particular contexts, is already inherently Western. As Asad put it, the idea that "religion is essentially a matter of symbolic meanings . . . and that it must not be confused with any of its particular historical or cultural forms, is in fact a view that has a specific Christian history."[52] The heart of that history was the transformation of Christianity from a medieval religion of outward public participation and social discipline into a modern religion of inward conscience: "The only legitimate space allowed to Christianity by post-Enlightenment society [is] the right to individual belief . . . The suggestion that religion has a universal function in belief is one indication of how marginal religion has become in modern industrial society."[53] It is this post-Enlightenment, internal, propositional version of religion, Asad argues, against which other religions are measured and found wanting.

As a critique of religion, Asad's reasoning is powerful. But note the work that belief does in his model: it stands as a proxy for that turn inward. The work of history, for Asad, was to raise belief onto a pedestal from which it gazes condescendingly at the world; but belief itself does not change in his model, it merely emerges. Thus, in order to create a genealogy of religion, Asad denies belief a history, participating in the broader tendency to essentialize the category. Like the scholars he criticizes, he treats belief as a coherent and stable epistemological object which one might either find or not find in a culture, rather than as a changing cultural space in which epistemology is negotiated.

By offering a history of belief rather than a genealogy of religion, this book will thus challenge some stubborn assumptions. What is desperately in need of critique is the very notion that belief has a fixed, universally viable meaning. Indeed, one argument of this book is that modern belief, as it developed historically in opposition to narrow and normative definitions of believing, in many ways prefigured the Asadian critical project. Just as Asad contends that "religion" normatively universalizes from an exclusive category, rendering other instantiations of religion incomplete, so modern belief developed in opposition to a categorical exclusivity that had left most people unable to believe. This is not simply to note a similarity, but to suggest more ambitiously that the historical transformation of Christian belief from fixed orthodoxy to human judgment, opening the category of belief to different ways of knowing, was the intellectual stuff of which modern critique is made. Crucial to my argument is that the kind of judgment at stake in the emergence of modern belief was *not* the Kantian version so deplored by critics of Enlightenment—the universalizing power of reason—but rather something more like subjective assessment. This formulation, while hardly innocent of discursive power, is not quite so obviously an attempt to control discourse itself.[54]

If we turn from anthropology to philosophy, a different disciplinary practice unfolds. Analytic philosophers generally begin with an "intuition" about what belief is, then trace that intuition forward to its logical conclusions, seeing where its consequences clash with other intuitions. Their goal is not transcendent truth but rather clarity of thought, exposing inconsistencies and helping to understand what is entailed by the positions we hold. Thus, it is informative to notice when the intuitions with which philosophers begin—the common ground shared by a wide range of thinkers, designed to appeal to the common sense of their readers—would *not* have been widely shared before the seventeenth century. Let me offer three examples.[55]

First, an important concern in modern philosophy is what "justifies" a belief. Most philosophers would hold that a belief is justified if the available evidence makes it likely: for any proposition p, the greater the evidence of it being true, the greater our justification for believing it. If it turns out that p is false, then our belief was untrue, but it was not unjustified if a large preponderance of evidence supported it. This intuition produces the sorts of problems philosophers love. So, for instance, consider the lottery paradox, available in many forms: I have bought a ticket for a lottery with a thousand tickets, the winner has been chosen, but I have not yet heard who has won. Given the vanishingly small odds of winning, I am *justified* in believing that I have lost. But by the same logic, I am justified in believing that each ticket has lost, and this is an impossibility, because one of the tickets has won.[56]

For a variety of reasons, this would not have made much sense before the seventeenth century. Statistical and probabilistic reasoning was embryonic if not nonexistent: not only had its mathematics not been elaborated, but the whole project of finding evidence in uncertainty was referred to divine providence rather than probability.[57] To put it another way, calculating likelihoods is poorly aligned with understanding God's eternal will. But more broadly, weighing or assessing a preponderance of evidence—at least in religion, the central issue in medieval discussions of belief—ordinarily would not have been accounted as belief at all; instead, it would have been understood as *opinion*. According to Thomas Aquinas, an opinion is an "act of the intellect inclined to one alternative while retaining respect for the other."[58] Religious belief did *not* retain respect for the alternative, but rather was by definition firm and certain. In this sense, Aquinas and his tradition suggest that *there can be no such thing* as "justified belief" in the modern sense of justification: if you hold the proposition p in proportion to the evidence for p, you either have knowledge (if the evidence is incontrovertible) or opinion (if the evidence is merely strong) but never belief.

Second, a fundamental debate in the philosophy of mind asks whether belief is voluntary: can you choose to believe? Bernard Williams, in his celebrated essay "Deciding to Believe," argued that belief is involuntary because by definition "beliefs aim at truth." Other philosophers, following in the tradition of John Henry Newman and William James, have responded that voluntarism remains compatible with the intuition that "beliefs aim at truth." Robert Nozick, for instance, inserted a practical component: beliefs do not *only* aim at truth, they also aim to benefit the believer. So, for instance, parents can decide to believe that their child is innocent, against the evidence presented in a courtroom, insofar as for them, as opposed to the jurors, the practical benefits outweigh the epistemic costs. In another version, Andrew Reisner asserts that the mere fact that "beliefs aim at truth" does not necessarily make belief involuntary, because there are conditions where having a belief will *cause* that belief to be true. William James had said something like this in the nineteenth century when he offered the example of believing that someone likes you: believing it helps them like you, so the unlikelihood of its prior truth need not prohibit believing it.[59]

All of this is very clever, but again its suppositions are relentlessly modern. While Christians in previous eras might have agreed that "beliefs aim at truth," the idea that this could therefore shape an argument about voluntarism would have made little sense. Augustine of Hippo famously argued that "to believe is to think with assent": an act of *will* is required to turn thought into belief, so all belief is in some meaningful sense voluntary. But this did not imply voluntarism in the modern sense, because the will (*voluntas*) was presumed to be fallen. If the will is in some sense disabled—"we are not able not to sin" as Augustine put it—then "voluntary" does not mean free choice.[60] In an Augustinian thought-world, you might well aim at truth by choosing to believe something false, because the will is so clouded and divorced from reason.

Third, another classic philosophical problem is "Moore's paradox." G. E. Moore identified a difference between applying the verb "believe" to yourself and applying it to others. For some reason, intuition tells us it is nonsensical to say, "It is raining, but I do not believe it is raining," while it is reasonable to say, in the third person, "It is raining, but *she* does not believe it is raining." Moore's explanation was that the assertion "It is raining" carries an implicit belief-claim, so the words "It is raining" really mean "I believe it is raining"; the first-person sentence therefore contains a direct contradiction while the third-person sentence does not. Ludwig Wittgenstein, however, noticed that more was going on in Moore's paradox: the verb "to believe" means different things in the first-person present tense because we are thinkers who can notice ourselves in the act of thinking. When I say, "I believe that p," I am potentially saying something about myself as much as I am saying something about the world: Wittgenstein sardonically described a man who asks if there is a fire in the next room, and when given the answer, "I believe there is," he replies, "Don't be irrelevant. I asked you about the fire, not about your state of mind!"[61] Moore's paradox has therefore progressed through modern philosophy as a way of analyzing the fragmented subject, for whom "I believe that p" knits together a series of potentially distinct dispositions and claims.[62]

But Moore's paradox would not have appeared so paradoxical before the rise of modern belief, because the statement "P, but I do not believe that p" would not have been intuitively nonsensical. We shall encounter many people claiming to know a thing is true without believing it, or even believing and not believing at the same time. One example is William Shakespeare's Sonnet 138: "When my love swears that she is made of truth / I do believe her, though I know she lies."[63] But more important examples concern the proposition "God is." Medieval and early modern Christians often took it for granted that everyone *knows* God is, but many do not *believe* God is, because belief was a more demanding epistemic condition. "Belief" was also taken to have distinct carnal and spiritual meanings. When the Bible says, "Thou believest that there is one God; thou doest well: the devils also believe, and tremble" (James 2:19), that did not mean that devils believe the same way Christians believe: they use different faculties, and their beliefs are directed toward different ends. This is what philosophers call "nonstandard semantics," but it is only nonstandard today.[64]

More examples could be offered of modern assumptions about belief that appear incompatible with earlier understandings. But I do not want to belabor the point; this analysis should already be sufficient to the task of denaturalizing the intuitions of the modern philosophy of mind. My project is not to argue against these philosophers, who battle valiantly for clarity against the dark forces of muddle, but to suggest that modern muddles evolved from different muddles past.

method

{⋙W⋘}

This is a history of ideas. I am concerned in these pages not with the ordinary pious business of believing, but with sites where Christians indulged in second-order thinking about what it meant to believe.[65] This is therefore *not* a history of belief as it was lived and practiced, a limitation that carries costs: I study belief outside its natural habitat, and among literate elites rather than the ordinary Europeans who must often have challenged their prescriptions. But the benefit of my approach is to escape the pious presumption that belief is simply the positive content of religion, equally and unproblematically present in every action or claim. This is crucial, because once we accept that the concept of belief has a history, we can see how it functioned as an axis of inclusion and exclusion, a framework through which some voices were authorized while others were silenced. By isolating belief as an intellectual problem, we can track the shifting claims that religious doctrine made upon the mind and upon the world.

This inevitably raises the question of whether this book is really a history of belief at all, or merely a history of belief-talk: does belief change over time, or is it only the way people describe belief that changes? At some level this is a philosophical question, beyond the cognizance of historians. We have direct evidence only for ink deposited on paper, not for processes of mind. But a partial solution is suggested by historians of the emotions, who argue that emotions are shaped by the cultural conditions in which they are experienced. If, for instance, there was a fad for emotional intensity and copious weeping in eighteenth-century Europe, does that mean that people's emotions changed? At the very least, it means that the way people *experienced* their emotions changed, and emotions are experiences of mental processes as much as the processes themselves. So it is with belief. If the Protestant Reformation unleashed new ways of describing belief, does that mean that Protestants believed differently? Well, certainly the way they *experienced* their belief changed, and belief is, at least in part, an experience of believing by self-conscious subjects.[66]

As these provisos suggest, *The Birth of Modern Belief* is an essay with an argument rather than an exhaustive survey of its vast subject, and this compression has required some hard choices. First, while I burrow down into details at many points, there are also places where I have been content to settle for generalities, letting an example or two stand for a more complex reality. In trying to achieve explanatory power, tracing the arc of my story across half a millennium, I have inevitably sacrificed some measure of analytical control. My hope is that the broad claims of this book will be sufficiently compelling to encourage others to nuance them. Second, while parts of this book map the terrain of belief broadly, other parts are unabashedly teleological, describing the emergence of new ideas because of their long-term historical importance. I do not feel the need to repeat endlessly the truism that the rise of one thing does not entail the fall of everything else; readers should take it for granted that change happens slowly and unevenly. But I believe that the purpose of history as a discipline is to explain change over time, hence my emphasis on strands of thought that signal the most significant transformations. Third, the range of this book is shaped by my own expertise, and I hope my specialist knowledge in some areas compensates for limitations elsewhere. This is a history of Christianity, not of Judaism, Islam, or other religions that played important roles in the West and have their own overlapping modernities.[67] In terms of subject matter, I focus on belief in God and formal doctrines, touching only occasionally on witchcraft, magic, and spirits.[68] Geographically, Britain plays an oversized role, followed by France, Germany, the Netherlands, Spain, and Italy. I hope that my argument would not be significantly altered by a different focus, but that is for others to determine.

A brief description of the argument is now in order. By the later Middle Ages, the category of belief possessed an elaborate topography in the Latin West. Belief did not necessarily entail knowledge-claims, because believing could adhere in baptism. Likewise, the doctrine of "implicit faith" meant that, by believing that everything the Church said was true, Christians could be said to believe a series of doctrines they neither knew nor understood. But atop these foundations, which made every nominal Christian in some sense a believer, there were many other kinds of belief as well, from the doctrinal belief that underlay rationalist theology, to the mystical belief of direct experience of God, to the rarefied belief that came from saving faith.

This framework came crashing down in the Reformation, as Protestants, Anabaptists, and Catholics all drew dark lines around belief. Protestants made the most difficult version the only one that mattered: no longer broad and complex, belief was narrowed and simplified, available only to a godly minority. Anabaptists went further, limiting belief to the perfection of the elect or even declaring belief too rarefied to subsist in a fallen world. Catholics responded by reducing belief to a form of obedience, putting belief into the hands of authority. Christians of all stripes adopted extreme positions, either borrowed selectively from the past or invented out of whole cloth,

to weaponize belief within the emergent confessional struggle. The result was a crisis in which Christians confronted the
daunting challenge of believing.

So in the seventeenth century, Christians contested the
logic of the confessional era, constructing broader and more
inclusive understandings of what it meant to believe. What
united these new perspectives against their medieval as much
as their confessional predecessors was a common emphasis on
sovereign judgment. Religious knowledge was redefined beyond the control of authority, justified in the world rather than
outside of it, much like opinion or natural knowledge. Thus,
the Christian category of belief became commensurate with
belief in science, society, and the self, resulting in an epochal
displacement of belief onto the secular.

My largest argument, then, is that Western modernity is
characterized not by a decline of belief but by its boundless
proliferation: today belief is everywhere, but in forms that
would not have been recognized as belief in previous eras. This
proliferation of belief does not imply that religion remained
the cornerstone of Western civilization; on the contrary, modern belief was the sharp edge that perforated Christianity,
breaching the wall that had separated religion from profane
ways of knowing.[69] This is, I hope, a considerable revision of
the ordinary view that in modernity religion has been rele-
gated to a separate, private sphere. Secularization in the West
was not about the segregation of belief from the world, but
the promiscuous opening of belief to the world.

Finally, while this is a book about belief, it is not *only*
about belief. Precisely because belief changes over time, it
can never be disaggregated from the culture it inhabits. It is
no coincidence, for instance, that the Middle Ages toggled
between versions of belief that were easy and versions that
were hard, befitting a Christian society in which everyone was

presumptively a believer, and yet no one could be understood to believe so successfully that they transcended the control of the Church. It is no coincidence that in the early modern era, as all foundations of knowledge seemed to be undermined, belief became a way of asserting exclusive possession of rare and valuable truths. And it is no coincidence that in a modern, liberal society designed around choice and competition, belief is presumed to be individual and free, so that religious belief is imagined essentially like any other sort of preference, permeable to incentives and market pressures, subject to social-scientific analysis. The category of belief, in the aggregate, is a distillation of social relations, epistemology, doctrine, and values, forming a window onto the thought-worlds of the past. Karl Marx claimed that he wrote about the commodity because it was the smallest unit of analysis that contains the whole social universe. Likewise, belief is the smallest unit of analysis through which Western society has expressed what it means to be an authentic and complete human subject, the subject who speaks the words *I believe*.

CHAPTER ONE

Medieval Varieties of Believing

CONSIDER THE STORY of the theologian and the child. A Middle English version from the 1380s, in John Mirk's popular collection of homilies, went like this. There once was "a great master of divinity" who worked tirelessly to write a book explaining "why God would be believed one God in three persons." One day, as he walked by the seaside contemplating this mystery, he found a "fair child" who "had made a little pit in the sand." The theologian asked what he was doing, to which the child replied that he was pouring "all the water in the sea into this pit." The theologian scoffed, "Leave off, son, for thou shalt never do that." The boy answered that he would just as soon accomplish his task as the theologian would accomplish his, then mysteriously vanished. After this mystical encounter, the theologian "left off his studying, and thanked God that so fair warned him." The story concludes, "Good men and women, this I have said to you, as God hath inspired me, willing you for to have full belief in the trinity."[1]

The tale is first attested in the early thirteenth century and occurs in countless manuscripts thereafter, with many variations. Sometimes the child is Christ or an angel. Often the

FIGURE 1.1. Detail of a cycle of scenes from the life of Augustine, depicting
Augustine with a boy on the beach. Painted by Benozzo Gozzoli in
1464–1465 in the Church of St. Augustine, San Gimignano.
Courtesy of SCALA / Art Resource, NY.

theologian is identified as Augustine of Hippo, a distinctly
odd choice given that Augustine did indeed finish his *De Trinitate*, an early masterpiece of systematic theology.[2] With Augustine as its protagonist, the story became a popular subject
of Renaissance painting, appearing first in Benozzo Gozzoli's
frescoes at San Gimignano in the 1460s (figure 1.1).[3] William

Caxton, founder of the first English printing press, included a version in his 1483 translation of the *Golden Legend*, even though it was not in his source text, because he had admired a painting of the scene on an altar in Antwerp.[4]

The tale obviously addressed the relationship between understanding and believing. But it also addressed a more fundamental paradox that troubled medieval Christians: how might finite and fallen creatures like themselves access an infinite and perfect creator? The trinity was in some sense an answer to this very riddle: God became man so that we might approach him. But because the trinity is an incomprehensible mystery, rather than solving the problem it was simply the most important instantiation of the paradox itself: with what flawed human faculty might we *know* that God became man? The problem was still the necessity of accessing perfection with our imperfection, which could all too easily be unmasked as an arrogant fallacy.[5]

The category of belief was, for medieval Christians, at heart a way of negotiating this characteristic predicament of a religion that posits an utterly transcendent deity but then desires to know him. Belief mitigated the potential hubris that adhered in every attempt to approach God, not only because it was biblically sanctioned—all who believe are saved—but because it was amphibious, a kind of knowledge-claim without implying knowledge. Belief was an ordinary human operation, as familiar in the tavern as at the university; and yet, when sanctified, belief might reach all the way to heaven. As a concept with one foot in epistemology and another foot in saving faith, belief was ideally positioned to address the dilemma of how finite creatures might approach an infinite creator. Hence the story of the theologian and the child. On the surface, the story appears to posit belief as a radical alternative to understanding. And yet, when the story identifies the theologian as

Augustine, author of *De Trinitate*, the message becomes more ambiguous. Might belief be a prop to reason? Or might reason tell us what to believe, even if those things transcend reason? Or might a limited understanding be sufficient to raise human beings toward a God who agrees to meet believers halfway?

Another way to say this is that the same amphibious quality that made belief so useful also made it slippery and polysemous, because the Christian category of belief looked, smelled, and tasted like so many other, more mundane operations that could *not* reach to heaven. Everyone from the bishop to the ploughman knew that belief was required: belief in God, belief in Christ, belief in the fundamental doctrines of Christianity. But what was it, how did it function, and how could it be achieved?

<hr />

From the perspective of theologians, a fundamental issue was how belief related to knowledge, understanding, and intellect—that is, the business of theology itself as a science of God.[6] Was belief a species of knowledge, or was it the opposite of knowledge? Did belief utilize reason, or did belief reject reason? Besides being difficult questions, these were deeply personal issues for scholars, whose professional investment in rational inquiry left them—like the theologian walking on the sand—perpetually vulnerable to charges that Christianity demanded belief in, rather than analysis of, divine mysteries.

As on so many issues, the most influential source for medieval thought was Augustine. Perhaps surprisingly, given his famously pessimistic view of human nature, Augustine developed an essentially rationalist view in which "belief" opens human minds to intellective knowledge of God. "Belief," he wrote in his most fundamental observation on the subject, "is nothing else than to think with assent."[7] Since belief is fundamentally propositional, "thinking" must come first, "for no one believes anything unless he has first thought that it is to be believed."[8] Yet thinking of divine things is beyond our capacity without divine assistance; thus, despite the centrality of reason, belief is never a merely human operation. As he wrote elsewhere, "it is God who gave us even to believe" (*nam et ut credamus, Deus dedit*). Propositional truth comes from God, and then we use our will to "consent to the truth."[9] Augustine thus made belief a partnership between will and intellect: intellect learns of the truth from God, will directs that knowledge toward proper ends, and the resultant belief then seeks yet more knowledge. Understanding grows as belief grows.

In *On the Free Choice of the Will*, for instance, Augustine argued that it is proper that "we want to know and understand what we believe." Of course, believing takes priority. His proof text was Isaiah 7:9—a verse to which we shall return—which Augustine rendered as *nisi credideritis, non intelligetis*, "Unless you believe, you will not understand." But once we believe any "important question of theology," it is appropriate that we should then desire to understand it, according to Christ's promise, *Seek, and ye shall find*: "For what is believed without being known cannot be said to have been found, nor can anyone become capable of finding God, unless he has first believed what afterwards he is to know."[10] In a sermon, Augustine debated between two rival claims: "I understand in order to believe" and "I believe in order to understand." The second was fundamental, according to Isaiah 7:9. But Augustine admitted that the first also held a grain of truth, because understanding, if already grounded in belief, can produce more belief. Those who believe just a little are enabled thereby to *listen* to preachers—like Augustine himself, delivering this sermon. Thus begins a chain reaction, for auditors are exhorted with reason, which produces more belief. Here Augustine turned to the text of Mark 9:24, "I believe, Lord, help my unbelief," the oxymoronic prayer of a man who has just enough belief to know he needs more.[11]

Trying to understand Augustine in his own context is beyond our scope; what matters for the present argument is that, building upon Augustine, a rationalist strain in medieval theology stressed the partnership between belief and understanding. So, for instance, Anselm of Canterbury interpreted Augustine's *credere ut intelligam*—"believe in order to understand"—to mean that the highest purpose of belief is to open the *credenda* of Christianity to the intellect:

> I do not endeavor, O Lord, to penetrate thy sublimity, for in no wise do I compare my understanding with that; but I long to understand in some degree thy truth, which my heart believes and loves. For I do not seek to understand that I may believe, but I believe in order to understand.[12]

Likewise, in his *De Incarnatione Verbi*, Anselm suggested "that no Christian ought to question the truth of what the Catholic Church believes [*credit*]," but "rather, by holding constantly and unhesitatingly to this faith, by loving it and living according to it, he ought humbly, and as best he is able, to seek to discover the reason why it is true [*quaerere rationem quomodo sit*]."[13] As Marcia Colish notes, while Anselm shared with Augustine a core epistemological concern—"the theological problem of speaking about God"—Anselm developed a new sense that the task of theology was not just to express the divine *logos* but to *define* it.[14] Anselm's lifelong project to prove the rationality of Christian belief—that the trinity is theologically necessary, that atonement is a reasonable economy of exchange, and that logically the greatest thing that can be conceived must exist—is not a claim that Christianity can be independently derived from reason. Rather, *given* belief in revelation, we may approach God most effectively through our reason. Belief is not only an act of faith, it is also a series of propositions to be understood, creating for Anselm what Virginie Greene calls "a virtuous circle in which faith and intelligence feed one another."[15]

A similar maneuver can be found a generation later in a treatise on the trinity by the French Augustinian, Richard of St. Victor. Richard admitted that "some of the things which we are commanded to believe appear to be not only above reason, but also contrary to reason"; in these things "we are more accustomed to rely on faith than on reasoning, on authority rather than argumentation, according to that saying of the prophet: *unless you believe, you will not understand.*" But, Richard argued, Isaiah did not mean that understanding is impossible, he meant only that it is available "conditionally" to the faithful.[16] In particular, Richard deployed the theological commonplace that divine things are eternal, unchanging, and "entirely unable not to be." And, he argued in a crucial twist, "it is entirely impossible for any necessary being to lack a necessary reason." In other words, God and his will are knowable through reason: "It will be our intention in this work concerning those things which we believe [*credimus*], to adduce not only credible [*probabiles*] reasons but also necessary ones, and to preserve the teaching of our faith by clarification and explanation of the truth. For I believe without a doubt that although they may be hidden from our efforts for a while, there is no absence not only of probable but also of necessary arguments for the explanation of anything that has necessary being."[17] This argument, elaborating upon Anselm's concepts of necessity and *fides quaerens intellectum*, is as close as we are likely to find to a union of belief and reason.[18]

A more aggressive variety of rationalism can be found in Ramon Llull, a Majorcan theologian who learned Arabic in order to convert Muslims in Spain and North Africa around the turn of the fourteenth century. Llull denounced his predecessor, Ramon Martí, who had supposedly used reason to convince the King of Tunis that Islam was false, but when the king asked him to prove the truth of Christianity, he responded that it could not be proved—"It is simply necessary to believe." Llull, by contrast, insisted that he could indeed prove the truth of Christianity, because the principle of "necessary reasons" held that all truths, both spiritual and philosophical, must align together. By this logic, Llull offered the remarkable argument that Arab philosophers were really Christians rather than Muslims, because to be a philosopher is to distinguish truth from falsehood: "Educated Saracens do not believe that Mohammed is a prophet, because in the Quran, which contains their law, they find many things incompatible with holiness and true prophecy."[19] Here we see the potential violence of a rationalism in which only those who believe properly can be said to understand, and understanding is presumed to be the path to Christian belief.

And what is the Bible?

If Augustine established the rationalist uses of belief, other Church Fathers bequeathed to the Middle Ages a very different perspective, whose heirs willfully trampled the fences Augustine had built. Most importantly, an alternative tradition, originating in opposition to Gnostic rationalists, stressed that Christian belief was an alternative to understanding, and that Christianity required believing without or against reason and evidence. Tertullian, a bitter polemicist against the Gnostics, argued in his second-century *De Carne Christi* that the implausible and seemingly oxymoronic death of the incarnated God should be believed precisely "because it is absurd":

prorsus credibile est, quia ineptum est.[20] Likewise, his more restrained successor Lactantius, advisor to the first Christian Emperor Constantine, expanded upon an argument in Cicero's *On the Nature of the Gods*: "If you believe, why then do you require a reason, which may have the effect of causing you not to believe? But if you require a reason, and think that the subject demands inquiry, then you do not believe; for you make inquiry with this view, that you may follow it when you have ascertained it."[21] Two centuries later, Pseudo-Dionysius birthed a long tradition of apophatic or negative theology, insisting that God so transcends even the categories of our thought that true belief is as much about unknowing as knowing.[22] Pope Gregory the Great in the sixth century, considering the unbelief of Doubting Thomas, wrote, "If God's method of operating is understood through our reason, then it is no longer something at which we marvel. Neither does our faith have any value, if human reason furnishes it with experimental proof."[23] As Glenn Most has shown, this became the standard interpretation of Christ's words to Doubting Thomas—"Blessed are those that have not seen, and yet believe"—in the Latin West: "proof that we should not try too hard to understand." Christ's words functioned as a message for future generations who, unable to see Christ's resurrection for themselves, would have to believe the reports of witnesses without question.[24]

Following Gregory and other patristic theologians, belief was taken in some quarters to be authentic only when it clashed with reason. Here the most influential voice was William of Auvergne, Bishop of Paris from 1228 to 1249, whose work *De Fide* insisted that belief is virtuous when we believe what appears to be untrue. Our natural propensity to believe the evidence of the senses is not the same thing as authentic Christian belief: "Just as it is one thing to love someone because of his merit . . . and something else [to love] from the virtue of loving, so it is one thing to believe on the basis of probability or evidence, and something else to believe from the virtue of believing itself." Belief that requires proof is an injured faculty, like a person who needs a cane to walk. But propping belief with reason is not only unnecessary, it is actually misguided, even monstrous, because the knowledge of faith is far stronger and more certain than the knowledge of the intellect: belief perceives the deep, inner essence of the universe, rather than the mere outward shadows of worldly epistemology. For belief to rely upon evidence is thus a perversion of divine order.[25]

This impulse found its fullest expression in the mystical tradition, that element of Christianity that involves, in the words of Bernard McGinn, "the preparation for, the consciousness of, and the reaction to what can be described as the immediate or direct presence of God."[26] A whole host of practices or technologies were developed in the Middle Ages to unite with God or come directly into the divine presence, ranging from asceticism and mortification on one side of the spectrum, to meditation and contemplative exercises on the other. Belief was not always a central category for mystics: when Francis of Assisi received his stigmata, for instance, it was not "belief" but devotion that drove the nails into his flesh in the midst of a forty-day fast. Nonetheless, we can find in medieval mystical writings some of the most eloquent claims that belief is a radical alternative to understanding.

So, for instance, the fourteenth-century German mystic Henry Suso rarely spoke of believing; he was much better known for action. Not lucky enough to receive the stigmata from God like Francis, instead he stigmatized himself, literally carving the name of God into his own chest with a knife, and "because of his burning love, he enjoyed seeing this and hardly noticed the pain."[27] Yet when Suso did discuss belief, he imagined it as a substitute for unreliable intellection, a partner of mystical experience rather than theological speculation. In his *Little Book of Eternal Wisdom*, for instance, Suso ventriloquized Christ contemplating the Eucharist: "In what manner my glorified body and my soul, according to the whole truth, are in the sacrament, this can no tongue express, nor any mind conceive, for it is a work of my omnipotence. Therefore oughtest thou to believe it in all simplicity [*Darum sollst du es einfältig glauben*], and not pry much into it." The doctrine of the mass, as Steven Justice has noted, often crystalized medieval debates over the limits of reason, not least because of the horror that ensued when Christians thought too literally about the human flesh they were consuming.[28] But Suso then used this mystery as a wedge to insist more broadly upon unknowing belief. "Had I asked thee how the portals of the abyss are constructed, or how the waters in the firmament are held together," Suso asked, paraphrasing Job, "thou wouldst perhaps have answered thus: It is a question too deep for me, I cannot go into it; I never descended into the abyss, nor ever mounted up to the firmament." Suso's conclusion was, therefore, "Why shouldst thou wish, then, to understand what surpasses all the earth, all the heavens, and all the senses? Or why wilt thou needs inquire into it? Behold, all such wondering and prying thoughts proceed alone from grossness of sense, which takes divine and supernatural things after the likeness of things earthly and natural."[29]

In spiritualist critiques of rationalist theology, the advantage of "belief" was that it provided a conduit between humanity and God that required no understanding. As the fourteenth-century Flemish mystic John of Ruysbroeck put it:

> The incomprehensible and most high nature of God transcends all creatures in heaven and on earth. For all that a creature can comprehend is of the creature; but God is

above all creatures and within and without all creatures, and every created comprehension is too narrow to comprehend him. . . . We should believe the articles of faith [*articulos fidei credere*], and not desire to understand [*exploratos*] them.[30]

Vernacular English works of the fifteenth century were likewise saturated with a soft mysticism that advised readers, as the child on the beach advised the theologian, to abandon understanding and believe instead. The most eloquent example comes from an anonymous but often reproduced Middle English verse:

> Wytt hath wonder & kynde ne can
> How maydyn ys moder & god ys man
> Leve thy askyng & beleve þat wonder
> ffor myght hath maystry & skyll goth vnder.[31]

Now, while there were rationalist and non-rationalist understandings of belief in the Middle Ages, it would be wrong to imagine that these were opposing parties or schools. Admittedly, sometimes the issue could be a flashpoint of controversy, as when Bernard of Clairvaux denounced Peter Abelard in 1140 on that grounds that "He endeavors to scrutinize by the light of his reason alone the mysteries which are apprehended by the pious mind only by the intuition of faith: the faith of the pious, which believes and does not discuss." According to Bernard, Abelard "holds even God in suspicion, nor is willing to believe anything unless he shall have first considered it by reason. Though the prophet says, *If you will not believe, ye shall not understand*, that man blames spontaneous faith as mere credulity."[32] Yet despite Bernard's hyperbole, much more often thinkers tried to square these opposing tendencies. If we look, for instance, at the great medieval theorist of "learned ignorance" Nicholas of Cusa, or at the Chancellor of the University of Paris Jean Gerson, we find careers dedicated to the reconciliation of these alternative idioms.[33] The variety of medieval conceptions of belief was most often a sign of layered complexity rather than fundamental disagreement, a recognition that the kind of belief upon which the science of God was built was not necessarily the same kind of belief that led the mystic into the sight of God.

The issue of belief's relationship to understanding was closely tied to a different problem: how was religious belief similar to, or different from, other sorts of knowledge-claims? After all, people were said to "believe" lots of different things—about nature, about history, about objects of perception. But surely Christian belief, the kind referred to in the New Testament, could not be qualitatively the same as these mundane operations. The doctrinal beliefs of Christianity, encapsulated in the word credo (I believe) at the head of the Apostles' Creed, were not generally understood as propositional claims equivalent to more prosaic beliefs about the world: to believe them was not merely to attest their truth but in some other way to inhabit them.

Yet at the same time, if religious belief was never quite the same, neither could it be entirely divorced from more mundane ways of believing, because religious belief was beyond the capacity of human language to express or the human mind to comprehend. The word "believe" in every European language referred *both* to religion and to more banal truth-claims, because no alternative could capture the ineffable qualities that made religious belief different from ordinary intellective assent.[34] Thus, religious belief was in constant danger of collapsing back onto its profane homonym, haunted by the secular knowledge-claims from which it sought to separate itself. A sinful and fallen world inevitably forgot the difference between religious belief and other ways of knowing, and the Sisyphean labor of Christianity was to remind people that real belief was something more.

Crucial here was the medieval distinction between knowledge, opinion, and belief. *Scientia*, or knowledge, had a cluster of distinctive premodern meanings quite different from the modern concept of science. Scientia was secure and demonstrable knowledge, proved deductively and syllogistically from self-evident axioms. Achieving scientia was difficult and rigorous: syllogisms had to describe the very essence of their objects, or else risk conclusions that was merely accidental and particular rather than universally valid. This framework was common throughout late antiquity and the Middle Ages, but it was newly theorized and systematized in the Christian West with the rediscovery of Aristotelian texts (especially the *Posterior Analytics*) and their incorporation into Christian cosmology in the twelfth and thirteenth centuries, most famously in the work of Thomas Aquinas.

Christians like Aquinas claimed to know a surprising amount through rigorous scientia, because Christian revelation was taken to offer insights into the essences of so many things. Yet, on the vast majority of topics, knowledge was unavailable. Instead, according to medieval theorists, there were varying degrees of *opinio*, or opinion.[35] As Edmund Byrne has written in a fascinating book on probability and opinion in Aquinas, "The notion which Thomas wishes to express by the term 'opinion' has its roots deep in the fact of human ignorance."[36] Aquinas first defined opinion very broadly, in his *De Anime*, as "cognition of those things about which we do not have certain judgment [*iudicium*]." But later, in his *Summa*

Theologica, he clarified this definition by writing that opinion is an "act of the intellect inclined to one alternative while retaining respect for the other."[37] By this definition, opinions may well contain some truth, but by the same token they necessarily contain some falsehood. Thus, he argued, opinion is not virtuous; unlike knowledge, it is always corrupted. The dialectical process of disputation (Aquinas's own method) attempts to reach a higher proportion of truth, and at least in theory sufficient ratiocination might connect an opinion demonstratively to essential principles and so achieve scientia. But in practice, the human mind is so fallen that opinion, a corrupt compound of truth with falsehood, was often the most that was possible.

Crucial for our analysis, then, is that religious beliefs that depend upon revelation and cannot be deduced logically from first principles—the doctrine of the trinity, for instance—are not knowledge.[38] But at the same time, those religious beliefs are absolutely certain, not because they are demonstrable but because they are given by a perfect authority, containing no corruption, so they are not opinion either. They are instead a third category, and Aquinas devoted a great deal of effort to analyzing this separate category that had been unknown to his beloved Aristotle.

In the *Summa Theologica*, for instance, Aquinas glossed Augustine's classic definition of belief, asking whether to believe is to think with assent.[39] He approached this question through his habitual technique of dialectic, noting that "to think" can be taken in three ways. First, it can be taken "in a general way for any kind of actual consideration of the intellect." But it can also be "more strictly taken for that consideration of the intellect which is accompanied by some kind of inquiry," in other words, a stage of thought prior to a settled conclusion. And such inquiry can be further divided into two species: deliberation about "universal notions" and deliberation about "particular matters." Having made this division, Aquinas argued that "to think with assent" in the first sense does *not* constitute belief, "since, in this way, a man thinks with assent even when he considers what he knows by science." So belief is *not* knowledge. In the second sense, however, to believe *is* to "think with assent" because belief is always deliberative or speculative: it "does not attain the perfection of clear sight." In this respect, Aquinas admitted, belief is a close relative of "doubt, suspicion, and opinion" [*dubitante, suspicante, et opinante*] because it never achieves the clarity of demonstration. But, unlike these more problematic operations of the intellect, belief also has much in common with knowledge and understanding, because of the firmness that defines it. In sum, Aquinas wrote, "the act of believing [*credere*] is distinguished from all the other acts of the intellect."

Here Aquinas goes well beyond predecessors like John of Salisbury (1120–1180), who had described belief as an "exceedingly strong opinion" (*vehemens opinio*) rather than an altogether different category, and Hugh of St. Victor (1096–1141), who had defined belief as a certitude greater than opinion but less than science.[40] He is more in line with his recent predecessor at Paris, William of Auxerre, who defined faith/belief as *more* certain than demonstrative scientia because "the intellect illuminated by faith believes in the first truth more than in a syllogistic demonstration."[41] He also echoed Bernard of Clairvaux, who wrote that while faith and understanding both possess secure truth, "opinion" is merely "to hold something as true which you do not know to be false . . . Faith possesses nothing which is uncertain, for if it does, it is not faith but opinion."[42] The point for Aquinas, as Marcia Colish puts it, was that "faith transcends science. Faith, after all, deals with the noblest possible object of knowledge; it opens to the knower an infinitude of truth and goodness; and it is absolutely certain." To those who lack it, belief seems like nothing more than "a knowledge which cannot be verified," but those who have it know that it is the firmest way the mind can know.[43] The tremendous influence of Aquinas meant that, at least within formal university theology, his view would prevail: belief was absolutely certain assent to propositions that are given by perfect authority rather than known according to perfect demonstration. Of course, all human beings experience doubts about what they believe; but for Aquinas and his successors, this did not imply uncertainty, because certainty lies in the source of the proposition rather than in our grasp of it. By the same token, wrong belief is not really belief at all no matter how firmly held; it is rather opinion, because belief itself is guaranteed to be true.[44] Thus, while of course we all "believe" in mundane propositions as well as divine ones, those mundane beliefs, based upon flawed human authorities, are only a species of opinion; Christian belief is fundamentally different from the belief of the world because it rests upon the authority of God himself.[45] Here medieval thinkers followed Lactantius and other Church fathers, steeped in the classical rhetorical tradition, who had distinguished sharply between our belief in "a well-composed poem" or "a speech beguiling with its sweetness"—what Cicero had called "a plausible invention to generate faith [*fidem*]"—and religious belief.[46]

Recent historians have stressed that the rigorous framework of medieval scientia was in many ways unsustainable: the profound distance it posited between demonstrative knowledge and other kinds of truth-claims, while intended to increase the authority of academic reasoning, in fact generated skepticism and encouraged speculation about other, lesser but still meaningful categories of knowledge. Writers like Christine de Pizan, Henry of Ghent, William of Ockham, and Ockham's antagonist Jean Buridan all experimented with perceptual knowledge, or knowledge based on testimony, that was suitable for living if not for philosophy.[47] Opinion relentlessly flooded into the cracks of knowledge. But belief appears to have been considerably more robust. To the best of my knowledge, only one medieval writer willfully shattered the barrier separating opinion from belief, and he was, not surprisingly, a heretic: Reginald Pecock, the only English bishop deprived of his see for heresy before the Reformation. Pecock wrote, in vernacular English, that merely "opinial faith" is the kind Christians typically possess on earth, while "sciential faith" is reserved for "the bliss of heaven." Christian belief, for Pecock, was therefore decidedly uncertain, as befitting our fallen nature. Even the apostles, who saw Christ's miracles for themselves, had only "opinial belief" because it was the product of empirical observation. Pecock thus attacked his own Church for insisting upon blind faith in its theological pronouncements, calling instead for belief based upon the evidence of the senses. It is no wonder he was forced to recant his heresies and to burn his books with his own hand.[48]

{⟨⟩}

Aquinas developed the notion that belief flows from infallible authority, but he did not invent it. In late antiquity, Augustine had taken up this cudgel most famously in his influential polemic against the Manichaeans, *De Utilitate Credendi* (*On the Profit of Believing*). Again, his key proof text was Isaiah 7:9, which he rendered as *nisi credideritis, non intelligetis*, "Unless you believe, you will not understand." But here, we must notice that this was a mistranslation. As Augustine himself was honest enough to note in his *De Doctrina Christiana*, the Latin word "*intelligetis*" was a nonliteral translation, following the Greek Septuagint, of a Hebrew original that had nothing to do with "understanding." Already in Augustine's time, the Vulgate Bible had corrected the passage to "*Nisi credideritis, non permanebitis*": if you do not believe, you will not endure. It is remarkable that in all the hundreds of medieval and early modern Catholic books that cite this passage, it is hard to find a single one that uses the Catholic Church's own Vulgate. The reason will soon become clear: this passage became the lynchpin of the argument that what defines Christian belief and distinguishes it from profane knowledge-claims is that by definition it consists in obedience to the Church.

De Utilitate Credendi focused on the necessity of believing without understanding, against heretics who claimed that they should first understand a doctrine before they could believe it. The reason belief must precede understanding, Augustine wrote, was not merely that most people are incapable of comprehending theology, although that was of course true. No, the principal reason was that belief itself is characterized by the fact that when we believe, *we believe someone else*. Augustine distinguished between three adjacent categories of truth-claim: understanding, belief, and opinion (*intellegere, credere, opinari*).[49] As he summarized the difference: "What then we understand, we owe to reason; what we believe, to authority; what we have an opinion on, to error."[50] Just as we believe our father's identity on the authority of our mother, so we believe religious truths on the authority of the Church.[51] For Augustine, all religious belief—except the originary belief of inspired witnesses—is belief in some report: blessed are those who have not seen and yet believe. And given a choice of which authority to believe, the only sensible path is to believe the Church, which taught us to believe in the first place; otherwise there is no reason to believe at all. Or at least that was Augustine's message to the Manichaeans.

One potential inadequacy of Augustine's argument was that, while it usefully distinguished belief from understanding and opinion, it failed to distinguish between natural and supernatural kinds of believing: there is no intrinsic difference, so far, between believing that Brutus killed Caesar and believing that Pilate killed Christ. While never entirely solving this problem, Augustine deployed two separate solutions to mitigate it, both of which echoed down the Christian tradition. First, he stressed the categorical difference between believing a merely human authority and believing the Church guided by the Holy Spirit. As he bluntly put this sentiment, "I would not have believed the gospel unless the authority of the Catholic Church had moved me"—a gift to future defenders of the power of Rome.[52]

Second, Augustine used the preposition "in" to differentiate ordinary propositional assent from genuine Christian commitment: we do not just believe, we believe *in*. So, for instance, *Credere Christum, et credere in Christum, differunt*—"to believe Christ, and to believe *in* Christ, differ." Elsewhere Augustine wrote, "If he has faith without hope and without love, he believes that Christ exists, but he does not believe *in* Christ."[53] And yet again:

> He that believes him does not necessarily believe *in* him. For even the devils believed him, but they did not believe *in* him . . . What then is *"to believe in him"*? By believing to love him, by believing to esteem highly, by believing to go into him and to be incorporated in his members.[54]

Despite a superficial similarity to the modern English distinction between loving someone and being *in* love with them, Augustine's idiom carried different connotations. In Latin, the object of the preposition "in" can occur in different grammatical cases: "in" followed by the accusative, as here, suggests movement, often translated as "in*to*." Thus, Augustine's *credere in Christum* would be better translated as "to believe *into* Christ," except that we lack that idiom in English.

Both Augustine's idea of "believing *in*" and his distinction between believing ordinary human authority and believing an inspired Church became staples of the medieval tradition. So, for instance, on the subject of believing *in*, Anselm elaborated upon Augustine in an oft-cited formulation, stressing that even among those who ostensibly believe the Church's doctrine, not all are *believers*: "Living faith *believes in* that in which we ought to believe, while dead faith merely *believes* that which ought to be believed."[55] Peter Lombard, in his vastly influential *Sentences*, expanded upon Augustine with a threefold distinction between "to believe God" (*credere deo*), "to believe in a God" (*credere deum*), and "to believe *in* God" (*credere in deum*). Simply "to believe God" is to believe that what he says is true. "To believe in a God" is to believe that God *is*. Only "to believe *in* God," to be joined with God through belief, represents genuine Christian belief.[56] This distinction infused vernacular religious texts in the later Middle Ages. For instance, the 1491 French incunabulum *La Mer des Hystoires*, an abridged translation of a Latin compendium of world history, told its readers that to believe *in* God is not merely to believe that God is, but "to spread the news and honor the fact that he is. The good and the bad both believe God indifferently, but it is only the good who believe in God, as mentions the Master of Sentences."[57]

The idea that religious belief adhered in obedience to the Church was most influentially elaborated through the doctrine of *fides implicita*, implicit faith, designed to make belief easier for the uneducated masses. A succinct early version comes from William of Auxerre, professor of theology at Paris, who wrote that "to believe implicitly is to believe to be true in general whatever the Church believes."[58] That is, as long as you believe that everything the Church believes is true, you need not believe specifically in any of its doctrines, or even know what they are: belief is imputed to you. There was a great deal of dispute about exactly what had to be believed explicitly and what was suitably implicit. A baseline established by lawyers took Hebrews 11:6—"He that comes to God must believe that he is, and is a rewarder to them that seek him"—to delimit what had to be believed explicitly by all Christians, with everything else potentially numbered among the *implicita*. But this was an embarrassingly low bar, not least because it did not include Christ, so commentators like Thomas Aquinas and Denis the Carthusian stressed that Hebrews 11:6 implied a series of other, more obviously Christian imperatives.[59] Nonetheless, because elite theologians had such a low opinion of the rustic laity, it was hard for them to imagine requiring very much knowledge—in most of Europe, for instance, with Germany perhaps the exception, laypeople recited the *Credo* in Latin rather than the vernacular and did not generally know what they were saying.[60] Moreover, in the hands of Pope Innocent IV in the thirteenth century, *fides implicita* was interpreted to mean that you can believe a doctrine because you *think* the Church believes it, even if it later turns out that the Church believes no such thing. By this logic, a wide array of errors could be maintained provisionally, without fault, so long as they remained open to correction by the Church.

Of course, most expositors of implicit faith were apologists for the institutional Church that employed them, with a vested interest in arguing that belief consists in obedience. But this doctrine was also used in potentially subversive ways by those outside the hierarchy. One example is the English mystic Julian of Norwich, who suggested that because belief by definition flowed from the Church rather than her own supernatural experiences, those experiences could not disturb her belief.[61] Profane literature could also paradoxically benefit from the Church's monopoly on belief. At the conclusion of *Mandeville's Travels*, for instance, the traveler decides that because people are so incredulous, on his way home he would visit Rome "to show my book to the Holy Father the pope, and tell him of the marvels that I had seen." After reading Mandeville's writings, the pope allegedly "confirmed my book in all points."[62] Here the Church's privileged status as the font of belief becomes a celebrity endorsement.

Perhaps the most perverse claim that belief adheres in obedience comes from William of Ockham, so often accused of dissent and hounded by the papacy. Ockham argued that, according to the doctrine of implicit faith, you may in fact *doubt* that something the Church says is true, as long as you nonetheless believe generally in the authority of the Church. Ockham justified doubt in this way: "Someone doubting some particular article, however, does have a firm faith that the whole Christian faith is true and certain. He also has a firm implicit faith about the very article that he doubts. And therefore he is Catholic even if he does not have a firm explicit faith about that particular article."[63] In this wonderful reasoning, implicit faith grows to gargantuan proportions, cloaking all manner of free inquiry and speculation under cover of a generalized orthodoxy.[64]

An interesting derivative of Augustine's two arguments—about belief adhering in the authority of the Church, and about what it means to believe *in*—was a long-running debate over whether we ought to believe *in* the Church. The Apostles' Creed requires belief *in* each person of the trinity, but it is much less clear whether we ought to believe *in* other articles of faith, or merely believe them. The language in the Creed—"I believe in the Holy Spirit, the holy catholic Church, the communion of saints . . ."—was grammatically ambiguous, in Latin as in English: the preposition "in" might apply only to the Holy Spirit, or it might be interpolated across the subsequent articles.

There was significant patristic ammunition behind the claim that we should only *believe* the Church, rather than believing *in* it. Augustine had argued that "of his apostles we can say, we believe Paul; but not, we believe *in* Paul: we believe Peter; but not, we believe *in* Peter."[65] Elsewhere he wrote, "Believe *in* the Holy Spirit, believe the holy Church."[66] Rufinus explained, in the first great commentary on the Apostles' Creed, that "we are not told to believe *in* the Holy Church, but that the Holy Church exists, speaking of it not as God, but as a Church gathered together for God."[67] Faustus of Riez agreed: "He who believes in the Church believes in man . . . Abandon, therefore, the blasphemous notion that you ought to believe in any human creature."[68] By the ninth century, Paschasius Radbert summarized his predecessors this way: "No one can rightly say, I believe in my neighbor or in an angel or in any creature whatever. Everywhere in the divine scriptures you will find the right to this confession reserved to God alone."[69]

Yet on the other hand, a minority report from alternative authorities defended belief *in* the Church. Chrysologus, for instance, defended belief "*in* holy Church. Because the Church is in Christ, and Christ is in the Church; he therefore who acknowledges the Church, confessed that he believed in the Church."[70] Jerome, in his *Dialogus contra Luciferianos*, asked in quasi-creedal terms, "Do you believe *in* the holy Church?" expecting an affirmative reply, and many medieval authorities like Peter Abelard repeated his formulation until the offending preposition was deleted by later editors.[71] Hélinand of Froidmont, a French Cistercian of the early thirteenth century, defended Jerome's formulation this way: "Do you believe in holy

Church, that is, do you believe that no one can be saved without abiding faithfully in the unity of the body of the Church?"[72]

In light of this minority report, Thomas Aquinas fudged. While he admitted that "it is better and more in keeping with the common use to omit the *in*," he also allowed that if we want to say we believe *in* the holy Catholic Church, "this must be taken as verified in so far as our faith is directed to the Holy Ghost, who sanctifies the Church, so that the sense is, 'I believe in the Holy Ghost sanctifying the Church.'"[73] This was to become a huge hostage to fortune. We might speculate, for instance, that it authorized the German theologian and papal apologist Hermann von Schildesche, writing at the request of Pope John XXII in 1330, to argue that, "In our view, the beginning of all articles of the faith lies in believing in the holy church [*credere in sanctam Ecclesiam*]."[74]

And even if the weight of theological opinion was against believing *in* the Church, nonetheless the preposition was often included anyway for aesthetic reasons rather than theological ones.[75] Any medieval scholar poring over manuscripts would have found countless texts that included the dangerous prepositional proposition, "credo *in* ecclesiam."

Perhaps the most fundamental issue of all was the question of how easy or hard it was to believe. John van Engen has eloquently described the dilemma of how to define "faith" in medieval society, transforming what was originally an exclusive concept, designed to differentiate a Christian minority from the profane social body of the ancient Mediterranean, into an inclusive concept, designed to incorporate the entire social body. On the one hand, everyone (Jews being the exception that proved the rule) was numbered among the faithful; but on the other hand, for the concept to retain its utility, faith had to remain an aspiration toward which people strived and which some inevitably failed to achieve.[76] A parallel dilemma structured medieval discussions of belief, complicated by the fact that Christian belief had its worldly doppelganger: believing was not only a spiritual activity, it was also an ordinary cognitive operation which in some sense everyone practiced, whether Christian or not. So in essence the question became: how difficult was it for the profane act of intellective assent to reach beyond the opinion of the world and become a point of contact with the divine?

A useful place to explore this issue is the scholastic habit of distinguishing different types of "faith," which inevitably depended upon the vocabulary of belief to differentiate them. According to medieval theologians, the most basic kind of faith was *fides infusa*: infused faith, which was imparted to infants at baptism. We must be careful to keep this scholastic definition in mind, because the reformers of the sixteenth century radically altered the meaning of "infused faith," identifying it with saving faith; but in the Middle Aages, infused faith was the most generalized form, the kind that floated in the air of Christian society. When developed through instruction, this infused faith became an acquired faith, *fides acquisita*, and was termed *credulitas*: belief. But already there was controversy, because even fides infusa could sometimes be equated with belief. Augustine had argued that "an infant, although he is not yet a believer in the sense of having that faith which includes the consenting will of those who exercise it, nevertheless becomes a believer through the sacrament of that faith. For as it is answered [by godparents] that he believes, so also he is called a believer, not because he assents to the truth by an act of his own judgment, but because he receives the sacrament of that truth." In this sense, "believing is nothing else than having faith."[77] When Ivo of Chartres wrote a short chapter called "What it is to believe" in his *Panormia* around 1100, the sole content of the chapter was a version of this quotation from Augustine.[78] And an English Dominican of the thirteenth century, Richard Fishacre, wrote that "infants believe because they have an habitual faith, as sleeping persons have eyesight."[79]

Usually fides acquisita was imagined to be the kind of faith associated with belief as an act of substantive assent. However, in their usual manner of subdivision, the scholastics split fides acquisita into two species. First came *fides informis*, formless faith, sometimes termed dead faith. It was in this sense that the devils believe and tremble (James 2:19): they have the content of faith but their will does not assent to it or direct it toward proper ends. As Peter Lombard put it, fides informis is "that unformed quality of faith by which a bad Christian believes everything that a good one does."[80] But when fides acquisita is joined with good works, it becomes *fides formata*, or sometimes *fides caritate formata*: formed faith, or faith formed by love.

There was therefore a well-developed discussion of what role belief might play as a mark of distinction even within a society of believers. But the issue of whether belief was easy or hard could also be framed in ways that transcended scholastic taxonomies of faith. For instance, the question could be raised whether heretics, Muslims, and Jews ought to be described as unbelievers, or whether they were simply wrong believers—in other words, whether the category of "belief" is consistent with error. A late medieval vernacular understanding of belief was certainly capacious enough to allow that, for instance, Muslims "believed" in their Quran. Examples are easy to find. In the English version of the prose romance *Pontus et Sidonia*, for instance, an Islamic usurper "suffreth every man to live in what belief that ever he will."[81] In the *Golden Legend*, there is no incongruity in a pagan torturer telling St. Margaret, "Believe, and thou shalt live"—an offer she refuses, remaining true to Christ.[82] In *Dives et Pauper*, we are told that "Solomon sought the company of heathen women. The women were stable in their false belief, he was unstable in his right belief and followed her false belief, and forsook God's law in a great part, and worshipped false gods."[83]

Yet, as we have seen, Christian believing was generally understood, at least by theologians, to be qualitatively different from other, more mundane kinds of believing. Hence it was perfectly possible to argue that even though the word "believe" was used to describe Muslims, Jews, and heretics, they actually lacked belief, and were unbelievers, because they believed in religious matters only in the profane or quotidian sense of the term. Leo the Great provided patristic authority for this view. Writing to the Council of Chalcedon in 451, he denounced "the vain unbelief of heretics": "Let not that be defended which may not be believed." Likewise, in a sermon on the nativity of Christ, he used the wonderfully evocative phrase "all false believers' opinions" [*omnium fere falsa credentium opinionibus*] to emphasize that heretics who have "refused to believe the reality of the two natures in Christ" hold their views only as opinions, hence they possess belief only in the profane or vernacular sense.[84] The medieval Latin neologism credentia could mean not only beliefs but heresy, suggesting an ironic content: *mere* beliefs, in a worldly rather than properly Christian sense.[85]

Islam offered a particular challenge to medieval Christian conceptions of belief, because the Church was so unsure about what Islam was. Often it was portrayed as paganism and idol worship. In the twelfth century, it became more common instead to portray Islam as a heresy: worshippers of the true

God were corrupted by the false doctrine of Mohammed. Only gradually thereafter did some medieval Christians (notably the Dominicans) reach the conclusion that Islam was an alternative religion altogether. The question of whether Muslims "believed" in God or their own doctrine was therefore highly unstable. To the extent that they were imagined as rational, they might be given credit for "believing" as a way of indicating that they were open to persuasion; when Muslims failed to convert after receiving the Gospel, however, they were instead described as irrational, with false opinions rather than belief.[86] So, for example, John-Jerome of Prague described a miracle story he had heard while traveling in the Holy Land around 1430: the body of a Saracen, whose murder had been falsely blamed on Christians, rose from the grave and announced that "Our Mohammedan faith [*fides*] which you call holy is not a faith [*fides*] at all, but a fable [*fabula*]."[87]

Thomas Aquinas, in his *Summa Theologica*, put theological meat on these bones. In attempting to provide a rigorously philosophical definition of faith, he asked whether "to believe in a God" [*credere deum*] constitutes an act of faith, given that heathens appear to believe in a God too, but surely cannot be reckoned to have faith. He determined in response to this riddle that "unbelievers cannot be said to 'believe in a god' as we understand it in relation to the act of faith. For they do not believe that God exists [*non enim credunt deum esse*] under the conditions that faith determines; hence they do not truly believe in a God, since, as the Philosopher observes, 'to know simple things defectively is not to know them at all.'"[88] This argument was, as we shall see, dangerously portable: by its simple logic, any defect in knowledge of God could be grounds for arguing that the defective agent does not believe that God exists at all. This was part and parcel of the Christianization of reason by scholastic theologians, which made it increasingly

possible to argue that, for instance, Jews lacked reason altogether, or that they were deliberate disbelievers who rejected
evidence that should lead any rational person to Christian
truth.[89] In general, the twelfth and thirteenth centuries saw
an exponential increase in arguments for the unbelief of out-
siders, as the Church formalized its doctrines and theorized its
own authority to define belief.[90]

Besides heretics and non-Christians, the putative "belief"
of wicked Christians was also open to debate, raising the question of how far belief could be ascribed to most people even
in an outwardly Christian society. Was someone who claimed
to believe, but acted in ways that defied that claim, really a
believer? Again, in a vernacular sense anyone could be said to
believe; but if they believed the promises and threats of God
only in the same mundane way they believed the gossip of their
neighbors, they could also be said not to believe at all. Two
Anglo-Norman expositors of the articles of faith, for instance,
William of Waddington and William Peraldus, concurred that
"He who is in mortal sin lies when he says, 'I believe in God.'"[91]

This raises the question of "embodied belief": in what sense
could belief be understood as a category of action? Should we
so radically distinguish intellective belief from somatic activity
in the Middle Ages?[92] Certainly Augustine, despite his usual
view that belief is "nothing else than to think with assent,"
sometime equivocated: in one relatively obscure fragment, for
instance, he explained that concerning religious truths, which
must be first believed and then subsequently understood, "understanding is achieved through observing those commandments which concern virtuous living."[93] This equivocation was
normal in the Middle Ages: beneath the dominant theme of
belief as a work of the intellect was a leitmotif stressing that it
was nonetheless a *work*, part of a broader ethical framework
of faith formed by love.[94] John Mirk's *Liber Festivalis*, for

instance, invoked "works of belief" to suggest that belief adhered in outward holiness: "He that believeth and is christened shall be saved and follow the works of belief . . . and he that believeth not nor doth the works of belief shall be damned. The works of belief be meekness and charity, for without these two shall no man be saved, and he that hath these two, he is written in the genealogy of our lord Jesus Christ."[95] Good works and true belief were certainly distinguishable; whether they were separable was less clear.

Finally, within this swirling variety, the most fundamental question was whether belief was the default condition of practicing and professing Christians, or whether it was a special condition, the difficult labor of remaining Christian in a fallen world. Again, there was a vernacular rhetoric that flattened Christian belief onto other kinds of truth-claims, rendering Christian belief no harder than believing that the sun will rise tomorrow. But others were less forgiving.[96] The *Theologica Deutsch*, an anonymous late-medieval mystical text that would become a favorite of Martin Luther, claimed that Christ's statement, "He that believeth not . . . shall be damned," did not refer merely to "the articles of the Christian faith, for everyone believeth them, and they are common to every Christian man, whether he be sinful or saved, good or wicked." Christian belief was instead "a certain truth which it is possible to know by experience, but which ye must believe in, before that ye know it by experience, else ye will never come to know it truly."[97]

Thomas Aquinas likewise described "believing" as fundamentally alien to a fallen world. He began his commentary on the Apostles' Creed by describing two theological doctrines so fundamental to God's essence that there can be no belief in God without them: monotheism and divine providence. The name God itself, Aquinas wrote, signifies nothing else but "the ruler and provider of all things." "He therefore believes in

God"—and here Aquinas used *credit Deum esse*, believes God to exist—"who believes that everything in this world is governed and provided for by him." Aquinas then used the logic of monotheism and providence to suggest that countless outward Christians demonstrate, "not by their words and hearts, but by their actions," that they actually believe in many Gods, and thus do not believe that there is a God at all, QED. Those who "believe that the celestial bodies influence the will of man and regulate their affairs by astrology," for instance, "make the heavenly bodies gods, and subject themselves to them." In the same category "are all those who obey temporal rulers more than God, in that which they ought not; such actually set these up as gods." The ranks of polytheists also included those who "love their sons and kinsfolk more than God," and those who "love food more than God."[98] For Aquinas, all these sinners—not only sorcerers and astrologers, but the throngs who put worldly loyalties above spiritual obligations, or who followed their bodily urges—in a very real sense did not believe in God.

The medieval category of belief was baggy; after a thousand years of speculation, a variety of views is no surprise. But within this expanse, the overwhelming impression is of theologians, mystics, and other Christian thinkers defending the specificity and preeminence of Christian belief against other sorts of truth-claims, especially that bugbear of classical epistemology, opinion. The Christian Middle Ages were almost wholly innocent of the notion that "belief" consisted in a person's individual views of religion; with rare exceptions, belief was instead some form of participation in the collective and indubitable *credenda* of the Church. Presumably, popular religion was less precise: we have little evidence that Europe's peasants accepted, or even knew about, elite theological views of belief, any more than they knew or cared about elite theological views of Christology, charity, or sex. Yet the official view was enormously consequential, because it yoked individual religious speculation with error rather than truth, more akin to village gossip or even heresy than to conscience.

For all the debate that surrounded belief, and for all the repressive possibilities latent in its starker definitions, it nonetheless appears that, with rare exceptions, in the Middle Ages Christian opponents did not usually accuse one another of not believing. Rather than precipitating conflict, controversies over belief in the Middle Ages were largely debates over the internal condition of Christians: what did it take to transcend the default belief that permeated the sinful world and achieve real access to God? People answered in different ways, but they usually framed their answers within a presumptive community of believers. At least by comparison with earlier and later centuries of Christianity, belief was not an issue that generated much heat.

But this peaceable kingdom was a chimera. The exceptions that proved the rule—Jews within Christendom, Muslims on its borders—show how belief could, with little or no intellectual effort, be turned into an exclusive category. And we might speculate that these shadowy Others, the unbelievers who endlessly intruded upon the pious fantasy of a believing society, were on the minds of medieval writers whenever they considered what it meant to believe. It thus did not take much for the violent potential of belief to be applied, for instance, to heretics, whose alleged misapprehension of divinity could so easily be read as denying divinity altogether. It did not take much for the scholastic distinction between belief and opinion to be used to deny the belief-status of all error, or even to deny the belief-status of truth held in merely worldly or profane ways. It did not take much for the rationalist program of belief to insist that believing incorrectly was a sign of irrationality.

What prevented diverse understandings of belief from descending into chaos was the fact that, in most times and places in Western Europe before 1500, there was little incentive for authorities to inquire too deeply into how their subjects believed. But that does not change the fact that belief itself, as a category, could bear so little weight. Pushing too hard on belief would inevitably lead to conflict, not only because different versions contradicted one another, but because so many versions had been honed to differentiate authentic religious belief from the profane world. We thus might posit a kind of continuity across the medieval/early modern boundary: conflict latent in one intellectual context was actualized in the next. For if ever the fantasy of religious unity were to collapse, the medieval tradition contained all the resources necessary to redefine belief as exclusive rather than inclusive, a condition characterized by scarcity rather than ubiquity. When ideas that had been developed to understand an inward spiritual condition were redeployed to police outward community, Europe would face a revolution.

CHAPTER TWO

The Reformation of Belief

IT IS DIFFICULT, across the gulf of half a millennium, to recall how eccentric Martin Luther's ideas first seemed. Centuries of use have worn down their sharp edges, normalizing some claims while silently occluding others. Only with great effort, then, can we imagine the surprise of sixteenth-century Christians when Luther first explained that most of them were unbelievers. In the winter of 1517–18, in the midst of the controversy over indulgences that ignited the Reformation, Luther continued as professor of Bible at the University of Wittenberg, lecturing on the Epistle to the Hebrews. When he got to Hebrews 11:6, "he that cometh to God must believe that he is," Luther offered a strikingly original interpretation. "To believe that God exists," Luther wrote—he used the Latin *credere deum*, which his university audience would have recognized immediately as Peter Lombard's term for belief that there is any God at all—"seems to many to be so easy that they have ascribed this belief both to poets and to philosophers." But this was a categorical error, for mundane assent was not really belief at all: "Such human faith is just like any other thought, art, wisdom, dream of man. For as soon as trial assails, all those things immediately topple down."[1]

It was scandalous for Luther to suggest that belief in the existence of God was exceptional rather than ubiquitous. As we have seen, a rare and demanding version of Christian belief had been available in the Middle Ages, alongside more quotidian varieties, as a condition to which Christians might aspire and occasionally as a lever of differentiation from religious adversaries. But Luther made the starkest and most rarefied variety of belief the only one that counted: all others were mere simulacra, the debased epistemology of the world, so that people who lacked the full benefits of faith did not really believe that God is. The result was a topography of Europe's religious landscape as unrecognizable to Luther's first auditors as it is to modern historians: Luther argued that Christian belief was vanishingly rare in European society, belonging only to a small minority within a seething mass of infidels.

However novel and frightening, this vision proved immensely powerful, and not only within the movement Luther began. For more than a century, it became normal for Protestants, Catholics, and Anabaptists to radically limit the category of Christian belief. The rival confessions of Christianity, unwilling to grant belief to their enemies or to dissidents and backsliders in their ranks, participated in a common project to make belief *hard*, denying belief-status to most putative Christians and their religious claims. They thus launched a revolution in religious epistemology. The reformations of the sixteenth century have been endlessly studied, and "faith" has been a prominent part of that enterprise, yet only a handful of scholars have noticed that at the center of the maelstrom was the problem of religious knowledge.[2] This chapter thus seeks to restore to its proper place a significant and largely unnoticed rupture in European ideas: the reformation of belief.

What did Luther mean when he said that "to believe that God exists" is so difficult? How could he defend that claim when, like so many contemporaries, Luther also insisted that knowledge of God was imprinted on all human souls? It is useful to begin with a cycle of sermons he preached in the late 1530s, summarizing and systematizing his ideas on the relationship between Christian belief and carnal epistemology. Luther was a prodigious preacher, but in 1537 he received a special opportunity. The pastor of the town church of Wittenberg, Luther's disciple Johannes Bugenhagen, was invited by King Christian III to oversee the Reformation in Denmark, leaving his Wittenberg pulpit empty. Other Lutheran ministers agreed to share the daunting task of preaching in their hero's presence on Sundays; but Luther himself volunteered to give the regular Saturday lectures, dedicated to the Gospel of St. John.[3] Luther found in this most spiritual New Testament text an object lesson in the radical distinction between law and gospel that was at the heart of his new movement, using the law-to-gospel paradigm to redefine what it meant to believe.

In his sermon on John 1:18, "No man hath seen God at any time," Luther addressed a familiar problem in Christian exegesis: how to harmonize this passage with Romans 1:19–25, where St. Paul explains that all men have knowledge of God. Theologians had been working through this knot at least since John of Damascus in the eighth century, but Luther suggested what appears to have been a novel approach: the two passages could be reconciled by noticing that "there are two kinds of knowledge of God: the one is the knowledge of the Law; the other is the knowledge of the Gospel." Reason, Luther wrote, "is familiar with the knowledge of God which is based on the Law." The philosophers had this legal knowledge of God, which is why they could distinguish right from wrong;

indeed, everyone has it to some degree. But legal knowledge is insufficient:

> The other sort of knowledge of God emerges from the gospel. There we learn that all the world is by nature an abomination before God, subject to God's wrath and the devil's power, and is eternally damned. From this the world could not extricate itself except through God's son, who lies in the bosom of the father. He became man, died, and rose again from the dead, extinguishing sin, death, and the devil . . . This is the true and thorough knowledge and way of thinking about God.

Thus, Luther wrote, reason is capable of only a "left-handed and a partial knowledge," the way "a blind man discusses color." That is all that Turks, Jews, and papists can manage, conceding the existence of God legally but without "evangelical and Christian knowledge."[4]

A few weeks later, in a group of interconnected sermons on John 3:16—"God so loved the world, that he gave his only begotten son, that whosoever believeth in him should not perish, but have everlasting life"—Luther explained how the distinction between legal and gospel knowledge pertains to the concept of belief. Luther acknowledged that legal or "historical" knowledge of Christ can be found among outwardly professing Christians, like the papists. But belief in Christ requires not merely legal knowledge that he is the son of God, but also trust that he will fulfill the promises of the gospel, for "he is very God not only in his person, but also in his office and his works." In a particularly important extrapolation from this argument, Luther insisted that the gospel promise that "whosoever believes in him has eternal life" is "a definition of his essence" (*essentialis definitio*); hence genuine belief in Christ must necessarily include trust that by that belief alone you are saved.[5] In this remarkable argument, Catholics who sought to be saved by their works—so many millions of men and women with their confession, penance, and absolution—were in fact unbelievers.

Throughout Luther's vast corpus of writings, we can find him arguing that Catholics do not really believe in God or in Christ, because their reliance upon works shows that their supposed belief is merely carnal rather than spiritual, the de-based epistemology of the world rather than properly Christian belief at all. So, for instance, Luther asked, "What is a greater contempt and rebellion against God than not to trust [*credere*] his promises? . . . Is not the person who does this denying God? . . . Those who imagine they are fulfilling the law by doing works of chastity and mercy that are legally re-quired . . . are nevertheless included under the sin of unbelief [*incredulitatis*]."[6] For Luther, belief remained a rarity even in an outwardly Christian society, "for there are many who speak the words 'I am a Christian' with their mouth but do not be-lieve this in their heart."[7] As he put it in his tract on secular au-thority, perhaps one person in a thousand is a true Christian.

In this view, unbelief rather than belief becomes the normal or default condition of a sinful world.[8] As Berndt Hamm has written, for Luther "all human speculation, speech, and judg-ment about God is untrue"; Luther's intellectual crisis was pre-cisely to have "reached the end of his human possibilities . . . as an epistemological subject."[9] And while the novel theology of *sola fide* restored something like reliable religious knowl-edge to the justified minority, it left the majority wallowing in unbelief, from which all sin emanates: "Unbelief [*Unglaube*] alone commits sin, and brings forth the flesh . . . Unbelief is the root, the sap, and the chief power of all sin."[10] In his lec-tures on Genesis, Luther described the original sin of Eve as "unbelief or doubt [*Incredulitatem seu dubitationem*] of the

Word and of God." Thus, "The source of all sin truly is unbelief and doubt and abandonment of the Word. Because the world is full of these, it remains in idolatry, denies the truth of God, and invents a new God." By this stark logic, unbelievers are everywhere.[11]

Luther also doubled down on that strand of the Christian tradition which insisted that belief requires absolute assurance, not subject to doubt or reconsideration: belief was not opinion.[12] In his commentary on Genesis 15:6—"And he [Abraham] believed the Lord; and he [God] reckoned it to him as righteousness," which Luther called "one of the foremost passages of all scripture"—Luther defined what he meant by believing: "The very fact that God promises something demands that we believe it, *that is, that we conclude by faith that it is true and have no doubt that the outcome will be in agreement with the promise.*"[13] He contrasted this firm belief with "an uncertain and wavering opinion" (*vaga opinione et dubia*); only "this very belief" (*ipsum credere*) is "imputed by God himself as righteousness."[14] In *The Bondage of the Will*, Luther wrote, "The Holy Spirit is no skeptic, and the things he has written in our hearts are not doubts or opinions, but assertions—surer and more certain than sense and life itself."[15]

Finally, Luther rejected the (mis)translation of Isaiah 7:9 that was at the heart of the Catholic tradition: instead of "*Nisi credideritis, non intelligetis*"—if you do not believe, you will not understand—Luther insisted "*Nisi credideritis, non permanebitis*": if you do not believe, you will not endure. Against scholastic rationalism or reliance upon the Church's authority, this was the doctrine of sola fide, framed explicitly in terms of what and how you "believe." As Luther put it in his lectures on Isaiah, while "the ancients" had mistranslated the passage, Isaiah meant that the promise of God is "useless unless faith is added . . . for those who believe God make and reckon him to be true . . . and they themselves also become truthful through faith. On the contrary, to the unbelieving all things become deceptive, unreliable, and unsure."[16]

⟶ Luther's vision was in large part woven together from the most rigid strands of the medieval tradition, now pushed to a conclusion that would have seemed deeply uncharitable to his predecessors. But it was also supplemented by a healthy dose of innovation. Perhaps the most genuinely novel aspect of Luther's argument was the notion that to believe, you must not only hold correct doctrine, you must also apply that doctrine experimentally to yourself. That is, just as you cannot believe in God or Christ without believing in salvation by faith alone, so you cannot believe in salvation by faith alone without believing that *you yourself* are saved. Other Protestants, working to systematize Luther's defiant rumblings into a coherent theology, developed this idea. Most importantly, in the 1521 *Loci Communes*, the first systematic theology of the Reformation, Luther's colleague Philip Melanchthon identified faith as *fiducia*—that is, confidence, trust, or reliance—in the divine mercy promised in Christ.[17] All other kinds of faith were merely human and thus not really faith at all. This did not mean that knowledge of doctrine (*notitia*) and assent to that doctrine (*assensus*) were irrelevant, but rather they were incomplete without the fiducia that applied doctrine to one's self. As Melanchthon put it, "You do not believe unless you believe that salvation has been promised to you."[18] The "impious," who take the promise of the gospel only in general terms, "do not believe, but hold a frigid opinion to which the depth of the heart does not adhere." By contrast, believers are those who "believe these things will happen to themselves (*quae credunt SIBI eventura*)."[19] The Reformed tradition closely followed the Lutherans on this issue. Zacharias Ursinus, in his influential commentary on the Heidelberg Catechism, wrote: "When I say, I believe in God, I mean I believe that he is my God . . . to believe in God is to be persuaded that he will make all things attributed to him subservient to my salvation, for the sake of his son."[20] This also precluded the possibility of implicit faith, for as John Calvin wrote, "It is not enough to believe implicitly without understanding [*implicite credit quod non intelligat*], or even inquiring. The thing requisite is an explicit recognition of the divine goodness, in which our righteousness consists."[21]

In sum, we are seeing here a collapsing of propositional belief onto saving faith, so that people cannot be said to believe the truth-status of religious propositions unless they believe them with the kind of fiducia, or trust, which Protestants identified with grace and salvation.[22] In the scholastic tradition, belief had likewise been distinguished from opinion, but what mitigated the rigor of that separation was that you could achieve certainty by believing with the Church. Luther and his followers eliminated this possibility for implicit faith, without at the same time granting belief-status to mere opinion, leading quickly to a condition where, theologically speaking, most people did not believe at all.

This new configuration produced an awkward relationship between belief and doctrine, emphasizing formal knowledge while at the same time insisting upon its insignificance. On the one hand, because belief was so closely tied to justification by faith, belief necessarily entailed at least some theological sophistication. Without *knowing* that you were saved by Christ rather than works, you could not *be* saved by Christ rather than works. Of course, this did not mean that the uneducated could not be believers. Protestants denied any elitism: one of the thieves was saved on the cross next to Christ, after all, evidence that true belief could be found in the most unlikely of places. Luther, bound by his association of belief with saving faith, even argued (like his hero Augustine) that elect infants were in some sense believers, a point on which Anabaptists would catch him in his own pretzel logic.[23] But true belief, however embryonic or potential, was still *doctrinal*: the thief was saved because he believed correctly. This did not require the learning of the schoolmen, but neither could it be ignorant of the fundamental truth of man's total depravity and the gratuitous gift of God's grace, for as John Foxe asked, "How can we believe the promises of God when we know them not?"[24] In the words of the great Heidelberg theologian Zacharias Ursinus, "It is indeed necessary to have learned a doctrine first before you believe it."[25] Philip Melanchthon advised readers to "exercise the spirit in meditating accurately on the promises, for by no means can Christ be known outside of the promises."[26]

Thus, the reformation of belief was inherently didactic: in a world without implicit faith, every Christian had to know what she believed. The result was an avalanche of pedagogy to teach the illiterate masses the doctrinal knowledge necessary for salvation. In a terrifying claim, effectively demanding the first academic test for Church membership, Luther argued in the preface to his 1529 *Large Catechism* that anyone who does not know its contents "should not be numbered among Christians nor admitted to any sacrament, just as artisans who do not know the rules and practices of their craft are rejected and considered incompetent."[27] Countless other catechisms followed. The catechism of Andreas Osiander was published in fifty-four separate editions.[28] In the Netherlands alone, sixty-two editions of the 1563 Heidelberg Catechism were printed before 1585.[29] Ian Green has identified some 680 different English vernacular catechisms published between 1530 and 1740.[30]

The century and a half after the Reformation was thus the great age of creedal Christianity: as belief became a marker of social and political association, every social and political body needed its own creed. And not only the volume of creedalism increased, but its detail: Christians were now required to "believe" in structures of Church government, the theology of sacraments, justification by faith, predestination, and other arcane doctrines. Given the infighting between Protestants, especially in the Holy Roman Empire between 1570 and 1600, many of the new confessions and articles of faith included sections on what *not* to believe as well. The *Saxon Visitation Articles* of 1592 included four positive doctrinal articles affirming Lutheranism, followed by four articles condemning the "false and erroneous doctrines of the Calvinists." And over the course of the confessional era, the new creedal statements gained quasi-canonical status for their adherents. While most required subscription only *quatenus* (insofar as) they agreed with scripture, the 1655 *Reaffirmed Consensus of the Truly Lutheran Faith* required subscription to its articles *quia* (because) they agreed with scripture.[31]

But despite this new creedalism, we should not be fooled into thinking that the "reformation of belief" was fundamentally propositional. Belief was much harder than creedal assent, hence the Reformation was much more than a conflict over doctrine. The English puritan Arthur Dent, for instance, insisted that even among his Protestant neighbors, "few will believe the scriptures. Few will believe this, because few feel it; where it is not felt, it can hardly be believed. Only the elect do feel it, and therefore only the elect do believe it. As for all others, they are the very [ap]prentices and bond-slaves of the devil, which is a thousand times worse than to be a galley-slave."[32]

Most important, to distinguish Christian belief from creedal knowledge, Protestants deployed a devastating pejorative term: *fides historica,* or historical faith.[33] In other contexts, that term had enjoyed a long, non-pejorative history. In classical Latin, fides historica (or *fides historia*) glorified historical truth over literary distortion; in early modern Europe it remained in some quarters a defense of historical reliability against skeptics.[34] Among humanist scholars, the phrase came to signify a critical approach to history, determining the proper criteria of credibility and which authorities were worthy of fides—questions to which we shall return.[35] But perhaps because of the importance of these issues for the emergence of modern critical scholarship, it has not been appreciated that when Protestant theologians transported the term fides historica to a religious context, it became an ironic insult, *mere* historical faith. In particular, fides historica was used to disparage propositional assent to Christianity: mere acceptance that the facts of religion are true. It was called fides historica—a term widely condemned by Catholics—because it implied that you believe in scripture only in the same sense you believe secular histories, as if believing God or Christ were no different than believing Caesar or Thucydides.[36] Hence, Melanchthon preferred the term *historica opinio*, to emphasize that it was not really faith at all but mere opinion, correct only in the sense that even a broken clock is right twice a day: "This sophistic faith, which they first call 'formless' and then 'acquired,' and by which the impious give assent to the evangelical histories much as we are accustomed to do in the case of Livy or Salust, is no faith at all but is merely opinion. It is an uncertain, inconstant, fluctuating cogitation of the human mind concerning the word of God."[37] Fides historica was what the devils possess, according to James 2:19, "the devils also believe, and tremble": no one knows better than devils that God exists, but that is not equivalent to Christian belief. As John Calvin wrote in his *Institutes*, "Multitudes undoubtedly believe that God is, and admit the truth of the gospel history, and the other parts of scripture, in the same way in which they believe the records of past events, or events which they have actually witnessed." But this, Calvin wrote, could be considered belief or faith only by the rhetorical figure of *catachresis*, the intentional misuse or straining of a figure of speech. In fact, whatever bare assent they manage toward God "by no means penetrates to the heart," hence they are "not a whit superior to devils."[38]

Countless examples can be found of reformers using the term fides historica to distinguish authentic religious belief from its creedal content. The Italian reformer Peter Martyr Vermigli called historical faith a "vulgar and cold assent" and "a belief induced . . . by human persuasion," rather than the "certain, firm, efficacious" assent that comes from "the inspiration of the Holy Spirit."[39] To the Scotsman Robert Rollock, historical faith is a "judgment of the mind," whereas justifying faith is also "in the will and heart."[40] Real belief, according to the Englishman John Smith, is not like the belief of the world. When we say "I believe" in the Creed, it means "I not only understand and conceive it, but assent unto it in my judgment as true, and consent to it in my will as good, and build my comfort upon it as good to me: this act of belief carries the whole soul with it."[41] Or, as his countryman George Walker explained as England was on the verge of civil war, fides historica "is only an assent unto the word of God, that it is true, arising from carnal reason and arguments convincing the judgment"; by contrast, the belief of the elect "is not a naked assent ruled by human and natural reason, but guided by God's spirit, and joined with a relying on God."[42] Protestants have here displaced belief almost entirely from the intellect onto the will, so that doctrine is radically insufficient, no longer a load-bearing wall in the house of the godly. Thus John Milton: "A man may be a heretic in the truth."[43]

There is an abiding tension here between on the one hand emphasis on doctrinal content, and on the other hand denial that doctrinal assent can ever constitute Christian belief. It is insufficient to know the truth, Protestants insisted, just as it is insufficient to rely upon the Church to know it; instead we must yield to that truth, trusting wholly in something alien to our fallen nature. For this reason, Protestants often substituted *agnitio* for *cognitio* in their discussions of belief: acknowledgment rather than knowledge.[44] The Reformation's remarkable new emphasis on belief thus contained two very different and potentially contradictory impulses. First, the Reformation unleashed a new creedalism the likes of which had not been seen in the West for a thousand years. As Christians parsed their doctrinal differences ever more obsessively, Christianity itself was transformed, in John Bossy's classic formulation, from a body of people to a body of beliefs.[45] Second, the Reformation privileged belief by identifying it very closely with saving faith and thus effectively limiting it to the community of the elect: if the Gospel promised that all who believed were saved, then the reprobate must not really believe at all. The reformers of the sixteenth century, by simultaneously emphasizing belief as forensic creedalism *and* belief as absolute trust, thus rather remarkably demanded absolute trust in arcane, controversial doctrine. No wonder they thought belief was so hard.

{≈≈≈≈⟩W⟨≈≈≈}

The pressures of the Reformation led Roman Catholics, no less than Protestants, to embrace stark and exclusive new understandings of what it meant to believe. For Catholics, scouring their tradition for resources to meet the threat of heresy, this meant first and foremost identifying belief with obedience to the authority of the Church. There were many reasons why this should have been so. For one thing, independent belief-claims had proved dangerously fissiparous: in a world where the devil suddenly seemed to be everywhere, planting false opinions in the minds of those who questioned the Church's authority, it seemed only natural that belief must adhere to obedience. Nor could the doctrine of implicit faith be so broadly interpreted as it had been before; certainly the laity who did not understand doctrine could still believe with the Church, but in a world full of rival doctrines, they had to know which beliefs the Church held. Moreover, the Catholic Church had little choice but to sharpen its understanding of what made people believers. Some medieval Catholics had argued that the *fides infusa*, which instilled a habit of grace at baptism, was sufficient to constitute Christian belief; yet now there were millions of baptized Christians who were not in the Church at all. Thus, Catholics inadvertently followed Protestants down the rabbit hole of anthropological pessimism, finding that baptism alone did not do nearly as much to heal the injury of original sin as some had thought, so "belief" could only result from a faith acquired in the Church.[46] For Catholics as well as Protestants, belief became much, much harder.

The most (in)famous sixteenth-century example comes from Ignatius of Loyola, founder of the Jesuit order, who wrote in his *Spiritual Exercises*, "We must always hold, in order to be right in all things, that I believe the white that I see is black, if the hierarchical Church so determines it."[47] Loyola's yoking of belief to obedience appears to clash with other early modern conceptions that stressed the imperviousness of belief to worldly command. Luther's "Here I stand," and Galileo's "And yet it moves," represent metonymically an alternative tradition of belief that speaks truth to power. Yet, as Loyola was attempting to underscore, the whole concept of creedal Christianity presumes the ability to believe corporately with the Church, against the evidence of experience. Seeing white but believing black, Loyola tells us, is no more or less jarring than seeing bread but believing flesh (for Catholics), or seeing death but believing eternal life (for Protestants as well). Belief is *not* knowledge based on evidence; it is rather trusting that your own worldly experience is wrong. Thus, Loyola argued, experience is deeply fallible: the flesh is weak, the devil can appear as an angel of light, so we ought not to believe our senses; but the authority of the Church, guided by the Holy Spirit, cannot err on questions fundamental to faith, so we ought to believe it instead.

It did not have to be so; the increasing dominance of this position was driven by the dynamics of confessional conflict more than any necessities of Catholic theology. In the early 1540s, even as Pope Paul III was approving the Jesuit Order, there remained room for maneuver. In Italy, the so-called *spirituali*, Catholics who emphasized individual and internal faith, engaged in their own attempts to revise the idea of belief, in many ways paralleling Protestant arguments. When in 1541 one of the leaders of the *spirituali*, Cardinal Gasparo Contarini, was appointed papal legate to the religious colloquy between Protestants and Catholics at Regensburg, it appeared for a fleeting moment that belief might not come to rest so unequivocally in obedience. Contarini helped to negotiate a compromise with the reformers Philip Melanchthon and Martin Bucer on justification, after which he adopted the Protestant terms *fiducia* and *assensus* and accepted, against what would later become Tridentine orthodoxy, that faith is an act of the will. But a month later this compromise was roundly rejected by Contarini's superiors and he received a vicious scolding from Cardinal Farnese in Rome. Over the subsequent two decades, the Roman curia systematically purged opposing views from their ranks.[48] The decision to emphasize authority in the construction of belief was thus a process that only gradually gathered momentum over the course of the sixteenth century.

Its decisive moment, although certainly not its final stage, was the election of the head of the Holy Office of the Inquisition, Michele Ghislieri, as Pope Pius V in 1566.

Sometimes, as in new articulations of "implicit faith," the issue for post-Reformation Catholics was a division of labor between the laity and the clergy, with clerics required to believe doctrine while the laity, unable to comprehend theological niceties, had to believe the Church. As Cardinal Jacques Davy Du Perron put it, "Besides the things that particular people are held to believe with a distinct and explicit faith, there are many others which they are obliged to believe [*obligez de croire*] with a faith of adherence and non-repugnancy, which is called in the schools 'implicit faith.'" Laypeople were not obliged to believe more arcane doctrines in their own right; instead, they must "adhere and consent to the Church which believes them": "For making profession to believe all that the Church in which they are incorporated believes, their faith embraces in general, by the merit of their obedience, all that that Church believes distinctly."[49] It must be stressed here that implicit faith, while designed in the Middle Ages to make belief easier, in the context of the Counter-Reformation made belief harder: no longer about ignorance, excusing laypeople from having to believe for themselves, implicit faith was now about obligation and obedience, forbidding laypeople from believing for themselves.

In other contexts, the issue was not a division of labor, but rather the idea that belief by definition consists in obedience to the Church because the authority of the Church is what separates "belief" from mere opinion in the first place. Catholics routinely stressed that "belief" could not be based upon individual experience, or at least that experimental belief was inferior, no better than profane epistemology, built upon the shifting sands of human fallibility rather than the rock of the Church. Roberto Bellarmino taught explicitly that belief meant believing with the Church: in his catechism, when the Disciple asks what is meant by the word "*Credo*," the Teacher responds, "That is to say, I believe firmly and without doubt all things which are comprehended in these twelve articles [of the Apostles' Creed], which God himself taught to his Apostles, the Apostles truly taught the Church, and the Church truly handed down to us."[50] Peter Canisius likewise explained that faith is "the gift and light of God, by which the illumined firmly assent to what God reveals and the Church sets forth to us to be believed (*nobis per ecclesiam credenda preposuit*)."[51] As an Irish Jesuit wrote in the middle of the seventeenth century, "To believe like a Christian, is to believe the mysteries of Christian religion because they are sufficiently proposed as divine revelation by the testimony of the Church; not of every Church, but of the true Catholic one, which only giveth lawful authority."[52] As Susan Schreiner has shown, in the sixteenth century to believe was to be certain, and certainty lay with the Church.[53]

An elaborate example comes from Simon Vigor, a notoriously polemical court preacher at Paris and sometime delegate at Trent, in a cycle of sermons on the Apostles' Creed printed in 1585. Those who search religion with their natural reason, Vigor wrote, fall into heresy and atheism, because "natural reasons are repugnant to the articles which we must believe."[54] That is why we must believe without understanding: we can never understand the truths of religion, but we are nonetheless bound to believe them, hence the faithful do not demand a reason but say simply, *Credo*.[55] This discussion, as Vigor was well aware, replayed a series of arguments pioneered by Augustine in *De Utilitate Credendi* a thousand years before. But Vigor more explicitly emphasized against a new breed of heretics that the incessant Protestant demand *first* to be shown scriptural warrant and *then* to believe was in actuality a species of doubt, because it depended upon the corrupt inclinations—that is, the hermeneutical sensibilities—of the fallen individual. In the Christian religion, Vigor wrote, "it is necessary to believe first."[56]

What authorized and guaranteed belief, and indeed what rendered it belief rather than opinion, was the universal Church. Vigor wrote that heretics are misguided when they claim to search for the truth, because the truth is already located in the Catholic Church and "it is not necessary to look for what has been found."[57] This is why, Vigor wrote, "it is necessary for us to believe in the Catholic Church and to adjust faith, without the least doubt, in what she proposes to us."[58] As he wrote in a later sermon, if an "idiot" is asked why he believes something, it suffices for him to respond, "*Credo Ecclesiam Catholicam.*" In this sense, the ninth article of the Apostles' Creed—believing the Church—trumps all the others, because we are all "idiots" and our natural reason is unreliable; only believing the Church provides a solid foundation for belief in God, the trinity, and other points of doctrine.[59] When a Turk or a Jew is converted to Christianity, he is first taught the ninth article of the Creed, that there is one holy and universal Church, even before affirming Christ, because "it is this holy Church which tells him that he must believe in Jesus Christ."[60] In sum, "I believe all that the Church believes, it is enough for me to be so well founded on the faith of this Church that cannot err."[61]

These sorts of arguments, even when they echoed the medieval tradition, acquired new meanings in a context when suddenly the world was filled with unbelievers. So, for instance, the Bishop of Verona, Luigi Lippomano, wrote in a 1568 Italian commentary on the Apostles' Creed that to believe in God means that "you come to him in love and charity, which produces good works." This was a perfectly ordinary account of what the scholastics called *fides caritate formata*. But now this traditional view was accompanied by a novel language of exclusion: religion, Lippomano writes, "consists solely in persuading to believe," and those who do not believe in the *credenda* of the Church are not wise but fools, a reference to the psalm "The fool says in his heart there is no God."[62] In May 1591, a public disputation on the nature of "infidelity" at the Jesuit stronghold in Catholic Bavaria, the University of Dillingen, held that heresy is worse than either paganism or Judaism, because it is about choice, and mere opinion can never rise to the level of religion. As the printed précis of the disputation put it: "The doctrine of our faith is not properly speaking accepted by human choice or discovered by human ingenuity."[63]

Catholics also stressed in newly rigorous ways that Christian belief had to be transformative, wholly unlike profane epistemology; as for Protestants, unbelief rather than belief became the default condition of a fallen world. So, for instance, the French Carmelite Thomas Beauxamis argued that while "many evil people can believe that what God says is true," they do not truly believe, because "while they had known him as God, they did not glorify him as God. And this is the greatest ignorance."[64] A French catechism from 1575 held that mankind believes more in the devil than in God. Belief is fundamentally contrary to our fallen nature; it requires the greedy to renounce their riches, the bawdy to renounce their lusts, and all of us to denounce our "false gods." In these texts, the habitual failure of human belief is tied to the fact that most false claims to believe are based upon empirical evidence or rational argument, whereas real belief must rely upon authority. The French catechism, for instance, refers to Christian belief as "belief without experience" [*croyance sans experience*]; the belief of Abraham, and of the martyrs, was "against natural experience," hence it was agreeable to God.[65] Likewise, the Catechism of the Council of Trent affirmed that "when God commands us to believe, he does not propose us to search into his divine judgments, or inquire into their reasons and their causes, but demands an immutable faith, by the efficacy of which the mind reposes in the knowledge of eternal truth . . . Faith, therefore, excludes not only all doubt, but even the desire of subjecting its truths to demonstration."[66] Ours is not to reason why.

An interesting barometer of changing Catholic attitudes was the willingness of authors to embrace what had previously been an unpopular minority position: that people ought to believe *in* the Church. As we saw in chapter 1, most medieval writers denied that the Apostles' Creed should be taken to read "I believe *in* the Church," because the special condition of "belief *in*" should only have God as its object; but Thomas Aquinas left more wiggle room than he probably intended when he admitted that belief *in* the Church was acceptable insofar as it meant "I believe in the Holy Ghost sanctifying the Church." This was a big enough loophole that, when the Reformation made the authority of the Church controversial, Catholics hurled themselves into the breach. The first important Catholic to reassess the thorny preposition was Luther's early opponent, Tommaso De Vio, Cardinal Cajetan, in his 1531 tract on papal authority. Cajetan, noting his dissent from some authorities, wrote that if we take "Church" to mean the entire Church Triumphant that includes Christ as its head, then we may believe *in* it, because the "final decision of our faith" pertains to that Church. But we can also believe *in* "the Church on earth" insofar as it is "connected to the Holy Spirit": believing in an infallible institution is equivalent to believing in the Holy Spirit that guides it.[67]

An influential locus for these arguments was the issue of prayer to saints. Protestants had argued that if only God can be believed *in*, then prayer to saints was idolatrous, often invoking Romans 10:16, "How then shall they call on him in whom they have not believed?" The English Catholic translators of the 1582 Douai-Rheims Bible responded in their annotation of this passage that scripture also allows us "to believe *in* men," as in Exodus 14:31, *They believed in God and in Moses*, "and the ancient fathers did read in the Creed indifferently, I believe *in* the Catholic Church, and I believe the Catholic Church."[68] This was to become a standard argument. The English Jesuit John Gibbons, also defending prayer to the saints, used Philemon 1:5—"thy love and faith, which thou hast toward the Lord Jesus, and toward all saints"—to argue that "the ancient fathers" read the article of the faith "indifferently: I believe *in* the Catholic Church, or I believe the Catholic Church."[69] A generation later, the Jesuit philosopher Francisco Suárez ran sympathetically through all the objections to believing *in* the Church, from Augustine to Erasmus. But he also expanded upon Aquinas to suggest that believing *in* the Church was licit insofar as "it is nothing else than to believe it to be one and holy, or at most, to believe it to be such as bears witness to an infallible rule of faith, and propounds out of the motion of the holy spirit."[70] And while many Catholics continued to stress the earlier tradition, it became increasingly common for even the most traditionalist writers to cite the Thomist exception as a way of acknowledging the infallibility of the Church.[71]

Finally, it is important to emphasize the Catholic program of catechism and education. While Catholics never demanded that everyone should *understand* doctrine, nonetheless the Church did demand, in essence, that everyone should fail to understand the *same* doctrine. Uniformity was the greatest safeguard against heresy, to prevent people from wrongly imagining that they believed with the Church when in fact they did not. So belief became fundamentally propositional, not in the sense that you believed whatever you thought, but in the sense that you believed when you gave your assent to what the Church taught.

The Counter-Reformation was thus a giant educational machine, first to teach the clergy proper doctrine, then through them to educate the whole body of Christians. The Jesuit order invested vast resources in education, not least to train new recruits to serve in their missions. Already by the time of Loyola's death in 1556, there were dozens of Jesuit colleges located from Portugal to Austria. After the 1599 *Ratio Studiorum*, these schools shared a curriculum: by 1640, more than four hundred Jesuit institutions operated under the *Ratio Studiorum*, and by the height of the order in the eighteenth century, there were more than six hundred schools and colleges plus nearly two hundred seminaries.[72] At the same time, the new "congregations" of the Roman Curia—essentially departments of ecclesiastical government—acquired various portfolios intended to promulgate and unify doctrine. The Sacred Congregation of the Roman and Universal Inquisition, also known as the Holy Office, was founded in 1542 to defend the integrity of the faith; we think of the inquisition as a technology of enforcement, but its policing function cannot be separated from the enormous enterprise of correcting theological errors. Many other congregations were established by Sixtus V in 1588, including the Congregation of the *Sapienza* which oversaw university education. The Sacred Congregation for the Propagation of the Faith—or *Sacra Congregatio de Propaganda Fide*, from which derives the English word "propaganda"—was founded in 1622 to propagate Catholicism in non-Catholic countries.

But perhaps the most important revolution was in catechesis, for it was no longer sufficient for the laity simply to recite the Creed, the Lord's Prayer, and the Ten Commandments, now people also had to know the Church's interpretation of those texts. The most famous Catholic catechism, known as the Roman Catechism, was produced by the Council of Trent and simultaneously published in Rome, Venice, Antwerp, and Paris to ensure that doctrine was shared throughout Christendom, and then translated and reprinted in almost every European language. But, as Lee Wandel has noted, the Roman Catechism was primarily for priests. For the laity, the crucial educational texts were the catechisms written by Peter Canisius at the behest of the Holy Roman Emperor. No fewer than 331 separate editions of Canisius's catechisms had already been printed before his death in 1597.[73]

Slowly and unevenly, but relentlessly driven by the pressures of confessional difference, belief for Catholics thus became far more difficult than it had been before—not least because the ideal of believing with the Church, previously a way of making belief easier for the uneducated masses, now became a way of excluding dissenters and freethinkers from belief. Whereas for Protestants the issue was largely about psychological depth—you may think you believe, but really you do not—for Catholics the pressing issue was control: anything outside of the Church's authority potentially failed the test of belief. The doctrine of implicit faith, which had allowed and even encouraged variety within the medieval Church, became under the pressure of this creedal age a doctrine of indoctrination and domination. Slowly but surely, the de facto diversity of views that had subsisted in the medieval Church was redefined as mere opinion or imagination. Belief became instead the credenda of what the Church taught, and disobedience to the Church, or even independent traditions outside of the Church, were increasingly species of unbelief. Thus, peasants with their own interpretations of Christianity, and mystics who sought God by looking inward, and scholars who sought to understand God through their intellect, all grew to resemble the throngs of unbelievers who seemed to crowd around the Church on all sides.

⟨⟩

How hard was belief? Just ask the amateur historian and professional soap-boiler Sebastian Franck, whom we may take as our point of entry into the "radical Reformation."[74] According to Franck, "There is not a single believer on earth."[75]

This was, needless to say, an extreme view. But the small minority of Anabaptists and other radicals are crucial to understanding the reformation of belief. While their views never became prevalent—indeed, they will soon be squeezed out of our story under pressure from the gathering forces of both Protestant and Catholic orthodoxy—they suggest just how divisive belief became. Quite apart from the fact that Calvin and other Protestants developed their views of belief explicitly against the radicals, attention to radical theology suggests how hard it was to construct any stable understanding of belief out of the jagged and inconsistent inheritance of the Middle Ages.

Franck's mystical classic *Paradoxa* (1534) used the same pessimism about the spiritual condition of fallen man that was at the heart of both Protestantism and the Catholic apophatic mystical tradition to challenge the notion that belief is possible at all. Franck insisted that "in the hearts of all natural human beings . . . everyone says, 'There is no God,'" because mankind is flesh and God is spirit, so the two "must needs clash like fire and water." Within this intense dualism, the carnal world can *only* deny God's existence: when Adam fell he made the devil his God, and our world is nothing more or less than a manifestation of the denial of God generated by the Fall.[76] This nearly

Manichaean system yielded one of Franck's central paradoxes: "The world does not even believe what it believes." Naturally, the world wishes to appear faithful [*gläubig*], but the life and work of the world demonstrates "that it does not believe even what it believes and confesses with its lips. Indeed, it cannot believe."[77] Here, in what we can easily imagine as a natural extension of the Protestant program, belief is not merely difficult but impossible.

Yet in response to this ubiquitous unbelief, Franck offered another paradox: *Der Glauben glaubt im Unglauben*, "Belief believes in unbelief." What he meant was that God cannot tolerate the idolatry of the carnal world, so he deprives people of their idols, stripping them of hope and terrifying them into despair. Only then does God offer grace:

> Nothing then is left after such despair but unspeakable sighing to God which a person who is stuck in this hell does not himself know, since he stands over against God in spiteful resistance, grumbles, complains, blasphemes God, and in his heart accuses him of lies, fully resolved in this unbelief. God then comes to rescue this now-extinguished brand, blows on him the breath of his grace, and pulls the devoured sheep by its ears out of the wolf's clutches . . . God has no closer friends than these unwilling blasphemers who are all together in unbelief yet believe amidst this unbelief with an inexpressible sigh in the ground of their soul.[78]

This is heady stuff. It rejects the Protestant consensus that human beings, convicted by the law for their works, must throw themselves on the mercy of God; for Franck, this too is unbelief, a species of works theology, a mere pantomime of religion, because human beings cannot know God sufficiently to throw themselves on his mercy. Human beings do not, in fact, believe in God. What is needed instead is something that draws upon the German mystical tradition of Meister Eckhart and Johannes Tauler, whose work Franck knew well: an evacuation of the self, not faith but a rejection of the whole world in which faith cannot subsist. Hence Franck's reference to an "extinguished brand": a person emptied of self, whose fire has gone out so that God's fire can replace it. A believing person [*gläubigen Mann*], Franck tells us, is like a "rare, strange phoenix who, in his nakedness and stripping himself of all idols (to whom alone the world looks and in whom it hopes), stands totally surrendered to God."[79] Only through such absolute surrender [*ergeben*] does "a person becomes a believer" [*wird der Mensch gläubig*].[80] This yielding to God cannot be learned from books, sermons, or even scripture. Instead, belief is the fruit of direct experience of divinity.[81] The greatest of Franck's paradoxes, then, is his forthright claim that "there is not a single believer on earth," even though he locates belief in a small minority of godly Christians.[82] The answer to this riddle is simple: true belief is, by definition, not upon earth, and only by leaving earth behind can it be discovered.

Sebastian Franck thus offers a sort of asymptotic limit or event horizon, an understanding of belief so refined that it disappears entirely. And while he was undoubtedly extreme, Franck's view well represents the tendency among the radical reformers to push belief beyond the ordinary capacity of human beings. This should not fool us into thinking that belief was any less important to the radicals. On the contrary, their implication was that, since belief is so far beyond ordinary human capability, those who do believe become more than human. This is a thread worth pulling: in the hands of many radicals, belief became a sign of perfection.

So, for instance, the French-born reformer Sebastian Castellio, formerly Rector of the College of Geneva before he was banished from the city, is best known for his controversial defense of religious toleration. In the context of John Calvin's notorious execution of Michael Servetus for heresy in 1553, Castellio evoked the intentionally offensive image of Christ returning to earth to oversee tortures and executions, asking in strikingly modern terms: whom would Jesus burn? Less famous but more important for the present inquiry was Castellio's robust claim for the power of belief.[83] For those who successfully renounce their own will and follow Christ, Castellio wrote, an extraordinary conversion follows: "There is a first and imperfect faith, whereby a man is driven to renounce himself. This being increased, the man persevering, becomes daily greater, til at length he comes to such perfection that he doth believe all God's words, precepts, promises, threats, as certainly as you believe it will be day after night. Hence arises that omnipotence whereby he removeth mountains."[84]

Moving mountains: this was a reference to a cluster of biblical proof texts which both enticed and worried early modern readers. Twice in the gospel of Mark, Jesus seems to suggest that through belief, human beings can bend nature to their will. In Mark 9, a father brings his possessed son to Jesus requesting an exorcism, to which Jesus responds, "If thou canst believe, all things are possible to him that believeth." Two chapters later, a fig tree cursed by Jesus dries up and withers; responding to this miracle, Jesus says, "Whosoever shall say unto this mountain, Be thou removed, and be thou cast into the sea; and shall not doubt in his heart, but shall believe that those things which he saith shall come to pass; he shall have whatsoever he saith." The parallel text of Matthew 17:20 has the apostles asking why they were having trouble driving out devils, to which Christ answers: "Because of your unbelief: for verily I say unto you, If ye have faith as a grain of mustard seed, ye shall say unto this mountain, remove hence to yonder place; and it shall remove; and nothing shall be impossible unto you." Here, the power of belief appears unlimited.

Needless to say, most exegetes did not understand these passages to refer to human "omnipotence." To understand Castellio's unusual reading, we need to look at how he understood the difference between Christian belief and the ordinary truth-claims of the world. On the one hand, he insisted that Christian belief is fantastically hard: if we truly believe God's promise, for instance, then "no earthly care should trouble us," therefore anyone troubled by earthly cares does not believe.[85] Castellio contrasted this with the ease of worldly belief: children believe their parents, soldiers believe in their right to plunder, and so forth.[86] The problem, then, is that human beings believe in the world, but not in God. Castellio's most elegant proof was that belief in the world can overcome lust, while belief in God cannot: you would hesitate to fornicate in the presence of a child, yet you do not hesitate in the presence of God.[87]

To redirect belief from the world to God, Castellio wrote, you must learn "to hate your self," and this utter surrender is what we call belief: "You must so depart from your own will, that if you be asked what you would, you may answer, nothing but what Christ willeth. And all this you shall do by faith, for unless you did believe [*crederes*], you would not do."[88] Here, then, is the wellspring of belief's unlimited power: to "do by faith" is to evacuate the self and fill up with God. This is how "omnipotence" becomes not only possible but assured: the believer cannot really will something unless God wills it, hence everything she wills—even moving a mountain!—really and truly comes to pass.

Castellio was a latecomer to the web of ideas and movements known as the "radical Reformation," and many details of his theology were atypical. But what *was* typical was his high view of human sanctification, in which "belief" is indelibly associated with righteousness, blamelessness, or perfection. The radical Reformation, to the extent that it cohered at all, cohered around the separation of a small remnant of true believers from the reprobate world. Typically this separation was enacted through a series of practices—adult believers' baptism, Christian communism or "community of goods," and the "ban" or excommunication as a means of maintaining the purity of the church. The theology behind these practices was almost always a rejection of the Protestant doctrine of "imputed righteousness," in which God mercifully covers sinners in a cloak of righteousness that remains alien to their temporal condition. This, for the radicals, was not enough to mark off the godly as different and purer than their neighbors. Instead, despite considerable theological variety, the radicals stressed that the godly became truly righteous.

So, for instance, Menno Simons was explicit, in *The New Creature* (c. 1537), that belief keeps the commandments of God. Addressing the typical Protestant, Menno asks:

> If your faith (*geloove*) is as you say, why do you not do the things which he has commanded in his word? His commandment is, repent and keep the commandments. And it is evident that you grow worse daily; that unrighteousness is your father, wickedness your mother, and that the express commandments of the Lord are folly and foolishness to you. Since you do not do as he commands and desires, but as you please, it is sufficiently proved that you do not believe (*gelooft*) that Jesus Christ is the son of God, although you say so. Nor do you believe that his word is truth, for faith and its fruits are inseparable.[89]

Like so many other Anabaptists, he rejected the doctrine of *sola fide* as an excuse for easy living, without the discipline that true belief demands. To those who "boast that you believe (*gelooft*) in Christ," he demanded, "If you believe rightly (*gelooft . . . recht*) in Christ, as you boast, then manifest it by your lives that you believe."[90]

And like Castellio, Menno thought that belief could work miracles. His example, in *The Foundation of Christian Doctrine* (1539), was the biblical story of the parting of the Red Sea: "Moses believed the word of the Lord (*geloofde des heeren woordt*), stretched out his hand, and smote with the rod. The waters were divided and Israel was redeemed." Of course, God rather than Moses performed the miracle, but nonetheless, "if Moses had not believed (*gelooft*) the word of God, and had through disobedience failed to strike the sea, then undoubtedly it would not have gone well with an affrighted and fearful Israel."[91] Menno then expanded this lesson into a larger argument: "Whoever hears the word of the Lord and believes it with his heart (*met der herten gelooft*)," according to Menno, "faithfully observes all things the Lord has commanded him." He continued, "If Noah and Lot had not believed (*gelooft*) the word of the Lord, they would have fared ill. If Abraham had not believed (*gelooft*), he would not have obtained such glorious promises. But now have they believed and done the right (*nu hebben sy gelooft, recht gedaen*) and are become heirs of righteousness."[92]

Menno was not the only radical reformer to insist that belief would manifest in extraordinary ways. Chief among these manifestations was "community of goods" or Christian communism. So, for instance, Peter Walpot, bishop of the Moravian Hutterites in the second half of the sixteenth century, argued that true belief is impossible without practicing communism: if anyone claims "that he believes [*glaub*] in one holy Christian Church and the community of the saints, but there is no community in his Church and he himself is against having things in common [*ist er auch kein gmainschaffter*] in deed and truth, then his faith is a dead faith."[93] Walpot's point was not only that believers *ought* to practice community of goods, but that the renunciation of private property adheres to belief itself, and is encoded in the very act of believing, so that in believing in God you renounce all possession: "Whoever says that he would like to follow Christ" without "forsaking all that is creaturely" and denying "that he owns or possesses anything . . . does not really believe in Christ [*glaubt nit in Christum*]."[94]

Especially within religious groups who defined their community around what they called "believers' baptism," the category of belief necessarily separated the small number of true Christians from their adversaries.[95] While Luther had been forced by his theology to admit some residual sense in which elect infants might believe, for the Anabaptists believing became much harder, limited to those who thought, felt, and lived as God commanded.[96] Thus, despite the relative absence of catechisms and other explicitly creedal material among Anabaptists, there was in effect an even stricter litmus test for what it meant to believe among radical reformers than there was among Catholics or Protestants. But once this test was passed, belief functioned like a pulsating power line, filling the elect with divine energy. With belief, the radicals could move mountains; such power could only be granted to a select few.

In his landmark 1942 book *The Problem of Unbelief in the Sixteenth Century*, Lucien Febvre argued that atheism was impossible in early modern Europe, because religion structured even the very thought that might have challenged belief in God. Hence so many alleged harbingers of secular modernity—from

the mischievous impiety of François Rabelais, to the sober theorizing of the scientific revolution—were instead visible signs
of "a century that wanted to believe."[97] Yet, for all his brilliance, Febvre's influential attention to the problem of *unbelief*
obscured the complexity of belief itself. Scholars following in
his footsteps, searching for nascent incredulity in the Christian
West, have been so concerned to ask *whether* people believed
that they have rarely noticed that the great problem of the sixteenth century was *in what sense* people believed.

Over the lifetime of the generation born around 1500, the
category of belief was fundamentally transformed according
to the divergent obsessions of Europe's emergent confessional
communities. For Protestants, belief came to mean not only
adherence to correct doctrine but the saving faith that applied
that doctrine experimentally to yourself. For Catholics, belief
came to mean not only adherence to correct doctrine but resting one's assent in obedience to the Church. And for radicals,
belief came to mean not only adherence to correct doctrine
but transformation and transcendence. In sum, belief became
hard, sometimes so hard that it ceased to be capable of the task
for which creeds and confessions had been developed in the
first place: defining communities according to shared views of
the divine.

Of course, these were aspirations rather than realities, poles
toward which people, ideas, and institutions were attracted
rather than lived conditions. As we shall see, part of the historical importance of these stark visions was their impossibility,
and hence the reactions they inevitably spurred. But the reformation of belief nonetheless reshaped the world in its image.
Among Protestants, those who internalized new ideals of belief
found awesome new responsibilities alongside complex psychological pressures; those who did not experienced coercion,
discipline, and the possibility of exclusion. For Catholics, a vast

new institutional infrastructure was created to authorize true belief while simultaneously anathematizing and punishing all that remained unauthorized. Anabaptists and other radicals, who only rarely sought or won worldly authority, enforced their exclusive vision of belief through a relentless series of purges and separations, policing the boundaries of belief with the only weapon they had—the power to divide yet again. And of course, all those who found themselves living in territory controlled by their religious opponents might be identified, to their horror, as unbelievers. The sum of these divergent innovations was an epochal transformation of "belief" in European society: previously valued for its ubiquity, belief now obtained value from scarcity.

CHAPTER THREE

The Invention of
the Unbeliever

THE ENGLISH MINISTER George Gifford is most famous for an historical accident: as a chaplain in the Earl of Leicester's army, he was present at the 1586 Battle of Zutphen and so attended at the deathbed of Philip Sidney. But he was also a prolific author whose most influential book was a dialogue between Atheos and Zelotes—that is, Atheist and Zealot—known as *The Countrie Divinitie* (1581). Modern students, when confronted with this stark puritan attack on popular Christianity, assume that it must have been intended ironically as antipuritan satire: surely no author could really have preferred the uncompromising meanness of Zelotes over the goodhearted neighborliness of Atheos! But Zelotes was the hero of the work and Atheos the villain, so it is instructive to consider in what Atheos's alleged unbelief consisted.

Atheos represents the post-Reformation Everyman: he expects that good people will be saved and wicked ones will be damned, and within this commonsensical framework he is a very paragon of Christianity. He claims to have "as good a faith and as good a soul to Godward as the best learned of them all." His creed is simple, direct, and unimpeachably orthodox: "I mean well; I hurt no man, nor I think no man any hurt; I love God above all, and put my whole trust in him. What would ye have more?"[1] On this basis he expects to be saved: "I hope if there be but three in all this country go to heaven, I shall be one of them, I mean so well."[2] Atheos, in other words, is a pious Christian.

The zealot's goal is to unmask this pious Christianity as unbelief. In part, this is an attack on doctrinal ignorance, accusing all men of unbelief who fail to engage deeply with the Bible and its doctrines: "There are a number of ye which are indeed very atheists, and set not a straw by the knowledge of God's will. For let a man tell ye of any duty which ye should be taught out of the holy scriptures, by and by, this is your answer: those things are not for us to meddle withal."[3] But the zealot's more pressing point is that Atheos's failure to apply Christian doctrine experimentally to himself is literally unbelief. In an important passage, Atheos bluntly rejects Zelotes's allegation that he and his neighbors are damned, because the Gospel promised that all who believe are saved: "How can ye say their state is damnable, so long as they believe? Can men do more than believe?" Zelotes responds with a concise statement of the new Protestant position: "They do *not* believe: for if they believe, then are they sure that God loveth them, what is it else which they believe?"[4] Elsewhere, Atheos indignantly tells Zelotes, "Let me alone; I believe as well as you." Zelotes responds that he will test whether Atheos really believes, asking a question which sounds absurd to modern ears: "Ye believe that Christ was crucified and suffered upon the cross, but are ye able for to *prove* that ye believe in Christ crucified?" Atheos, furious at this challenge, answers, "I say I do. Are you able for to disprove me?" To which Zelotes responds, "Sin is not slain in ye, therefore ye do not."[5]

In Gifford's *Countrie Divinitie,* we thus find an epitome of the Reformation project of belief, now expressed through a new idiom: the atheist. The words "atheist" and "atheism," and their cognates in other languages, were coined in the middle decades of the sixteenth century, simultaneously throughout Western Europe. They soon exploded into common usage; by the 1580s, accusations of atheism were everywhere. As historians have pointed out, "atheism" did not mean in the sixteenth century precisely what it means today: it could refer to a whole series of moral and religious offenses besides intellective denial of God's existence. Likewise, accusations of atheism, even when they do refer to intellective denial of God's existence, do not prove the actual presence of such a position: the atheist was the characteristic bogeyman of the confessional age. So, what might the invention of the unbeliever signify?

Generations of scholars have trawled through these materials for evidence of "real" atheism, with limited success. More recently, a number of scholars have demonstrated that early modern atheism was a coherent concept with its own contours and meanings rather than simply a derogatory slur.[6] But this book is not about unbelief; our concern is the transformation of belief itself. As we have seen, the Reformation and Counter-Reformation collaborated to transform belief into a principle of exclusion, making belief *hard.* We need now to consider the effects of this new confessional logic: the intellectual consequences of discovering that a supposedly Christian society was in fact populated by legions of unbelievers. For it turns out that, once deployed, the logic of atheism—all the myriad arguments by which wrong believers or insufficient believers could be denounced as unbelievers—carried daunting corollaries and implications, committing both sides to versions of belief so harsh and unyielding as to be unsustainable. The invention of the unbeliever, in the hands of zealots like George Gifford, was both

a major component of the sixteenth-century revolution in belief and an important reason why that revolution failed.

MAIN
ARG
chapter

{~~~~~~~}

Historians interested in the emergence of atheism have described at considerable length the variety of meanings attached to the term in the sixteenth century, arguing that it did
not generally signify the absence of belief in God. What these
historians mean, however, is that atheism did not signify the
absence of what *we* would call belief in God. Yet, as we have
seen, their belief was not ours: in the sixteenth century, belief
was transforming, coming to be seen as an arduous task, far
more difficult than mundane epistemology. That leaves open
the question: how did accusations of atheism relate to *their*
understandings of belief?

Our starting point is necessarily the Greek word ἄθεος
(*atheos*), literally "without God." This word was, of course,
known to scholars, and the exponential growth of Greek learning in Renaissance Western Europe undoubtedly encouraged
the emergence of atheism as a modern term. But the vernacular words that evolved in the sixteenth century were burdened
by the fact that, in the classical tradition, atheos contained a
variety of meanings to confuse the learned. Crucially, atheos
always carried the connotation of denying God's existence; but
it also carried a series of other meanings, and the history of belief will turn on the way these alternative meanings came to depend upon and imply one another.

As early as Plato's *Apology*, we find the first great debate
over the meaning of the term. At his trial, Socrates tells his
prosecutor Meletus that he does not understand the charges
against him: is he accused of being atheos for believing in
gods who "are not the gods whom the state believes in," or is

he accused of being atheos because he does not "believe in gods at all?"[7] According to Plato, Meletus opted for the latter alternative, accusing Socrates of not believing in gods at all. Yet this should not blind us to the ambiguity revealed in this passage: the first alternative offered by Socrates—that an atheist was someone who rejected *certain* gods—would have been familiar to Plato's readers and to later Greeks. As A. B. Drachmann has noted, in the Greek tradition atheos often meant "the point of view which denies the existence of the ancient Gods," hence Jews and later Christians were routinely taken as *atheoi* for their monotheism.[8] The term also carried more ethical meanings: to be atheos was to be ungodly, like Orestes, whom Aeschylus called atheos (despite his conversations with Apollo) after he violated religious norms by murdering his mother.[9] It could also mean (literally) godless, like Oedipus, who according to Sophocles was abandoned by the gods.[10] So atheism was from the beginning a polysemous notion, as befitting any attempt to comprehend the absence of something that is always already invisible.

In a Christian context, ambiguities multiplied: atheos always contained the possibility of Meletus's stark meaning—denial of all divinity—while never foreclosing other meanings. The term appears only once in the Greek New Testament (Ephesians 2:12), where it refers to "strangers from the covenants of promise, having no hope, and without God (*atheoi*) in the world"—in other words, gentiles. Moreover, the Greek Fathers sometimes used the word to turn the tables against pagan persecutors who had accused them of atheism for denying the gods of the pantheon: Polycarp denounced the crowd at his execution, saying, "Down with the atheists!" and Justin Martyr admitted in his *First Apology* that Christians are atheists with respect to the pagan gods, but not with respect to the true God. As Alan Kors notes, Clement of Alexandria "used the term *atheist* equivocally, for he applied it to explicit disbelief, to certain forms of erroneous belief (denial of providence, for example), to those who used God as 'accomplices to man's own evil,' and to those who infused the Divinity with the worst passions of men."[11] Plutarch described the atheist in something like a modern sense—someone who "thinks there are no gods"—but his point was that the atheist is not as bad as the superstitious person "who wishes there were none."[12]

In Latin, the word *atheos* or *atheus* existed but was vanishingly rare. Probably its only classical usage was in Cicero's *De Natura Deorum*, where he twice referred to the Greek philosopher and poet Diagoras, "who is called the Atheist."[13] It is unclear whether Cicero meant this as a Latin coinage, or whether he was simply using a Greek epithet for a Greek; but regardless, Western medieval manuscripts rendered the word atheos in Roman script, because the scribes who produced them had no Greek.[14] Thus was a Latin word born—later rejected by snobbish modern editors, who render the word ἄθεος to keep their Golden Age Latin pure. But it saw only occasional use by Christians, and hardly ever outside its original Greek context. The early Christian apologist Minucius Felix used the term *atheon*; but he was merely paraphrasing Cicero referring to Diagoras. Augustine used it just once, in his *Answer to Petilian the Donatist*, where he Christianized Cicero by referring to "the atheist Diagoras, who denied that there was any God, so that he would seem to be the man of whom the prophet spoke beforehand, 'The fool has said in his heart there is no God.'"[15] Lactantius referred to Diagoras as atheos in his *De Ira Dei*, and he referred to Theodorus as atheos in his *Epitome Divinarum Institutionum*.[16] According to the *Patrologia Latina*, the Psalms commentary of the fifth-century mystic Arnobius the Younger lamented the taunts of *athei*; but since this phrase was omitted from Erasmus's seminal printed edition in 1522, it was evidently unknown to early moderns.[17] St. Hilary used *impii athei* to describe the unduti-ful, like children who despised their parents.[18] In *Against the Nations*, Arnobius of Sicca refuted the charge that Christians were atheistic, impious, or sacrilegious for doubting the pagan gods, throwing those epithets back in pagan faces: "It is fitting that none should be called by such names, more than your-selves."[19] That is virtually the entire inventory of atheos in the late antique West, and as with the Greeks, we can see that it connoted inappropriate relationships to divinity as much as denial of divinity.

Subsequent Latin usages remained extremely infrequent in the Middle Ages and early Renaissance. We can occasionally find the word, as when the twelfth-century English bishop Gil-bert Foliot used *atheum* to describe impious people who "re-proached the Lord."[20] But the word had virtually no footprint, and on the eve of the Reformation, atheos sounded distinctly odd. The Vulgate had translated *atheos* in Ephesians 2:12 as *sine Deo* (without God) rather than using the Latin word, and when Marsilio Ficino came to translate Plato in the fifteenth century, he likewise used circumlocutions like *divinitatis ex-pers* and *absque deo*, or semi-synonyms like *prophanissime* and *impietate*.[21] As late as 1536, when Philip Melanchthon de-scribed Epicureans as "*atheoi*," he used Greek rather than Ro-man letters for the word, which he may not have imagined to be properly Latinate.[22]

Thus, on the eve of its vernacular emergence in the middle of the sixteenth century, the rarely used concept of "atheism" already contained, among the learned, a crucial ambiguity. On the one hand, it unquestionably referred to atheism in something close to the modern sense, insofar as it was best known as an epithet for a handful of ancient Greeks who were accused of denying the existence of divinity. And yet, on the other hand, the same word referred to other things as well—most importantly, wrong religion and gross impiety. What was the relationship between these potential meanings when the vernacular word burst onto the scene?

⊰━━◈W◈━━⊱

In English, the first uses of the term atheist already show a debate over how broadly or narrowly to construe the concept. Sometimes writers were relatively clear. So, for instance, in 1560 the Scottish reformer John Knox responded to an unnamed Anabaptist who had attacked Protestants as worse than "athei, that is to say, such as deny that there is any God."[23] In this definition, helpfully provided for English vernacular readers who were not yet expected to recognize the term, there is not much room for confusion. When this Anabaptist defined athei so narrowly, he could easily have had in mind Thomas Elyot's pathbreaking Latin-English dictionary of 1538, where the Latin word atheos was defined as simply "he that doth not believe that God is."[24]

But things were not so simple: from the first, atheist could also refer to error, hypocrisy, and other forms of profanity. The Protestant émigré John Véron, for instance, wrote in 1561 that Roman Catholics who denied predestination were "a sort of atheists and swinish epicures," and for English readers unaccustomed to this new word, he provided a helpful marginal note: "Atheists are in English called godless."[25] Now, Véron was not a native English speaker, so we might take his literal translation with a grain of salt. Nonetheless, it is intriguing that "godless" was itself an English Protestant neologism, first used in William Tyndale's 1528 *Obedience of a Christian Man* to describe religious hypocrites.[26] Six years later, the Protestant George Joye used the word to describe Thomas More and other Catholics who saw merit in good works as "godless barkers against God."[27] This Protestant connection between the Greek term "atheist" and the more bluntly Anglo-Saxon "godless" was repeated in Philip Sidney and Arthur Golding's 1587 English translation of Phillipe Mornay's *De la verité de la religion chrestienne*: "And so what shall those other religions be, but either idolatry or atheism, that is to say, utter godlessness?"[28]

Nor did Elyot's dictionary sweep the field when it defined *atheos* so narrowly as "he that doth not believe that God is." In 1552, another dictionary, Richard Huloet's *Abcedarium anglico latinum*, translated the English word "infidel" into Latin as *atheos*. In 1572, Huloet's revised *Dictionary*, now translating from Latin into English, offered for *atheos* two English words: "infidel" and "miscreant." Both are interesting, and neither meant simply "he that doth not believe that God is." "Infidel" sometimes referred to those who did not believe in Christianity—especially Muslims—but it also referred more generally to the damned. "Miscreant," without its modern sense of social depravity until relatively late, in the Middle Ages meant literally wrong-believing and was applied to Turks, heretics, and bad Christians. The 1525 English translation of Froissart's *Chronicle*, for instance, rebuked a Christian leader for seeking "alliance with a king miscreant, out of our law and faith."[29]

The word atheist was also often used to refer to "Epicureans," both ancient and modern. A 1569 work, for instance, described with apparent synonomy "so many Epicures, so many Libertines, so many Atheists and people abandoned to all filthiness and dissolution."[30] But here was another ambiguity, because Epicureanism (quite apart from its atomist physics) had two related but non-identical religious meanings for sixteenth-century Christians: on the one hand denial of God, providence, or the immortality of the soul; and on the other hand debauchery and wicked living. The interconnection between these was crucial. It was a commonplace that denial of divinity would lead to all manner of sins; but on the other hand, that does not necessarily mean that alleged Epicureans were being accused of thought-crimes. Instead, they *acted* as if they did not believe, which made them in some important sense atheists, but left ambiguous the question of their intellective views.

Thus, in the roiling and churning religious controversies of the sixteenth century, it was often hard to tell whether a narrow or broad sense of atheism was intended. And this was exactly the point, for it was only by virtue of the narrow definition that the broad polemical usage of this brand-new word acquired its sting, while at the same time it was only by virtue of its broad polemical usage that the narrow definition acquired real power in a nominally Christian society. So, for instance, in a 1565 English translation of the Portuguese Catholic Bishop Jerónimo Osório, a helpful marginal note glossed Osório's claim that it takes great effort for heretics to reach the heights of abomination: "Sects be the steps to atheism; that is, of denying that there is any God." That sounds pretty clear. But then, on the very next page, another marginal note undermined that clarity and posited instead, "Our heretics be guilty of atheism."[31] So which was it? Was heresy a step on the path to denial of God, or was heresy ipso facto denial of God, or was denial of God not the only meaning of "atheism"?

Comparable complexities can be found when we turn to the French case, made more bluntly consequential by the torture and execution of the printer Éstienne Dolet as *athée* in 1546. The sixteenth-century French word *atheistes* and its cognates (*athéisme, athée*) seem to have been popularized by the Swiss Protestant Pierre Viret. In perhaps the first printed usage, a 1543 letter warning Protestants against trying to live peacefully under Catholic rule, Viret wrote, "There is no great difference between hypocrites, condemners and mockers of God, and blasphemers who lie against the Holy Spirit. They are all close cousins, and we see by experience that by degrees the one falls into the other. Because many of those who have become atheists and without God, who have first had some knowledge of the truth and then blaspheme against it, are fallen into these abysses by degrees."[32] Here, an *atheiste* is essentially an apostate, a lapsed Protestant who falls back into the old religion or outwardly conforms to it. We can therefore associate the rise of the term atheist in French with John Calvin's campaign, beginning in 1544, against so-called Nicodemites, those who claimed to be Protestants in secret while remaining publicly Catholic.

In his *Dialogue on the Disorder Present in the World* (1545), Viret explained in more detail what he meant by the term. "By these Epicureans and Atheists," he wrote, "I intend a new sect . . . who have previously recognized the Evangelical truth but have returned to wallow in the mud like pigs":

> I omit in part the ancient Epicureans, and those of the Roman curia who have almost always made profession of this philosophy, and who have for the first article of their faith, that there is no God but their bellies. But I speak here of a sect of new Epicureans, who have enough knowledge of the truth to understand the abuses of the pope, and to mock the idolatries and superstitions of the papal Church; but they have not yet learned to understand Jesus Christ truly. And yet for as much as they have abused this knowledge which has been given to them in order to reach a greater knowledge of Christ, and that they have converted it into carnal liberty, God has taken them for reprobate.[33]

Here again, without forgoing a jab at the atheists in Rome, the main targets are hypocrites and backsliders from the Protestant cause, now grown into a dangerous sect.

John Calvin also deployed the term atheist in ways that blurred the distinction between denial of divinity and other religious outrages. The most influential example was Calvin's 1551 *Des Scandales*, where he seems at first to assume something like the modern meaning of atheism, focusing on the dangerous notion that "all religions have their origins in men's brains, that God exists because it pleases men to believe so, that the hope of eternal life has been invented to deceive the simple, and that fear of judgment is a childish terror." But in the very next paragraph, this more formal understanding is transformed, without fanfare or apparent incongruity, into an attack on the *atheisme* that is "rampant everywhere throughout the world," especially in "the courts of kings and princes, in courts of justice, and in other distinguished walks of life." The reason for this plague of atheism, Calvin tells us, is that throughout the world, but especially in high places, conscience "is banished altogether."[34]

Among French Catholics, the word also had a variety of meanings. Often the issue was doctrinal, as in a 1555 work by François de Billon, where one sign of the nation's blessings was that "all the Gallic people have at all times had faith and believed in the worthy immortality of the soul . . . the inhabitants of this region have never had anything of atheism."[35] But on the other hand, atheism could also refer to godless living. For instance, Jacques le Fèvre's *Iuste Complaincte de l'Eglise Catholique* (1562) described heresy's intrinsic tendency to dissolve everything in its path. It subverts kingdoms and abolishes laws; it destroys distinctions between estates; and it "makes us live like brute beasts, and makes us fall into atheism."[36] Here the term implies moral depravity and the absence of conscientious restraint, free living rather than free thinking.

The invention of the atheist in the sixteenth century thus utterly depended upon, but was never limited to, a definition of "atheist" that meant "one who does not believe that God is." The word always contained that strict or narrow meaning, but it also cast a much wider penumbra of connotations, a semantic field that included godlessness, misapprehension of God, idolatry, paganism, debauchery, apostasy, and hypocrisy. These other, commonplace meanings were not *alternatives* to the idea that "atheist" meant "one who does not believe that God is"; rather, they were informed by an understanding of belief itself in which these other meanings might be *examples* of not believing that God is. In order to figure out what atheism was, in other words, early moderns had to wrestle with the problem of belief itself. Can a person who acts like there is no God really believe in God? Can a person who believes in many gods properly be said to believe at all? Is there a difference between being on the path to unbelief and actually failing to believe, or can the former be understood as an embryonic version that fully contains the latter? In the fraught atmosphere of the Reformation, the line drawn by Peter Lombard in the Middle Ages—between "to believe God," "to believe in *a* God," and "to believe *in* God"—could not be maintained. The new language of atheism was both a symptom of this slippage and one of its most potent instruments.

In the sixteenth century, two vast new polemical enterprises— the Reformation and the Counter-Reformation—had incentive to push as far as they could toward the most exclusive definitions of belief. The word atheist itself was central to this project, and its emergence is a barometer of changing conditions. But even without the word, combatants could deny belief-status to one another. In what became an infamous early example, at the first session of the Council of Trent, the Italian

Bishop Cornelius Musso of Bitonto expressed dismay that heretics had "turned away, as it were, with unanimous consent from religion to superstition, from faith to infidelity, from Christ to Antichrist, even from God to Epicurus to Pythagoras, saying with impious heart and shameless mouth, there is no God."[37] This kind of rhetoric, identifying opposing positions *within* Christianity with ancient atheists who had described all religion as a ruse, allowed little room for compromise or conciliation, little room for belief as a journey rather than a destination, little space on earth between God and the devil.

A relentless logic drove polemicists toward this position. From a Catholic perspective, one pillar of the new orthodoxy was that, if belief adhered in obedience to the universal Church, then those who systematically deviated from that Church became ipso facto unbelievers. In this argument, the problem was not simply the content of heresy but its method of truth-seeking, which depended upon human speculation and interpretation rather than the acceptance of authority, and hence could not be accounted belief at all. So, for instance, at a 1568 religious disputation in Paris, one argument for the atheism of the Calvinists was their rationalist and materialist rejection of miracles like transubstantiation: how could belief in God be compatible with testing his miracles according to mundane reason? Surely if it was impossible for God to appear in the form of bread, as the heretics allegedly insisted, then by the same logic so was God himself.[38] The Parisian printer Nicolas Chesneau, in the preface to a volume of sermons by François le Picart, argued that the mere act of individual scriptural interpretation, with its "illicit curiosity" and "experimenting," leads men to fall not only into heresy but "more often than not into atheism, forgetting God and his Church."[39]

The Irish Jesuit and future Archbishop of Dublin, Peter Talbot, was more explicit in a 1657 treatise explaining why the free choice of individuals could never constitute Christian belief. Left to their own devices, Talbot wrote, people might entertain an infinitude of opinions, like the Turks with their prophet, the Jews still waiting for a messiah, and the absurdities of the English puritans. "Turks, Jews, and puritans," Talbot wrote, "do not believe these fond articles of their own religion with any supernatural faith; their belief is merely historical, just as children believe the history of the Knight of the Sun, Don Quixote de la Manche, etc." That is to say, "They assent to the mysteries of the trinity and incarnation, not because God revealed it to them, but because they are pleased to judge it very probable, or certain, that God revealed some such thing." It is evident "that their own fancy or opinion, and not God's revelation, doth move Protestants to believe what they do believe of Christian religion" because they "choose to themselves amongst articles which the Catholic Roman Church proposed . . . All the rest (though equally proposed to them by the testimony of the said Roman Church as divine revelation) they reject as fabulous, or apocryphal, because it suits not with their liberty, fancy, and manners." Thus, regardless of the content of their opinions, and even when occasionally those opinions are correct, Protestants are unbelievers because they lack "the fundamental motive of Christian belief" which is that articles are "sufficiently proposed as divine revelation by the testimony of the Church": "Their faith be neither Christian nor supernatural; their own persuasion alone is not sufficient to supernaturalize their belief."[40]

As Catholic writers incessantly pointed out, the word heretic, and its Latin and Romance cognates, derived from the Greek word meaning "able to choose." Heretics were simply choosers, those who falsely supposed that belief consisted in selecting from a menu of options rather than accepting authoritative verdicts. Within this logic, Catholics argued that the very act of choosing was a rejection of God, who demands obedience rather than choice. This was a particularly common strategy among Jesuits. The Italian Jesuit Antonio Possevino, in his aptly titled book on the *Atheisms . . . of all the Heretics of Our Time* (1586), wrote that "heresy always hastens to atheism as its center or proper sphere," while the English Jesuit Thomas Fitzherbert wrote that "atheism is indeed the very center whither all heresies do naturally tend and finally fall."[41] The Flemish Jesuit Leonard Lessius argued, as a 1631 English translation had it, that all heresies "do finally propend and incline to atheism"—the Latin original had *dubitatio de toto religionis negotio*, doubt of the whole matter of religion—because, having departed from true religion, "man's understanding findeth nothing wherein it may firmly and securely rest."[42]

Protestantism was thus fundamentally a negative religion, a form of doubt rather than belief, subtracting from true religion until nothing remained. Listen, for instance, to the Elizabethan cardinal-in-exile William Allen:

> If thou cast an earnest eye upon their whole doctrine, thou shalt find that it principally and in a manner wholly consisteth in taking away or wasting another faith that it found before, so that the preachers thereof must ever be destroyers, pluckers-down and rooters-up of the truth grounded before. Will you see then what a Protestant's faith and doctrine is? Deny only and make a negation of some article of our belief, and that is a form of his faith, which is lightly negative. There is no free will; there is no works needful to salvation; there is no Church known; there is no chief governor thereof; there be not seven sacraments; they do not *conferre gratiam*, give grace; baptism is not necessary to salvation; Christ is not present on the altar; there is no sacrifice; there is no priesthood; there is no altar; there is no

profit in prayers to saints or for the dead; there is no purgatory; Christ went not down to hell; there is no *limbus*; finally, if you list go forward in your negative faith, there is no hell, there is no heaven, there is no God. Do you not see here a trim faith and a substantial? Look in Calvin's *Institutions* and you shall find the whole frame of this wasting faith. There is nothing in that blasphemous book nor in their apologies but a gathered body of this no-faith.[43]

A similar example is *La Doctrine curieuse des beaux esprits de ce temps* (1623) by the French Jesuit François Garasse. Book III was dedicated to the rebuttal of *atheisme* (or, as he sometimes called it, *libertinage*) on the one hand, and *heretiques* or *Huguenots* on the other. In a very limited and ironic sense, Garasse distinguished these categories and described the differences between them.[44] But the whole intent of the text was to argue that there was no essential difference between heretics who "half believe in God" and atheists who "believe nothing at all."[45] Or, as he put it, "heretics do not reject all articles of faith indifferently, but they choose whichever are to their taste, to believe whatever seems good to them," daring to tell God which bits of religion they will believe.[46] Their departure from the "common belief of the Church" is in fact unbelief, because the chooser claims to be his own master rather than admitting authority, which is the wellspring and definition of belief itself.[47] In Garasse's logic, Protestantism represented a series of subtractions from the faith, and atheism was merely the logical extension of that process until there was nothing left to subtract.[48] By diminishing religion they destroy religion, for "in articles of faith, it is impossible to take one away without snatching away a feather from the wings," grounding the whole bird.[49] Martin Luther, through his "careful diligence" in this process of subtraction, "reached all the way to atheism."[50]

By contrast, "true spiritual liberty consists in the simple and wise belief in everything the Church offers, indifferently and without distinction."[51] We must "honestly believe what the Church offers," without imagining that we as individuals have any choice in the matter. The difference between philosophy and Christianity is the difference between "wanting to know" and "believing."[52]

We find a similar argument in *The Reformed Protestant, Tending Directly to Atheisme, and all Impietie* (1621) by the English Jesuit Laurence Anderton, who argued that Truth is by definition affirmative, while error is negative, an absence of Truth: "Negatives in general are not so much the object of faith as rather waste and destruction thereof."[53] Yet, Anderton noted, everything positively affirmed by Protestants "they have received from the Church of Rome": the Trinity, the scripture, the Creed. The so-called Reformation, then, was nothing more than a process of subtraction or omission wherein great chunks of Catholic truth were taken away: the merit of works, images, relics, pilgrimages, prayers to saints, purgatory, prayer for the dead, bishops, and so forth.[54] Thus Protestantism "tended to atheism" in a literal sense: the farther reformation proceeded, the less religion was left, until finally nothing remained. This allowed Anderton to describe, with obvious relish, the process of continuous reformation over the previous century, in which "this alluring precept of a more refined reformation" had led every sect to murder its parent at the moment of its "viperous birth."[55] Luther's revolt subtracted four sacraments, several books of canonical scripture, and key doctrines; the subsequent reformation of Zwingli subtracted Christ from the sacrament; the third reformation of Calvin, Beza, and the puritans removed bishops and the universal grace of Christ's sacrifice.[56] After so many reformations, Anderton wrote, "a man would assuredly have thought that reformation had been at its height," yet nonetheless "from the puritans are now again last issued forth the Brownists and antitrinitarians, both of them urging as yet a further negative reformation" subtracting the Lord's Prayer, infant baptism, and finally the divinity of Christ.[57] "The most refined reformation made by Protestants from the Roman Church," wrote Anderton, is "that Christ our savior and redeemer is not God," after which Christians fell inevitably to "infidelity." In this logic, Protestants were only believers in the very limited and rapidly diminishing sense that they retained residual Catholicism; reformation was a vehicle for "unbelief," which was "the proper *terminus ad quem*" of such destruction.[58]

Another side to atheism was dissolute living, a phenomenological or "practical" atheism that adhered in the body. The English Jesuit Robert Parsons, in his 1582 *First Book of the Christian Exercise*—reprinted over forty times, and so popular that the Church of England gave up banning it and published its own expurgated version instead—explained succinctly how this worked. In a chapter on the sin of "negligence," Parsons clarified that by that word he meant more than its common usage, "for I do comprehend under the name of 'negligent' all careless and dissolute people, which take to heart nothing that pertaineth to God or godliness, but only attend to worldly affairs, making their salvation the least part of their cogitations. And under this kind of negligence is contained . . . a secret kind of atheism, or denying of God; that is, of denying him in life and behavior." Although these atheists "profess that they believe and trust in him, yet by their dissolute and careless doings, they testify that in their hearts they believe him not." For them, "the world is their only treasure, and not God. And consequently they prefer that before God, as indeed atheists."[59] There was nothing specifically Catholic about this argument. Yet Parsons deftly transformed it into anti-Protestant polemic by arguing that among the principal causes of practical atheism was heresy, which provokes "questions and doubts," and thereby "weareth out a mans wit, and in the end bringeth him to care for no part, but rather to condemn all."[60] There were other rationales, as well, by which Catholics could suggest an intrinsic connection between Protestantism and the practical atheism of debauchery. The Scotsman Nicol Burne, for instance, argued that "solifidean presumption"—that is, the doctrine of salvation by faith rather than works—"induces in man looseness of life," from which flows "atheism, barbarism, or Mahommet's faith at the least."[61]

While widely used by Catholics, the argument connecting atheism to sin became not just common but foundational for Protestants. The central issue in the Protestant polemic against atheism was not doctrine, but rather the overwhelming weight of sin that made unbelief such a ubiquitous condition. This argument can be traced directly to the famously dour leader of the Reformation in Geneva, John Calvin, whose most recent biographer summarized his disposition with two apt sentences: "The superior force of his mind was evident in all that he did. He was also ruthless, and an outstanding hater."[62] Calvin obsessed over the apparent failure of so many superficial Christians to believe in God. But like Luther before him, Calvin faced an apparent contradiction. On the one hand, there were good reasons to think that unbelief was more or less impossible, and the Christian tradition insisted that the existence of God was apparent to any thinking creature. As Calvin put it, "That there exists in the human mind, and indeed by natural instinct, some sense of deity [*divinitatis sensum*], we hold to be beyond dispute." Even those who claim to deny the being of a God "occasionally feel the truth which they are desirous not to know."[63] Yet on the other hand, Calvin organized the entire introductory section of his *Institutes*—perhaps the single most influential text of the Reformation—around unbelief. He argued that the seemingly impossible words of Psalm 14:14, "The fool hath said in his heart, there is no God," referred primarily to those who "stifle the light of nature and intentionally stupefy themselves. We see many, after they have become hardened in a daring course of sin, madly banishing all remembrance of God." These people, while they do not fully "disown his essence" [*essentiam . . . non adimant*], nonetheless "rob him of his justice and providence, and represent him as sitting idly in heaven." This, for Calvin, was the sort of atheism that saturated a sinful world: "Whosoever he be that, quenching the fear of the heavenly judgment, doth carelessly follow his own affections, he denieth that there is a God."[64]

I want to focus for a moment on this phrase—"he denieth that there is a God"—from the 1561 English translation by the Elizabethan lawyer, poet, and politician Thomas Norton. The standard modern translation of the *Institutes*, produced by Henry Beveridge for the Calvin Translation Society in 1845, deviates from Norton and renders this passage as "*virtually* denies that there is a God." This seems to have been an attempt to make Calvin more compatible with modern notions of atheism; it made no sense to Beveridge for Calvin to say that a careless follower of his own affections *literally* denies that there is a God. But Norton had it right, Calvin does not say *virtually*: the Latin is simply "*Deum esse negat*," and the original French has "*nient qu'il y ait un Dieu*." This blunt equation between the unregenerate sinner and the atheist was crucial for Calvin, displacing the specter of unbelief from an infinitesimal minority onto an immeasurable majority. It threatened every Christian with the possibility that their own inescapable inclination to live in the world *as if* there were no God might transform them into the monster who denied there was any God at all. For Protestants, so committed to the depravity of mankind, it was persuasive to argue that, with the veil of Catholic confession and absolution stripped away, atheism in a deep and real sense might be unmasked in every corrupt worldling.

This was not, in principle, an anti-Catholic argument; after all, Protestants used it against sinful and worldly Protestants. But on the other hand, it was characteristic of Protestant polemic to describe sinful and worldly Protestants as essentially Catholic, in the sense that they remained unreformed, still trusting in the world rather than faith. The Protestant argument linking sin with atheism also mapped neatly onto the structure of anti-Catholic polemic because, quite apart from Catholicism's alleged theological errors, Protestants routinely described the Catholic priesthood as corrupt worldlings, the principal tricksters and salesmen for a faux-faith that pardoned all manner of debauchery in return for cash.

An early example comes from the Lutheran Johann Rivius, who condemned atheists falsely living under the name of Christians.[65] The principal reason we refuse to repent our sins, Rivius wrote, is "our incredulity": if we really believed in divine judgment and the punishment of sinners as anything more than "womanish fables," we would work to amend our lives.[66] This logic could be applied to all sinners, but Rivius applied it first and most starkly to the "popish priests" (*pontificii sacerdotes*) with their whores, who do not "really believe" despite their "dreams of faith."[67] In the same vein, Pierre Boquin, professor of theology at the University of Heidelberg, described how, "In some of these governors of the [Catholic] Church, superstition and ignorance of heavenly doctrine grows stronger every day; in others, contempt of true religion increases;

and in most, either atheism or Epicurism openly rule. Their manners are most corrupt; all discipline, even that of which the popes themselves are inventors and architects, is wholly overthrown."[68] The Englishman Matthew Sutcliffe, hip-deep in anti-Jesuit polemic, attacked "the ambitious and luciferian popes, the carnal cardinals, the fleshy friars and priests, and popish atheists, that have no God but the pope and their belly; men in condition swinish and brutish, and in their religion hellish."[69]

This is not to deny that Protestants also associated Catholic *doctrine* with atheism: just as Luther denounced works theology as unbelief, so the English theologian William Perkins, among others, argued that belief in God was impossible without the doctrine of predestination.[70] But even this doctrinal atheism was often focused on its moral effects. Just to take one example, the English minister Francis Marbury, preaching at England's premier pulpit at Paul's Cross at the beginning of the seventeenth century, claimed that, "It would allure a pirate indeed to be of their religion, if he might be sure to buy out his punishment after his death with the robberies and rapines of his life. In the meantime such doctrine as this hath brought atheism into the world." Marbury continued, "A popish atheist is an hideous mongrel, even a very centaur. As to say the very truth, popery and atheism are very coincident, and their differences very obscure. Popery is a sensual dissembling with God."[71]

All of this suggests that, while the division of atheism into "practical" and "speculative" branches became a mainstay of Protestant polemic in the seventeenth century—a particularly influential example was Francis Bacon's oft-cited essay "Of Atheism"—the practical and the speculative were rarely very far apart. Usually the purpose of the distinction was to uncover the horror of atheism even where it was least expected, rather than to admit that some kinds of atheism were less real than others. So, for instance, the taxonomic impulse reached its zenith with the Dutch Calvinist theologian Gisbert Voetius, who constructed an extended family tree of atheism. First, he divided atheism into practical and theoretical branches—atheism of life versus atheism of thought. Further subdivisions differentiated people who were atheists themselves (*atheismus proprius*) from those who promoted atheism in others (*atheismus participatus*), direct and indirect atheists, external atheists (negating God) and internal atheists (ignorance, doubt, opinion), and so forth.[72] But the point of this taxonomy, and many others Voetius constructed during his long polemical career, was not to construct a hierarchy of atheism but to demonstrate how deeply atheism could penetrate and how widely atheism could permeate an outwardly Christian society.[73]

From this polemic flowed a stark and dangerous corollary: all unrepented sin was atheism, even in friends and neighbors who were not otherwise theologically suspect. There is no more cogent example than *The Drunkard's Character* (1638) by the Englishman Richard Younge, who argued that drunkards may seem to believe God's promises—they hope to be saved—but evidently they do not believe God's threats of punishment. Younge told the drunkard, "Either thou believest there is no God at all, or else that God is not just and true, nor speaks as he means in his word, which is worse." Therefore, "Thou art but one of David's fools, which say in their heart, there is no God."[74] According to Younge, "It is hard for men to believe their own unbelief . . . For he, whose heart speaks atheism, will profess with his tongue that he believes there is a God and that he is just and true."[75] But this was demonstrably a lie, for if men really believed that sinners would burn forever, they would not dare "continue in the practice of these sins without fear or remorse or care of amendment." By definition, "if they did in good earnest believe that there is either God or devil, heaven or hell," then "they could not but live thereafter and make it their principal care how to be saved."[76]

For John Calvin, not surprisingly, the difference between the atheist and the believer mapped onto the difference between Israel and her enemies, the elect and the reprobate, with all its Manichaean simplicity. Calvin summarized this vision in an extraordinary passage in his *Commentary on the Acts of the Apostles*:

> Those are called worshippers of God spiritually, who gave their name to the God of Israel. Religion is attributed to them alone, therefore there remaineth nothing else for the rest, but the reproach of atheism (*atheismi*), howsoever much they toil and moil in superstition. And that for good considerations, for of whatsoever pomp the idolaters make boast, if their inward affection be examined, there shall be found nothing there but horrible contempt of God.[77]

Atheism, then, was not for Protestants an amorphous and free-floating accusation but a very specific one; it only appears amorphous and free-floating because it could justly be applied to almost all the world. When you have a hammer, everything looks like a nail.

And so the Reformation filled up the world with unbelievers. By privileging the starkest and most unforgiving interpretations of what it meant to believe, polemicists were able to transcend the argument that the ungodly were like atheists, and reach the conclusion that they were, or for practical purposes could be considered, atheists indeed. Always relying upon the possibility that atheism could mean something other than simply not believing in God's existence, early modern religious writers inserted the word into the conversation and then, in a devastating but theologically plausible bait-and-switch, insinuated or sometimes overtly argued that many professing Christians did not believe in God at all.

Scholarship on early modern atheism has, naturally, focused on unbelief rather than belief. Proceeding from Lucien Febvre's seminal argument that unbelief remained unthinkable in the sixteenth century, historians have sought to discover when and how it became thinkable. They have analyzed doubt and skepticism as precursors to full-blown unbelief; they have studied the underground spaces where unbelief might have been expressed and the regimes of censorship that prevented its public articulation; they have studied a stubborn undercurrent of materialism in popular culture; they have studied the ways religious writers invented reasonable arguments for unbelief in order to refute them; and most important, they have ceaselessly hunted their quarry—genuine denial of the existence of a deity—wherever they could run it to ground, springing hidden atheists from the historical bush.

This whole scholarly enterprise is based upon the obstinate but rarely examined assumption that atheism is a subject of transcendent historical importance. This view is perhaps most clearly articulated by the historian Jonathan Israel, for whom the emergent possibility of atheism in the "radical Enlightenment" marked the seminal watershed of human history when ideas were emancipated from their reliance upon God. Before the possibility of genuine atheism, Israel argues, every new idea, however robust, persuasive, and secular, could always be trumped by reference to an infinite and omnipotent God. With the emergence of atheism, however, ideas had to be judged on their own terms, and the whole edifice of modern thought emerged from God's shadow.[78]

Yet must we regard atheism as so fundamental? Israel's argument, like others that take atheism to mark the boundary between premodern and modern worldviews, presumes that there was a coherent and unified object called "belief" to begin with, whose absence could be clearly defined. But this is untrue: belief was complex and contested, meaning different things to different people, shading imperceptibly into other cognitive operations and dispositions. People believed in many different ways, and many failed to believe, depending upon what belief was taken to be. The invention of the unbeliever in the sixteenth century was thus just as consequential as the later emergence of "modern" atheism, because it necessitated a fundamental transformation: after the Reformation filled the world with unbelievers, European society was slowly reorganized around the absence rather than the presence of belief. I want to end this chapter by briefly considering this reorganization, because it goes to the heart of my argument that the Reformation did not inaugurate new habits of mind that led to the Enlightenment, but rather the Enlightenment emerged in reaction against habits of mind that began with the Reformation.

It is a hoary commonplace that Protestantism represented a turn toward interiority and individualism, and that the historical importance of the Reformation lies in the way it privileged the sovereign believer—like Luther declaring, "Here I stand"—as the authentic modern subject. We are told by Protestant, Catholic, and secular historians alike that, for good or ill, Protestantism empowered individuals to reach their own conclusions on a wide range of propositions, leading both to liberal freedoms and to the moral relativism of modernity.[79] It should by now be apparent why a properly historical account of "belief" makes this untenable. The Reformation's new emphasis on belief could not produce liberal individualism, because what Protestants meant by "belief" was severely restricted. Catholics and Anabaptists were not believers, in this view. Neither was Atheos, George Gifford's pious Christian Everyman who occasionally went down to the pub to drown his sorrows. They could make no claims for conscience. They could make no demands about where to stand. They were the objects of this new regime of creedal apartheid rather than its subjects, because atheists had only opinion rather than belief. So, far from liberalizing an authoritarian Catholic world, the invention of the unbeliever in the Reformation structured a new form of authoritarianism.[80] While Catholics disciplined populations to believe, Protestants learned how to discipline populations of unbelievers.

Lutherans began this process with the state-sponsored policing of the unregenerate majority, now presumed to be genuinely reprobate rather than merely pious sinners in need of penance and absolution. As Marc Raeff has noted, "We encounter the first significant examples of the intervensionist and regulatory *Polizeistaat* [police state] in the Protestant states of Germany, such as Saxony and Hessen, in the second half of the sixteenth century."[81] But the disciplinary apparatus of the Calvinist Churches, generated by what Lyndal Roper calls "a view of all human relationships . . . as being structured around authority and submission," is better known.[82] In Amsterdam, for instance, the city fathers in 1596 created the first House of Discipline or *Tuchthuis*, where the undeserving poor were sent to labor for the public good and were given moral instruction to make them into productive citizens. Those who violated the code of conduct in the House of Discipline, demonstrating their depravity by swearing, gambling, singing, or failing to meet their production quotas, might be starved, or might be put in solitary confinement, or might be put into something called the "Drowning Cell," an idiosyncratically Dutch form of correction. The prisoner was put into a sealed room. Water was pumped in. The only way to remove the water was for the prisoner to pump it out by hand. At first the prisoner would complain and refuse to cooperate, but once the water reached the prisoner's head, generally he would be "cured of his idleness." After he had pumped out all the water and fell exhausted to the floor, the newly motivated worker would be allowed to return to the general population.[83]

In Scotland, there were different mechanisms of discipline. The "stool of repentance," for instance, made moral offenders visible to the whole community, so that they might receive the opprobrium of their neighbors.[84] But the most famous instrument of discipline in Scotland was the Branks, an iron cage placed over the heads of unruly women, fitted with long metal spikes or plates to be inserted into their mouths to keep them from speaking. Imported into England as the "Scold's Bridle," it provided "for correction of scolds . . . such a bridle for the tongue as not only quite deprives them of speech, but brings shame for the transgression and humility thereupon . . . which being put upon the offender by order of the magistrates, and fastened with a padlock behind, she is lead round the town by an officer to her shame, nor is it taken off till after the party begins to show all external signs imaginable of humiliation and amendment."[85]

The consistory of Calvin's Geneva, a partnership between reformed ministers and city magistrates, heard thousands of accusations by godly citizens against their ungodly neighbors—and sometimes against the godly themselves in moments of weakness—shaming and intimidating them into obedience. So, for instance, there was Jean Renault, known as "The Braggart," who got drunk and told his minister to leave town and go away. When questioned, Renault told the consistory that he was merely quoting the words of Mark 16:15, "go and preach

the gospel to all the world."[86] Jacques Duval, a servant originally from Paris, offended the godly by saying that going to
church was only for the rich, while he had to work Sundays to
feed his children.[87] Another man was dragged before the consistory for naming his dog Calvin; he claimed rather preposter-
ously that he had been misheard, and the dog's name was really
"Carlin."[88] Bertold Maurys named his penis "The Redeemer"
and was in the habit of wielding it like a club, asking men,
women, and children, *"N'est-il pas beau, le Redempteur?"*[89] Of
course, sinners like these would have been prosecuted by Catholics, too, but Protestant strategies and goals were different.
For Catholics, through the theology of penance, the point was
to save souls, and for those who refused to repent there were
increasingly draconian penalties. For Protestants, by contrast,
the state of souls was essentially beside the point: true repentance was presumed to be vanishingly rare, a gratuitous gift of
God's grace rather than the routine end to routine petty proceedings in the Church courts. So, rather than producing belief,
these proceedings were intended to manage the efflorescence
of unbelief in our sinful world, punishing or shaming offenders
until they hid their sinfulness deep inside where it belonged.
Of course, inward conversion was desired, but it was never expected; salvation was God's business, not the consistory's.

So, while the Reformation can with some justification be
seen as a rebellion against authoritarian attempts to enforce
belief, its alternative was not liberal, tolerant, emancipatory, or
modern. Protestant arguments for the freedom, sanctity, and
authority of belief were not defenses of private opinion or judgment, they were arguments against private opinion or judgment. To credit Protestants with the advent of modern pluralism makes about as much sense as crediting Catholics with
the advent of Protestantism: any regime can be said to create
the reaction against it, but that does not mean that the first

dawn of one movement is radiant with the promise of its successor. Rather, Protestantism offered an alternative authoritarian project designed around the novel premise of an unbelieving world, intended to maintain order in a society now re-envisioned as chock full of atheists. This project was "secular," not in the sense of making space in the world outside of religion, but only in the ironic sense that it demanded religious discipline over an unbelieving world. Modern belief would only emerge when the Reformation project of belief collapsed under its own weight.

CHAPTER FOUR

The Unbearable
Weight of Believing

FRANCESCO SPIERA, a lawyer from the small town of Cit-tadella within the Republic of Venice, was denounced to the Inquisition in November 1547. He had doubted purgatory. He had read the banned best seller of Italian reform, the *Beneficio di Cristo*. He had claimed that Christ alone atoned for all his sins. In May 1548, rather than leaving his family destitute—he had ten children and another on the way—Spiera chose not to risk prison or death for his beliefs, but agreed to the sentence of the Inquisition: he publicly abjured his heresy, then paid twenty-five ducats to buy a tabernacle for his parish church. This was unremarkable: the vast majority of victims of the Holy Office saved their lives by renouncing their errors and throwing themselves on the Church's mercy. But Spiera's sub-sequent trajectory made him notorious: rather than either re-turning to Catholicism, or practicing Protestantism in secret, he determined that he was in fact an unbeliever. Abandoned by God, unable to call on Christ's mercy, he died in despair be-fore the end of the year. Spiera's recantation and death quickly became one of the most popular cautionary tales in Reformation Europe.[1]

Among many accounts, the version penned by the law professor Matteo Gribaldi was printed in Latin, Italian, German, Dutch, and nearly two dozen English editions. On the surface, the moral of Gribaldi's fable was simple: better martyrdom than recantation. But much more was at stake. Spiera's life and death served as an object lesson in the thin line between belief and unbelief. Before his recantation, Spiera was to all appearances a true believer: "He had attained abundant knowledge of the truth, through faith, by the manifest testimonies of the holy scripture." He had tasted in his heart "the gifts of the Holy Ghost, as faith, hope, charity, meekness, gentleness, and all manner of quietness and tranquility of the mind, as he that did possess Christ."[2] After his recantation, however, Spiera felt "the terrible indignation of God against him" and fell into "utter desperation," saying he had sinned against the Holy Ghost, and "Christ neither suffered nor paid for him, but for the elect only."[3] Now, as Spiera and his Protestant colleagues knew well, this apparent fall from election was theologically impossible: either he had not really been assured of salvation before, or he was not really abandoned by God after. Thus, the bulk of Gribaldi's account described how some thirty Italian Protestants spent weeks gathered around Spiera's bedside, attempting to discern which was true. God's mercy is infinite, they told him, enough to forgive Peter's thrice apostasy and the sins of the thief on the cross. All he needed was belief: "Have a sure confidence, Master Francis, and rise, and doubt ye not at all [*nullatenus dubitetis*], God hath already mercy upon you." Spiera answered, "I do not believe" [*Non credo*].[4] After explaining that many worse men had been saved, they asked him, "Why do ye not believe this? Will ye not that God should have mercy upon you?" Spiera answered, "I believe all that ye say. Yea, the devils believe, and are afraid, but all this availeth me nothing . . . My heart is full of hatred, cursing, and blasphemy. I believe and feel [*credo et sentio*] that God is against me." In a harrowing moment, Spiera's attendants convinced him to say the Lord's Prayer with them. He prayed "with plentiful tears, so devoutly and gravely, and with such inward affection, as we thought, that all we [who] stood by did weep with him." But it was all for naught. Spiera admitted that his prayer was but an outward show of hypocrisy. "I know all this and I believe that the infinite mercy of God doth far surmount all the sins of the world, and that every man that believeth and hath faith easily obtaineth pardon," he told them, but alas for himself, "I can neither hope nor believe."[5]

Thus, Spiera's companions came to understand that he had never really been elect at all. Despite appearances, he had possessed only temporary rather than saving faith, for it was impossible that anyone who "had once perfectly and firmly believed, should fall."[6] Spiera finally realized, upon examination of his life, that his belief had always been feigned, and soon thereafter he fell dead of his despair. Besides the moral that it is better to die than recant, then, a second moral intruded upon readers of this tale, one that applied to Protestants universally rather than only those who faced the possibility of martyrdom: you, too, may be an unbeliever. However assured you may feel in your belief, you, too, could be another Francesco Spiera. Who could read this story without anxiety about their own belief?

The tale of Francesco Spiera therefore represents a crack in the façade of Reformation belief and an early warning sign that belief could not support the vast new weight that both Catholics and Protestants had placed upon it. The crisis of belief that beset Europe in the later sixteenth and seventeenth centuries was the harvest of what the confessional project of

belief had sowed. Protestants and Catholics alike had conspired to make belief hard. Rebelling against the debased epistemology of the world, they determined that only particular
doctrines, and only particular ways of holding those doctrines,
and only particular sources of assurance of those doctrines,
constituted Christian belief. This was intended, of course, to
fortify godly lines against legions of newly recognized enemies.
But like poison gas blowing back across Reformation trenches,
it soon threatened the very people who proposed and internalized such rigorous definitions of belief in the first place. For if
belief were suddenly so hard, and if unbelief were not merely
possible but commonplace, then how safe or reliable could
any belief be? If sin might at any moment be unmasked as
unbelief—and who among us does not sin—how were Christians to manage the terrifying discovery of their own unbelief?
Luther and his successors, it turns out, had released a potent
solvent into European religion. Once belief was so hard, unbelief became not the absence of belief but its failure, a ground
state onto which all belief threatened to collapse unless enormous energy were expended to keep it aloft. Protestants and
Catholics alike had sought in the Reformation to make belief
hard; by unleashing the specter of unbelief upon Europe, they
succeeded.

❦

For Protestants, belief became pressure. Not for everyone, of
course. Many still tried to live as if belief were easy, blithely
ignoring their new burdens, and some succeeded. Others became the enforcers of belief, accumulating cultural capital
through identification with the new regime. But for those on
the receiving end of stringent new criteria of belief, whether
out of commitment or loyalty or necessity, what had previously

been the unobtrusive background radiation of Christian society now shot through their souls like an X-ray, exposing every crack and imperfection. As Protestants tried to accommodate this unprecedented exposure, many presumably experienced moments of joy and confidence; but many also experienced moments of terror, and some found the weight of belief more than they could bear.

The pressure of belief was principally generated by a tension that adhered in the core Protestant doctrine of assurance.[7] Protestants insisted that true belief was by definition *certain*. If you had it, you had it entirely and forever. You could not believe in God with 51 percent certainty, or believe that the resurrection of the dead was likely; these were examples of unbelief rather than belief. Moreover, if, as we have seen, belief in God was belief that you yourself were saved by believing, it followed that doubt about your own salvation amounted to doubting God. Examples are easy to find in the writings of all the major reformers, like the early Lutheran leader and Augsburg preacher Urbanus Rhegius, who argued (in John Foxe's translation), "He that doubteth of the will and favor of God, and is not assured that He will be merciful to him for Christ's sake, and that all his sins be pardoned in him, he is no true Christian and in his incredulity cannot but be condemned."[8]

Yet on the other side, Protestants also made a seemingly contradictory argument: all sin flows from unbelief, and since no human being is free from sin, even the elect are guilty of unbelief. As the English theologian William Perkins put it, "Howsoever this faith be strong, yet is it always imperfect, as also our knowledge is, and shall so long as we live in this world be mingled with contrary unbelief and sundry doubtings."[9] Calvin put it similarly: "In all men, faith is always mingled with incredulity."[10] This latter position was, of course, a crucial bulwark for Protestants against the perfectionism of radicals who insisted that belief was only possible by transcending sin. For Calvin and the Protestants, by contrast, belief was transformative, but it was only finally victorious in heaven, hence even the godly remained tethered by law and conscience as they sought God's forgiveness for their unbelief.

One fault line in the Protestant system, then, was the inherent tension between an understanding of "belief" utterly incompatible with doubt, and a theology of human depravity demanding that even the elect remained mired in uncertainty.[11] Belief was absolutely certain, but at the same time always incomplete. This contradiction was, on the one hand, a useful accommodation to psychological reality: the literature of consolation reassured Christians that even the elect feel doubts. But on the other hand, consolation offered no litmus test to distinguish the merely temporary insecurity of the elect from the crippling unbelief of the damned. Reformers wallowed in this tension rather than resolving it. It epitomized the "cultivation of a sense of crisis," and the quest for spiritual intensity, that Alec Ryrie has described as characterizing the psychology of early modern Protestantism; as Ryrie notes, "even bleak landscapes can have their own appeal."[12]

Heinrich Bullinger, for instance, admitted that as long as we live in the world, even true believers experience fluctuations.[13] Man's mind is "at no time so enlightened or confirmed, but that cloudy mists of ignorance and doubtings [*nebulae ignorantiae dubitationisque*] do sometimes arise."[14] Yet at the same time, he insisted upon absolute assurance: "Whatsoever we believe in the word of God, we do believe it most assuredly, without wavering or doubting, being altogether as sure to have the thing, as faith doth believe to have it."[15] Citing a classic proof text of belief—Abraham's trust in God's ridiculous promise that he would sire a child in his old age, and in God's appalling demand that he murder that child—Bullinger wrote that Abraham "gave no place to unbelief [*incredulitanti*] to be tempted of it; he fell not to his own reasons and doubtful inquisitions, as unbelievers [*diffidentes*] are wont to do."[16] Bullinger's conclusion, characteristic of the reformers, was to differentiate the infidelity of unbelievers from the "infirmity of faith" [*fidei imbecillitas*] against which believers struggle; but as Bullinger himself admitted, the problem was that this difference was not necessarily visible to anyone except God.[17]

The Lutheran Johann Gerhard, whose *Meditations* were first printed in 1606 and then widely translated throughout Europe, addressed this conundrum by appealing to the text of Mark 9:24, a verse that had been largely dormant in the medieval tradition: "Lord, I believe, yet help thou my unbelief!" He confessed that he was just as guilty of unbelief as the damned, yet "the acknowledgement of my guiltiness, and the saving knowledge of thee, doth disjoin me from them." By confessing his unbelief, and praying for belief, he might hope that his fault was merely "weak faith [*fide languida*], but faith." And with the strengthening of this faith through time, he might achieve assurance against his doubts.[18] This was a standard strategy in the Reformed world as well. Richard Greenham, the great English doctor of conscience, advised a godly man who was "much tempted with unbelief" that if he could pray, "Help, Lord, my unbelief," and if he could sincerely say, "In this unbelief I am grieved, as in my belief I am wont to be comforted," God might restore to him the grace whose fruits would assure him of his salvation.

Greenham's protégé, the English puritan Nicholas Bownd, argued that the great unbelief of St. Thomas, demanding to touch Christ's wounds, shows "that we are all as full of unbelief as he, and much more; yet Christ will not refuse us, if we do not obstinately remain in it, but . . . have a desire to believe."[19] In *A Plain Man's Pathway to Heaven* (1601) by another

English puritan, Arthur Dent, the honest Philagathus asked the minister Theologus, "how, or in what respects, the child of God may both have doubtings and yet be fully assured?" Theologus answered by comparing the elect to a man tied to the highest steeple in the world, who cannot help but feel terror when he looks down, even if he knows he is bound securely: "Even so when we look downward to ourselves we have doubts and fears; but when we look upward to Christ and the truth of his promises, we . . . cease to doubt any more."[20]

True believers, then, battle their unbelief and ultimately persevere against it. Yet it requires vast energy to suppress the unbelief that lurks within us: so long as we live in the world, unbelief will keep welling up from inside. Calvin expressed this difficulty in the first person: "So deeply rooted in our hearts is unbelief [*incredulitas*], so prone are we to it, that while all confess with the lips that God is faithful, no man ever believes [*persuadeat*] it without an arduous struggle."[21] The English Presbyterian Obadiah Sedgwick described "the difficulty of believing in Jesus Christ," likening belief to rolling a boulder up a hill: "A stone having a natural propension and impetus to descend, if you do but quit the hand of it, it will down. But now to make a mighty stone mount the hill, to get it up into the air, there being no natural aptness to this, it is a hard and difficult attempt." Belief was a Sisyphean task.[22]

The most terrifying part of this system was how hard it could be to distinguish belief from unbelief, what Sedgwick called "the facility of error and mistake about believing."[23] Let us take Calvin's *Institutes* as a field guide to this "facility of error and mistake." On one side, Calvin wrote, "believers have a perpetual struggle with their own distrust," and they must "examine themselves carefully and humbly, lest carnal security creep in and take the place of assurance of faith."[24] That is, sinful trust in one's self rather than God could stealthily oust belief; this was the stuff of nightmares, like some bodysnatcher taking up residence inside us and making us atheists before we are aware of it. On the other side, and equally disturbing, the merely temporary and hypocritical faith of the reprobate could produce something that looked precisely like true belief, and those unbelievers felt just as assured of salvation as true believers. "It is correctly said," Calvin wrote, "that the reprobate believe God [*Deum credere*] to be propitious to them, inasmuch as they accept the gift of reconciliation, though confusedly and without due discernment; not that they are partakers of the same faith or regeneration with the children of God, but because under a covering of hypocrisy they seem to have a principle of faith in common with them."[25] In a fallen world where carnality still binds the godly, belief and unbelief appear to converge.

So, because the Holy Spirit works temporarily even in the hearts of unbelievers, "the better to convict them and leave them without excuse," phenomenologically the only difference between belief and unbelief might be their duration.[26] The temporary faith of the reprobate can look exactly like true belief for a time: "Just as a tree not planted deep enough may take root, but will in process of time wither away, though it may for several years not only put forth leaves and flowers, but produce fruit"—that is, just like Francesco Spiera.[27] Even the most secure belief could, paradoxically, be a sign of unbelief, while subjective unbelief could be a sign of true belief. Richard Greenham argued that when you are most assured of your salvation, that is when you "least fear and suspect yourself, and by that means lie open to unbelief again," whereas belief is strongest when you are humbled by your own sinfulness and admit your unbelief: "We show we have belief, when we mourn for our unbelief, and then our faith may be least, when we think it to be most."[28] This was the Protestant hall of mirrors, where belief and unbelief stared back at one another in hope and terror.

The crisis of belief for Protestants, then, was that their theology exposed the lethal third rail of atheism and refused to bury it again. Absolute assurance of salvation was the only guarantee that you were not in fact an atheist, but such absolute assurance was an aspirational ideal or asymptotic limit rather than a lived condition. The perseverance of the saints was a theological axiom, but as a practical matter it could only be proved posthumously. Those who persevered to the end were saints, QED, but those who did not were not; and as John Bunyan famously noted, there remained a way to hell even from the gates of heaven.

Hence self-examination—that great Protestant alternative to the confessional, whose highest expression was the spiritual diary—became a crucial technology for discernment of belief. Already quite early in the Reformation, this impulse was described by the Lutheran preacher of Augsburg, Urbanus Rhegius: "Let every man examine and search himself well, lest he deceive himself. Many men there be which say they believe when they have no belief."[29] The early seventeenth-century English divine Nicholas Bownd wrote, "If men for want of due examination and trial of their own heart, do presume of that that is not in them, and so imagine that they believe when they do not, or to have more faith than they have, they shall one day find that their fantasy hath deceived them . . . For many think that it is the easiest thing in the world to believe, when as indeed it is the hardest."[30]

A striking example is an English text first published in 1586, *The True Tryall and Examination of a Mans Owne Selfe*, attributed to the Flemish Protestant Andreas Hyperius but probably more extrapolation than translation.[31] Its opening advice was incandescently invasive: the godly man must "gropeth and inwardly rippeth up every corner of his conscience."[32] You must remember that you are "nothing else but sin: thou art, every whit of thee, a wretched sinner and guilty of everlasting damnation."[33] Like the traditional Catholic genre of confessors' manuals, the book used the Decalogue as a system for probing the depths of human depravity, beginning with the First Commandment (as Hyperius's Lutheran Church numbered it): "I am the Lord thy God which brought thee out of the land of Egypt." What is so striking is the text's expectation that sins against this commandment were ubiquitous. Besides "godless doubting" and "curious questioning," ignorance of doctrine was a sin against the first commandment, as was a failure to thank God for adversity and torment, as was distraction during divine worship. Any lapse, however small, "makes thee guilty."[34] Indeed, if "in the causes and points of Christian religion, thou have at any time spoken otherwise with thy tongue than thou hast inwardly thought and believed in thy heart . . . this is an horrible offense and a plain preferring of man before God, and this is a sin against the Holy Ghost."[35]

No Christian could undergo such a rigorous trial and emerge unscathed. That was precisely the point: all men violate the first commandment every day, doubting God just as blithely as they covet their neighbors' goods. The Protestant project of belief required absolute assurance but insisted upon the necessity of doubt, intentionally generating anxiety in even the most devout Christians about whether they truly believed in God. This was the brave new world of belief, theologically assured but subjectively experienced as a series of partial victories and mortifying defeats.

Thus, as the weight of belief generated new genres of self-examination, increasing numbers of Protestants experienced and described belief as a problem in their lives. Of course, historians have long noted the torments experienced by Calvinists seeking evidence of their own election. The psychic turmoil generated by predestination, its capacity to produce despair as well as assurance, was integral to the doctrine itself, forcing Christians to recognize their own depravity as a condition of their apotheosis. But it has not been noticed how deeply *belief* was the subjective center of these miseries. Calvinists, even after their supposed conversions, discovered their incapacity for the sort of utter reliance on God and immaculate freedom from doubt that they had been taught was the definition of authentic belief. The result was a plague of subjective atheism and hypocrisy, accompanied by existential terror. How could it have been otherwise, unless a century of books and sermons designed to keep people balanced on a knife's edge between consolation and despair was just so much hot air?[36]

A useful introduction to this phenomenon is the diary kept from 1634 to 1638 by Samuel Rogers, fellow of Emmanuel College, Cambridge and then a parish minister.[37] Protestant diarists had always obsessed over their own unworthiness, but Rogers made unbelief a central theme. When he was in the depths of despair he wrote, "I am much sunk and pressed in spirit, and mourn under a dead, unbelieving, disturbed heart"; but even in periods of temporary recovery he wrote things like, "Unbelief somewhat beat down," a poignant reminder that unbelief rather than belief had become the default condition of the world.[38] Rogers's diary is often a record of his depression. In March 1635, for instance, a brief entry recorded, "Neither life nor spirit to write, all upon a melancholy distemper taken in the day which I could not conquer." The following day, "The same holds still, and scarce can find in my heart to pray; and unfit for Sabbath tomorrow." And again the following day, "Sabbath, poor, poor, poor, and wretched, heartless, dead, nothing, nothing."[39] The subjective cause of this recurrent depression was Rogers's impression that God had abandoned him: "O my deadness and unbelief," he wrote in September 1636, "the lord frowns, and I am strained what should a poor creature do."[40] His spiritual highs and lows came at an alarming rate, often daily, so that belief and unbelief appear to be simultaneous rather than consecutive, warring parties within his soul, neither able to vanquish its enemy.[41]

Michael Wigglesworth, Harvard College don and paragon of New England godliness, is best known for his 1662 epic poem *The Day of Doom*, which is nearly as cheerful as it sounds. Yet Wigglesworth also kept a spiritual diary in which he revealed that he was haunted by his own "atheism." Among the sins he confessed were contempt for the tedium of Christian worship, overweening pride in his academic studies, and—always in cipher to prevent discovery—a burning lust for his (male) students. Wigglesworth's diary reveals a constant struggle with what he called unbelief, punctuated by a series of abortive conversions in which he temporarily acquired what he supposed was saving faith, only to fall back into godlessness again. During those terrifying five years, he scribbled dozens of times as a sort of mantra the words of Mark 9:24: "Lord, I believe, help my unbelief."

There were moments when Wigglesworth admitted to full-blown doubts about God and religion. "I found much deadness and little brokenness of heart for my sins this day, and some risings of atheistic thoughts," he wrote in September 1653. "I find that the clearest arguments that can be cannot persuade my heart to believe the being of a God."[42] The following month, in a more academic mood, he wrote, "Innumerable evils compass me about, vain thoughts on God's day in his ordinance break in upon me like a flood . . . I was sadly assaulted after noon when I heard of God's truth with doubting whether ever word of the scripture were infallible because of possibility of mistakes in the writings and because of the points in the

Hebrew and the various readings in the text and margin."[43] In November, he recorded, "My vileness breaks forth again whilst I am hearing the Word. An atheistic irreverent frame seizes upon me; and whilst God is bidding me see his glory I cannot see it; vile and unworthy conceptions concerning God come into my mind."[44] Three weeks later he was still "questioning the most palpable truths . . . as whether God be; [and] whether the scriptures be his word."[45] Toward the end of his diary, Wigglesworth found himself "musing about this point, that God is," and the first proof he adduced was almost shocking in its desperation: "If there were no God, men's hearts would not be full of enmity against God as they are, ergo there is a God."[46]

But when Wigglesworth wrote about his own "atheism," he did not simply mean doubt about God's existence: he experienced all of his sins and temptations as unbelief. "Sensuality, and delighting more in the creature than in God," for instance, was a sign of "greatest atheism" because it implied that pleasures of the flesh were real while the Holy Ghost was "but a fancy."[47] He described his boredom with religious worship as "great unbelief" and a sign of "atheism and no apprehending of God there present."[48] His insecurity about salvation indicated "an unbelieving heart, which questions God's love."[49] All of this was experienced as agony by a man wrestling with his sexuality and self-proclaimed "whoredoms" which "open a gap to unbelief": "I am ashamed to lift up mine eyes to heaven and call God my gracious father . . . I believe, Lord, help my unbelief, which is great."[50]

Samuel Sewall was a 1671 graduate of Harvard College and later a prominent judge in Massachusetts Bay Colony, most famous for his role in the prosecution of the Salem witches, which he eventually repented. But quite apart from that infamous attack on God's enemies, nearly two decades earlier

Sewall first recorded terror at his own unbelief. In 1675, on the night of a local tragedy when a ten-year-old girl was "consumed to ashes" in a fire, Sewall dreamed that he held a child in his arms, the child's mother weeping behind him, as he climbed a stairway to heaven. "I went up innumerable steps and still saw nothing, so that I was discouraged, doubting with myself whether there was such a place as *sedes beatorum*." In the dream, "all things began to seem more vile," and when he awoke he was "much troubled."[51] More bouts of unbelief followed, but the most extraordinary occurred when Sewall joined one of Boston's Congregationalist churches. For weeks he had been tormented about his own "unfitness and want of grace." When he arrived to take communion for the first time, he experienced a crisis:

> I could hardly sit down to the Lord's Table. But I feared that if I went away I might be less fit next time, and thought that it would be strange for me who was just then joined to the Church, to withdraw, wherefore I stayed. But I never experienced more unbelief. I feared at least that I did not believe there was such an one as Jesus Christ, and yet was afraid that because I came to the ordinance without belief, that for the abuse of Christ I should be stricken dead.[52]

Among the more palpable impressions in this troubled passage is Sewall's awareness of contradiction: disbelief accompanied by fear of divine punishment. This paradox is simultaneously what pries Sewall away from God and what unites them together again. Belief is the always incomplete work of holding unbelief at bay.

Women, too, internalized unbelief. Hannah Allen attempted suicide at least a dozen times after having convinced herself she was a "hypocrite" whose assurance of salvation was only feigned. She described herself as a "cursed apostate" who found within herself "a scorning and jeering at religion, and them that professed it."[53] She repeatedly located this unbelief in the inadequacy of her relationship to divinity, her inability to achieve the settled trust in God's promise that Protestants insisted was authentic belief, despairing at her own "wretched, unbelieving heart."[54] When her grandmother explained the depths of God's mercy through Christ, she responded, "What do you tell me of a Christ? It had been better for me if there had never been a savior, then I should have gone to hell at a cheaper rate."[55] This understanding emerged at least in part from her close reading of the puritan hero Richard Baxter: "I now saw that my faith was only a fancy, and that according to an expression of Mr. Baxter's in a book of his: that the love I formerly had to God, was carnal and diabolical."[56] As this allusion to "diabolical" faith suggests, central to Allen's doubts was the scriptural problem raised by James 2:19 and obsessively analyzed by Protestant commentators, that "the devils also believe, and tremble." Allen felt only this *unbelieving* belief, and she, too, trembled: "When I complained of those dreadful sins I said I was guilty of, some would ask me if I would be glad to be rid of them, and to be in another condition? 'Yes,' said I, 'so had the devils. Who do you think would not be happy? But I cannot desire it upon any other account.'"[57] Here the problem of belief speaks in the voice not of systematic theology but of fathomless sorrow.

But the most famous example is undoubtedly John Bunyan. Like the diary of Michael Wigglesworth, Bunyan's autobiographical *Grace Abounding to the Chief of Sinners* (1666) records serial conversions and apostasies. Unbelief is a recurring experience for Bunyan, and belief is painfully temporary, its final victory always just beyond the next bend. So, for example, Bunyan recounts one fairly typical crisis: "In these days I should find my heart to shut itself up against the Lord, and against his holy word. I have found my unbelief to set, as it were, the shoulder to the door to keep him out."[58] Soon afterward, however, he experienced a conversion: "Now was my heart filled with comfort and hope, and now I could believe that my sins should be forgiven me. Wherefore I said in my soul with much gladness: Well, I would I had a pen and ink here, I would write this down before I go any further, for surely I will not forget this forty years hence."[59] But rather than lasting forty years, this settled assurance did not last forty days, and the next crisis was far worse, plunging Bunyan into abysmal doubts:

> For about the space of a month after, a very great storm came down upon me, which handled me twenty times worse than all I had met with before . . . Whole floods of blasphemies, both against God, Christ, and the scriptures, was poured upon my spirit, to my great confusion and astonishment. These blasphemous thoughts were such as also stirred up questions in me against the very being of God, and of his only beloved son, as whether there were in truth a God or Christ, or no? And whether the holy scriptures were not rather a fable and cunning story, than the holy and pure word of God?[60]

In case after case of subsequent apparent conversions, Bunyan believed that now, finally, he had transcended these doubts, only to fall into unbelief again.[61] Once, a bout of unbelief lasted two and a half years. At another time, in another mood, he recalled that "my peace would be in and out sometimes twenty times a day."[62] But always the same unbelief returned—"a great cloud of darkness which did so hide from me the things of God and Christ that it was as if I had never seen or known them in my life"—followed by yet another conversion in which "my former darkness and atheism fled away, and the blessed things of heaven were set within my view."[63] Was this unrelenting cycle evidence of perseverance or backsliding? Both and neither, as every wave was pregnant with the next trough. At the end of his autobiography, Bunyan, now a minister, admitted being tempted to blaspheme God from the pulpit.[64] Even in prison, a martyr for his beliefs, "all the things of God were hid from my soul."[65] And on the final page, now speaking in the present tense of authorship, Bunyan still has moments when he is tempted "to question the being and truth of the gospel," he still finds in his heart "inclinings to unbelief."[66]

Although both had perfectionism

If for Protestants the problem was the necessity of an impossible perfection, for Catholics the problem was the necessity of an impossible obedience. Catholics were constitutively committed to the authority of the universal Church, over and above their own individual experience, in defining belief. Yet at the same time, Catholics faced a broad array of spiritual choices, not just about what to believe but about how and why to believe it. Navigating this incongruity—figuring out how to believe as individuals while still subordinating belief to authority—was the great dilemma of early modern Catholicism.

I want to take as my avatar of this dilemma Teresa of Avila. The daughter of a Toledo merchant, who by her own account wasted her childhood reading chivalric romances before joining a convent, Teresa's background was ordinary. But by vocation she was extraordinary, not only for her ecstatic religious mysticism and remarkable literary talent, but for her administrative and reformist energy, founding a new religious order and sustaining it against fierce opposition. Teresa in part understood belief as the fruit of individual spiritual experience, and it was for that experience that she became famous. Yet at the same time, Teresa defended the larger Catholic project of belief in authority, subjecting all opinion to official correction, only transforming it into belief when it participated in the doctrine and life of the universal Church. Navigating between these conflicting impulses—endlessly parsing what it meant to "believe" an independent revelation from God and agonizing over how such belief was authorized—was one of Teresa's consuming preoccupations.[67]

Before jumping into Teresa's writings, I want to contextualize her dilemma by discussing a famous visual representation: Gian Lorenzo Bernini's *Ecstasy of St. Teresa*, one of the great masterpieces of baroque sculpture, completed in 1652, seventy years after her death. The sculpture was commissioned by the Venetian Cardinal Federico Cornaro, a member of the Sacred Congregation for the Propagation of the Faith, for the chapel where he intended to be buried, at Santa Maria della Vittoria in Rome. The scene frozen in stone by Bernini showed an angel piercing Teresa with a spear, the most famous moment in Teresa's *Autobiography* and one of the most famous mystical visions in the Western tradition:

> I saw in his hand a long spear of gold, and at the iron's point there seemed to be a little fire. He appeared to me to be thrusting it at times into my heart, and to pierce my very entrails; when he drew it out, he seemed to draw them out also, and to leave me all on fire with a great love of God. The pain was so great, that it made me moan; and yet so surpassing was the sweetness of this excessive pain, that I could not wish to be rid of it. The soul is satisfied now with nothing less than God. The pain is not bodily, but spiritual; though the body has its share in it. It is a caressing of love so sweet which now takes place between the soul and God,

FIGURE 4.1. Ecstacy of St. Teresa. Completed in 1652 by Gian Lorenzo
Bernini for the Cornaro Chapel, Santa Maria della Vittoria, Rome.

that I pray God of His goodness to make him experience it
who may think that I am lying.[68]

Generations of readers, following Bernini, have dwelt upon
the overt sexuality of this passage. Part of what makes the
statue extraordinary is how perfectly it captures Teresa's baroque blending of dissonances: soul meets body, a virgin saint experiences orgasm at the hands of a Christian angel who could
pass for a pagan cupid. But the sexual intensity of the first part

of Teresa's vision has overshadowed another dissonance at the end: Teresa's expectation that unless God sends to readers their own mystical visions, they would not believe hers.

The problem Teresa signals in this final sentence is not whether *she* should believe her own visions—although this was often her concern—but rather whether *we* should believe them. Teresa, after all, had no authority to pronounce upon religion; so if belief is acceptance of authority, then disbelieving Teresa is entirely justified. In her writings, Teresa was deeply conflicted on this issue, following a long line of women mystics who had confronted the Church's insistence upon authorization earlier and more intensely than their male counterparts, and had struggled to make their voices heard. In some places, as a dutiful child of the Counter-Reformation, Teresa admitted that she "justifiably is not believed."[69] Because seemingly divine visions can come from the devil or the imagination as well as God, Teresa told her nuns, "My desire, sisters, is that you realize you are doing the right thing if you refuse to give credence to them."[70] It is "with reason" that she is disbelieved, she wrote, because rapture cannot be diagnosed from the outside.[71] Yet in many other places, Teresa desperately wants her experiences to teach others: "I believe they will not be lost who, humbling themselves, even though they be strong, do not believe by themselves, but believe this one who has experience."[72] "Let them believe me," she pleads, "believe for the love of the Lord this little ant, for he wants it to speak."[73] The pole star of consistency among these swirling heavens was that Teresa remained convinced throughout her life that no one *would* believe her who had not seen God for themselves: "There is no one who believes this if they haven't experienced it."[74]

One half of Teresa is therefore a rebel against the Counter-Reformation project to make belief the product of authorization rather than experience; the other half of Teresa struggles

in reaction. Bernini's masterpiece settles this dispute and re-
stores authority to its throne. Commissioned by a Cardinal
of the Roman Curia, the sculpture is Teresa's canonization in
marble: it authorizes us to believe the truth of what it depicts.
Its intense realism provides a simulacrum of mystical experience for the crowds who come to see it, defying Teresa's own
insistence that if we have not experienced the divine for ourselves, we cannot believe her.[75]

The Church wanted us to believe Teresa on their authority,
hence they made her a saint and made her the subject of sub-
lime art; but Teresa was certain that we could not believe, and
sometimes argued that we should not believe, unless authorized by our *own* experience of divinity. So should we listen to
the artist or the saint? The conflict between authority and experience offered a hall of mirrors for Catholics no less baffling
than the one into which Protestants had inadvertently wan-
dered with their theology of human depravity. The Catholic
Church's drive to structure belief around authority could never
succeed in the face of individual experience, any more than
individual experience could succeed in structuring belief for a
population whose religious identity was defined by obedience
to a hierarchical Church. Teresa's dilemma thus speaks, across
the chasm of centuries, to the historian who wants to "take belief seriously": what might it mean to take seriously the belief
of a woman so conflicted about her own credibility? If we take
Teresa's belief seriously, should we believe or disbelieve her?

To understand how Teresa experienced the new weight of
belief, we must step back and examine the broader landscape
of unauthorized Christianity her revelations inhabited. One
problem with the newly emphasized connection between belief and authority was that Catholic Europe had always been
saturated with unauthorized religious claims: much of the
content of Western Christianity existed outside the space of

the Church's authority rather than either for or against it. Colorful examples are innumerable. Galician folktales described a vengeful Virgin Mary who commanded the sea to rise up and drown villages that had refused her hospitality when she visited Spain.[76] Peasants argued that fornication was no sin, and that no one would be sent to hell for sex between consenting adults, apparently without understanding that the Magisterium would beg to differ; but few probably went so far as the Castilian man who claimed that "Christ our Lord, at the time that he was in the world, must also have fornicated."[77] In Portugal, special prayers offered anyone who recited them "whatever you ask, such as royal favor, great revenge upon your enemies, a higher salary, or escape from any danger."[78] Stuart Schwartz has demonstrated how many Iberian Christians claimed that "all can be saved," including Jews and Muslims, if they obeyed their own religious laws.[79]

There were countless examples of more elite and scholarly unauthorized religious claims as well. Indeed, every time a churchman (or occasionally a laywoman or layman) made creative theological arguments, or reported their own individual spiritual experience, he or she perforce made unauthorized religious claims. In theory, all Catholics made these claims "subject to correction" by the Church, and resistance to correction, rather than the claims themselves, constituted heresy; as the medievalist R. I. Moore has noted, heresy is literally the product of persecution, because the canonical definition of heresy is the "obstinate defense" of opinion against authority.[80] Spectacular examples include John Wycliffe, Meister Eckhart, and Martin Luther. After his 95 Theses denouncing indulgences, for instance, Luther was told in an interview with Cardinal Cajetan to "recount your error, for the pope requires it, whether you will or no"; only afterward did Cajetan ask the now fatal question: "Do you or don't you believe it?"[81] But, of course, the vast majority of opinions never received adjudication by the Church, never received either correction or approval.

Thus, if in some significant sense early modern Catholics "believed" a thousand things upon which the Church had not seen fit to pronounce, it is crucial to acknowledge that they "believed" them loosely or contingently: these were the fruits of individual experience in an era when the individual had not yet won sovereignty over belief.[82] In the ordinary course of things, their religious claims remained suspended. Only when authority stepped in to arbitrate was this loose form of belief forced to tighten; experience had either to yield sovereignty over belief by accepting correction or claim sovereignty over belief by resisting. This form of arbitration became vastly more common as the early modern era progressed. In the fifteenth century, the Church had needed only to pronounce authoritatively on a relatively narrow band of issues. On most questions of religious life—whether a local hero was a saint, or whether a particular dream was a vision from God, or whether a village fertility rite was a legitimate manifestation of Christian devotion—there was no official position, hence opinion could diverge without belief entering into it. Those unfortunate dissenters who were declared heretical—Lollards, Hussites, and others—were the exception rather than the rule, and they represented only a small fraction of de facto diversity. In a world newly characterized by ecclesiastical fragmentation, however, the Fathers of Trent and subsequent Catholic leaders pronounced authoritatively on innumerable issues, and a vast penumbra of what previously had been diversity of opinion was redefined as contrary to true belief.[83]

Take, for instance, Menocchio, the Friulian miller whom Carlo Ginzburg's research has made the most famous peasant in early modern Europe. A walking illustration of the adage that a little knowledge is a dangerous thing, Menocchio gleaned from the few books he had read that God was created alongside the angels, formed out of chaos like worms spontaneously generating in moldy cheese. When Menocchio made a nuisance of himself, "always arguing with somebody about the faith just for the sake of arguing," his words were described by himself and others as "fancies" or "opinions," more akin to imagination than belief. Only priests ever described him as heretical; to his neighbors his offense was blasphemy, *lèse majesté* against God and a social offense to the community, a crime of behavior rather than thought. Later, however, when Menocchio came before the Inquisition, we can watch the very moment when belief entered the conversation:

> It is true that I said these things, to various people, but I was not telling them they should believe all this. On the contrary, I urged many of them, "Would you like me to teach you the true way? Try to do good and walk in the path of my ancestors and follow what Holy Mother Church commands." But I uttered those other words because I was tempted to believe them and teach them to others. It was the evil spirit who made me believe those things and who also persuaded me to say them to others.

In the examination that followed, Menocchio admitted to "believing" dozens of heterodox things, but his statements of "belief" came in response to direct questions that demanded belief-talk in response: What do you believe the Holy Spirit to be? Which person of the Holy Trinity do you believe to be in the Eucharist? And yet even then, faced with the awful power of the Church to define belief, he denied again that he believed his own opinions. "I have an artful mind," he told his interrogator at the end, "and I have wanted to seek out higher things about which I did not know. But I do not believe that what I have said is the truth, and I want to be obedient to the Holy Church. And

I have held opinions that were wicked, but the Holy Spirit has enlightened me, and I beg mercy of almighty God."[84]

In principle, then, Catholic belief depended upon the authorization of the Church. But in practice this was fantasy. The Church's drive to structure belief around authority could never succeed in the face of individual experience, and Catholics tied themselves into knots, and experienced more than a little despair, attempting to reconcile their own unauthorized religion with their belief in the Church. Sometimes the unauthorized religion in question was philosophical, like the claims of Bruno or Galileo. But sometimes it was enthusiastic or inspired, resulting in a remarkable drive by the Catholic Church to silence its own saints. This is the phenomenon at the heart of Michel de Certeau's modern masterpiece *The Mystic Fable*: the "extraordinary devotion" that was so worrisome to ecclesiastical authorities, because its "manner of speaking" was an alternative language into which the requirements of the Council of Trent could not be translated. All over Europe, the Catholic Church of the later sixteenth and early seventeenth centuries found itself suppressing its most pious subjects, who wondered whether their own luminous piety was a blessing or a curse. As Certeau recounts, for instance, a priest from Bordeaux wrote to his bishop in 1627 to apologize for a "whiplash from on high" that had struck him during Mass: feeling God within himself, he sang a hymn to the Holy Spirit when he was supposed to be reading the prayer for the day. Recoiling from this experience of inspiration, he promised that he would "no longer be so pious" and humbly begged the bishop "to write to me whether I should absolutely reject all extraordinary devotion."[85]

Which brings us back to Teresa of Avila's lifelong attempts to reconcile her own visions from God with the Church's insistence that she believe nothing upon which authority had not

[margin handwritten note: imp. observation]

pronounced. Teresa was inconsistent about how the category of "belief" related to her mystical life. There are places where she denigrates "belief" as mere intellection and therefore inferior to mystical experience; yet these passages are few.[86] Most of the time, belief is among Teresa's central categories because the fruit of mystical experience *is* belief, with intellection its pale shadow. So, for instance, one sign that her visions are truly from God is that they are believed more strongly than mere human words: "Even if the words are spoken by men who are very important and learned, or concern the future, we do not have them engraved on our memory, or believe them [*las creemos*], as we do these. The certitude is so strong that even in things that in one's own opinion [*en cosas muy*] seem impossible, and in which there is doubt as to whether they will or will not happen, and the intellect wavers, there is an assurance in the soul itself that cannot be overcome."[87] Union with God produces "such certitude . . . that the soul cannot help believing in the truth of it."[88] For Teresa, this sort of belief is involuntary: "Nor was I able to force myself, even though I did all I could, to believe and desire another road; it wasn't in my power to do so."[89] And this intense belief—what she calls "knowledge of a truth that is the fulfillment of all truths"—is extremely rare: "To me it seemed I had always believed this, and that all the faithful believed it. He [Truth] told me: 'Alas, daughter, how few there are who truthfully love me! For if they loved me, I would reveal to them my secrets.' "[90]

But if Teresa makes belief central to her spirituality, what sort of belief was it? In some passages, Teresa accepts the Counter-Reformation commonplace that belief is not an individual exercise but consists in obedience to the Church, so that individual opinion only becomes belief when it is properly authorized. She wrote, for instance, that a soul with a strong, living faith "always strives to proceed in conformity with what the Church holds . . . All the revelations it could imagine—even if it were to see the heavens open—wouldn't move it one bit from what the Church holds."[91] But in many other places, experience seems plainly to trump authority. So, for instance, Teresa offered an analogy, telling her confessors that "if they were to tell me that a person whom I knew very well, and with whom I had just finished speaking, were not that person, but that I had imagined it, I would without doubt, as they knew, believe what they had said rather than what I had seen."[92] This is the standard, Ignatian position: her senses lie, but she is bound to obey the Church. However, she continued, "if this person were to leave me some jewels, and they were left in my hands as tokens of great love, I would not believe what they said [*que no podría creerlo*], even though I desired, because I hadn't any jewels before and was poor, whereas now I found that I was rich."[93] This, she claimed, was equivalent to her visions, whose effects overruled the authority of the confessors. In her *Spiritual Testimonies* she was more explicit that her own experience authorized her to believe revelations despite the authority of the Church: "[If] all the learned men and saints in the world were to join together and torture me with all the torments imaginable, and I wanted to believe them, I wouldn't be able to make myself believe that these things come from the devil; for I cannot. When they wanted to force me to believe that the devil was the cause, I feared, upon seeing who said this, and I thought they must be saying the truth and that I, being what I was, was being deceived. But at the first locution, or experience of recollection, or vision, all they had told me was blotted out; I couldn't do anything but believe God was the cause."[94]

Teresa wrestled with this contradiction throughout her life, and while she never achieved a settled synthesis, her attempts to square the circle reveal the anxiety and confusion of a Catholic milieu newly buffeted by belief. One way to resolve her dilemma was to claim that direct experience of God *cannot* be otherwise than according to the Church; apparent contradictions between authority and experience, like apparent contradictions within scripture, are ruled prima facie out of bounds. So, in the case of one revelation, she wrote, "I believed that since it didn't go against sacred scripture or against the laws of the Church, which we are obliged to keep, the revelation was true."[95] Later, she told the Inquisitor of Seville that "if any of her experiences were to induce her to turn against the Catholic faith . . . she would have no need to go in search of proof [*pruebas*], for then she would see it was the devil."[96] This maneuver was put under enormous strain, however, by Teresa's confessors and superiors, whose frequent insistence that she was delusional or possessed by demons challenged her belief in her own experience. At these moments of stress, her consistency buckled. When one confessor told Teresa that her project to found a religious order was based upon her own dreams rather than genuine revelations, she was distraught and feared that she really had been deceived; she very nearly yielded experience to the adjudication of the Church. However, at the last minute, God spoke to her again and told her that, while the project was indeed his will, she should nonetheless obey her confessor and keep "silent for the present, until it would come time to return to the task." In this way, Teresa tried to believe her revelations while accepting the necessity of obedience to the Church; never mind that the Church's explicit command was not to believe her revelations.[97] Here Teresa's contradictions mirrored those of the Church, which authorized Teresa's experiences even when they stressed the importance of unauthorized experience.

These tensions are neatly encapsulated in *The Interior Castle*. In one passage, Teresa gives perhaps her most eloquent statement that opinion is not belief until it is authorized by the Church: "In difficult matters, even though it seems to me

I understand and that I speak the truth, I always use this expression 'It seems to me.' For if I am mistaken, I am very much prepared to believe what those who have a great deal of learning say. Even though they have not experienced these things, very learned men have a certain 'I don't know what'; for since God destines them to give light to his Church, he enlightens them that they might acknowledge a truth when presented with it."[98] And yet on the very next page, she condemns the confessors who had misled a women she knew (herself, thinly disguised) despite their authority: "After asking a half-learned man of the kind I mentioned—he knew as little as she had known before God enlightened her—she was told that God was present only by grace. Such was her own conviction that even after this she didn't believe him."[99] A bit later, Teresa tells us that when God engraved words on her heart, despite having been told by her confessors that the words were foolishness, "there remains a spark of assurance so alive . . . that even should the soul desire otherwise, that spark will stay alive."[100] This higher order of credence trumps both the intellectual and the institutional authority of the Church.

This was the context, then, for the agonism with which we began: the problem of whether, to the extent that Teresa believed her own revelations, other people should believe her as well. Teresa wavered endlessly on this issue: the audacity of her words and deeds demanded assent, yet she repeatedly insisted upon her own humility and worthlessness. There was, of course, something deeply gendered about this dilemma: by refusing to keep silent Teresa transcended the bounds of her sex, hence the very words that established her credibility at the same time undermined it. But Teresa also reflects a problem at the heart of early modern Catholicism, whose project to subsume private experience under authorized belief trapped men as well as women, priests as well as laypeople—even no less a priest than Ignatius of Loyola, who was himself a mystic and wrote his defenses of the authority of the Church in part to shield himself from charges of unsanctioned piety. Countless early modern Catholics wrote and spoke so that others would believe them; but without authorization they were outside the bounds of credulity, shouting into the wind.

⟨⁓⁓⁓⁓⁓⁓⟩

While obviously the depth of Teresa's spirituality was atypical, her dilemma was paradigmatic: belief was internal, individual, and radically grounded in experience, and yet authority over all belief rested with the hierarchical Church. So what exactly did it mean to believe what you were told? How could belief as obedience be reconciled with belief as conscientious assent by free, ethical beings? One of the first and boldest attempts to resolve this dilemma appears in the writings of Teresa's ally, confidante, and sometime confessor, the Spanish mystic John of the Cross (1542–1591). While much later canonized and hailed, like Teresa herself, as a Doctor of the Church, in his lifetime John was deeply controversial and spent most of a year in prison for disobedience to his superiors in the Carmelite order. Also like Teresa, he struggled endlessly with the problem of how to square his own mystical spirituality with the demands of an authoritative Church. John's answer was to construct a version of "belief" that was radically free of content, allowing him to obey authority while removing the core principle of belief from any human control.[101]

Following the apophatic tradition of the so-called *via negativa* or negative theology, John understood faith as a subtraction rather than an addition, a suppression of all human faculties—the intellect, the senses, experience—to make room for the divine. If we denude ourselves of "any understanding, feeling, imagining, opinion, desire," we might successfully "pass beyond everything to unknowing."[102] So, for instance, John reimagined the three cardinal virtues (faith, hope, and charity) as ways of blinding or emptying ourselves: "Faith causes darkness and a void of understanding in the intellect, hope begets an emptiness of possessions in the memory, and charity produces the nakedness and emptiness of affection and joy in all that is not God."[103] John's metaphor to explain the requirement of negation was the sun shining through a window: the window contributes nothing to the sunlight, rather it must be cleaned and polished to allow the full brilliance of the sun to illuminate the room within.[104]

From our perspective, the most remarkable thing about John's negative theology was that it rejected the category of "experience" in the formation of belief.[105] In sharp contrast to the mystical tradition (including Teresa of Avila), John rejected visions and locutions from God, not because their provenance was suspect, but because even genuine revelations were impediments to the subtractive process of unknowing. Even if God really sends manifestations of divinity, John wrote, "one must never rely on them or accept them. A person should rather flee from them completely and have no desire to examine whether they be good or bad."[106] Whereas Teresa was obsessed with the discernment of spirits—the problem of whether her visions were of divine, human, or demonic origin—John regarded the whole question as "profitless, a waste of time, a hindrance to the soul, an occasion of many imperfections as well as spiritual stagnancy."[107] No discernment of spirits should be attempted, and the only purpose of telling spiritual advisors about supposed visions was that they should teach us "how to void the memory of these apprehensions. Whatever these apprehensions may in themselves be, they are not as great a help toward the love of God as is the least act of living faith and hope made in the emptiness and renunciation of all things."[108] These passages, bluntly rejecting revelations from God, confused John's first readers as thoroughly as they confuse modern students.

The reason even authentic visions from God should be ignored is that they necessarily appear to us "in some limited mode or manner" rather than in God's own infinitude without form or likeness.[109] People who discover that their visions are genuinely from God develop attachments to those finite visions, hindering the path to darkness.[110] In a remarkable passage, John tells us that "God is rightly angered" with anyone who admits supernatural communications, however authentic, because of the presumption in trying to reach God through knowing rather than unknowing.[111] Thus, *all content* of religious experience is dangerous because, however authentic, it hinders those who would "journey to God through the negation of all things."[112]

Given the feebleness of individual experience, then, the content of religious belief was wholly dependent upon, and coterminous with, the pronouncements of the Church. John interpreted Matthew 18:20—"Where two or three are gathered . . . there I am in the midst of them"—to mean that individual experience cannot generate true belief: "Thus God announces that he does not want the soul to believe only by itself [*a solas se crea*] the communications it thinks are of divine origin, or for anyone to be assured and confirmed in them without the Church or her ministers. God will not bring clarification and confirmation of the truth to the heart of one who is alone. Such a person would remain weak and cold in regard to truth."[113] Thus, "although individuals may consider their knowledge certain and true . . . they must not, because of this conviction, fail to believe and to give assent of reason to the instructions and commands of their spiritual director, even though these may be extremely contrary to what they feel."[114] Even in scripture, although God spoke to human beings, "what God said at that time did not have the authority or force to induce complete belief, unless approved by the priests and prophets." God "definitely does not want us to bestow our entire credence on his supernatural communications, or be confirmed in their strength and security, until they pass through this human channel of the mouth of another human person."[115] Hence, new spiritual experiences should never be believed, only the Church should be believed, "and if individuals want to escape delusion they should not adapt their credence [*crédito*] and understanding to those truths of faith revealed again, no matter how true and conformed to the faith they may seem . . . It greatly behooves souls not to want to understand the truths of faith clearly, so that they may thereby conserve pure and entire the merit of faith and also pass though this night of intellect to the divine light of union."[116]

The irony running through this argument is palpable. John gives a plenitude of authority over belief to the Church, but the sort of belief that he has in mind—that is, intellective belief in the content of religion—he denounces as not only peripheral to true faith but an impediment to it. Because cognitive commitments and assent to propositions basically mean nothing, John's apparent reliance upon authority over belief is effectively a feint, giving with the left hand what the right hand takes away (or perhaps robbing Peter to pay Paul).

But on the other side of the ledger, when John denounces experience as irrelevant or harmful to belief, this, too, is a feint. Repeatedly in his work, John associates authentic belief, the sort that really matters, with mystical union. So, for instance, "Those who want to reach union with God should advance neither by understanding, nor by the support of their own experience, nor by feeling or imagination, but by belief in

God's being [*sino creyendo su ser*]."[117] Indeed, part of the reason John insists that people must let the Church overrule their
own cognitive commitments is that "in this way they will be
led by faith to divine union, for a soul must journey to it more
by believing than by understanding [*más creyendo que enten-
diendo*]."[118] John offered tantalizing glimpses of this mystical
belief, but of course it was by definition indescribable. In some
places he called it "vague, dark, and general knowledge," infinitely superior to distinct and particular knowledge.[119] Elsewhere it was "general knowledge . . . so recondite and deli-
cate . . . that the soul does not perceive or feel it"; you cannot
know that you know something in this way, because the act of
knowing would destroy it.[120] Again, John employed his master
metaphor of the sun shining through the window: we know it
is shining because of the particles of dust that are illuminated
in the beam, but only by removing those particles may the
beam itself, now imperceptible, pass undisturbed.[121]

When John says that experience has no role in belief, then,
he is invoking a technicality to limit the disorder generated by
a project whose whole purpose is to make individual union
with God, rather than the corporate Church, the essence of
belief. By defining the process and achievement of union as
non-experience, because it is too subtle and rarefied to register
phenomenologically, he is in fact reserving to the individual
the only kind of belief that really matters.[122] In sum, John of
the Cross answers the problem of belief by yielding to authority all knowledge-claims and positive religious commitments.
He cannot possibly be accused of heterodoxy or improper discernment, because, in the doctrinal sense of the term, he refuses to believe outside his obedience to the Church. In this
sense, like Ignatius of Loyola, he would have no trouble believing that white is black. And yet, for John, the point of this obedience is not that the Church is infallible; indeed, it makes no

difference to him whether his beliefs with the Church are right or wrong. They matter only because they rid him of the burden of thinking about the unthinkable or imagining the unimaginable. Believing with the Church opens for John an essentially private space of belief that is impermeable to the world.

In the end, what makes John of the Cross important to our story was not his particular solution to the Ignatian paradox—epistemic content would become more rather than less important to the category of belief in the seventeenth century—but the creativity with which he demonstrated that the paradox admitted solutions. The notion that we must believe that white is black if the Church says so was not a minority position; it was almost universally accepted by Catholic writers. But this was the beginning rather than the end of their imaginative engagement with belief, authority, and experience. Following in John's wake, the inventive energy of Catholics poured into trying to figure out how, *given* the authority of the Church over belief, their beliefs could still be their own. While they reached different conclusions, it is nonetheless striking how much basic conceptual architecture they shared. Like their scholastic forbears, who answered every paradox by subdividing terms, they splintered the category of belief in order to argue that the version owed to authority was the least important of all. There were other kinds of belief, deeper or stronger or more subtle, where experience ruled.

<hr />

Calvinists, Lutherans, and Catholics obviously did not experience the weight of belief in the same way, and within the different confessions there was enormous variety, not only in terms of class and gender, but in terms of each person's affective relationship to religion. I would not want to suggest that these

→ more accepted now?

few examples speak for all of early modern Christianity. What I would suggest, however, is that the weight of belief really did increase exponentially, hence early modern religion was in many ways defined by struggle and experimentation with how to manage that new weight. Some people, of course, managed it by not caring: we can imagine, although we cannot prove, that something like doubt really did emerge from this maelstrom as people found themselves unable to believe in the ways they were taught. But this is a book about belief, not unbelief; for us the crucial point is that many people did care, but caring was not always enough. For them, the new weight of belief was a terrible burden: they despaired, or they faced persecution, or they hid inside their own minds. Sometimes they died, sometimes they persevered, but we do not have to imagine too many cases like Hannah Allen or Teresa of Avila to understand the damage done when belief was made so very hard.

By the end of the seventeenth century, this weight would be lifted. Not everywhere or for everyone, and certainly not always to the same degree; but real options became available to both Protestants and Catholics to believe in ways that were not so hard, to conceive of their own religious opinion outside the framework the confessional era had created. It is to that story that we now turn.

CHAPTER FIVE

The Birth Pangs of Modern Belief

TO SEE HOW early modern Christians began to reject the confessional project of belief and grope their way out of the hall of mirrors, consider two allegorical paintings of the same subject. The Synod of Dort met in the Dutch town of Dordrecht (in English called Dort) in 1618–1619 to reinforce Calvinist orthodoxy, much the way the Council of Trent had bolstered Catholic orthodoxy in the previous century. In particular, Dort condemned the so-called Arminians or Remonstrants, dissidents who had, over the previous quarter century, challenged the Reformed doctrine of predestination and dared to assert the role of free will in human salvation. Both paintings reject the legitimacy of the synod and its rigid Calvinist canons; but their divergent ways of doing so signal a fundamental shift.[1]

The first image, now in Delft, was painted around 1622, probably by a Catholic. Following the conventions of medieval allegory, the participants at the synod are travesties of the natural world: a whale chairing the council represents England, Walachia is an immovable rock, the Dutch ruling house of

FIGURE 5.1. Symbolic representation of the Synod of Dordrecht.
Artist unknown, 1622. Courtesy of Collection Museum
Prinsenhof Delft, The Netherlands.

Orange-Nassau is a monkey, and so forth. Below them are the tragic fruits of their efforts: not consensus but discord. The political protector of the Arminians, the Land's Advocate of Holland Johan van Oldenbarnevalt, who was executed less than a week after the Synod ended, lies on the floor clutching his own decapitated head. The secretary sobs into his hand as he dutifully records the Calvinist orthodoxy affirmed by the canons of Dort. Overall, the anonymous artist depicted a scene of dark power and supernatural foreboding: demonic chaos has replaced divine order.

The second painting, now in Lyon, was painted a century later, in 1721, by the Dutch artist Abraham van der Eyk. The scene could not be more different: instead of supernatural chaos, we find a perversion of earthly judgment. The image is dominated by a set of scales. On the left side are the Arminians,

FIGURE 5.2. Disputes between Remonstrants and Counter-Remonstrants in 1618. Abraham van der Eyk, 1721. Musée des Beaux-Arts de Lyon.

who have placed on the balance a Bible, along with their own statements of religious belief, each duly authenticated with a wax seal. On the right side are the Calvinists, who have placed on the balance a book on which can be read the word "Calvin"— perhaps it is the *Institutes*. On top of the book, the Prince of Orange, Maurice of Nassau, has laid his sword, hence worldly power has wrongfully tipped the balance in the Calvinists' favor. The allusion is to a story from the Roman historian Livy.[2] When the Gauls conquered Rome, there was a dispute over the weighing of the gold tribute they demanded. When the Romans complained that the measurement was unfair, Brennus, chieftain of the Gauls, disdainfully added his sword to the balance and declared, "Vae victis": woe to the conquered!

I begin with these images not only because the Arminians will be central to the story that follows, but because I think the latter painting can stand for a striking novelty: the choice between two theological positions is here not a matter of divine or satanic intervention, but a careful weighing of opposing views, an orderly process of deliberation in which authority has unjustly intervened. By the eighteenth century, something had changed: belief was now associated with sound and judicious consideration, and the struggle to believe correctly was no longer simply about defeating the gathering forces of evil, it could also be about overcoming the forces of intolerance that seek to corrupt human judgment. This transformation was far from universal, but it was influential and pervasive: by the early eighteenth century, it was commonplace to suggest that human beings use their own judgment to assent to religious propositions and that such judgment is their religious belief.

This chapter explores how this transformation began, mapping the reaction against the confessional project of belief that had defined the sixteenth century, and sketching the intellectual resources that allowed an alternative project to replace it. I call this first stage "birth pangs" because modern belief enjoyed neither a peaceful nor an easy delivery. Its protagonists were either dissidents within the confessions, or representatives of those confessions far out on the periphery of Christendom where the ordinary rules failed, figures who suffered for their religion no less than the martyrs of the previous century. These marginal actors were forced by circumstances, and enabled by their own fertile imaginations, to invent rationales by which opinion or judgment, qualitatively indistinguishable from other sorts of truth-claims, might qualify as Christian belief. A second revolution had begun.

We must begin with the French Catholic lawyer Michel de Montaigne, a towering figure in the history of belief even if his principal role was to clear ground rather than to plant new vineyards.[3] Richard Popkin's magisterial *History of Scepticism* calls Montaigne "the womb of modern thought." His radical skepticism was a clarion call to generations of intellectuals, as was his "fideist" claim that in the absence of stable knowledge there can only be faith.[4] But scholarly focus on these two poles has obscured what we might call the middle register of Montaigne's *Essais*, where he was concerned less with faith and knowledge in the abstract than with a practical question: given the simultaneous uncertainty of knowledge and necessity of faith, how and when might we believe things? In interesting ways, Montaigne's answers stage the same conflict between authority and experience that we saw in the writings of his contemporary, John of the Cross, and like John he uses the dialectic between them to pry open new space for individual belief.[5] But for Montaigne, unlike for John, that space was conceived as a mode of open inquiry about the world.

It is, of course, no revelation to say that belief was a problem for Montaigne: near the heart of his *Essais* was the revival of Pyrrhonist skepticism, recommending a pure suspension of judgment, for it is "better to remain in suspense than to entangle yourself in the many errors that the human fancy has produced."[6] Because the senses and reason are unreliable, all knowledge-claims must be contingent rather than dogmatic. This is why Montaigne invented the essay as his pet genre, with all its rambling uncertainty: "If my mind could gain a firm footing, I would not make essays, I would make decisions; but it is always in apprenticeship and on trial."[7] Religious belief was a particularly pressing concern for Montaigne insofar as he blamed dogmatism for the carnage of the French Wars of Religion. The fact that Christians on both sides had killed for their beliefs proved that at least one side's assurance was misplaced, and if one side was wrong, then surely the other side could be too. In Montaigne's view, religious beliefs are merely human—we believe true things the same way we believe false, with fallible human faculties—so no belief should be held with certainty. Montaigne therefore offered a model for undogmatic religion, organized around opinions rather than beliefs: "I set forth notions that are human and my own, simply as human notions considered in themselves, not as determined and decreed by heavenly ordinance and permitting neither doubt nor dispute; matter of opinion, not matter of faith; what I reason out according to me, not what I believe according to God [*ce que je discours selon moy, non ce que je croy selon Dieu*]; as children set forth their essays to be instructed, not to instruct; in a lay manner, not clerical, but always very religious."[8]

But Montaigne was not simply arguing that his own "opinions" were less certain or reliable than another, higher species of knowledge-claim called belief. On the contrary, much of the intellectual work of the *Essais* was to show that *all* knowledge-claims occupied the uncertain and unreliable space of "opinion," even those that masqueraded as belief. So, as he put it in the *Apology for Raymond Sebond*:

> How diversely we judge things! How many times we change our notions! What I hold today and what I believe, I hold and believe it with all my belief [*je le tiens et le crois de toute ma croyance*]; all my tools and all my springs of action grip this opinion and sponsor it for me in every way they can. I could not embrace or preserve any truth with more strength than this one. I belong to it entirely, I belong to it truly. But has it not happened to me, not once, but a hundred times, a thousand times, and every day, to have embraced with these same instruments, in this same condition, something else that I have since judged false? . . . Nevertheless, whether fortune moves us five hundred times

from our position, whether it does nothing but empty and pour back incessantly into our belief, as into a vessel, more and more different opinions, always the present and the latest one is the certain and infallible one.[9]

The problem with belief, then, is that it is built upon the shifting sands of human cognition. "Some make the world believe that they believe what they do not believe. Others, in greater number, make themselves believe it, being unable to penetrate what it means to believe."[10] This inability to penetrate what it means to believe, this incapacity to believe in any way that transcends opinion, is for Montaigne almost universally representative of the human condition.

One consequence of this discovery for Montaigne was that, lacking any reliable basis in individual experience, belief must yield entirely to authority. Montaigne submitted his essays "to the judgment of those whose concern it is to regulate not only my actions and my writings, but even my thoughts."[11] He performed this obedience "not perfunctorily but in sincere and complete submission . . . I speak as an ignorant inquirer, referring the decision purely and simply to the common and authorized beliefs [*aux creances communes et legitimes*]."[12] His reason was not that the Church was always right—far from it!—but that there was no reliable reason to prefer a different position above it. The skeptic can seek truth but not test it, so he obeys.[13] If human reason "strays however little from the beaten path and deviates or wanders from the way traced and trodden by the Church, immediately it is lost, it grows embarrassed and entangled, whirling round and floating in that vast, troubled, and undulating sea of human opinions, unbridled and aimless. As soon as it loses that great common highroad, it breaks up and disperses onto a thousand different roads."[14] Montaigne's solution was thus a sort of pure propositional conservatism: "Since I am not capable of choosing, I accept other people's choice and stay in the position where God put me. Otherwise I could not keep myself from rolling about incessantly. Thus I have, by the grace of God, kept myself intact, without agitation or disturbance of conscience, in the ancient beliefs [*creances*] of our religion, in the midst of so many sects and divisions that our century has produced."[15]

So, like John of the Cross, Montaigne yields belief entirely to the authority of the Church. And yet, again like John, the belief that he surrenders is effectively neutered, because the real business of the individual is something else entirely: freethinking inquiry and doubt. As he puts it in his essay *Of Prayers*: "I hold it as execrable if anything is found which was said by me, ignorantly or inadvertently, against the holy prescriptions of the Catholic, Apostolic, and Roman Church, in which I die and in which I was born. And therefore, always submitting to the authority of their censure, which has absolute power over me, I meddle rashly with every sort of subject."[16] Authority trumps experience when push comes to shove, but Montaigne's whole project is to avoid push ever coming to shove.

So, for Montaigne, "believing" with the Church is not Ignatian dogmatism; it is itself a kind of skepticism, admitting that we can only ever believe for contingent reasons and in fallible ways. Belief does not end doubt: while we cannot come to settled beliefs against the beliefs of the Church, we most certainly can speculate and entertain opinions. And since Montaigne has effectively downgraded all belief to the level of opinion, this becomes a distinction without a difference. So, for instance, when discussing belief in God, Montaigne calls for "*simple croyance*": not faith as required by the Church, but merely the kind of belief we invest in "any other history"—a concept to which we shall return. We ought to limit ourselves to a kind of belief that falls within our human capacity, rather than striving for a doomed assurance.[17] Elsewhere, Montaigne argues that theological doctrines should not be accepted "in the train of ancient beliefs, by authority and on credit, as if they were religion and law."[18]

Thus, Montaigne wrote, his own capacity to sift the truth amounts to "free will not to enslave my belief easily."[19] This kind of belief-*manqué* was always contingent and fallible, never rising to the level of belief the way the Church defined it; but it was nonetheless for Montaigne superior to the propositional pseudo-certainties owed to the Church. In sum, while propositional belief had to conform to authority, the kind of belief that really mattered was a process or disposition toward a truth that could not be known, rather than a settled confidence in that truth itself. Belief, now reimagined as something very like opinion, was the fruit of individual experience, even if it could never yield the sort of categorical truths that dogmatic religion had taught people to expect.

Montaigne thus reduced all belief to the belief of the world: if we believed in God "just as in any other history, if we knew him like one of our comrades, we would love him above all other things."[20] In one sense, then, it is reasonable to see Montaigne as the progenitor and first apostle of what I am calling "modern belief." Yet there is a problem: it is hard to imagine a worse poster child for a new constellation of belief that embraced individual propositional judgment, because few individuals in history have been so unwilling to assent to any propositions about anything! That is, while the history of skepticism is undoubtedly important, it is not the history of belief; Montaigne undermined old certainties, but to trace the emergence of a new paradigm of belief we must search elsewhere.

Another version of how human judgment might constitute Christian belief can be found in the works of the Italian philosopher and Dominican friar Giordano Bruno, burned at the stake for heresy in Rome in 1600, a notorious freethinker whose hatred of the Reformed church was equaled only by hatred of his own. Bruno is most famous for his heterodox claim that the universe is infinite, containing not only our own solar system but an infinitude of similar systems, worlds without end. This conception shaped Bruno's philosophy of knowledge, because if the created universe is infinite, he argued, then it cannot be wholly separate from an infinite God. On this basis, Bruno embraced rationalism: there are not separate lights to illuminate the natural and the supernatural, instead all can be understood using the same human faculties.[21] Bruno thus proposed that on any question, a man must "judge and take up his position, not on the basis of hearsay or according to the opinion of the majority of their age, merits, or prestige, but according to the persuasiveness of an organic doctrine."[22] So Bruno, too, might be seen as a progenitor of modern belief. But again, while not untrue, this identification is strained: Bruno belonged to an esoteric tradition in which hiddenness is a characteristic of the universe and the role of the philosopher is to commune with that hiddenness. While Bruno challenged the content of established belief, often in his writings belief itself appears to be a kind of stance in relationship to mystery rather than a positive judgment or statement of opinion.

So, if the Roman Catholic world did produce an apostle of modern belief, far out on a limb inventing the idea that believing is the open-ended space of sovereign judgment, that brilliant but unfortunate soul was Tommaso Campanella (1568–1639).[23] A radical Dominican friar, who among other enormities was a millenarian communist, Campanella spent much of his life in a Neapolitan prison. But that did not make him obscure or unimportant; his prison writings were widely known, and after being released in 1629 he became an advisor to Pope Urban VIII and a courtier of Louis XIII of France. His *Atheismus Triumphatus* (*Atheism Vanquished*) was written in Italian around 1605 while Campanella was in prison; condemned repeatedly by Church authorities when he tried to publish it, and described by censors as "slippery as an eel," it was published and then quickly suppressed in Rome in 1631, and then finally published in an unexpurgated Latin edition in Paris in 1636.[24] Written by a man whose creativity was outside the pale of orthodoxy, it was driven by a desire to re-inscribe belief outside the authority of the Church and instead within the sovereign judgment of the individual Christian.

The book opens with a flourish: "I, as a human mind, examined all religions in the universe . . . led by common reason and sensible experiments, so that with firm resolve I might rehearse for myself and others the belief of the teachings of the true faith."[25] This is a rebellion, not in content but in category: Campanella demands the autonomy to judge the beliefs of the Church for himself and is happy to report that they have passed muster.[26] After this fanfare, the first chapter is a taxonomy of "the order of believers" (*ordo credentium*) divided into six different categories, each of which challenged the Church's conception of what belief was. The first sort, for instance, "believes whatever is proposed to him" by the religion in which he is born because he does not critically examine its claims; here Campanella includes Jews, Muslims, and gentiles alongside those born under the "true law." The second sort of believers reason independently, but then, for worldly and self-serving reasons rather than apostolic obedience, believe whatever the regime tells them to believe. Yet another sort of believer does not really believe that God exists, but rather believes the religion of prudence and policy; these included Machiavellians, libertines, and Calvinists. There are also those who believe contrary to reason, those who believe out of weakness or fear, and the skeptical philosophers who regard all beliefs equally and indifferently.[27] Thus, even before Campanella's infamous second chapter, where he parroted atheistic views so sympathetically that he convinced many readers he shared them, his first chapter established "belief" as an almost infinitely broad category.

Yet at the same time, even from this opening chapter, Campanella suggested that there might be rational criteria to choose between different beliefs. This is why Campanella was accused of being an atheist in disguise. If "atheism" was taken to mean putting rational judgment above the authorization of the Church, then indeed he was.[28] But the point of Campanella's freethinking was nonetheless, as his title indicated, to vanquish atheism by establishing new and more solid grounds for belief. He began this project in chapter 14, where, having already considered objections to Christianity, he asked on what basis it might nonetheless be believed. Campanella suggested a series of criteria, drawn from the Roman law tradition and rules of evidence, by which a rational person might believe one religion over another: its production of miracles and martyrs; its prediction by previous prophecy; its ability to prophecy the future correctly; the constancy of its believers; its temporal duration.[29] He argued that other religions failed these tests, but Christianity passed them all and was therefore credible.[30]

Campanella was here elaborating a preexisting apologetic tradition, which we shall examine further below; he was outside the bounds of orthodoxy, but not inventing a whole new path. But then in chapter 15, Campanella widened his apologetic considerations into more broadly epistemological ones. Every proposition, Campanella wrote, is either true or false, but truth and falsehood can only be known by "trial [*experimento*] of all the senses" or by rationally weighing the credibility of "testimony."[31] Just because everything may be doubted, that does not make all things equally uncertain: the quality of evidence matters.[32] Ancient writers had denied the existence of another hemisphere, for instance, but now the testimony of the "unlearned [*idiotae*] sailor" Christopher Columbus was rightly believed above the opinions of so many philosophers and theologians.[33] This became, for Campanella, a robust attack on Montaigne and the skeptics: while it was formally true that we might doubt all things, many things—like the paternity of sons who resemble their fathers—are effectively proven by our senses. Other things, like the well-documented miracles of Christ, are effectively proven because of the quality of witness to them. While Campanella did not use the term that would soon develop for this sort of non-demonstrative proof—"moral certainty"—he came close when he argued that anyone who denies them "utterly deserves no faith."[34]

What sort of testimony, then, is worthy of trust? Campanella proposed eight commonsensical rules: we trust those who testify from their own senses rather than hearsay, who are not directly contradicted by other testimony, who have nothing to gain by lying, and so forth. Here Campanella was partaking of the new critical spirit of the *artes historicae,* in which he participated; he had written his own contribution to critical historiography in 1600, and he was an avid reader of the Catholic ecclesiastical historian Cesare Baronio among others.[35] And, as Campanella discussed at length, the conditions of credible testimony are satisfied by the books of the New Testament, which harmonize together, were predicted by prophets, and were confirmed by miracles. Only a fool, he writes, would doubt the eyewitness (*testificans oculatus*) of the apostles because of his own blind imagining (*coecus opinans*).[36] There is nothing surprising about Campanella's conclusions—Aquinas

and others had made similar arguments for the reasonableness of believing Christianity. Instead, his radicalism lies in re-
making belief itself as, by definition, an outcome of individual
interpretation of "evidence and testimony" (*indicia et testimo-
nia*).[37] Building upon skeptical predecessors like Montaigne,
who had reduced all belief to the level of opinion, Campanella performed a second and more important maneuver, constructing a spectrum of belief based upon the likelihood of its
claims. This was a world away from the so-called probabilism
of Jesuit moral theology, which argued that any course of action could be followed if there were probable arguments for it,
even if more probable arguments supported a different course
instead—a position for which the Jesuits were denounced as
amoral hypocrites.[38] For Campanella, by contrast, belief in its
religious sense was collapsing onto the kind of belief found in
the study of rhetoric, from which Christians had so long distinguished it: the persuasion of the mind by evidence.[39]

⟨≈≈≈⟩W⟨≈≈≈⟩

As in Catholic Italy, so in the Protestant Netherlands, dissidents
led the way. Jan van den Driesche (1550–1616), better known
by his Latin nom de plume Johannes Drusius, was among the
greatest biblical scholars of his era. Born in Flanders, he was
caught up in the first stages of the revolt of the Netherlands
against Spanish rule. In 1567, young Drusius was forced to flee
from the University of Leuven to England, where he enjoyed
a meteoric rise, first learning Hebrew with a private tutor in
Cambridge and then, at the tender age of twenty-two, becoming
Professor of Oriental Languages at Oxford. He returned to the
Netherlands after the temporary peace of 1576, first as professor at Leiden and then at Franeker, far to the north of the conflict zone, where he thought he would not be bothered for his

religion. He was wrong. His friendship with the controversial scholar Jacobus Arminius, and his association with the so-called Arminians or Remonstrants who tried to reimagine Dutch Protestantism without the stark theology of Calvin, meant that for his last twenty years he lived under constant suspicion. Despite his fame and learning, he was considered too dangerous to be included in the Bible translation project sponsored by the nascent Dutch Republic; instead, he wrote arcane notes on the Old Testament, not published until after his death.

The Arminians were crucial challengers to Calvinist hegemony throughout Northern Europe, so we should not be surprised that they played a prominent role in challenging the confessional regime of belief. Drusius, while not the lead player in this drama, deserves pride of place for striking an early blow. In his *Observationum Libri XII* (1584), a scholarly if snide correction of errors in biblical philology, Drusius challenged the long-standing claim that we should not believe *in* men, we should only believe *in* God. As we have seen, some Counter-Reformation Catholics argued that the Church, too, should be believed *in*. But Drusius offered a more comprehensive critique: "I do not agree with those who want 'to believe God' to be different than '*in* God,' because the Hebrews, whose phrase it is, do not recognize this distinction, which elsewhere the laws of the Latin language changed. So they said 'to believe God' and '*in* God' indifferently."[40] It was in vain, Drusius continued, for theologians to claim that we should not "believe *in*" men, since there are four Old Testament passages where the prepositional phrase "believe *in*" refers to human beings in the original Hebrew, some of which are translated using the Latin preposition *in* and some not. Likewise, Greek sources employ phrases like "to believe *in* eternal life" and "to believe *in* the resurrection of the dead." There is simply no such thing as a higher, religious meaning of "believing *in*": a single, indiffer-

ent "belief" is all the Bible can offer, whatever corruptions may
have crept into later Latin theology.[41]

Drusius was not yet an "Arminian" when he wrote these
passages, because Arminius had not yet developed his controversial doctrines. Moreover, he often claimed that his biblical
scholarship was utterly innocent of doctrine: "All my meager
knowledge revolves around grammar and history. Religious
dogmas I leave to others to handle. In history there is no heresy, much less in grammar."[42] With the benefit of hindsight,
however, we can see that it was no coincidence Drusius would
become an Arminian, nor that his arguments would find fertile
soil among Arminians in both the Netherlands and England.
Jacobus Arminius (1560–1609), erstwhile student of Theodore
Beza at Geneva, later pastor in Amsterdam and then Professor
of Theology at Leiden, was the first theologian of real standing
in the Calvinist community to break with Calvin and Beza on
the core issue of predestination. Arminius argued that instead
of God predestining people to damnation or salvation irrespec-
tive of their merits (the Calvinist position), and instead of God
predestining them in light of his foreknowledge of their sins
or repentance (the Catholic position), God predestined people
according to his "middle knowledge": his *conditional* knowledge of cause and effect. In this system, very cleverly, people are
damned for the sins they actually commit, hence they retain a
version of their free will; yet at the same time, God retains his
absolute sovereignty because he determines the circumstances
in which free will will be exercised, so whether people are saved
is a direct effect of the circumstances he ordains. The details of
this system are beyond our scope. What is important is that Arminianism intentionally undermined the normative Protestant
understanding of Christian belief.[43]

So, for instance, in a 1605 letter to his disciple and successor
Johannes Wtenbogaert, Arminius seemed at first to echo the

ordinary Protestant argument that belief in Christ requires assurance that you are saved. And yet, Arminius offered a crucial novelty, distinguishing between assurance *in the present*, and *conditional* assurance.

> In these expressions, therefore, "I believe that Christ is the savior of the world, yea that He is the savior of believers and of me," the following are *not* included, "I believe that I have remission of sins, I believe that I have eternal life." But this is included in them, "I believe that I *shall* have these in his name." For since I believe that I shall obtain these blessings on my believing in him, I believe in him that I may actually have them, and then I actually receive them. The confounding of these matters is the cause why our divines occasionally speak with less propriety concerning justifying faith.[44]

Arminius was arguing that his Calvinist predecessors had oversimplified, eliding a crucial distinction that made belief less stark and absolute. It was not the case that Christians must rest in a settled state of assurance in order to believe. Instead, belief is a process in time, a journey rather than a destination: doctrinal belief induces a desire for salvation, and desire for salvation induces Christians to apply salvific doctrine to themselves, which leads to salvation. The first stage, while not complete, was nonetheless real belief. Downgraded in this way, the category of belief could, in principle, build bridges rather than burning them.

While Arminius was writing in the Netherlands, Richard Hooker was writing in England from a similar theological perspective. Hooker is sometimes described as an Arminian, a label that would be correct except that Arminius was not yet widely known for the positions that would bear his name; it would be nearly as accurate to call Arminius a Hookerian.

And Hooker, like the Dutchman, wrote remarkably heterodox things about belief. In 1585, for instance, Hooker preached a sermon at the Temple church that launched a famous debate with the Presbyterian Walter Travers. Hooker's sermon, on "the certainty and perpetuity of faith in the elect," argued against the possibility of assurance of salvation: spiritual realities cannot be evident to us, they are obscured by our fallen natures. In the absence of a "certainty of evidence," all we may achieve is a "certainty of adherence" to God. No wonder Travers, in a complaint to the Privy Council, condemned Hooker's alleged claim "that the assurance of that we believe by the word is not so certain as of that we perceive by sense."[45]

Eight years later, in his influential *Lawes of Ecclesiastical Politie* (1593), Hooker argued that all belief was essentially the same, regardless of whether its source was scripture, reason, or the authority of the Church.

> Since the ground of credit is the credibility of things credited, and things are made credible either by the known condition and quality of the utterer, or by the manifest likelihood of truth which they have in themselves, hereupon it riseth, that whatsoever we are persuaded of, the same we are generally said to believe.

"The ground of credit is the credibility of things credited": here Hooker approaches the principle that we are properly said to believe whatever we judge to be true, according to our own persuasion. That is, we can believe "by reason or by sense."[46]

This propositional understanding of belief came to fruition in the work of Thomas Jackson, one of England's leading Arminian theologians, who became Dean of Peterborough and President of Corpus Christi College, Oxford when his faction rose to power under Charles I. Jackson is an obscure figure today, but in his own time he was both renowned and controversial. According to his nemesis, the puritan William Prynne, Jackson's work was "blanched and blasted by a parliamentary examination, excepted against by the convocation house, answered by some, disavowed by most."[47] In 1631 he received the dubious honor of a seven-hundred-page rebuttal by the Calvinist William Twisse against his neoplatonist treatise on the nature of God. The following year he was one of the dons lambasted in "The academicall army of epidemicall Arminians," a satirical ballad that was passed around Oxford University. To his allies, however, he was a man of deep insights. His collected *Works* were published in the 1650s, again in the 1670s, and then again in the nineteenth century during the Oxford Movement.

Jackson's first major salvo, *The Eternall Truth of Scriptures, and Christian Belief* (1613), attacked both the Calvinist and Catholic concepts of belief. Against Calvinist assurance, he wrote that "belief, taken generally, doth neither exclude all certainty, nor necessarily require any," because belief is simply assent to something that is not evident, and this assent "may be weaker or stronger." As he put it most bluntly, "They may truly and properly say they believe, if their assent to it be greater than to the contrary"—a concept of belief as a mere preponderance of opinion that cut against virtually the entire Christian tradition. Against the Catholics, Jackson rejected the notion that "belief" is distinguished from "other assents or opinions" by being grounded on "the authority of the teacher . . . of the points proposed to be believed." While true sometimes, in many cases we believe because we *test* authorities rather than simply accepting them.[48]

This was preparatory to Jackson's most important work, *A Treatise Concerning the Original of Unbeliefe . . . with Directions for Rectifying our Beliefe or Knowledge* (1625). Here Jackson's goal was to attack the idea that belief was hard. In a careful taxonomy, he distinguished between heretics, infidels, and atheists. Heretics were those who denied any articles of the Apostles' Creed; infidels were those who denied the particular articles concerning Christ; and atheists were those who denied the particular articles concerning God. Thus, while every atheist was necessarily a heretic, not every heretic was an atheist.[49] Jackson therefore argued that "belief, as it is terminated to the first words of the Creed"—that is, *I believe in God*—is the "line or axis which severs atheism or irreligion from religion, whether true or false, and doth as it were constitute two distinct hemispheres of men."

Jackson knew that other Protestants would dislike this framework: "*To believe in God* hath gone current so long, for as much as *to put trust or confidence in him*, that now to call it in, or make it go for less, will perhaps be thought an usurpation of authority." Yet, Jackson argued, the authors of the Creed meant by its first article "no more than to believe there is a God, or to give credence to his word." Thus, he wrote, "We may safely acquit from actual atheism" those who merely fail to be as good Christians as they wish to be: to put all our trust in God is "the mark whereat the belief of novices must aim, not the first step they are to make in this progress."[50] Bare belief—"to hold it more probable there is such a God or judge than none"—Jackson proposed as the hinge or pivot point, "the lowest degree imaginable of belief, if not rather the one extremity or *ultimum non esse* of infidelity or unbelief."[51] The sixteenth-century project of belief was coming under attack, and a new project was beginning.

The centerpiece of this new project was the rehabilitation by Protestants of *fides historica*, or historical faith: intellectual assent to the factual matter of Christianity, the stories and doctrines of the Bible, came to be accounted authentic Christian belief.

One crucial context for this rehabilitation was the transformation of history itself and the growing sophistication with which later Renaissance historiographers articulated analytical criteria for historical faith. Whereas at the outset of the Reformation, history was still widely considered a "species of rhetoric, primarily valued for its ability to inflame auditors to virtue," by the end of the century, history was a distinct methodology that demanded "an empirical and inductive approach," as Nicholas Popper has written.[52] In the hands of virtuosic scholars like Francesco Patrizi, François Baudouin, and Jean Bodin, rules of historical evidence were developed that mirrored jurisprudence; increasing attention was paid to the quality of evidence for facts rather than the authority of the person attesting them; and "integrated" history used more reliable information to assess less reliable claims. In the Protestant world, these methods were deployed in the pioneering ecclesiastical history that began appearing in 1559, the *Magdeburg Centuries*, and they were at the heart of the enterprise of Joseph Scaliger, Isaac Casaubon, and other academic luminaries.[53] But this raises the question: just because new rules had been developed to defend faith in history, why did it suddenly make sense for Protestants to apply those rules to religion? New techniques placed historical faith on allegedly firmer ground, but it was still plainly probabilistic rather than indubitable, human rather than divine; so why did some Protestants come to regard as sufficient what their predecessors had rejected as insufficient?

To find the answer, we must turn to the genre of "apologetics," the ancient project of defending the credibility of Christianity, which gradually came to rely upon history.[54] Apologists had long argued that it was *reasonable* to believe in Christianity: natural reason points toward supernatural truths even if it can never reach them.[55] The fountainhead of the scholastic tradition was Thomas Aquinas's *Summa contra Gentiles*, which argued, ostensibly to Jews and Muslims, that vast swaths of Christian doctrine were accessible to natural reason: God's existence, the immortality of the soul, divine providence, and much else besides. But in the final section, Aquinas turned to truths accessible solely through revelation, arguing that while mysteries like the trinity could not be derived from reason, it was nonetheless reasonable to believe them because historical evidence pointed to their truth: the "wonderful conversion of the world to the Christian faith," despite vicious persecution, must have been miraculous, hence its revealed doctrines must be true.[56] Historical evidence here offered support for Christian belief.

In the 1430s, other rational proofs for the credibility of scriptures were added to this discussion by Raymond Sebond, regius professor of theology at Toulouse, in his *Theologia naturalis, sive liber creaturarum*. So, for instance, Sebond argued from literary style: while other books try to persuade, the Bible simply asserts things which seem incredible, thus proving that its author needed no arguments. Likewise, since the Bible contains mysteries far above human understanding, no human could have written it, QED.[57] These arguments represented a departure from the Church's usual claim to authenticate scripture by continuous tradition; for Sebond, the world itself provided evidence for belief in sacred history. Sebond's torch was taken up by the Spanish humanist Juan Luis Vives in *De Veritate Fidei Christianae* (1543), who defended the use of empirical evidence in matters of faith.[58] Much of his empiricism involved the much older technique of "understanding the architect from the building," as Vives put it.[59]

But it also occasionally involved assessing the credibility of the gospels themselves as histories, which were written by eyewitnesses and corroborated by their agreement in all points of significance.[60]

There was similar practice in the Reformation. Calvin's *Institutes*, of course, stressed that rational arguments could never prove to infidels that scripture was the word of God; without assurance based upon faith, "the authority of scripture remains in suspense." Yet nonetheless, "secondary helps to our weakness," like arguments for scripture's credibility, could confirm preexisting beliefs and edify Christians. Thus, a substantial chapter of the *Institutes*—much of it added for the third Latin edition in 1543, perhaps in response to Vives— offered arguments for the credibility of Moses, the prophets, and the evangelists: their unadorned style, their use of self-deprecating material, the later fulfillment of their prophecies, and so forth.[61] A generation later, the fully developed Protestant analogue to Vives was *De la verité de la religion Chrestienne* (1581) by Philippe de Plessis Mornay, who wrote rather more about the specifically *historical* credibility of the Bible. That is, using examples drawn from Calvin and elsewhere, and deploying the extensive arsenal of the Renaissance *ars historica* for assessing credibility, he explained why the authors of the Bible should be trusted as historians.[62] Mornay thus came closest, in this long tradition, to using history as evidence for faith; yet Mornay certainly did not equate belief in scriptural history with Christian belief itself.

The real innovation must therefore be credited to one of the most infamous heretics of the Reformation, the Sienese reformer Fausto Sozzini, better known by his Latinized name Socinus (1539–1604). Socinus migrated all over Europe, from Catholic Italy to Protestant Geneva to the bastion of Anabaptism in Transylvania; he spent his last quarter century in

Poland, where he led the radical church known as the *Ecclesia Minor* or Polish Brethren, progenitors of the Unitarians. Already by 1563, he had rejected the divinity of Christ and the immortality of the soul, and then he turned to the question of scripture. Socinus's *De auctoritate sacrae scripturae* was written circa 1568 but not published until twenty years later, under the false name of the Spanish Jesuit Dominicus Lopez. It was not initially known that Socinus was the author, and the work was taken seriously by contemporaries. Devoted to defending the historical credibility of the scriptures, it offered the novel thesis that belief in scriptural history is sufficient to induce, and can be accounted, Christian belief.

Socinus suggested that we must assess the historical truth of scripture using our reason, just like any other histories.[63] Here he drew inspiration from the *artes historicae* which were busily developing rules for assessing historical credibility. In particular, the years immediately preceding Socinus's composition saw the publication of two profoundly influential guides for historical judgment, which Socinus presumably had in mind: François Baudouin's *De Institutione Historiae Universae* (1561) and Jean Bodin's *Methodus ad Facilem Historiarum Cognitionem* (1566).[64] Confronting the inevitable criticism that this methodology was insufficient for Christian assurance, Socinus answered angrily: the same credence "commonly yielded to many other histories or books . . . might be enough to incline men at length to become true Christians."[65] To make this remarkable claim, he appealed to the *Catholic* rather than Protestant notion of faith:

> An infinite number of those who are called Christians, especially the subjects of the Church of Rome, will have faith to be progressive, in its beginning weak and small, and afterwards gradually augmenting and gathering strength.

And that any one with good works, although he has but very little faith, if he be endued with but an infirm persuasion of the truth of the evangelical history [*minima fide, id est, persuasione veritatis historiae evangelicae*], may render himself capable of receiving that divine grace, by the efficacy whereof, he will afterwards be made thoroughly sensible of the evidence of the truth of what the above-named writers report concerning Jesus of Nazareth.[66]

Here Socinus combined the Protestant view of the authority of scripture with the Catholic view of "faith formed with love," to argue that fides historica is sufficient for Christian faith: "Whoever assents to the history, must in like manner of necessity assent to the doctrine. And what's more, the very doctrine is part of the history."[67]

Socinus's conclusion was that if people genuinely believed the history of the New Testament, then "everyone would not only profess the religion therein proposed, and pretend to be a Christian, but be so in reality [*reipsa*], that is, sincerely obey Jesus Christ the son of God." His reason was close to Pascal's famous wager a century later. Consider, he suggested, whether you would risk one small coin (he used the Latin *teruncius*, a small denomination of base metal, what the English would call a brass farthing) for a chance to win millions in gold. If you believe the history recounted in the New Testament, then you accept the analogy between this wager and making sacrifices in the world to obtain the felicity of heaven. Thus, Socinus wrote, anyone who believes intellectually that the scripture is true is also bound to believe its promises and attempt to fulfill their obligations: "He who is good, ingenuous, and tractable in his mind and will . . . will easily believe [*facile credit*] what he hears of the immense reward promised to them who shall practice those things . . . and so believing [*ita credens*], will use his utmost endeavors to obey and fulfill the precepts of Christ."[68]

So how did this treatise by one of the Reformation's most notorious renegades enter the mainstream of European thought? Through the Arminians, who, as Sarah Mortimer has noted, shared with the Socinians the view that "reason . . . dealt with religious claims in the same way as all other propositions."[69] One of Arminius's most fundamental breaks from his Protestant predecessors was, like Socinus, to insist upon the primacy of the intellect over the will in Christian faith.[70] Arminius understood faith as "an assent of the mind" [*adsensus animi*].[71] He argued that "knowledge is antecedent to faith; for the Son of God is beheld before a sinner believes on him. But trust or confidence is consequent to it . . . The instrument [of faith] is the gospel, or the word of faith, containing the meaning concerning God and Christ which the Spirit proposes to the understanding, and of which he there works a persuasion."[72] This position allowed the Arminians to appreciate the arguments of Socinus about propositional assent to biblical history, in essence adopting the Catholic argument that the factual history of Christ's sacrifice contains all that we need for faith, but divorcing that argument from dogmatic belief with the Church. Now, for the first time, the individual, propositional, *historical* judgment of Christians becomes the essence of faith. Thus, the Arminian leader Conrad Vorstius published a definitive new edition of Socinus's *De auctoritate sacrae scripturae* in 1611. Vorstius probably did not yet know who had written it; like many Arminians he would soon find himself publicly denying that he was a Socinian. Thereafter, the Arminian leader Simon Episcopius, and then his disciple Stephanus Curcellaeus—a close friend of René Descartes— adopted and enlarged Socinus's biblical hermeneutic, arguing that the historical veracity of the Bible was identical to the truth of Christianity, so that historical faith was essentially the only kind of faith there was.[73]

In England, the great expositor of this new doctrine was the indomitable Thomas Jackson. As early as 1613, in order to explain how assent to Christianity could be elevated above the 50 percent threshold that constitutes belief, Jackson borrowed and translated—that is, stole—Socinus's image of wagering a *teruncius* for the chance to win millions. The key to increasing belief, Jackson wrote, was to convince people of the veracity of scripture: if they believe the Bible is the word of God, belief in Christian doctrine follows. Of course, there is no absolute proof; but given the enormity of what is potentially to be gained, "presumption and probability" is sufficient reason to believe. Jackson put it this way: "Could men consider these things seriously, and account of them but as probable, what is there in this life, which in any reason they should not venture for the obtaining of so great a good? . . . For this life compared to that to come, hath not the proportion of a farthing to whole millions of gold, or all the treasures in this world."[74]

Two years later, in his 1615 *Iustifying faith*, Jackson addressed fides historica in detail. He announced that while of course "every assent unto supernatural truths, of what rank soever, sufficeth not to the attaining of supernatural and eternal bliss," nonetheless saving faith is "not opposite, but subordinate, or rather coincident to historical assent."[75] He thus suggested a series of "grounds or motives" to induce historical assent, including "experiments." For example, we give credence to Caesar's description of the Roman conquest of Britain because Roman coins bearing Caesar's image have been found buried in Britain, providing external reasons to believe his account. These kinds of experiments, Jackson argued, are "exactly answerable to the exact relation of prophets and evangelists": we believe them because they are experimentally validated by subsequent events. Thus, he concluded, "our faith is not to be reputed unsound or non salvifical, because historical; but rather oft times therefore unsufficient to save, because not so fully historical as it might be."[76]

So what sort of assent is due to the historical truth of scripture? Jackson distinguished between the "certainty," the "stability," and the "strength" of assent: certainty arises from clarity of understanding, stability from the proper correspondence between our understanding and its object, and strength from the proper valuation of the object itself.[77] Given this matrix, we can have an infinitely "strong" assent in religion, because God can never be valued too highly; but "certainty" cannot be required, and indeed is very dangerous. Jackson described "every degree of certainty we get in belief," beyond what is appropriate to its object, as "a step to sorcery." This was, according to Jackson, an "especial root of popery": "This certainty of persuasion which they thus enforce upon themselves, without proportional increase of evidence or perspicuity apprehended in the object, hath the same proportion to lively faith, that stubborn foolhardiness [has] unto true valor."[78] Given this discussion, it is plausible that Jackson's title—"Justifying Faith"—was a pun, meaning not only the faith which justifies, as in the normal Protestant usage, but faith which Jackson himself *justifies* in something like the modern philosophical sense: justifying faith is an act of persuasion.

Jackson's influence was largely limited to England. But on the international stage, the most influential Arminian voice was Hugo Grotius, whose *De veritate religionis Christianae* (1627) redeployed almost all of Socinus's arguments (and those of Jackson, Mornay, Vives, and their predecessors) for the historical credibility of scriptures, elaborated with an encyclopedic knowledge of classical and Jewish history.[79] Grotius also added, or newly emphasized, that *all* Christianity was based upon a rational consideration of the credibility of reports. Like his predecessors, Grotius asked why Christ's contemporaries, men of good judgment brought up in other religions, should have followed him despite there being no honor or profit to be had in Christianity. Grotius's answer was remarkable: "Why, I say, they should do thus, there can be no reason given but this one: that upon a diligent inquiry, such as becomes prudent men to make in a matter of the highest concern to them, they found that the report which was spread abroad concerning the miracles that were done by him, was true, and founded upon sufficient testimony."[80] There is nothing here of grace and revelation, nothing of saving faith, only the diligent inquiry of prudent men whether to believe a proposition. We must not expect certainty or assurance, Grotius argued. Because Christianity is an historical religion, we are obliged to accept probability rather than certainty, and God had made the scriptures credible rather than certain as a "touchstone to try men's honest dispositions."[81] Grotius, through his immense fame, thus offered something like modern belief not only to his own Arminian brethren but to the whole of Europe.

In the early seventeenth century, among influential writers on both sides of the Reformation, *probable* belief, based upon the judicious weighing of evidence, emerged as Christian belief indeed. And here, our story begins to overlap with one of the most important developments in the history of science, the epistemological innovations of the seventeenth century which shaped the scientific revolution. Some of our most insightful scholars have explored how and why the ancient concept of *scientia* slowly disintegrated. Beginning with Bacon and Galileo, we are told, then reaching maturity with the experimental program of the Royal Society and the mathematics of probability discovered by Pascal, Fermat, and Huygens, the medieval paradigm demanding deductive demonstration as the basis for knowledge was gradually replaced by induction, experimentation, and probabilistic reasoning.[82] This story is unassailable as far as it goes; but like so much truth in the new inductive era, it does not tell the whole story. In particular, it describes how two kinds of epistemic claims, knowledge and opinion, gradually merged; but it only rarely and inadequately acknowledges the role of a third epistemic category, belief.[83] The handful of scholars who have noticed that there *was* a transformation of belief, for all their perspicuity, have not suggested that religious knowledge might have been a leading rather than trailing indicator.[84] Without a sense that belief can experience revolutions the way science does, it has been virtually impossible to notice the priority of religious belief in the history of modern knowledge.

⟨⟫⟩

While Tommaso Campanella was developing his arguments on the ideological periphery of the Catholic world, and Thomas Jackson and Hugo Grotius were developing their arguments on the ideological periphery of the Protestant world, others were experimenting with similar notions on the geographical periphery. It has long been noticed that the Jesuits in Asia—who, unlike the Dominicans and Franciscans of the Spanish Empire, were not accompanied by armies—found that missionizing required sophisticated intellectual engagement and strategies of accommodation. This was why the Italian Jesuit Matteo Ricci was widely suspected of converting to Confucianism even as he sought to convert the Chinese to Christianity: his project required at least a modicum of commensurability between these systems, famously represented in his own work of apologetics, *The True Meaning of the Lord of Heaven*.[85] Rather than focusing on the Jesuits in Asia, however, I want to focus instead on the Jesuits in Canada. For their own spiritual purposes, and in very different ethnographic circumstances, these missionaries erased traditional lines between knowledge, belief, and opinion, in the process activating something very much like modern belief. Their story is long, but worth the telling.[86]

In January 1612, the Jesuit missionary Pierre Biard wrote to his superior in Paris from a small toehold of French settlement on the banks of the Annapolis River in Acadia, lamenting the difficulties of converting the Mi'kmaq. Exasperated with his failures of communication and deploying all the cultural prejudices we might expect in his generation of Frenchmen, Biard noted that, "as the savages have no definite religion, magistracy, or government, liberal or mechanical arts, commercial or civil life, they have consequently no words to describe things which they have never seen or even conceived." They were relentlessly carnal rather than spiritual, so "all their conceptions are limited to sensible and material things." In particular, Biard lamented: "We are still disputing, after a great deal of research and labor, whether they have any word to correspond directly to the word *credo*, I believe. Judge for yourself the difficulty surrounding the remainder of the Creed and fundamental truths of Christianity."[87]

The context for Biard's admission was the controversial decision by the Jesuits to focus their missionary activities on something called belief rather than simply baptism. The Jesuit order had long been more concerned with interior religiosity than most other sixteenth-century Catholics. Certainly in France since the end of the religious wars, the Jesuits had endeavored to build a Catholicism organized not just around the requirements of the Council of Trent but around the spiritual conversion of a troubled populace. Hence their attitude toward conversion in Canada.[88] In the years before the arrival of Biard and his Jesuit colleague Ennemond Massé in 1611, several dozen indigenous men and women had been converted by secular priests, but they had "accepted baptism solely as a sign of friendship"; the Jesuits were shocked to discover that "when asked if they were Christians," they "made signs to show that they had never heard the word."[89] This was embarrassing, reminiscent of Spanish conquest a century earlier, when the Mesoamericans had received baptism "without knowing either the Creed or confession" and thus continued "to sing to the devil their usual sorceries."[90] So, instead of repeating the hasty approach of their predecessors, the Jesuits refused to baptize any adults except those on the brink of death unless they had received rigorous doctrinal instruction and showed evidence of divine grace.[91] As late as 1637, Father François Joseph Le Mercier claimed, with some exaggeration, that they still had "not yet baptized anyone who had the use of his reason, unless he were in danger of death."[92] This slow pace exasperated French settlers, who hoped to see Christian converts rather than Christian corpses; but despite objections, the Jesuits held doggedly to their slow-and-steady approach. Most of the new Christians in New France, then, were either deathbed converts who had unexpectedly survived, or children who had been raised as Christians. Thus, unlike in English North America, where converts were known by terms like "praying Indians," in Canada this small but growing community was known, simply and universally, as "the believers."[93]

It is likely that this term arose from the French perception that belief itself was a novelty among indigenous peoples, whose mythologies required other forms of commitment. This is not to deny that the Jesuits were familiar with Renaissance comparative religion, which had been developing since the fifteenth century.[94] Rather, it suggests that their understanding began from the premise that belief in other religions was not the same kind of thing as belief in true religion; it was more like the profane belief of the world, the kind of belief you invest in neighbors or rumors, filled with error and without any credible foundation. According to the Jesuits, indigenous peoples perceived very dimly, "through the twilight, as it were, that some deity does exist," but they identified that deity with dogs or bears, or with the sun, because they could not conceive of an immaterial God.[95] They had some knowledge of the immortality of the soul, but their materialism led them to bury food with the bodies of their dead so that their souls did not starve.[96] The more the Jesuits learned, or thought they learned, about indigenous peoples—espeically the Wyandot, whom they called "Huron"—the more examples abounded of their alleged carnality. In 1639, a Jesuit claimed that "it is useless" to explain to them the blessings of heaven: "Some say that they do not see how, as they have so weak legs, they can make so long a journey and reach heaven. Others assert that they are already afraid, and dread lest they may fall from so great a height."[97] Whether the Wyandot people's dim view of divinity could be understood as believing at all was a matter of some disagreement, but minimally they did not believe in the proper, religious sense of the term. To the extent that the Wyandot could be said to have beliefs, these were merely "idle fancies . . . founded upon lies" and easily displaced by truth.[98] As an example of this debased epistemology among another nearby nation, Father Paul Le Jeune noted that the Montegnais (Innu) word for the creator of the world, *Atachocam*, actually means "fable."[99]

Attempts to convert the indigenous people of North America were thus allegedly frustrated by the absence of a "spiritual" vocabulary. At first, the Jesuits learned words by "inquiring of the savages how they called each thing," which worked well enough for what "could be touched or seen." But when it came to terms for "internal and spiritual acts, which cannot be demonstrated to the senses," communication foundered:

The words and proper phrases for all those things are lacking: Holy, Blessed, Angel, Grace, Mystery, Sacrament, Temptation, Faith, Law, Prudence, Subjection, Authority, etc. Where will you get all these things that they lack? Or, how will you do without them? O God, with what ease we make our plans in France! And the beauty of it is that after having racked our brains by dint of questions and researches, and after thinking that we have at last found the philosopher's stone, we find only that a ghost has been taken for a body, a shadow for a substance, and that all this precious elixir has gone up in smoke![100]

Or so they said. Yet, despite so much talk by the Jesuits of a great divide between the spiritual belief of Christians and the material epistemology of indigenous peoples, in fact belief proved a crucial space of convergence. What emerges urgently from their accounts is that the Jesuits accepted—and were prepared to exploit—the absence of any stark line between knowledge, opinion, and belief. In a context where people had to be *convinced* to believe through reason and experience, the Jesuits found themselves rethinking the assumptions of the Counter-Reformation. As Mark Waddell has argued, Jesuit scientists in seventeenth-century Europe launched a broad project of epistemological naturalism and probabilism, making the world—including the holy and preternatural—more knowable in order to differentiate it from an unknowable God.[101] On the colonial periphery, it thus made perfect sense for Jesuits to dismantle the confessional project of belief from the inside, much the way Montaigne and Campanella dismantled it from the outside.

So, for instance, Father Joseph Jouvency much later described the following scene from 1611. The Innu, when they first heard of eternal hellfire, were impressed in principle with the idea of a punishment for sins, but nonetheless they "obstinately withheld their belief because, as they said, there could be no fire where there was no wood." Jouvency regarded this as a typical example of indigenous materialism, apt for "physical man" in whom "the entire system of knowledge is based on vision." After some perplexity, one of the priests came up with an answer, declaring that, instead of burning wood, the earth of hell burned by itself. When his indigenous audience laughed— what kind of earth could burn by itself?—the priest offered to show them a piece of the underworld, "in order that, since you do not believe the words of God, you may trust the evidence of your own eyes." Thus, with the people gathered to watch, the priest produced a lump of sulfur and cast it into the fire; at which point, having seen and smelled, the crowd "believed (*credidit*) in the word of God that there is a lower world."[102]

This was the first of a long series of what can only be described as religious experiments. So, for instance, on one occasion Father Le Jeune challenged an indigenous healer to test empirically whether his drumming and singing was better medicine than Christian belief. Seeing that the healer himself was gravely ill, Le Jeune offered a modest proposal. First the "sorcerer" would beat his drum and sing for ten days, to see if it cured him. If he were not cured, he must confess that his methods were ineffective. Thereafter, the healer had to "abstain ten more days from all these superstitions; give up thy drum, and all these wild noises; ask of the God whom I adore that he give thee knowledge of himself; reflect, and believe [*pense & crois*] that thy soul must pass to a life other than this."[103]

Similar negotiations between belief and empirical evidence—in both causal directions—were commonplace. On one occasion, an indigenous healer told a patient that in order to be cured, he had to obtain a pair of stockings like the Jesuits wore, so the patient's family begged Father Buteux for a pair. Buteux

answered that "these dreams were but nonsense," and to prove
it, he offered a deal: "He would give him what he wanted, on
condition that after he had worn them four days, more or less,
if he did not recover he would abandon these idle fancies and
believe [*croiroit*] in God."[104] Another incident involved the
need for snow to enable hunters to track game: "As to the pro-
posals we make to them to believe in God, one of them said
to me one day, 'If we believe in your God, will it snow?' 'It will
snow,' I said to him. 'Will the snow be hard and deep?' 'It will
be.' 'Shall we find moose?' 'You will find them.' 'Shall we kill
some?' 'Yes, for as God knows all things, as he can do all things,
and as he is very good, he will not fail to help you.'"[105]

One dramatic example occurred in 1628 when, in the midst
of a drought, the Wyandot "sorcerer" Tehorenhaegnon claimed
that he could not make rain because (as a Jesuit described it),
"The thunder, which they pretend is a bird, was afraid of the
cross that was in front of the Frenchmen's house, and that the
red color with which it was painted was like a fire burning and
flaming, which divided the clouds in two when they passed
above it." The head of the village demanded that the French
remove their cross, which they refused to do, claiming that the
cross had been there more than a year and it had rained within
that span. But rather than precipitating a confrontation, one
of the Jesuits thought of a plan: he told the Wyandot to paint
the cross some other color, and if it immediately began to rain,
then Tehorenhaegnon told the truth, but if it did not then he
was an imposter. The plan worked: they repainted the cross
white, it still did not rain, so the villagers denounced Tehorenhaegnon and instead asked the Jesuits how to make it rain.
And here is the most interesting part of the story: far from
denouncing the whole carnal edifice of rainmaking as sorcery,
they held a festival of repainting, reciting prayers, and kissing
the cross. And according to Father Jean de Brébeuf, "They did

so well that on the same day God gave them rain, and in the end a plentiful harvest, as well as a profound admiration for the divine power."[106]

In these examples, Jesuits presented belief to indigenous people as an empirical exercise. In what amounts to a travesty of traditional miracles stories, in which the divine will is made manifest by God's manipulation of nature, here nature is manipulated and then observed to produce evidence of the divine. Under pressure from Protestants who regarded implicit faith as mental slavery, and in backlash against the coerced baptisms of Spanish missionaries, these Jesuits experimented openly with experimentalism, breaking down the partition wall between profane epistemology and Christian belief. These were not the straw-man Jesuits mocked by Blaise Pascal in his *Provincial Letters*, demanding that authority should be believed even if it contradicted itself; on the contrary, these Jesuits were busily producing the epistemological categories of the scientific revolution, in the name of Christian belief.[107]

It is also remarkable how, under the ostensible sign of accusing indigenous peoples of materialism, the Jesuits in fact challenged indigenous spirituality with materialist critiques of their own. For instance, in 1634 Father Le Jeune confronted the Innu people on a "fine article of their faith" [*bel article de leur croyance*], as he sarcastically put it: the destination of souls. He was told by his hosts that after death, souls go "very far away, to a large village situated where the sun sets." Le Jeune responded with what looks much like materialist skepticism: "All your country, I say to them (meaning America) is an immense island, as you seem to know; how is it that the souls of men . . . can cross the water to go to this great village that you place where the sun sets? Do they find ships all ready to embark them and take them over the water?" No, they answered, the souls go on foot and ford the sea. And here,

Le Jeune thought he had won the debate: "How can they ford the great ocean, which you know is so deep?" But Le Jeune had not won at all: "Thou art mistaken, they answer, either the lands are united in some places, or there is some passage which is fordable over which our souls pass." There was still one region the French had not explored where there might be a bridge: "We know that no one has yet been able to pass beyond the north coast." But Le Jeuene would not take this argument lying down: they could not go north because "of the great cold in those seas, so that if your souls take this route, they will be frozen and all stiff from cold before they reach their village."[108]

This turned out to be only the beginning of a surprisingly long debate. What do these souls eat on their long journey? Bark from trees, Father Le Jeune learned, to which he replied sarcastically that it was no wonder the Innu feared death, if that was the finest fare they could look forward to. What do these souls do when they arrive at their dwelling place? They rest during the day, and then at night they work, hunt, and play. Aha, Father Le Jeune rejoined: "But they cannot see at all during the night." His interlocutors were unimpressed: "Thou art an ignoramus, thou hast no sense [*tu es vn ignorant, tu n'as point d'esprit*] . . . Souls are not like us, they do not see at all during the day, and see very clearly at night." Le Jeune then tried a different line of questioning: what do these souls hunt? "They hunt for the souls of beavers, porcupines, moose, and other animals, using the soul of the snowshoes to walk upon the soul of the snow." Father Le Jeune then asked: when they kill the soul of a beaver, does that soul die entirely, or does it have another soul which goes to yet another village? He received a curt response: "Be silent, thou hast no sense [*esprit*]; thou askest things which thou dost not know thyself; if I had ever been in yonder country, I would answer thee." But once again, the Jesuit could not let things lie, and now, finally fed up, he offered a full rebuttal. "Europeans navigated the whole world," he said, and no one had ever found the alleged village of souls, which was a bunch of nonsense. Only human souls are immortal, and if they are good they go to heaven, if they are bad they descend into hell, "there to burn forever," each according to his works.[109]

What is remarkable about this exchange is the way natural knowledge is so imbricated with religious belief. A material understanding of souls cannot be correct, Le Jeune asserts, because material souls would drown in the deep ocean, or freeze in the cold north; they would be unable to see in the dark, and their village would be found by travelers. Of course, by exactly the same argument, Christian souls could not burn in hell—an objection in fact raised, at almost exactly the same time, by the Italian freethinker and materialist-atheist Giovanni Francesco Loredan[110]—but the Christian answer would be much the same as the Innu: you are an ignoramus, of course souls are not like us, the same rules do not apply. Yet for the Jesuits, the very act of trying to distinguish Christian belief from worldly knowledge relied upon the resources of material skepticism: in trying to make materialist religion more spiritual, Father Le Jeune met his interlocutors halfway and made Christianity more material, its beliefs connected to the same epistemology that comprehended the depth of oceans and the temperature of the frozen north.

Sometimes the Jesuits bluntly doubted spiritual effects whose causes they could not see. So, for instance, when the Wyandot insisted that the *Manitou*, or devil, "caused sickness and death," the Jesuits pleaded material causes: "It is not the *Manitou* that spoils these organs, but too great cold, too much heat, excess of any kind. Dost thou not feel thyself burn when thou hast drunk brandy? That consumes thy liver and dries it up, it impairs the other internal organs, and causes sickness, which, becoming more aggravated, entirely destroys some organ;

whence it happens that thy soul goes away, thou art dead, and this without the *Manitou* having touched thee."[111] For another example, when the harvest god *Iouskeha* was reported in 1636 to be thin and sad, it was taken as "an indubitable sign of a very bad year." In response, the Jesuits were indignant: "The fun of it is, no one can be found in the country who will say, 'I have seen him,' or 'I have spoken to a man that has seen him'; and yet every one deems this an indubitable fact [*croit cecy comme une chose indubitable*], and no man takes the trouble to make a more searching inquiry into the truth of it."[112]

A more searching inquiry: here is the key.[113] The real problem the Jesuits had in converting indigenous people was not that they were too materialist to believe in things unseen, but rather that they were so spiritual that Jesuit attempts to undermine their religion by invoking profane epistemology were ineffective. So, when the Wyandot recounted one of their creation myths—which involved the founder of the human race, who lived on an island along with a fox and a marten—a Jesuit challenged the myth on rationalist grounds: "How [could he] become the father of all these nations, since he was alone and had no companion?" They responded, "We do not know; we were told so; our fathers never taught us any more about it." This was the very essence of belief, as the Jesuits were forced to admit: "This solution . . . would not be bad, if their religion were good."[114]

At the heart of these interactions was the fact that conversion required judgment: people had to be convinced to believe. If one part of judgment depended upon empirical evidence, another part depended upon the reliability of testimony: the Jesuits had to convince the indigenous peoples that they themselves were credible witnesses. Raw power played its part: "The more imposing the power of our French people is made in these countries, the more easily they can make their belief [*creance*] received by these barbarians."[115] Yet natural knowledge also made an unexpected appearance, because the foremost proof the Jesuits could offer of their own credibility was their knowledge of material things. So, for instance, in December 1637, the Jesuits successfully predicted a lunar eclipse, which "gave us great repute here, securing approval of what we believe."[116] A more elaborate example occurred when an Innu man asked Father Le Jeune about geography. Le Jeune drew a map of the earth, "and after having traced Europe, Asia and Africa, I came to our America, showing him that it is an immense Island. I described for him the coast of Acadia, the great Island of Newfoundland, the entrance and gulf of our great river Saint Lawrence, the people who inhabit its banks." Having listened, the man exclaimed, "This black robe tells the truth . . . for we are acquainted with the greater part of these lands and tribes, and thou hast described them as they are." Le Jeune then laid his cards on the table: "As I am truthful in speaking about things of the earth, also thou shouldst persuade thyself that I am not lying when I speak to thee about the things of heaven; and therefore thou oughtst believe [*croire*] what I have told thee about the other life."[117]

We are finding here the origins of what Amos Funkenstein described as "secular theology" in the seventeenth century: "Theological concerns were expressed in terms of secular knowledge, and scientific concerns were expressed in theological terms. Theology and other sciences became almost one."[118] Necessity is the mother of invention, and unlike in France or Mexico where belief could so easily be reduced to a form of obedience, in Canada the Jesuits had to invent new ways of believing. Forced by circumstances to be no less skeptical than their countryman Michel de Montaigne, the Catholic Church's own emissaries left the Counter-Reformation project in tatters. Modern belief had emerged.

CHAPTER SIX

Enlightened Belief

IN WHAT SENSE did René Descartes believe in God? The point of asking is not to question *whether* he believed, like contemporaries who saw the specter of atheism in his mechanical philosophy, but rather to underline the novelty of *how* he believed.

When Descartes questioned the foundations of all knowledge in his *Discourse on Method* (1637) and *Meditations* (1641), he ostensibly exempted Christianity from his investigations. Because the path to heaven "is open no less to the most ignorant than to the most learned," and because "the revealed truths which lead to it are beyond our understanding," he would not dare submit Christian truths to his weak powers of reasoning.[1] Descartes also practiced obedience, deleting defenses of heliocentrism from his writings after he learned of the Church's condemnation of Galileo; given his voluntarism, we might generously stipulate that he was not a hypocrite but instead convinced himself to believe with the Church.[2] Nonetheless, in his famous experiments in radical doubt, Descartes manifestly submitted authoritative religious truths to the judgment of his own mind, rather than submitting his own mind to the judgment of authority. He could not have done otherwise. His desire to believe only things that were certain and indubitable, and to treat uncertain knowledge as if it were false, created a compelling need for him to generate a beneficent God from first principles, as a rock upon which other knowledge could be built.[3] Without that firm foundation, nothing could be certain outside his own mind. Descartes escaped solipsism by reasoning that if his mind could conceive of a being more perfect than itself, then that being must have a real referent, because his mind could not have constructed it from its own inferior resources. And from the premise that all deceit flows from some defect, he concluded that such a perfect being could not be a deceiver, hence God does not systematically pervert human senses. Descartes therefore established, from his own internal resources, the credibility not only of God but of the external world.

Descartes's decision to submit the Church's dogma to the judgment of his own mind was therefore not contingent but absolutely central. His argument for God's existence was not simply one example from a list of things he could prove rationally, but rather was the wellspring of all argument, the fundamental theorem that allowed him to establish secure knowledge in other fields. The whole ground of judgment, for Descartes, was the mind's capacity to discover a truth external to itself; only after independently proving that God exists could he believe anything else. Descartes's belief in God thus challenged not only the post-Tridentine emphasis on belief as an act of obedience, but also the framework of his hero St. Anselm—on whose "ontological argument" he based his reasoning—who had famously declared that we "believe in order to understand." For Descartes, complex acts of ratiocination must necessarily *precede* belief, and the individual reasoning person must believe for himself if belief is to have any meaning.[4]

Descartes rode the crest of a wave that was about to break over European Christianity. If the early seventeenth century had introduced Christians to the idea that belief was sovereign judgment, then the problem necessarily arose of how that judgment should be exercised: on what grounds should I believe? The question of *criteria*, while crucial in the fields of law and logic, simply had not attracted much attention previously in the domain of religious belief.[5] In a world where epistemology focused on demonstrable certainties, and where religious belief focused on obedience to authorities or trust in God, individual judgment had most often been dismissed as mere opinion, a failure to recognize the overarching circumstances that removed judgment from human hands. Even to the extent that authorities conflicted with one another, the role of the interpreter was to locate the most properly authoritative voices rather than to develop an independent opinion.[6] But with the emergence of an alternative space of belief that privileged human judgment rather than condemning it, the question was inescapable: how could individuals navigate competing claims to religious knowledge?

The answers occupied the space where belief met the Enlightenment—less the so-called radical Enlightenment than the vast new project of more mainstream thinkers to reestablish Christianity on new grounds. The Enlightenment was a heterogeneous movement—an Italian in the 1730s, for instance, described a five-cornered war between Aristotelians, Spinozists, Lockeans, Cartesians, and Leibnizians—with many geographical and chronological variants.[7] Certainly there was no single Enlightenment understanding of how judgment should be exercised: different figures and schools disagreed about the capabilities of reason, about the relationship between reason and experience, and much else besides. But they nevertheless shared, against the confessional framework, a common aspiration to privilege the subjectivity of the individual whose belief remained free. Over the course of the century between 1650 and 1750, as Enlightenment thinkers eroded the scholastic architecture of the mind, ancient distinctions between belief, knowledge, and opinion collapsed in the face of the sovereign believing subject. As they deflated the bloated claims of dogmatism, they preserved the category of Christian belief while at the same time perforating that category and leaving it open to the profane beliefs of the world.

⟨━━━◆※◆━━━⟩

I began with Descartes because he so influentially posed the question: on what grounds should I believe? Perhaps the most historically significant part of Descartes's answer was to focus resolutely on the internal resources of the believer. As Klaus Scholder puts it, "For Descartes, the thinking subject takes the place of the object to be thought as the given starting point for philosophizing."[8] It is crucial here that Descartes was not a theologian: one of the most profound transformations he set in motion was that, by making belief a resource of the self rather than an artifact of doctrine, he raised the possibility for Christian belief to transcend theology. It is no accident that, in our search for discussions of the nature of belief, the era from Aquinas to Descartes has focused mostly on clerics, while the era from Descartes to Kant will include scientists, philosophers, artists, mathematicians, and other laypeople. As Jonathan Sheehan writes, "The Enlightenment engagement with God . . . would take place in a wildly expanded set of cultural and intellectual registers."[9] Crucial to that engagement was a new space of belief where the function of the believer was to judge rather than submit to judgment.

But another controversial part of Descartes's answer was to focus on rigorous, a priori reasoning as the ground of belief, blurring the distinction between belief and knowledge upon which so many of his predecessors had insisted. Descartes's rationalism generated a profound debate over what kinds of resources the believer might bring to bear.[10] Much of this chapter will explore different parts of that debate, including critiques of reason, but we must begin with a foundational disagreement among the so-called rationalists. On one side were those who imagined reason as a technology of discernment: Christians must necessarily believe unreasonable things, but reason could tell you which unreasonable things to believe. On the other side were those who imagined reason to be constitutive of belief, so that belief and knowledge converge.

In the Catholic world, the former position runs through Jansenism. Inspired by the teachings of Cornelius Jansen (1585–1638), Professor of Biblical Exegesis at the University of Leuven and later Bishop of Ypres, Jansenism placed human depravity at the center of the Catholic theology of atonement. Jansen's disciples, like Jean Duvergier and Antoine Arnauld, also denied free will in salvation, insisting that God's grace cannot be resisted and strongly implying that Christ died only for the elect. This quasi-Calvinism does not make the Jansenists sound like good candidates for a "rationalist" understanding of belief. But some of the Jansenists at their stronghold of Port Royal Abbey in Paris also acquiesced to Descartes's powerful new argument that the quality of our reason shapes our capacity for ethical action; their spiritual puritanism combined with Cartesian rationalism made for a potent but unstable compound.[11]

The occasion for its combustion was the condemnation of five propositions in Jansen's posthumously published tome *Augustinus* (1640) by Pope Innocent X in 1653. Arnauld and his colleagues dutifully accepted that the pope had de jure authority to determine heresy: if the pope said that a proposition should not be believed, then it should not be believed. However, they argued that the Church had no authority over matters of fact. So, while they agreed that they *would* disclaim the five condemned doctrines if those were found in Jansen's book, the Jansenists argued that on their own reading the book contained no such doctrines, and the pope had no authority to tell them that it did. In the controversy that followed, the doctrinal issue of grace and free will thus quickly faded into the background, replaced by a long conflict over the role of individual reason in religion. That is, the Jansenists, despite their generally pessimistic view of humanity, committed themselves to the position that there was an alternative kind of belief, based on individual judgment, that ran parallel to the kind of belief that consisted in obedience to the Church. They thus proposed a version of Catholic belief that privileged the individual finder of fact.[12]

The centerpiece of this view was *La logique, ou, l'art de penser* (1662), colloquially known as the Port Royal Logic, by Antoine Arnauld and Pierre Nicole. A true cornerstone of the Enlightenment, *La logique* effectively supplanted Aristotle's *Organum* for the first time as the standard textbook of philosophical reasoning in European universities. After hundreds of pages of more or less formal logic, the authors abruptly turned to the criteria of belief, declaring that there are "two general ways which lead us to believe that a thing is true":

> The first is, the knowledge which we have of it ourselves, from having known and sought out its truth, whether by our senses or by our reason. This may be called, generally, reason, since the senses themselves depend on the judgment of reason—or science, taking that term more generally than it is taken in the schools, for all the knowledge of an object derived from the object itself. The other way is the authority of persons worthy of credence, who assure us that such a thing is, although we ourselves know nothing

about it. This is called faith or belief [*creance*], according
to the expression of St. Augustine—*Quod scimus debemus
rationi; quod credimus autoritati.*[13]

We have seen this quotation from Augustine before: it was
the claim in *De Utilitate Credendi* that formed the basis of
so much Catholic argument that belief derives from authority. But Arnauld and Nicole had transformed the meaning of
this famous dictum, even before it was uttered, by introducing
both reasonable knowledge and assent to authority as parallel
"ways which lead us to believe that a thing is true." That is,
these were both subsets of a higher-order belief. In the Port
Royal Logic, then, belief is an individual judgment reached
after weighing evidence: the difference between the first and
the second methods consists in the kind of evidence weighed,
where the latter is the evidence of testimony. In Christian
belief, when reason and the senses are insufficient, we judge
whether revelation is credible. The similarity here to the Arminians is obvious, although incongruous given their incompatible theologies; perhaps Arnauld and Nicole had been
reading Tommaso Campanella instead.

A key purpose of this section of the Port Royal Logic was to
propose rules of discernment: when does reason demand that
testimony should be believed? The answer was that "it is necessary to pay attention to all the circumstances," both the "internal" facts of the matter and the "external" quality of the evidence attesting it. If a fact is unlikely, then its witnesses must
be exceptionally credible; if a witness is incredible, then the
fact attested must be exceptionally likely. Belief rightly occurs
when "all the circumstances are such, that it never or rarely
happens that the like circumstances are the concomitants of
falsehood."[14] The qualifier "or rarely" [*ou fort rarement*] is crucial: this is a probabilistic calculus rather than a demand for

assurance. While the Port Royal Logic employed a hierarchy of knowledge-claims ranging from "metaphysical certainty" to "moral certainty" to mere "probability," it carefully avoided linking "belief" to one of these more than the others. In sum, while the authors insisted that Catholics are sometimes right to believe authorities despite their apparent defiance of reason, they must not believe authorities blindly, like the followers of false religions; rather, Christians must only "bring our understanding into captivity to the obedience of Jesus Christ" when they have "sufficient proofs" that it is "a reasonable action" to do so.[15]

While ostensibly orthodox, this profound new emphasis on individual judgment would prove powerfully disruptive. As Arlette Farge has argued, Jansenism was at the heart of the emergence of "public opinion" in eighteenth-century France: "Once one had admitted that individuals were capable of thinking about the church and about Jansenism, one realized perforce that they could have opinions on *any* aspect of public life."[16] In particular, beginning in 1728, the wildly popular Jansenist newspaper *Les nouvelles ecclésiastiques* openly insisted that ordinary men and women had a natural, intellectual capacity to enter theological debate over the 1713 papal bull *Unigenitus*, which had condemned Jansenist heresies. Thus, the Jansenist model of belief provided an unusually early and explicit archetype for what was to become a touchstone of the Enlightenment, the competence of individuals to judge within "new spaces where every man was his own arbitrator." As Farge puts it, there emerged "an ever growing conviction that people had a right to know and to judge. This, in the eighteenth century, was something new: thinking about things might be forbidden, but it was also, and triumphantly, legitimate."[17]

Against these early Enlightenment writers who saw "reason" as a resource to help believers judge what to believe, another very different post-Cartesian position suggested we should believe whatever leads us to the rational truths of philosophy. Here the most influential example was Baruch Spinoza, famous for describing God as the necessary unfolding of nature rather than a being with will and purpose. On this logic, there could be no miracles: God cannot act against the order of nature, because God *is* the order of nature. With this necessitarian metaphysics in mind, Spinoza equated belief with understanding, insisting that on metaphysical matters it is impossible to believe further than we understand. Against those who argued that "there is no need to understand God's attributes, but only believe them"—virtually all of the Jewish and Christian traditions!—Spinoza answered that this position was literally nonsensical, because "invisible things, which are objects of the mind alone, can not be seen with any other eyes than through conceptual demonstrations." Therefore, people who "do not grasp the demonstrations, see nothing at all of these things, and therefore whatever they report from hearsay about such questions, neither affects nor indicates their minds any more than the words of a parrot."[18] People might say that they believe something without understanding it, but in fact all that they believe is the part that they understand.

So how can this rationalism be squared with Spinoza's equally famous and controversial claim that we must believe pious dogmas rather than true ones, even if what we believe is false? The answer lies in the deconstruction of biblical interpretation in Spinoza's toweringly heretical *Tractatus Theologico-Politicus* (1670).[19] There had been radical reconsiderations of the Bible before, not least Thomas Hobbes's 1651 *Leviathan*, followed by Lodewijk Meyer's 1666 *Philosophy as the Interpreter of Holy Scripture*, both of which used "reason" to undermine traditional interpretations. While Hobbes insisted that reason teaches the hermeneutic authority of the political sovereign, Meyer insisted that reason itself *is* the hermeneutic authority, so that, for instance, creation *ex nihilo* was impossible and the doctrine of the trinity was a meaningless jumble of words.[20] Building on these arguments, Spinoza radically distinguished the philosophical truth of the Bible—its moral *message*, that we must obey God and love our neighbor—from the factual credibility of the Bible, which, Spinoza suggested, to the general astonishment of Europe, was extremely limited. Spinoza argued that scripture was written by flawed human beings, with limited understanding, whose reporting of events was clouded by emotion and interpretation. Those writings were then corrupted as they passed through subsequent generations of transmission. The result is that, while the ethical message of scripture is certain because it accords with reason, the facts of scripture, and the words in which it is written, are riddled with errors.[21] Spinoza thus argued that divine law does not require *"fidem historiarum"*: historical belief in scripture gives us "no knowledge of God, nor consequently love of God either."[22] This was a revolution not only against traditional interpretation but also against the newer, probabilistic arguments of Grotius and the Arminians.

But that does not mean that Spinoza denounced belief in the Bible. On the contrary, he accepted that reaching the rational truth of scripture often required believing the stories of the Bible, in all their baroque irrationality, along the way. Belief in scriptural history, he wrote, is necessary for "ordinary people" [*vulgo*] whose lack of philosophical training means that they are "not competent to perceive things clearly and distinctly"—a philosophical term of art for rational certainty— and who therefore require stories to teach them moral truths.[23] For the philosophically competent, however, those truths can be deduced rationally rather than accepted on report. By this argument, vulgar belief in revelation, when placed properly, is not irrational at all but arrives exactly where reason says it should. Reason and belief converge.

It was in this seemingly paradoxical sense that Spinoza's "belief" was hyper-rationalist even while he admitted belief in irrational things: the content of all true religious belief is reducible to philosophy, even if philosophy and theology are radically different things and in practice most people reach truth non-philosophically. For instance, whether I believe factually in a Bible story, like Moses parting the Red Sea, is entirely beside the point, because the essence of belief happens at the next level of abstraction, where the brute facts of the perceived world yield to the absolute truths of reason. I believe correctly if my belief in Moses parting the Red Sea leads me to the philosophical truth of love and obedience; but philosophy might produce that same correct belief without Moses entering into it at all, while contrariwise I might *wrongly* believe in Moses parting the Red Sea if that belief leads me to cruelty and rebellion instead. So, to return to Descartes's question—on what grounds should I believe?—according to Spinoza, reason dictates that people must believe whatever doctrine produces in them the kind of piety that is the essence of true, rational religion.

In the Port Royal Logic and Spinoza's *Tractatus*, we see two very different sides of rationalism already emerging by the 1670s, both fruits of Descartes's efforts to ground proper belief in the resources of the human mind. On the one hand, we have a *structure of discernment*: reason is the faculty that adjudicates between conflicting claims on our belief. On the other hand, we have a *principal of construction*: reason is the stuff belief is made of and the goal belief seeks. These two visions would resonate into the eighteenth century. The former position was taken up, for instance, in Gottfried Wilhelm Leibniz's "principle of sufficient reason"—a theory of intelligibility, that even contingent truths would be reasonable if their conditions were known—which undergirds his *Theodicy*, and on which he clashed with the necessitarianism of Spinoza. A generation later, it can be found in the *Logic* of Christian Wolff, Leibniz's successor as the foremost philosopher in Germany, who suggested that both secular and Christian knowledge are syllogistic and deductive—"doctrines propounded in scripture may be divided into the very same classes of truths into which the secular or natural are, and hence may with great benefit be examined in the same manner"—differing only in the sources of their premises.[24] The latter, more radical position can be found in the deist arguments of the Irishman John Toland, whose *Christianity not Mysterious* (1696) was burned by the public hangman in Dublin for suggesting that Christianity contains nothing that could not be deduced from natural principles, hence revelation is irrelevant to religion.[25] It can commonly be found thereafter among the *philosophes* of the high Enlightenment in France. Both alternatives, however powerful their differences, conspired to make Christian belief a product of individual ratiocination, like other kinds of knowledge-claims.

<hr/>

Insofar as the Port Royal Logic was probabilistic, weighing preponderances of evidence without definitive proof, it appears to prefigure another great monument of Jansenist scholarship, the posthumously published *Pensées* (1670) of the illustrious philosopher and mathematician Blaise Pascal. This resemblance is not a coincidence: Pascal was a close associate of Arnauld and Nicole and may well have contributed to *La logique*. But the oddity is that, while the Port Royal Logic is usually associated with rationalism, the *Pensées* are associated with anti-rationalism: "The heart has its reasons of which reason knows nothing." They are similar in that both want to explain why we should believe unreasonable things. But while the Port Royal Logic offers reasonable criteria for judgment, Pascal uses the *absence* of reasonable criteria as the fundamental datum that our reason must judge. Considering the *Pensées* thus gives us an opportunity to consider how fideism—the turn to faith in the ruins of certainty—fared in the century after Montaigne.

Around 1655, the Port Royal priest Isaac Louis Lemaistre de Saci sat down with Pascal to discuss the skepticism of Montaigne. If the reminiscence of Saci's secretary is to be believed, Pascal's admiration for the author of the *Essais* was mixed with revulsion. Of particular concern was that Montaigne, far from being a "disciple of the Church by faith" as he claimed, instead "acts like a pagan": "From the premise that without faith everything is uncertain, and that so many search for the true and the good without achieving any degree of tranquility, he concludes that one ought to leave the matter to others." That is, much to Pascal's frustration, Montaigne's fideism was what the modern critic Terence Penulhum calls *conformist* fideism, abdicating individual judgment in favor of tradition and authority.[26] For Montaigne, Pascal continued, "since the probabilities on both sides are equal, precedent and convenience overcome the balance and determine his conduct. Hence he conforms to the customs of his country because it is easy; he mounts his horse, like those who are not philosophers, simply because the horse permits him to do so. Yet he mounts it without believing that he has a right to do so."[27] Pascal thus regarded Montaigne's version of fideism as no more than a simulacrum: the path of least resistance is a sign of bad faith.

So how did the fideist Pascal differ from the fideist Montaigne? Throughout his sprawling *Pensées*, Pascal vehemently insists that there is insufficient reason to believe—in God, in religion, in virtually any proposition—given the inadequacies of reason and the senses. In this he is much like Montaigne. But on the question of God he also insists, with equal vehemence, that there is insufficient reason *not* to believe, and therein lies Pascal's central paradox: "It is incomprehensible that God should exist, and it is incomprehensible that he should not exist."[28] This was more radical than many of Pascal's predecessors, including Descartes, because not only God's attributes but God's existence is inaccessible to reason. "Let us now speak according to natural lights," he tells us. "If there is a God, he is infinitely incomprehensible, since, having neither parts nor limits, he has no affinity to us. We are then incapable of knowing either what he is or if he is. This being so, who will dare to undertake the decision of the question? Not we, who have no affinity to him."[29] God is neither credible nor incredible, since the created universe provides enough information neither to believe nor to disbelieve. Pascal is clear that God has designed nature this way on purpose: to frustrate the verdict of reason.[30]

Faced with this contradiction, Pascal condemns Montaigne's skepticism as wrongheaded, acknowledging one-half of a dialectic at the expense of the other. Montaigne cannot sidestep the question of belief, however much he tries: he cannot help but believe or disbelieve. Hence Pascal's famous wager, and its substitution of one kind of reason for another: instead of reason functioning as a technology of discernment, reason tells us what to do when our discernment fails. We are all betting on the question of God's existence: "You must wager. It is not optional. You are embarked." Either "God is, or he is not," but no appeal to reason can solve the question; indeed, reason will be equally offended by either choice. So how should we choose? The method Pascal proposes is "to weigh the gain and the loss in wagering that God is." The potential payoff of believing in God's existence is "an infinity of an infinitely happy life," which outweighs any possible risk of loss.

Thus, while belief in God cannot possibly result from a rea-
soned weighing of evidence, reason requires you to believe in
God anyway. What is probative for Pascal is not the evidence
of God, but the context of man.[31]

So Pascal was certainly a fideist rather than a rationalist,
arguing that the demands of faith exceed what can be deduced
from reason. But his paradoxical use of reason to reach that
conclusion launched a powerful current in modern Christianity, to be found, for instance, in Søren Kierkegaard's ideas of
the "leap to faith" and the "teleological suspension of the ethical": whatever reason may dictate in any particular situation,
the general context—a universe that makes no sense without
God—dictates that reason should yield to faith. That is, the
fideist does not *lack* reason to believe, she simply believes for
different sorts of reasons, no less dependent than Descartes on
the internal resources of the believing subject. Modern belief
was thus not simply the victory of rationalism: important instantiations of fideism also privileged the subjective judgment
of individuals to determine what sort of reasons they find most
probative. Pascal was, in his own way, as much an apostle of
modern belief as the rationalists. As he put it in a pensée called
"Authority": "So far from making it a rule to believe a thing because you have heard it, you ought to believe nothing without
putting yourself into the position as if you had never heard it.
It is your own assent to yourself, and the constant voice of your
own reason, and not of others, that should make you believe."[32]

Fideism: doctrine that
knowledge depends
on faith / revelation

While rationalists were blurring the distinction between belief
and knowledge, a different set of arguments blurred the distinction between belief and opinion. Instead of insisting upon
a priori reason, this alternative species of belief privileged

reason a posteriori which judged from experience. To trace the origins of this empirical understanding of belief, we must return to our story of *fides historica*, and the emergence of ever more robust and sophisticated arguments that believing the historical truth of Christianity was equivalent to being a Christian believer. This connection between empiricism and history is essential: history provided the template for belief that was provisional rather than certain.[33]

Trust in historical knowledge was a significant problem for Descartes and his followers in France, who argued that historians have no knowledge of objects in themselves but only unreliable hearsay supplied by others.[34] The issue subsequently leapt into prominence in Germany: following Johann Eisenhart's *De Fide Historica* (1679), leading German academics like Johann Ryssel and Christian Thomasius published treatises debating the credibility of historical witnesses and the status of "moral certainty." The religious dimension of their debate was never far from the surface: Hermann Conring, for instance, in a letter to his pupil Eisenhart, noted that "today every revealed religion rests on the certainty of human faith (*certitudini humanae fidei innixa sit*)."[35] But the story of historical knowledge as it relates to Christian "belief" is native to England, because it was there—first during the reign of Charles I from 1625 to 1640, and then more permanently after the failure of the puritan revolution in 1660—that Arminianism, previously a dissident movement, became for the first time the dominant theology of one of Europe's major Churches.[36] English Arminians, following in the footsteps of Thomas Jackson and Hugo Grotius, expanded their defenses of historical faith and more generally argued for a less demanding and more inclusive understanding of what it meant to believe. Historians of science have referred to them as the "royal society group"; it would be more accurate to call them the Arminian group, and then to notice how interesting it is that so many of these Anglican ministers were also scientists.

Consider one of their progenitors, William Chillingworth (1602–1644): godson of the Arminian Archbishop William Laud, sometimes accused of Socinianism for, as the later archbishop John Tillotson put it, "no other cause but his worthy and successful attempts to make the Christian religion reasonable." In his influential 1638 work *The Religion of Protestants*, Chillingworth admitted that "historical faith" has much in common with mere "opinion": both are built upon fallible evidence, and both admit stronger or weaker degrees. Yet, rather than concluding that historical faith was therefore insufficient, he instead demanded that "this ill-sounding word, opinion, should be discarded" because its negative connotations undermined the centrality of imperfect or provisional belief for Christianity. According to Chillingworth, God does not require us to believe any conclusion further than the premises deserve. Since the proposition "all the articles of our faith were revealed by God" is an intrinsically historical proposition, it admits only moral certainty rather than absolute certainty; hence God cannot require of us any more than historical faith. Chillingworth attacked those who insisted upon the impossible standard of assurance: those who argue "that it is in vain to believe the gospel of Christ with such a degree of assent as they yield to other matters of tradition" quickly fall into either despair or atheism.[37]

An equally prominent example is Isaac Barrow (1630–1677), poster child for early modern interdisciplinarity, who held an unprecedented number of Cambridge professorships: he was successively professor of Greek, professor of geometry, Lucasian professor of mathematics, and for a brief stint he even substituted for the professor of astronomy. But Barrow's real passion was divinity, and in 1669 he gratefully resigned the Lucasian professorship to the young Isaac Newton so that he could dedicate himself to the service of God. Barrow's *Brief Exposition of the Creed* offered as clear an expression as we are likely to find of the new, semi-official stance of the Church of England: religious belief is an empirical process of weighing evidence. In a remarkable moment, paraphrasing John 14:11, Barrow even claimed that Christ himself said, in effect, "You were not obliged to accept my testimony as true, if it were not also accompanied with other convincing reasons," and hence "believers did then argue themselves into faith upon our savior." Faith, Barrow wrote, is not a product of the will but "a result of judgment and choice." He attacked Augustine, "the father of scholastic distinctions," for his false dichotomy between believing and believing *in*: they both refer merely to "being persuaded" that a proposition is true. More broadly, he noted that "belief" has two simultaneous definitions, "one more general and popular, the other more restrained and artificial." The more commonplace definition is merely "being well persuaded, or yielding a strong assent unto the truth of any proposition . . . So we are said to believe what our sense represents, what good reason infers, what credible authority confirms to us." The more artificial definition, however, distinguishes between different kinds of persuasion, so that belief refers only to "that kind of assent which is grounded merely upon the authority (the dictate or testimony) of some person." According to Barrow, the phrase "I believe" in the Apostles' Creed refers to the "more general and vulgar notion": the assent of the mind to uncertain propositions through reason and the senses.[38]

Now, the question of how far the Arminian belief of the mid-seventeenth century intersects with the Enlightenment is complex, and certainly neither Chillingworth nor Barrow would properly be included in a study of the Enlightenment.

But in their emphasis upon the capacity of the mind to eman-
cipate human beings from bondage, and in their explicit rejection of so much theological subtlety as irrational obfuscation,
these Arminians paved the way for later discourses of belief.
We need not accept that the Arminians were tolerant or irenic
in order to realize that, as Martin Mulsow and Jan Rohls have
suggested, they were conduits between the precocious rationality of Socinianism and the early Enlightenment.[39] As J.G.A.
Pocock notes, Arminianism bled into these other movements
at the point where "the doctrine that humans might be saved
through the exercise of human capacity became enlarged to
include the exercise of intellectual capacity for criticism and
debate."[40]

The most influential fruit of their endeavors was John
Locke's *Essay Concerning Human Understanding* (1689),
which confidently discussed belief in terms that would have
been impossible a century earlier. After first defining "probability" as "likeliness to be true" based upon "arguments or
proofs," Locke wrote: "The entertainment the mind gives
this sort of propositions I called belief, assent, or opinion."[41]
While modern readers tend to regard the equation of these
three terms as self-evident, in fact this was the culmination
of a revolution. Locke continued: the rational person must
weigh the credibility of evidence before believing. The evidence of the senses is most convincing, while evidence from
testimony is suspect, and the longer the chain of transmission
the less credible it becomes.[42] Now, Locke admitted, there is
one sort of testimony that demands absolute assent without
any judgment or weighing of evidence: the testimony of God.
However, we must be sure that testimony is really from God,
and that we understand it correctly, before granting assent,
otherwise we are left vulnerable to enthusiasm and error.
Thus, even concerning divine revelation, "our assent can be

rationally no higher than the evidence of its being a revelation, and that this is the meaning of the expressions it is delivered in." In sum, Locke wrote, "He that believes without having any reason for believing, may be in love with his own fancies; but neither seeks truth as he ought, nor pays the obedience due to his maker . . . For he governs his assent right, and places it as he should, who, in any case or matter whatsoever, believes or disbelieves according as reason directs him. He that does otherwise, transgresses against his own light, and misuses those faculties which were given him to no other end, but to search and follow the clearer evidence and greater probability."[43]

Locke expanded these arguments in *The Reasonableness of Christianity* (1695). After unceremoniously dismissing any idea that "believing *in*" was stronger or different from mere belief, he declared that to believe in Jesus Christ is simply to believe "that Jesus was the Messiah, giving credit to the miracles he did, and the profession he made of himself . . . This was the great proposition that was then controverted concerning Jesus of Nazareth, whether he was the Messiah or no; and the assent to that, was that which distinguished believers from unbelievers."[44] The whole thrust of Locke's argument was to reduce Christian belief to assent to this proposition, no different from any other truth-claim. This did not make propositional assent the whole of Christianity; Locke emphasized that repentance is equally necessary, which is why the devils cannot be saved despite believing—a new solution to an old theological problem.[45] But assent to this single proposition was nonetheless the entirety of Christian belief:

> To this, 'tis likely, it will be objected by some, that to believe only that Jesus of Nazareth is the Messiah, is but an historical, and not a justifying or saving faith. To which I answer: that I allow to the makers of systems and their followers,

to invent and use what distinctions they please; and to call things by what names they think fit. But I cannot allow to them, or to any man, an authority to make a religion for me, or to alter that which God hath revealed. And if they please to call the believing that which our savior and his apostles preached and proposed alone to be believed, an historical faith, they have their liberty. But they must have a care how they deny it to be a justifying or saving faith, when our savior and his apostles have declared it so to be, and taught no other which men should receive, and whereby they should be made believers unto eternal life; unless they can so far make bold with our savior, for the sake of their beloved systems, as to say, that he forgot what he came into the world for.[46]

{~~~~~~~~~}

For these empiricists, Christian belief resembled opinion: judgment, with varying degrees of certitude, forged in contact with probative but non-demonstrative evidence.[47] But by the same token, other sorts of non-demonstrative claims, particularly claims about the natural world, were beginning to look a lot more like Christian belief. An important novelty of the Enlightenment, at least in its anti-Cartesian guise, was the equation of scientific theories with belief rather than knowledge. This innovation was not, originally, what it would much later become: a response by theologians hoping to dethrone science's normative claims. On the contrary, it was the work of scientists themselves, who found in probabilist theology the resources to defend the legitimacy of experimental hypotheses.[48]

The paradigmatic example was Robert Boyle (1627–1691), who has as much claim as anyone to be the progenitor of experimental science, and who also, not coincidentally, sponsored and bankrolled the translation of Hugo Grotius's *De Veritate Religionis Christianae* into Arabic.[49] In *The Excellency of Theology Compar'd with Natural Philosophy* (1674), Boyle wrote, "Even in many things that are looked upon as physical demonstrations, there is really but a moral certainty." He took as his example the argument by "Descartes and other modern philosophers"—the villains in his account of inductive reasoning—that "there are diverse comets that are not meteors." As Boyle archly noted, Descartes and his colleagues "had never the opportunity to observe a comet in their lives"; instead, they accepted evidence "upon the credit of those astronomers that had such opportunities," with the result that, though the argument pretends to a demonstrable certainty, in fact it has "but an historical one." Boyle wrote:

> The presumed physico-mathematical demonstration can produce in a wary mind but a moral certainty, and not the greatest neither of that kind that is possible to be attained; as he will not scruple to acknowledge, that knows by experience, how much more difficult it is, than most men imagine, to make observations about such nice subjects, with the exactness that is requisite for the building of an undoubted theory upon them. And there are I know not how many things in physics, that men presume they believe upon physical and cogent arguments, wherein they really have but a moral assurance.[50]

These and similar sentiments are often quoted in connection with Boyle's views on scientific epistemology: Boyle regarded hypotheses not as theorems to be proved but as "superstructures, looked upon only as temporary ones, which . . . may be preferred before any others, as being the least imperfect, or, if you please, the best in their kind that we yet have."[51] What has not received equal attention, however, is what it meant when

Boyle declared that such imperfect hypotheses should nonetheless be believed.

Boyle repeatedly accorded parallel status to "believing" the results of scientific experiment and "believing" the results of religious speculation. Often this involved arguing that hypotheses should not be rejected simply because they appear irrational. So, for instance, in *The Christian Virtuoso* (1690) Boyle argued that "it is very rational to believe" that heavier bodies fall faster than lighter ones, yet "notwithstanding this plausible ratiocination, experience shows us [otherwise]." Likewise, no one "would believe that a light black powder should be able . . . to throw down stone walls," were it not that experience demanded such belief.[52] The point of these examples was that Christian mysteries like the resurrection of the dead were not irrational; nothing that is possible should be dismissed a priori, because the accumulation of further evidence might show that we are making too great a metaphysical claim from limited data.

In other places, Boyle was more explicit that to believe as a scientist and to believe as a Christian were parallel exercises in judgment according to available evidence. In a tract attributed to Boyle on the reconciliation of reason and religion, he described how in science, as in religion, one must first query the credibility of the evidence upon which hypotheses are built. "A skillful astronomer" must examine whether his telescope is trustworthy; only then can he "confidently believe the discoveries it makes him, however contrary to the received theories of the celestial bodies, and to what he himself believed before, and would still, if the telescope did not otherwise inform him." Likewise, "a well qualified inquirer into religions, though he will be very wary, upon what terms he admits scripture; yet if he once be fully satisfied, that he ought to admit it, he will not scruple to receive upon its authority whatever supernatural truths it clearly discloses to him; though perhaps contrary to the opinions he formerly held."[53] The results of scientific inquiry are thus believed in much the same way as the results of religious speculation.

A very different argument for the parallel belief-status of religion and science can be found in Pierre Daniel Huet's *Demonstratio Evangelica* (1679), a work of apologetics seeking to demonstrate the historical truth, and therefore the theological truth, of Christianity.[54] Besides being a Catholic priest and a renowned humanist, Huet was co-founder of the provincial *Academie du Physique* in Caen, an avid student of geometry, and an admirer of the inductive method of the Royal Society against *"l'arrogance des dogmatiques."*[55] The *Demonstratio Evangelica* attempted to demonstrate Christian truths in the manner of a rigorous mathematical proof, in defiance of the Cartesians who claimed that history could never be more than opinion. Yet, as April Shelford has noted, quite apart from Huet's fascinating but ultimately misguided attempt to raise sacred history to the level of geometry, just as interesting was his parallel project to lower (although Huet would not have put it that way!) geometry to the level of history. Huet sought to show that there was no such thing as demonstrative science, hence historical faith could not be considered inferior to the claims of mathematics and the mathematical sciences.

Huet argued, like the ancient skeptics, that the axioms upon which geometry is built are not self-evidently true. If geometers defined a line as a length with no breadth, for instance—a concept not even its inventors could conceive in the mind—in what sense were their conclusions secure? Throughout the history of geometry, there had been more dispute over supposedly "demonstrated" conclusions than there had ever been over purely historical conclusions like the fact that

Augustus was emperor of Rome. "Certain moral and practical theses—or, if you prefer, positions or principles that rely on experience or historical credibility—have more who agree with them and fewer who object than geometrical principles do."[56] As Shelford has summarized Huet's argument: "Because geometrical notions were no less based on our experience of the world than 'common notions,' because they were the products of induction from particulars, they could be no more certain. Geometers were not wrong to use them, but they had to accept their lesser certainty. They had to accept, too, that it was possible to construct an equally rigorous and deductive proof from 'common notions.'"[57]

And this is precisely what Huet did, to his own satisfaction at least. He designed a series of simple definitions and axioms—"True Religion," for instance, is that which "has proposed only true things to be believed"—in order to prove that if books describing the historical fulfillment of prophecies are true, then the religion taught by those books is also true.[58] Only then did Huet launch into seven hundred pages of detailed apologetics to establish the historical truth of scriptures. Now, it could be argued that Huet failed in his project, because his definitions and axioms were no more self-evident than those he attacked in the mathematics, thus hoisting himself on his own petard. But this was not a failure, because his argument was that religio-historical proofs were no *less* rigorous than mathematical-scientific ones, and he had already knocked those mathematical-scientific proofs down a peg to the level of conviction based upon reasonable arguments: in other words, belief. Huet had put the claims of religion and the claims of mathematical sciences on an equal level; instead of one resting on rational deduction and the other resting on irrational belief, both were the products of a newly inductive style of believing.

John Locke was also a key player in this drama, for his *Essay Concerning Human Understanding* was committed to the notion that deductive demonstration was impossible in natural philosophy. Locke noted that genuine *scientia* depends upon an understanding of essences, "the being of any thing, whereby it is what it is."[59] In geometry, for instance, we understand the essence of a circle because anything that has that quality is a circle, and any circle has that quality. More surprisingly, Locke also wrote that there were moral examples of scientia, for example, "No government allows absolute liberty": "The idea of government being the establishment of society upon certain rules or laws which require conformity to them; and the idea of absolute liberty being for any one to do whatever he pleases; I am as capable of being certain of the truth of this proposition as of any in the mathematics."[60] Concerning objects in the world, however, we have no capacity for scientia, because all our information comes from the senses. We can learn a great deal about gold by studying it, for instance, but if we were capable of demonstrative knowledge, "it would be no more necessary that gold should exist, and that we should make experiments upon it, than it is necessary for the knowing the properties of a triangle, that a triangle should exist in any matter, the idea in our minds would serve for the one as well as the other."[61]

Locke thus declared that the natural world cannot be known, only approached. "Rational and regular experiments" can permit us to "see further into the nature of bodies, and guess righter at their yet unknown properties, than one that is a stranger to them; but yet, as I have said, this is but judgment and opinion, not knowledge and certainty."[62] Locke provided many examples of how natural knowledge partakes of belief, particularly when he distinguished "grounds of probability" based upon our own observation from "grounds of probability" built upon the testimony of others. Since we cannot observe all things ourselves, our judgment of natural things depends upon how testimony relates to our experience. If someone tells me that a man walked across a frozen river in winter, I am likely to believe it, because it corresponds to my experience of cold; but to the King of Siam, "whose experience has always been quite contrary, and who has never heard of anything like it, the most untainted credit of a witness will scarce be able to find belief."[63]

Thus, despite the efforts of Cartesians and Hobbesians, induction and empiricism swept over natural philosophy, and science became a study of the way things are rather than the way things must be. For all that the eighteenth century would see the rise of universalizing claims for scientific rationality, nonetheless that rationality would be represented by concepts like "theory" and "hypothesis," always provisional and incomplete. In the high Enlightenment, no less an observer than Voltaire celebrated (against Pascal) partial knowledge as knowledge indeed: "Let us console ourselves for not knowing the possible connections between a spider and the rings of Saturn, and continue to examine what is within our reach."[64]

The great philosopher of this incompleteness was the Scotsman David Hume, who insisted that all natural knowledge is based upon a finite supply of experience. Hume's 1739 *Treatise of Human Nature*, in a remarkable departure from the unanimous verdict of his predecessors, argued that belief is not assent at all but simply "a lively idea" associated with a "present impression" upon the mind.[65] That is, first there must be an "impression" caused by some external stimulus: a sound is heard, an image is seen. According to Hume's philosophy of induction, experience causes us to associate this impression with particular ideas: for instance, if a sound has on all past occasions coincided with the ringing of a bell, when we hear that sound our mind produces the idea of a bell. But a mere idea is not enough: to constitute belief, it must be a *lively* idea, as if its object were really present.[66] Crucially for Hume, lively ideas do not produce belief, lively ideas *are* belief: belief is simply the strong and present idea of one thing that we conceive when confronted by something else.[67]

This argument produced radical consequences, whether or not we regard Hume as a radical skeptic.[68] Whereas Locke had argued that it is *reasonable* to believe in accordance with a preponderance of evidence, for Hume, belief is not a function of reason at all, but simply of custom or habit.[69] No matter how many times a sound has been associated with bells in the past, its bell-ness is only a matter of probability. And since we cannot know the denominator in this probabilistic equation, not reason but custom makes us believe we are hearing a bell now. As Hume put it, in one of his countless statements of the induction problem: "There can be no demonstrative arguments to prove, that those instances of which we have had no experience, resemble those of which we have had experience."[70] Or elsewhere: "Tis not, therefore, reason which is the guide of life, but custom. That alone determines the mind, in all instances, to suppose the future conformable to the past. However easy this step may seem, reason would never, to all eternity, be able to make it."[71]

From this premise Hume famously argued that it can never be reasonable to believe in miracles. This was not only because all empirical claims are customary rather than reasonable, but because no empirical claim that a law of nature has been violated can ever outweigh the empirical evidence that had established that law of nature; if it did, that would not prove that a genuine law of nature had been broken, but only that we should not have accepted, upon limited evidence, that it was a law of nature in the first place.[72] This view could assume a fideist posture, as when Hume insisted that Christianity is inaccessible to reason: "Whoever is moved by faith to assent to it, is conscious of a continued miracle in his own person, which subverts all the principles of his understanding, and gives him a determination to believe what is most contrary to custom and experience."[73] But in the *Dialogues Concerning Natural Religion*, the relativist implications of his argument became clear. For instance, Hume's mouthpiece proposed as a thought experiment that the world might be a giant vegetable, scattering comets into the cosmos as seeds to produce new worlds. When asked, "What data have you for such extraordinary conclusions?" he produced the answer that was the point of the exercise: "This is the topic on which I have all along insisted. . . . We have no data to establish any system of cosmogony. Our experience, so imperfect in itself, and so limited both in extent and duration, can afford us no probable conjecture concerning the whole of things. But if we must needs fix on some hypothesis, by what rule, pray, ought we to determine our choice?"[74]

To conclude this discussion of the comparable belief-status of nature and religion in the Enlightenment, I do not wish to downplay the significance of subsequent developments in the epistemology of science, nor to pretend that Newton had the same epistemology as Locke or Hume.[75] Rather, my argument is that the Enlightenment forged a truce, as it were, between rationalism and religion on the ground of belief. This truce, assigning parallel epistemological status to very different sorts of claims, was based upon the notion that the world is forever mired in beliefs rather than demonstrable certainties. Thus, when theologians found themselves facing off against scientists in subsequent decades, they were on solid ground when they suggested that science was not a higher form of knowledge, but rather was just another species of belief. This argument, which would have been *literally nonsensical* a century earlier, had become in some sense a truism.[76] Hence Thomas

Jefferson's act for establishing religious freedom in Virginia: "Our civil rights have no dependence on our religious opinions any more than our opinions in physics or geometry."[77]

Some scholars have argued that this truce strained and eventually shattered as the epistemic claims and prestige of science grew.[78] But these arguments presume the vantage of scientists themselves rather than the vantage of laypeople asked to *believe* scientific claims. To the vast majority, new claims about the natural world—evolution, the big bang—do not rest upon a sturdy accumulation of experimental data but upon a series of potentially probative evidences which might sway their judgment: the authority of experts, the fit with spiritual assumptions, the evidence of their own senses. Because laypeople are empowered to believe science just as they are empowered to believe religion, they use their sovereign judgment—often to the dismay of scientists, who wrongly assume that people have only been empowered to trust in expertise. Thus, the truce has bent but never broken, as anyone living in the era of climate-change science can recognize.

⟨⟩

We have so far seen a variety of intellectual projects intended to make sense of a question that today we take for granted: on what grounds should I believe? Seventeenth-century movements like empiricism, fideism, Cartesianism, and Spinozism differed significantly in their understanding of belief, especially whether belief was more like knowledge or more like opinion. Even among Cartesians, Pierre Arnauld and Nicolas Malebranche wrote volumes of polemic against one another.[79] But these various positions shared a surprising amount of genetic material, all fundamentally derived from the novel premise that belief is human judgment.

It is in this light that I want to consider one of the great enigmas of early Enlightenment ideas, Pierre Bayle (1647–1706), a French philosopher of Protestant upbringing who spent most of his career in exile in the Netherlands. Bayle first scandalized the literati in his *Pensées diverses sur la comète* (1682) with the remarkable claim that atheists in history had lived virtuous lives, challenging the premise that religious belief was the foundation of moral order. But Bayle's magnum opus was the *Dictionnaire Historique et Critique*, published in 1697 and then expanded in 1702, which aimed to expose the errors and absurdities that littered theology and philosophy. Bayle's method was to provide succinct and unobjectionable articles on each subject, to which he appended a vast apparatus of footnotes combining the rambling skepticism of Montaigne's *Essais* with the sharp freethinking of Spinoza's *Tractatus*. The result was a vast treasury of demystification which Voltaire later called the "arsenal of the Enlightenment."

Another result, however, was an enduring mystery about how to classify Bayle within the intellectual ecosystem of his era. He has been called, by respectable modern scholars, an atheist, a fideist, a skeptic, a Cartesian, a Calvinist, a Socinian, and much else besides.[80] One possibility is that he hid his real views, and contradicted himself intentionally, to avoid persecution; on this view, the fact that his work so equitably undermined all varieties of religious doctrine must be taken as evidence that he was a closet atheist. But another possibility is that, if we consider Bayle's understanding of belief rather than the content of what he believed, he might resolve into a more coherent thinker at the intersection of different strands of the early Enlightenment project.

Let us begin with Bayle's fideism: his alleged claim that because reason is insufficient to discover religious truths—"Reason is like a runner who doesn't know that the race is over," he wrote—we must believe without reason.[81] Examples are plentiful, like the claim in his article on Spinoza that men lose their religion "from the moment that they seek it by the ways of human reasoning," and his praise of Pascal who "distinguished precisely all of his life the rights of faith from those of reason."[82] But Exhibit A is a series of "Clarifications" which Bayle appended to the second edition of his *Dictionary* to refute allegations of heterodoxy. There he stated that his skepticism could not be taken as an attack on religion, because on matters of revelation "no one should be admitted to examine if we must believe what God commands us to believe."[83] He quoted the ancient Fathers Lactantius and Tertullian to suggest that reason has no place examining the truth of revelation. As Bayle put it, "The merit of faith becomes greater in proportion as the revealed truth, which is its object, surpasses all the forces of our mind." If a belief is repugnant to reason, "we show ourselves more submissive to God, and we give him greater marks of our respect, than if the thing were moderately difficult to believe." The faith of Abraham was so profound because he believed against reason rather than with it: "There would not have been much merit in hoping on a promise of God for something that was naturally very probable [*très-vraisemblable naturellement*]."[84] Bayle thus rejected the whole framework of probabilism, instead stressing the need to triumph over the "temptations of incredulous and arrogant reason."[85] So here, surely, is a fideist.

But not so fast. In the same section, Bayle also pointed in a different direction. If, as he argued, "no one should be admitted to examine if we must believe what God commands us to believe," it follows that what may be examined "is only a question of fact, whether God wants us to believe this or that. Two kinds of people can doubt it: some because they do not believe that scripture is divine, others because they do not believe that

the meaning of the revelation is one thing or another."[86] Here
Bayle is very nearly quoting from Locke's *Essay Concerning
Human Understanding*: while we must believe any revelation
from God, nonetheless "our assent can be rationally no higher
than the evidence of its being a revelation, and that this is the
meaning of the expressions it is delivered in." Bayle refused to
engage with the first question: if one person accepts revealed
authority and another denies it, according to Bayle, they can
only speak past one another. Yet while the *fact* of revelation is
above dispute, the *meaning* of that revelation—what precisely
was revealed—remains open to speculation. And Bayle was a
vicious opponent of all attempts to require one interpretation
over another: each person's beliefs were free.

We have arrived, then, at a plausible pathway into Bayle's
Dictionary that can make sense of how he was *both* the great
fideist who insisted that reason and faith were wholly separate, *and* the great demystifier who so successfully exposed the
absurdities of received religion that he was taken for an atheist. That is, he required every Christian to use their own judgment about what revelation required them to believe. As Anne
Eusterschulte has noted, Bayle's critical technique was not to
relieve the reader of the burden of judgment, like some later
proponents of "reason" in the Enlightenment; rather, "given
the ambiguity of Bayle's demonstrations, the audience is challenged and involved in the process of criticism."[87]

Bayle's article on the biblical figure Abel, for instance, is
both illustrative of his broader method and contains a unique
statement about the intent of that method. After a bare, three-
sentence description of Abel, Bayle writes, "That is all that
Moses teaches us." But, he wryly notes, "if one wished to ex-
tend themselves to all that the curiosity of the human mind
has given rise to, there would be an infinity of things to say."[88]
For instance, we do not know how old Abel was when he was

slain, because we do not know the "duration of the state of innocence," and in a long footnote Bayle mocks attempts by so many divines to render an authoritative verdict. Next, he belittles Augustine's contention that Seth (third son of Adam and Eve) was the restorer of sanctity after the murder of Abel; this is only a matter of conjecture and the words of scripture "leave to our reflections all their natural liberty." Finally, Bayle notes that when the reader finds a jumble of "lies and errors" collected in his remarks concerning Abel, he must remember the purpose of the *Dictionary* is that the reader should pass judgment upon that heap. And he ends, "This is said here one time for all."[89] In this one entry, then, Bayle has allowed his wires to show: he presents absurdities not to foreclose the reader's judgment but to insist upon it.

Bayle had, by any standard, a minimalist view of what revealed religion required: the universe of accreted theology is treated as opinion to be critiqued rather than authority to be accepted. Individual judgment instead constitutes Christian belief, and the way we reach judgment in religion looks a lot like the ways we reach it in other arenas. So, for instance, in his article on Adam, Bayle once again recounts the bare story from scripture, writing, "That is all that we know for certain in this matter"—remember, in Bayle's version of fideism, the *fact* of truthful revelation is above dispute. Yet, he continues by discussing the "probability" of one of the cornerstones of Christian speculation about the relationship between religion and science, Adam's immaculate knowledge in paradise:

An infinity of other things which have been said of [Adam] are either very false, or very uncertain. It is true that some may be judged not to be contrary to the analogy of faith, nor to probability [*probabilité*]. I place in this last category what is said of his vast knowledge. We read nothing in Genesis

which is less fit to give us this idea than to take it away.
Nonetheless, it may be that Adam came out of the hands of
his creator with knowledge infused, and that he did not lose
it by his sin, any more than the wicked angels became less
learned since their fall, or that the crimes of learned men
make them lose the knowledge they possessed.[90]

The whole structure of this argument is a marriage of the
rationalist and the fideist. Having faithfully postulated that
scripture is indeed divine revelation, how might Christians
decide what to believe about that scripture without simply accepting the accumulated drivel of past ages? By weighing the
evidence and choosing the most probable interpretation for
themselves. The point is that for Bayle, as for so many of his
successors, much of what is taken to be skepticism is actually
a novel configuration of belief, now based upon judgment and
offered partially and conditionally rather than absolutely.[91]
Skepticism and fideism are not the opposite of intellective assent, they are the building blocks of a new kind of assent un-
tethered from old assumptions about authority and certainty.

{⸻}

I might be expected to conclude this chapter with a discussion of Immanuel Kant, who is often said to have "reconciled"
Cartesian rationalism with Lockean empiricism, and who proposed "judgment" (*Urteil*) as an innate mental faculty medi-
ating between them. I shall not do so, however, both because I
want to save Kant for the final chapter, and because, as I make
clear there, Kant represents only one idiosyncratic possibility
within a much broader set of outcomes. Instead, I want to conclude this chapter with a very different story, focusing on the
continued development of probabilistic belief.

John Locke's *Essay Concerning Human Understanding* noted what every child today knows from playing "telephone": the more links in a chain of testimony, the less reliable a report becomes. "Each remove weakens the force of the proof: and the more hands the tradition has successively passed through, the less strength and evidence does it receive from them." Never lacking humor, and never above a casual jab at Roman Catholics, Locke used this observation to attack the absurdity of trusting tradition, as if opinions "gain force by growing older." Opinions which "would not, to a rational man . . . have appeared at all probable" somehow grow "venerable by age," and a thousand years later "come, by an inverted rule of probability, to pass for authentic truths."[92]

An English philosopher made this observation, but it took a stubborn Scottish mathematician to attempt the remarkably literal-minded feat of actually calculating the decline of religious credibility. John Craige was a friend of Isaac Newton and an early adopter of the calculus—indeed, Gottfried Wilhelm Leibniz, with tongue firmly in cheek, ranked Craige among the originators of the calculus, ahead of Newton but behind Leibniz himself. Craige knew he was pushing against convention when he wrote his 1699 *Theologiae Christianae Principia Mathematica*, adapting Newton's famous title to claim that there are mathematical principles of Christian theology.[93] "Those who accept completely all the dogmas of religion," he wrote, "will doubtless think that I am undertaking something unsuitable to Christianity in trying to demonstrate its probability [*probabilitatem*]." But, to preempt that criticism, he offered this observation: "Faith is nothing other than that persuasion of the mind, derived from an indeterminate probability, by which we believe certain propositions to be true. If the persuasion arises from certainty, then it is not faith that is being produced, but knowledge. Probability generates faith, but destroys knowledge; certainty, on the other hand, generates knowledge and destroys faith."[94] In John Craige's remarkable project, then, we can find the apotheosis of the new, Enlightenment view that made belief synonymous with judgment rather than metaphysical certainty.

Belief, in Craige's view, is proportional assent to evidence: the stronger the probability for any claim, the firmer the belief. The "velocity of suspicion" is the scientific principle by which, over time, reports become less probable, and belief in their veracity declines. He argued mathematically that "suspicions of the probability of a history, transmitted through any length of time (other things being equal), increase in square ratio to the time passed since the beginning of the history."[95] The similarity of this equation to Newton's law of universal gravitation is perhaps too obvious to require comment. By this logic, belief in a reported truth would decrease rapidly over time, and "although a historical probability may never absolutely disappear, yet in the process of time it becomes so attenuated that the mind is hardly able to perceive its force."[96] Belief, according to Craige, is simply a percentage of mental assent, and when that assent becomes undetectable, even if technically non-zero, we cease to believe. In this model, belief and unbelief are different ways of expressing the same thing, just like probability and improbability.

The ostensible purpose of Craige's treatise was thus to "demonstrate a method for determining the time in which that degree of probability needed to produce a perceptible force on the mind disappears." According to the equation he developed, if belief in Christ were based upon purely oral testimony—and this is clearly a dig at Roman Catholics—it would already have disappeared in the eighth century. But because it is based upon written histories, it will disappear no sooner than the year 3150. Craige concluded that, since Luke 18:8 asks, "When the son of man cometh, shall he find faith on earth?" logically Christ cannot return before that year. His goal was thus to demonstrate "how seriously mistaken are all those who establish the advent of Christ so near to our own times."[97]

Craige's treatise was the object of criticism, and indeed ridicule. The German Johann Burkhard Mencken's popular catalogue of charlatans, *Zwey Reden von der Charlatanerie* (1716), made comedy of Craige's claim that human testimony remains merely probable regardless of divine impulses [*göttlichen Triebe*].[98] David Hume mocked the idea that belief in Julius Caesar had declined over time, while Alexander Pope in the *Dunciad* lampooned the "gloomy clerk . . . whose pious hope aspires to see the day / When moral evidence shall quite decay."[99] On a more serious note, the Jesuit Ignace de Laubrussel, tutor to the future King Louis I of Spain, argued that considerations of the probability of divine truths were fundamentally impious.[100] Yet nonetheless, among Craige's substantive critics—and there were many—it is remarkable how few shared Laubrussel's objection to the premise that belief was judgment according to probabilities. Most of the responses to Craige seem to have argued on his own ground.

The future Bishop of Bath and Wells George Hooper, for instance, submitted a paper to the Royal Society later in 1699 entitled "A Calculation of the Credibility of Human Testimony." Far from denying Craige's premise that belief adheres to calculations of probability, Hooper used the new mathematics of casualty insurance to explain why scripture was even more credible than Craige had argued. Hooper began by measuring the credibility of a witness according to how much insurance you would need to purchase on a proposition guaranteed by his word. For instance, you can imagine a person in whom you have so much confidence that you "would not give above one in six to be insured of the truth of what he says," in other words trusting him to the tune of £1,000 out of a £1,200 bounty. Over time, if this report passed through a series of witnesses each with a five-sixths credibility, the overall credibility would decline exponentially as Craige had suggested: 5/6 in the first generation, 25/36 in the second, and so forth. However, if there are multiple reporters, each fills in a portion of the improbability left by the others. If two distinct witnesses each have 5/6 credibility, their aggregate credibility is not 5/6 but 35/36, because the second witness provides a 5/6 probability to confirm the 1/6 left improbable by the first. By this method, Hooper calculated that if twenty reporters each had a credibility of 1/2, their aggregate credibility would be over two million to one. Hence Christianity will remain credible for an indefinite period because of its cloud of corroborating witnesses.[101]

Another Englishman named Peter Peterson apparently published a full-length rebuttal of Craige in 1701. Although the work no longer survives, descriptions of it from the early nineteenth century report that Peterson suggested an alternative law of decreasing probability, far more pessimistic than Craige's or Hooper's, according to which Christianity would cease to be credible by 1789.[102] The Frenchman Claude François Houtteville described Craige's work as "the greatest example of the vanity of human conjectures" in his 1722 *La religion Chrétienne prouvée par les faits*.[103] But Houtteville's principal objection was that belief depends upon the quality of evidence rather than its proximity: conviction does not weaken over time, because "the proof of a fact remains invariably the same." Thus, while Houtteville ridiculed Craige's mathematics, he conspired with Craige's understanding of belief as an empirically generated proportion of certainty.[104] Finally, Pierre Bayle praised Craige in the second edition of his *Dictionary*, but Bayle muddied the waters, as was his wont, by claiming that the Scotsman was actually a fideist. The fact that he was able to do so suggests quite a bit about how the new under-standing of belief could cross party lines and unite an incipient modernity against the older confessional regime. The ratio-nalist project of calculating probabilities could find common ground with the fideist project of believing against reason: be-lief in the merely "probable" could be read *either* as rationally playing the odds *or* as a leap to faith.[105]

The culmination of this history was the article on "Proba-bility" by the Genevan mathematician Charles Benjamin Lu-bières in the *Encyclopédie* (1754) of Diderot and D'Alembert. While not referring to Craige or his critics by name, Lubières described how over time testimony becomes "enfeebled ac-cording as it passes by many more mouths, according as the chain of witnesses is extended. It is easy to calculate, on the basis of established principles, the proportion of this enfeeble-ment." Using this method, he determined that if we have con-fidence of 95/100 in each witness, "the thirteenth witness will not transmit more than 1/2 certainty, and then the mater will cease to be probable, or there will no longer be any external reason for believing it." However, "if the testimony is transmit-ted in writing, the probability augments infinitely." He finished by exhorting the calculation of reasonable belief as a great step forward for human knowledge.[106]

So, was the credibility of Christianity preserved or under-mined by the Enlightenment trend toward probabilism and the new sense that belief must always be accompanied by its complement of doubt? As critical biblical scholarship eroded the authority of the received text, smug Protestant arguments about the reliability of written testimony would crumble. A belief is only as reliable as its witnesses. But on the other hand, that same critical scholarship offered Christians a rea-sonable leap to faith in a history now understood to be ap-proximate rather than definitive. With belief itself redefined as probability rather than certainty, the credibility of a compromised scripture could endure.[107]

[handwritten margin note: → key to why we still use scripture. we = Christians who practice in 21st century]

It is commonplace to divide Enlightenment intellectuals into parties or factions according to their views of the relationship between faith and reason. Fideists in one corner insisted that faith must be maintained without reason; Lockean empiricists clashed with Cartesian rationalists; deists like Anthony Collins followed Spinoza in reducing God to nature or philosophical ideals, thus challenging faith itself. But these divisions, important though they are, have blinded us to other trends. A common project of belief united these intellectuals: not agreement about what should be believed, or even what precisely belief was, but rather a second-order commitment to the autonomous judgment of the believing subject. Having smashed their way through the scholastic barriers that isolated belief from other categories of truth-claims like knowledge and opinion, belief became, in their view, simply the output of the human mind. Intellectuals differed on how that mind worked—this was a principal obsession of Enlightenment philosophy—but they agreed that its output was belief regardless, hence religious belief was no more or less than individual judgment about religion. The explosion of these ideas into the mainstream was a catastrophe for the confessional project that had tried, in an era of unprecedented religious competition, to prevent belief from being opened to the judgment of the world.

There is no better place to see the new framework of belief than in the Enlightenment's most concise, eloquent, and mature statement on the question: Denis Diderot's entry *Croire* in the *Encyclopédie*. Here is the article in its entirety:

Believe: to be convinced that a fact or proposition is true, either because one has not bothered to examine it; because one has examined it, but badly; or because one has examined it well. Only in the last case can our confidence in facts really be solid and satisfactory. It is both hard and unusual to feel at ease with ourselves when we have made no use of our reason or if the use we have made of it is bad. If we *believe*, without having any reason to *believe*, then we will always feel guilty of neglecting the most important aspect of our humanity, even if we discover the truth, and it is impossible for such a stroke of luck to compensate for such irregular conduct. The individual who makes a mistake, after calling on all the faculties of his mind, still proves to himself that he has done his duty as a reasonable human being. It would be as wrong to *believe* something without examining it, as it would be not to *believe* an obvious or clearly proven truth. We can therefore feel convinced in any given case or on any given subject only if we listen to the voice of our conscience and our reason. Acting otherwise is to go against our own intelligence and a misuse of faculties given to us for no other purpose than to accept the strongest probability and the best available evidence. These principles cannot be contested without destroying reason and throwing mankind into all manner of confusion.[108]

The second half is little more than a paraphrase of John Locke, but the first half clearly establishes the stakes of the Lockean position. By laying out three different options for believing—judgment based upon no examination, poor examination, or thorough examination—Diderot was not simply mocking the irrational pretensions of his unenlightened opponents. He was, rather, establishing a principle of commensurability: of course, rational judgment is best, but all kinds of judgment are equally examples of believing, and only internal conscience, rather than external authority, can arbitrate where reason really lies.

The idea that belief represents sovereign judgment, then, partially bridged the Enlightenment's debates over the relationship between reason and faith. It could even begin to bridge the gap between faith and unfaith, in the sense that atheism, itself a kind of judgment, could be accounted an authentic belief rather than merely belief's absence. Such was hinted by Pierre Bayle in a series of dictionary entries on atheists like Matthias Knuzen, and made explicit by Jacques Bernard, Bayle's successor as editor of the *Nouvelles de le république des lettres,* who in 1716 described atheism as a "creed" with "articles of belief."[109] Of course, we should not oversimplify; enormous disagreement remained. But the importance of this new ecumenism lay in the way it allowed for a common conversation, not only within religion, but also across religion, science, and society. A person accused of wrong belief in any of these arenas could respond with evidence, not necessarily to demonstrate the truth of the thing—in this inductive era, so much had ceased to be provable—but to justify their belief. This collapse of the boundaries between belief, knowledge, and opinion structured the emergence of a modernity in which belief, far from declining, flourished and proliferated, colonizing the natural sciences and the sciences of man. A new age of belief had begun.

CHAPTER SEVEN

Belief in the Human

THE PARADOX that art contains truth has always followed civilization; it might even be constitutive of civilization itself, opening space where human beings can find value in their own works. But in what sense do we *believe* in the products of our own imagination? Is "belief" so capacious that it can embrace the artificial? In 1739, David Hume denied it: "Whatever emotion the poetical enthusiasm may give to the spirits, 'tis still the mere phantom of belief or persuasion."[1] Yet by the nineteenth century, Hume's view would appear obsolete, and in 1817 Samuel Taylor Coleridge provided the canonical answer: art provokes from us "that willing suspension of disbelief for the moment, which constitutes poetic faith."

The phrase "willing suspension of disbelief" so subtly captured modern intuitions that we tend to take it for granted, as if Coleridge had described the timeless process by which human beings believe in their own creations. But a brief glance at the phrase's origin suggests how novel his vision was. The context was Coleridge's description of how he and William Wordsworth planned to co-author the *Lyrical Ballads*.[2] As Coleridge explained, they designed a literary experiment in which the "two cardinal points of poetry," naturalism and imagination, would merge. In Wordsworth's contributions, "subjects were to be chosen from ordinary life," but the poet's task was to "give the charm of novelty to things of every day, and to excite a feeling analogous to the supernatural, by awakening the mind's attention to the lethargy of custom, and directing it to the loveliness and the wonders of the world before us." In Coleridge's contributions, by contrast, "the incidents and agents were to be, in part at least, supernatural" but the goal was to portray "the dramatic truth of such emotions as would naturally accompany such situations, supposing them to be real. And real, in this sense, they have been to every human being who, from whatever source of delusion, has at any time believed himself under supernatural agency." Coleridge's task was thus to provide "a semblance of truth sufficient to procure for these shadows of imagination that willing suspension of disbelief for the moment, which constitutes poetic faith." So Coleridge's "willing suspension of disbelief" was not at all what it is usually taken to be. The "shadows of imagination" requiring poetic faith were not only poetry but the supernatural itself. His whole discussion presumed the disenchantment of the world, and his remarkable proposition was that belief in the supernatural is belief in human artifice: the mundane and the imaginary, the human and the supernatural, converge on the ground of belief.[3]

I begin with Coleridge, not because I propose to discuss literature, but because the last stage of our story is the process by which people came to believe in human invention. As we have seen, Europeans influenced by new ideas in the seventeenth century were freed to believe in spiritual objects in much the same way they believed in mundane ones, as acts of sovereign judgment. With the category so perforated, there was no intrinsic reason why belief had to remain bound to objects judged "true" in a transcendent or universal sense; it might also alight upon objects judged true in more provisional or instrumental ways. Crucially, this included the social world: ephemeral human creations, the ideas and things that we ourselves make. When Thomas Hobbes argued that political sovereignty was not ordained by God but conjured into being by man, for instance, his point was not to delegitimize what he called the "artificial person" of the state, but to convince people of its truth and make its artificial reality the basis of human action. When Giambattista Vico argued that we can only ever know things that we have made, he was not despairing at the human condition but acknowledging that civilization itself is the result of believing in human invention. In this sense, Coleridge's "willful suspension of disbelief" stands for the whole intellectual transformation by which works of human ingenuity—the state, the economy, the law—became legitimate objects of belief, functionally equivalent to belief in the supernatural.

The context for this transformation was the emergence of what Jonathan Sheehan and Dror Wahrman have called "self-organization": theories of immanent order in the world that reduced God to a remote cause or formal stipulation.[4] Orthodox writers of the later seventeenth and eighteenth centuries shared an abiding concern that God was disappearing from the world. The problem was not that many people questioned God's existence, but that God's existence seemed to have become so much less relevant. While previously the fall of a sparrow proclaimed God's special providence, now many Christians heard only the distant echo of God's prime motion. While previously the "powers that be" were ordained by God, now they were conjured into existence by contracts. While previously religious unity reflected the seamless identity of God, now religious competition reflected the worldly logic of the market. It appeared obvious to traditionalist observers that banishing

God from the world would erode the foundations upon which society was built: if God were removed, surely all would crumble, for how could people put their faith in the artificial?[5]

But in stubborn defiance of expectations, modern subjects did not stop believing in things. David Bell has described how the early Enlightenment constructed new "foundational concepts"—like society, the nation, the public, and civilization—none of which owed its existence to any "principal external to itself." By investing their belief in these products of human imagination, at least some Europeans shifted the whole frame of belief from one in which "the human terrestrial order was seen as subordinated to exterior (particularly divine) determinations, to one in which it was seen as autonomous and self-regulating."[6] The rise of social science had begun, not because of the new authority attached to science, but because the human became a proper object of belief.

Early modern observers who questioned the legitimacy of this displacement had a fair point. To invent something and then believe in it was as irrational as pulling yourself up by your own bootstraps, as absurd as Don Quixote modeling his life on chivalric romances. But people did, and people do. It turns out—and it must be stressed how very odd this is—that people do not have to accept that something is natural, divine, or eternal to believe in it: people also believe in what they have made. This ability of modern subjects to believe in the human, in something like the way they believe in the divine, explains why, in an era of disenchantment, belief did not decline but proliferated.

The "science of man," as David Hume memorably labeled it, was a characteristic project and principal obsession of the

Enlightenment.[7] This was not quite *social* science as it would later be understood: human beings were conceived as individuals rather than populations, hence Michel Foucault argued that a true social science was impossible before 1800.[8] But nonetheless, during the Enlightenment humanity became the object of knowledge in ways which for the first time mirrored the search for knowledge in nature, and "putative sciences of society sprang up like mushrooms, in all shapes and sizes."[9] Jean-Jacques Rousseau noted in 1750 that, after having finally understood the heavens (he had Newton in mind), humanity had now done something "even grander and more difficult— come back to himself to study man and know his nature, his duties, and his end."[10] Some theorists even suggested that *all* science was really the study of man. Hume wrote, "Tis evident, that all the sciences have a relation, greater or less, to human nature . . . Even mathematics, natural philosophy, and natural religion are in some measure dependent on the science of man, since they lie under the cognizance of men."[11] A 1774 Swiss encyclopedia entry on psychology declared, "It is to ourselves that we relate all things, it is the influence of things upon ourselves that leads us to applaud or condemn them; it is therefore the relation of things to ourselves that makes them of interest to us, and without knowledge of the nature, faculties, qualities, state, relations, and destination of the human soul, we can pass judgment on nothing."[12] Alexander Pope put it best in 1733:

> Know then thyself, presume not God to scan,
> The only science of mankind is man.
> Plac'd on this isthmus of a middle state,
> A being darkly wise, and rudely great.[13]

One reason for this new emphasis on self-knowledge was the transcendently influential empiricism of John Locke's *Essay*

Concerning Human Understanding (1689). If our minds are blank slates waiting to be inscribed by experience, as Locke argued, then each of us is the product of our environment. Hence, in addition to human beings making the social world, the social world makes human beings, and if we improve society, we improve ourselves. This was the optimism of the Enlightenment, the sense that man was, as the Scotsman Adam Ferguson put it in his 1767 *Essay on the History of Human Society*, "in some measure the artificer of his own frame."[14] Humanity was a creature of infinite possibility, alone capable of innovation; hence the study of ourselves was not an analysis of the immutable universe, but rather a creative process intended to generate the next stage of human development.

The possibility of social science was, of course, predicated upon the transformation of science itself. The old *scientia* had been an understanding of necessity, of how things must be according to their fixed natures. But the new science, as an inductive study of the way things are, could plausibly encompass the transient and mutable world of human beings. Yet *belief* in the human also required two further innovations. First, it required the rehabilitation of artifice itself, reimagining the products of human innovation not merely as secondary harvests of nature or providence but as worthwhile and independent objects of judgment. Second, it required instrumental belief. That is, to believe in the social, not only must I assent to propositions *for the moment* rather than absolutely, I must also assent to propositions because my assent can *produce* a truth that is not already there. This instrumental understanding of belief is necessary because, in the social world, human belief changes the very things on which it passes judgment.

To begin with the first issue: the seventeenth century saw a remarkable rehabilitation of things fictional, artificial, and imagined. We might plausibly attribute this transformation to the era's expanding commerce and the emergence of political economy, which encouraged invention as a basis for sound policy; we might just as plausibly attribute it to the rise of Baconian natural philosophy, in which the artificial conditions of experiment reveal nature's hidden potential.[15] Regardless of the cause, the wild heterogeneity of different examples in different fields suggests something of the breadth of the phenomenon. Take, for instance, the extraordinary rehabilitation of so-called artificial beauty—that is, the use of cosmetics.[16] According to a misogynist view of women's sexuality hardwired into Western morality, makeup had been widely condemned as concupiscence, its artificiality imagined as a kind of deception, rejecting divine truth and providence. Cosmetics were, of course, widely used anyway, but it is difficult to find principled defenses of the practice until the middle of the seventeenth century, when suddenly "artificial beauty" was vindicated as simply one more way that human ingenuity improves upon nature. Among the progenitors of this rehabilitation was the Parisian literary and intellectual *salon* known as the *conférences du bureau d'adresse*. In 1633, the French physician and journalist Théophraste Renaudot began a series of weekly conferences on the Île Saint-Louis where invited speakers publicly debated controversial questions. In a 1636 conference "Concerning Makeup" (*Des Fards*), three out of four speakers defended artifice. "Natural beauty," one claimed, "is like a rough diamond if art does not polish it." The most beautiful palaces are only beautiful because of their marble, gilding, and paint. Rhetorical eloquence is a sort of "makeup upon natural discourse." All the compliments and civilities we pay to others are merely "makeup and disguises upon our thoughts." Another speaker argued that, as Jesus had let his feet be anointed with ointments, "why should it be a crime for art to perfect nature, to aid in this work, by removing what is superfluous and adjusting what is lacking, which are also the two parts of medicine?"[17] After the publication of the debate in both France and England, suddenly it became commonplace to defend "artificial beauty."

Far from the world of cosmetics, artifice also found new defenders in mathematics: two different sorts of "artificial numbers" were crucial to the emerging vernacular mathematics of commerce. The first were simply what we call decimals; and it is hard to remember how unnatural the division of the world into tenths at first appeared to early modern minds. The concept of decimal mathematics was introduced into Europe by Simon Stevin in his 1585 *La Thiende* ("The Tenth"), published almost simultaneously in Flemish and French, then translated into English in 1608. Stevin stressed that decimals were an invention of human ingenuity, saving time that had previously been wasted adding up "broken numbers" (that is, fractions) within Europe's ponderous systems of weights and measures.[18] The English subtitle referred to the "art of tenths," and Henry Lyte's 1619 popularization was called *The Art of Tens*, after which decimals became widely known as "artificial numbers." Thus, Thomas Willford's influential *Willfords Arithmetick* (1656) divided calculation into two sorts, natural and artificial: "The first of these is so denominated from having proper figures and numbers significant of themselves, whereas the other is figurative, or founded upon art."[19] The figurative nature of decimals is partially explained by the fact that the use of the "point" to represent decimals was still unknown, so that Willford was, for instance, asking his readers to replace the natural number 3/4 by the artificial number 75, as if decimals were a kind of secret code.[20]

The other kind of "artificial numbers" were logarithms. These new tools to facilitate calculation had been introduced by the Scottish mathematician John Napier in 1615, but logarithms were popularized by the bestselling mathematical author Edmund Wingate, an English lawyer who lived in France and became tutor to Princess Henrietta Maria. Wingate's *Arithmetique Made Easie* (1630) was divided into two books, the first on natural arithmetic, where "operations are performed on the numbers themselves," and the second on "artificial arithmetic," where operations are performed using "borrowed numbers" or logarithms.[21] The following decade, the Jesuit Professor of Moral Theology Pierre Bobynet, who had a passionate interest in clocks, introduced the concept into French in his *L'Horographie Ingenieuse* (1647), where he praised the utility of *"nombres artificiels."*[22]

Perhaps the most unexpected place to find praise of artifice was the rise of "imaginary accounts" in double-entry bookkeeping.[23] The first example in English comes from Stephen Monteage's popular textbook *Debtor and Creditor Made Easy* (1675). Monteage's example was a joint-stock company in which three partners purchased a quantity of cochineal (used in making red dyes) for resale. Each partner had become indebted when they provided capital for the purchase; but where should the balancing credit be assigned, when it was temporarily in the form of warehoused goods rather than cash? The partners were not literally indebted the amount, because they had the goods; but no cash value could yet be assigned to those goods, because the sale price was not yet known. Monteage's solution was that "a *supposed* account is to be framed to bear this credit," much as dummy values are assigned in algebra. Monteage wrote, "So, by this imaginary or substituted account to be framed, will the difficulty of intricate company accounts be made easy to thy understanding.[24]

This treatment was expanded enormously in *A New Treatise of Arithmetick and Book-Keeping* (1718) by the Scotsman Alexander Malcolm, who made "imaginary accounts" into a general category to be used whenever "there is no giving or receiving, neither is there any absolute obligation," and yet the "posture of things" changes in ways that must somehow be represented. Examples included the accounting of goods in transit at sea, the money held in a wager before it is concluded, and conditional debts. These "imaginary accounts," Malcolm noted, are sometimes called "mediate accounts," but he preferred the term "imaginary" because their outcomes remained an image in the mind rather than a fixed certainty.[25] Like Schrödinger's Cat, they remained in suspension until future events reduced them to a classical state. The popularity of Malcolm's treatise was probably why the term exploded into general usage in the eighteenth century, despite the frisson of illegality that the term imaginary accounts always evoked. In a commercial world newly alert to the dangers of fraud, the term suggested that, just as jurisprudence was an artificial reason that required legal fictions, so bookkeeping required real but controlled acts of imagination.

The rehabilitation of artifice and imagination in so many different practical fields went hand in hand with their rehabilitation in philosophy. The first stone was thrown by Thomas Hobbes, who argued in his *Leviathan* that human "understanding" is simply "imagination" put into words.[26] We shall return to Hobbes soon, but because our business is to show how this rehabilitation intersected with belief, I instead want to begin with Baruch Spinoza, who argued in his *Tractatus Theologico-Politicus* that the prophetic content of the Bible was the product of human imagination.[27] Spinoza did not deny that the Old Testament prophets were inspired by God, but he argued that their prophesies reported sounds and visions in their minds rather than real things they had seen or heard. Prophets were thus people with unusually "vivid imagination" [*vividiore imaginatione*], whose revelations were filtered through the creative apparatus of their own minds. This explains, for instance, why "Isaiah saw seraphim with six wings each, while Ezekiel saw beasts with four wings each; Isaiah saw God clothed and seated on a royal throne, while Ezekiel saw him as a fire. Each undoubtedly saw God as he was accustomed to imagine [*ipsum imaginari*] him."[28] Spinoza's argument had profoundly corrosive effects for traditional biblical exegesis. The fact that prophets referred to devils and angels, for instance, did not mean that devils or angels really existed, only that human prophets perceived divine truth through the filter of their own imaginations.[29] As Spinoza summarized, "Many things are reported in scripture as real, and were actually believed to be real [*realia esse credebantur*], though they were nothing but representations and imaginary things . . . All these were undoubtedly only visions, adapted to the opinions of those who passed them on to us as they appeared to them, namely as actual events."[30]

Spinoza's crucial interpretive move, however, was not therefore to debunk the veracity of scripture, but to delineate a sense in which we ought to "believe" these imaginations despite knowing they are not real. That is, he separated the true *meaning* of biblical passages from what he called their "truth of fact." If we are to believe the Bible's sense or message rather than its facticity, then it makes no difference if a passage conflicts with reason, or if different passages conflict with one another; our goal is to understand the minds of the biblical authors and hence the philosophical meaning they intended to convey, so that these might have their proper effect on believers.[31] Quite apart from his reduction of God to nature, this unyoking of belief from objective truth is part of what led so many contemporaries to accuse Spinoza of atheism: rather than abandoning belief, Spinoza transferred some part of his belief to the human.

This untethering of truth from facticity had a remarkable parallel in the world of mathematics—not the practical mathematics of "artificial numbers" described above, but the treatment of so-called imaginary numbers by Spinoza's younger contemporary, the German polymath Gottfried Wilhelm Leibniz (1646–1716).[32] Earlier mathematicians, notably Gerolamo Cardano in the 1540s and Rafael Bombelli in the 1570s, had discovered that formulaic solutions to higher-order equations sometimes produced impossible answers: the square roots of negative numbers. These impossibilities were usually ignored by mathematicians who were, quite reasonably, looking for real answers rather than phantoms created by their formulae. Thus, in 1637, René Descartes named these phantoms for all time: he called them "imaginary numbers," arguing that we need pay no attention to answers when "there exists no quantity that corresponds to what we imagine."[33] But imaginary numbers could not be dismissed so easily. It was simple enough to jettison non-existent *answers*; but a much more perplexing question was what to do with imaginary terms that appeared in the course of the algebra but then cancelled out, yielding real results. If mathematics was supposed to be the last rigorous science, in which every step was demonstrable from a small handful of premises, by what standard could you defend the manipulation of objects those premises had never contemplated?[34] This was, on the one hand, simply one more iteration of an ancient problem, the ontological status of mathematical objects: was a circle a real thing in the world or an ideal thing in the mind of God? But it was also a new problem, because the mind of God did not seem to have thought of the square roots of negative numbers at all.

Enter Leibniz, stage left. Following Lord Herbert of Cherbury and others, Leibniz had already made distinctions between different kinds of "truths" central to his philosophy. In particular, he distinguished "truth of reasoning," which was demonstrative and necessary, from "truth of fact," which was contingent: truth of fact was the way the world was rather than the way it logically had to be.[35] Moreover, Leibniz's philosophy often featured speculation on the ontological status of exotic objects like monads and infinitesimals. So it should be no surprise that, faced with imaginary numbers, he waxed philosophical, believing in their use and significance as products of the human imagination without believing in their full metaphysical truth. In his most important contribution to the question, published in the Leipzig *Acta Eruditorum* of 1702, Leibniz offered a gnomic description: an imaginary number is "almost an amphibian between being and non-being." Leibniz pointed to the complex and stratified nature of reality, denying any simple division between the real and unreal: the "eternal variety" of the world would hardly permit "all things to be bound together under one genus." We can see in the magnificent oddity of imaginary numbers "a portent of the ideal world," so it would seem that imaginary numbers are, like other mathematical objects, reflections of the "divine mind." But not so fast. In fact, it is our imagination—*effugium*, a flight of fancy, an escape—that discovers imaginary numbers, and the verb Leibniz uses for "discover," *reperit*, can just as easily mean "invent." Thus, it is what our minds discover/invent that Leibniz describes as "almost an amphibian being and non-being." Within the phenomenal variety of existence, there is room even for inventions of the human imagination to serve the higher truth of mathematics.[36]

The imaginary number, then, is not simply a mathematical object that reflects divine perfection; it is rather suspended between human and divine creation. In an unpublished paper, describing his astonishing discovery that some real answers to equations *require* imaginaries in their solutions, Leibniz wondered, "How can it be that a real quantity, a root of the proposed equation, is expressed by the intervention of an imaginary?"[37] How could you believe a result obtained through what Leibniz called *fictions bien fondées*—"well-founded fictions"?[38] Almost always this question arose for Leibniz as he compared imaginary numbers to infinitesimals, the exotic new creations of the Calculus that likewise seemed both real and unreal. One answer was that these well-founded fictions were a sort of shorthand: not real themselves, but pointing to real things. So, for instance, in a 1706 letter to the Jesuit Bartholomew Des Bosses, Leibniz described imaginary numbers, like infinitesimals, as "fictions of the mind due to an abbreviated manner of speaking."[39] But in a 1702 letter to the French mathematician Pierre Varignon, Leibniz offered a more complex and interesting interpretation:

> Even if someone refuses to admit infinite and infinitesimal lines in a rigorous metaphysical sense and as real things, he can still use them with confidence as ideal concepts which shorten his reasoning, similar to what we call imaginary roots in the ordinary algebra, for example $\sqrt{-2}$. Even though these are called imaginary, they continue to be useful and even necessary in expressing real magnitudes analytically . . . In the same way we can also conceive of dimensions beyond three, and even of powers whose exponents are not ordinary numbers—all in order to establish ideas fitting to shorten our reasoning and founded on realities. . . . Furthermore, imaginary roots likewise have a real foundation [*fundamentum in re*]. . . . So it can also be said that infinities and infinitesimals are grounded in such a way that everything in geometry, and even in nature, takes place as if they were perfect realities.[40]

In the first part of this argument, imaginaries seem to exist as "ideal concepts" even if they do not exist in the world, a familiar Platonic argument to describe mathematical objects like circles. But there is a difference. A circle is something we can conceive, but we can no more conceive $\sqrt{-2}$ than we can conceive a Fifth Dimension or raising a quantity to the π power. These things have a real foundation—there is something beneath them that God created—but the mathematics itself is our own creation to access that reality. We are no longer in Plato's cave here: the shadow on the wall is not created by the divine and merely experienced by the human, but created by the human to make sense of the divine. "Well-founded fictions" are necessary for human beings to see further than nature allows, as if the denizens of Plato's cave invented flashlights to cast shadows for themselves.[41]

⟨⟩

Perhaps the first arena where the rehabilitation of artifice bore fruit in the "science of man" was the invention of fictitious origin stories, describing the emergence of humanity from a state of nature. By the late eighteenth century, the Scottish mathematician and philosopher Dugald Stewart had coined the term "conjectural history" to describe how, "when we cannot trace the process by which an event *has been* produced, it is often of importance to be able to show how it *may have been* produced."[42] But already in the seventeenth century, fictional narratives had become the foundation of real beliefs about the social world, not on the grounds that people had *really* behaved in a certain way, but rather if we agree how people *would* have behaved in certain conditions, we will have established a basis for understanding the real world. When John Locke wrote, "In the beginning all the world was America," for instance, he was not proposing an alternative to the biblical *In principio*. Rather, he told his just-so story—in this case, how money was invented—because anyone who granted its credibility was logically bound to believe his larger argument about the nature of property.[43] As with Spinoza and Leibniz, believing a meaning or truth was separated from believing facts.

The concept of a *status naturae*, or "state of nature," can be found in William of Ockham and other medieval writers describing the opening chapters of Genesis.[44] But, with some debt to Jean Bodin and the Renaissance tradition, it was most influentially introduced into political theory by the Dutch Arminian Hugo Grotius. He first used the phrase in his 1625 *De jure belli ac pacis*, but his discussion of what a state of nature looked like began much earlier, in his unpublished manuscript on the law of booty (c.1606) that became the kernel of his *Mare Liberum*, or *The Free Sea*, published in 1609.[45] In order to prove his argument that the sea cannot be a private possession, Grotius suggested that it was useful to consider the nature of possession in ancient historical epochs, "marked off perhaps not so much by intervals of time as by obvious logic and essential character."[46] Grotius thus recounted an idealized process of historical progression. "In the earliest stages of human existence," he wrote, "sovereignty" or "ownership" must have meant different things than they later came to mean in an epoch of settled societies. In a natural state, "which the poets sometimes portray as having existed in a golden age, and sometimes in the reign of Saturn," there could be no private property; the only kind of ownership was the privilege of an individual to use or possess common property. The transition to the "present distinction of ownerships" occurred gradually, as people noticed that certain sorts of possession (like food that is ingested) implied exclusivity, and then extrapolated from that observation to a more general theory. This narrative became the basis for Grotius's argument that ownership requires occupation, hence the sea, which can never be occupied, cannot be a private possession. Grotius thus began a process that would soon transform early modern political theory: believing fictional narratives in order to reach real conclusions.

Thomas Hobbes's view of the state of nature a generation later is too famous to require much elucidation here: "During the time men live without a common power to keep them in awe, they are in that condition which is called war, and such a war, as is of every man against every man." Life in this condition is "solitary, poor, nasty, brutish, and short," hence people voluntarily surrender their right of self-government.[47] But Hobbes was vague, perhaps intentionally, about the historical veracity of his state of nature. Sometimes it appeared to be an actual historical epoch; in the 1668 Latin *Leviathan*, for instance, he mischievously offered Cain's murder of Abel as historical proof of the war of all against all.[48] But much more often, Hobbes portrays the state of nature as a local condition, or an existential threat: it exists wherever sovereignty fails. The point of the state of nature, then, was not real history, but rather that if we believe it to be where Hobbes says it is, we must perforce follow Hobbes's logic that commonwealths are created when people in the state of nature "reduce all their wills, by plurality of voices, unto one will." The creation of commonwealths is "a real unity of them all . . . made by covenant of every man with every man, in such manner as if every man should say to every man, I authorize and give up my right of governing myself."[49] The remarkable phrase here is "as if": for Hobbes, real unity is created by a fictitious history.

This tradition continued in the work of Hobbes's successor and critic, the German jurist Samuel Pufendorf, whose 1672 *De jure naturae et gentium libri octo* has been called the "handbook" of Enlightenment anthropology.[50] For Pufendorf, the state of nature was a "supposed state" rather than a real one, "such a state as we may conceive man to be placed in by his bare nativity, abstracting from all the rules and institutions, whether of human invention or of the suggestion and revelation of heaven." It was, in other words, a thought experiment, intended to demonstrate that the movement from savagery to civilization could be explained in terms of natural processes.[51] We might trace Pufendorf's influence in many places, but an important case is Jean-Jacques Rousseau's *Discourse on the Origin and Foundations of Inequality Among Men* (1755). Rousseau noted that while "philosophers who have examined the foundations of society have all felt the necessity of going back as far as the state of nature," nonetheless "none of them has reached it" because it plainly never existed. So, he wrote: "Let us therefore begin by setting aside all the facts, for they do not affect the question. The inquiries that may be pursued regarding this subject ought not to be taken for historical truths, but only for hypothetical and conditional reasonings; better suited to elucidate the nature of things than to show their genuine origin, and comparable to those our physicists daily make regarding the formation of the world."[52]

Yet Rousseau absolutely insisted upon belief in this nonexistent state of nature. He painted a vivid picture of natural mankind, "wandering in the forests without industry, without speech, without settled abode, without war, and without tie, without any need of others of his kind and without any desire to harm them . . . subject to few passions and self-sufficient."[53] For this image to perform the intellectual work Rousseau assigned to it—proving that there is no such thing as "natural inequality"—it must be believed: yes, that is indeed the natural state of man, free and equal, hence any inequality is the work of society. But because he has already denied the possibility of man prior to society, what must be believed is the hypothetical conjecture rather than any reality undergirding it: that *if* man were abstracted from society, it would be so. This is belief about provisional rather than absolute truths, unmoored from their transcendent substance. They must only be believed for a time, so that they can do their intellectual work; once that hypothetical reasoning has been achieved, we need no longer believe in a state of nature.

⟨⟩

This brings us to our second building block for belief in the human: an instrumental understanding of belief, suitable to a world in which the truth itself is not fixed. That is, modern belief can sometimes assent, not to the prior truth-value of a proposition, but to the truth that is produced through the act of believing it. Here the progenitor was undoubtedly Thomas Hobbes.

The state, Hobbes wrote in *Leviathan*, is a creature of merely human rather than divine institution. It is an "artificial man" formed by "pacts and covenants," speech acts which analogically resemble the *fiat* by which God created natural man. According to Hobbes, the creation of this artificial man is essentially an act of self-defense, intended to create a synthetic body stronger than our frail natural bodies.[54] But the security provided by the state is always contingent upon assent to it, without which people put themselves back into a state of war, negating the purpose for which it was compacted in the first place. Hobbes's project, then, was to convince readers to believe in this artifice—that is, to believe that they should compact themselves into a commonwealth to increase their own security, and by so doing, to increase their security indeed.

According to Hobbes, faith itself is a human invention. Humanity in its natural state was devoid of faith, because by definition faith is the performance of a contractual obligation, and absent a commonwealth to make and enforce laws, there are no contracts.[55] In "the condition of mere nature, which is a condition of war of every man against every man," people might keep promises for their own purposes, but never as fulfillments of obligation, hence there is no faith.[56] Of course, fear of supernatural retribution was a great spur to the fulfillment of covenants.[57] But this did not constitute "faith" unless a person's fear of the supernatural was grounded upon direct, personal revelation from God, which by definition could not be transferred or demonstrated to another person. In the absence of direct revelation, religion was thus merely keeping promises to men who claimed to speak for God, and men remained free, in a state of nature, to break those promises as they pleased.[58] Thus the fountainhead of all faith, the creation of any religion beyond what you experience with your own senses, was the creative act of surrendering liberty to the sovereign. Hobbes therefore offered a radical new premise: instead of having faith first and then building institutions upon it, humans create institutions first and then build faith upon those institutions. To believe against the sovereign would therefore undermine all faith and religion. Hobbes's remarkable argument that the sovereign was the authoritative interpreter of scripture was an attempt to redeem rather than reject credulity: if the only two choices open to non-inspired human beings are either to refuse to believe at all, or else to believe in the merely human, then Hobbes chose belief in the human.[59]

Perhaps the most important result of these Hobbesian developments in the eighteenth century was a new social science of religion in which, remarkably, religion itself was declared to be artificial and yet, like the state, people were asked to believe in it anyway. Decades earlier, Machiavelli had so enthusiastically invoked Livy's description of the invention of pagan religion to keep the masses enthralled that many readers concluded that

Machiavelli himself thought all religion was a ruse. But for Machiavelli, crucially, the jig would be up if it were discovered that the gods were fictions; while he described the social benefits of invention, he by no means argued that those reading his book should knowingly believe fabrications. Hobbes came closer, arguing that all subjects must follow public religion because they had no legitimate grounds to prefer any alternative; but this argument was still not equivalent to asking people knowingly to believe in fictions. In Germany, Daniel Clasen's *De religione politica* (1655) addressed with terrifying seriousness the possibility that "religion is a human creation," but he hardly advocated that position.[60] Radical novelty was thus left to the scandalous Dutch émigré physician Bernard Mandeville, who told English readers that a great deal of morality and religion (if never quite all) was a human invention, but then asked them to believe it anyway because their belief in some sense made it true.

Mandeville argued that many of the truths his society took to be natural or essential were in fact artificial. This did not mean that there were no natural truths: Mandeville accepted, for instance, that knowledge of God's existence is available from nature, and that it is human nature to follow our appetites. But *The Fable of the Bees* (1714) and *The Fable of the Bees, Part II* (1729) were deeply anti-foundationalist, insisting that even these natural or essential truths were virtually insignificant until artifice shaped and perfected them. In particular, Mandeville insisted upon the transformative power of something called "society," which he described as a giant machine for transmuting natural things into artificial ones for the common good. A significant part of Mandeville's project was thus to promote belief in society, for the more we commit ourselves to this contrivance, the better it functions.

In his preface to *The Fable*, Mandeville promised to show how "by skillful management" the vices of each particular person had been made "subservient to the grandeur and worldly happiness of the whole."[61] From one perspective, this sounds relatively conventional: any theory of providence holds that vices are allowed by God to serve virtuous ends. But Mandeville played upon this commonplace to conjure a secular sort of providence in which "management" is human rather than divine. "It is the work of ages," he wrote, "to raise a politician that can make every frailty of the members add strength to the whole body, and by dexterous management turn private vices into public benefits."[62] Such a politician must "promote, and, if he can, reward all good and useful actions on the one hand, and on the other to punish, or at least discourage, everything that is destructive or hurtful to society."[63] Society is thus artificial, like the quintessential machine of the proto-industrial economy: "I know nothing to which the laws and established economy of a well-ordered city may be more justly compared than the knitting-frame. The machine, at first view, is intricate and unintelligible. Yet the effects of it are exact and beautiful."[64]

Crucial to this discussion was Mandeville's forensic distinction between the artificial and the natural: artificial things evolve and are perfected over time, while natural things "are all complete, and such as nature would have them, at the first production."[65] The honey made by the first bees was no worse than what their descendants produced, hence honey production is natural. Bees have never changed their architecture, hence their hives are natural as well.[66] It is not labor but improvement that constitutes artifice. Thus, Mandeville argued that *human society is not natural but artificial*. Society has a divine origin, as do all things, but only at several steps' remove; nature no more "designed man for society" than "she has made grapes for wine."[67] Man is the artificer of his own nature, created by the "labor of a sculptor" who is not God but himself; God created only the raw ingredients, but the work-manship that gives us value is our own.[68]

And not for nothing was the *Fable* condemned as a public nuisance by a Middlesex jury in 1723, for the centerpiece of Mandeville's narrative of secular providence was the invention of morality. "Morality," he wrote, was "contrived" by "skillful politicians, to render men useful to each other as well as trac-table."[69] Mandeville's point was not that moral precepts were therefore unworthy of belief; on the contrary, we should be-lieve in artificial morality because it produces public benefits. So, for instance, Mandeville wrote that the ideal of honor, so central to eighteenth-century society, "is a chimera without truth or being, an invention of moralists and politicians."[70] Yet we ought to believe in honor, because fear of dishonor—that is, shame—regulates our lives for the common good.[71] For an-other example, courage is a human invention. The only natural kind of courage is blind rage; all else is a contrivance of man to overcome reasonable fears of danger.[72] But Mandeville's pur-pose is not to denigrate this artificial courage: governors need men to fight in wars, so they invent a category called courage that corresponds to this need, and then produce it through flattery.[73] This whole discussion depends upon the need to be-lieve in social facts that are made true by our belief.

For Mandeville, religion, too, is artificial. Even though knowl-edge of God is available from nature, the natural result of that knowledge is simply fear; to transform fear into positive religious sentiment requires artifice.[74] Now, Mandeville ac-knowledged that this constructive work might be at least par-tially divine rather than human; he admitted that while false religion was created entirely by man, true religion included revelation. But nonetheless, despite some significant nods to Christianity, Mandeville's point was that religion—whether true or false—is sterile unless directed toward useful ends by the machine of society. Paradigmatic was his treatment of martyrdom. After having described courage as artificial, Mandeville pivoted to a special case of this contrived courage: "the joy and alacrity with which holy men in persecutions have suffered for their faith." Mandeville denied the usual argument that such bravery must be evidence of divine assistance: atheists have died just as bravely for atheism as Christians have died for Christianity.[75] All martyrdom is thus artificial, the result of social manipulation which leads people to act against their own natural interest in self-preservation. What matters is thus not which martyrdoms are real but which are useful to society; martyrdom, for Mandeville, is one of those private vices which leads to public benefits. In sum, Mandeville's project was not to undermine religious belief by demonstrating its contrivance, but to place it on new foundations. Belief in divine truths was radically insufficient without belief in fictions.

Which brings us to the Italian historian and philosopher Giambattista Vico. Not as famous in his own time as Bernard Mandeville, Vico was largely unknown outside his native Naples. But the two men share pride of place in the historical emergence of belief in the human. The heart of Vico's work was the intellectual principle usually known as the *verum factum*—"the truth is what is made"—first articulated in 1710. It was originally a linguistic proposition: for the Latins, he wrote, the words "verum" and "factum" are reciprocal, so that whenever something is said to be true that means it has been made, and whenever something has been made that means it is true. But Vico always argued for the deep metaphysics of language, and he converted the linguistic principle of *verum factum* into a philosophical one: we can know only the things that we have made.[76] In his *New Science*, published first in 1725, then revised in 1730 and 1744, this became the basis for an extraordinary analysis of the history of social and civil institutions: "The civil world is certainly the creation of humankind. And consequently, the principle of the civil world can and must be discovered within the modifications of the human mind. If we reflect on this, we can only wonder why all the philosophers have so earnestly pursued a knowledge of the world of nature, which only God can know as its creator, while they neglected to study the world of nations, or civil world, which people can in fact know because they created it."[77]

Vico's history of the civil world began with the "barbarous" peoples, descendants of Noah who had abandoned marriage and family in favor of promiscuous sexuality, and who thus lost their intelligence and were reduced to brute beasts. How could these creatures, whom Vico identified with the giants of the Old Testament, have returned to civilization? The answer, in short, was the invention of religion. Lacking the power of reason, Vico argued, they began with "a metaphysics which, unlike the rational and abstract metaphysics of today's scholars, sprang from the senses and imagination." With their senses they perceived things they did not understand, from which arose feelings of wonder, and whenever they felt wonder, "they imagined its cause as a god."[78] That is, they created religion and believed it, for, as Tacitus wrote, *fingunt simul creduntque*: frightened people imagine a thing and immediately believe. So, for instance, the ancients feared thunder and so imagined the god Jupiter with his thunderbolt, and "the figure of Jupiter was so poetic—that is, popular, exciting, and instructive—that its inventors at once believed [*credettero*] it, and they feared, revered, and worshipped Jupiter in frightful religions." The natural form of expression for this invention, Vico wrote, was poetry, the language of emotion rather than intellect. Thus arose the ancient myths, the foundational poetry of civilization, written in what Vico called the language of "believable impossibility" [*l'impossibile credibile*].[79] We are here approaching Coleridge's willing suspension of disbelief.

Yet Vico did not condemn this paradoxical act of inventing gods and then believing in them, *because what we create is true*. The purpose of religion is the manufacture of humanity: fear of the divine leads men to build civil institutions and thus emerge from savagery.[80] As the historian Amos Funkenstein described it, for Vico "the very humanity of man is an artifact."[81] The mythology of pagan antiquity is thus, for Vico, a record of how barbarous peoples used their poetic imaginations to build civilizations by believing in fictions. And, in Vico's cyclical view of history, the same process recurred in the Christian Middle-Ages, as Catholic superstitions recreated civilization out of the ashes of medieval barbarism. Even in the "modern" age of reason, society depends upon believing in what human beings have created, according to the principle of the *verum factum*:

> My *New Science* has shown in detail how providence caused the world's first governments to base themselves on religion, which alone made the state of families possible. Next, as they developed into heroic civil governments, or aristocracies, religion clearly provided the principal stable foundation. Then, as they advanced to popular governments, religion likewise served as the people's means of attaining democracies. Finally, as they come to rest in monarchical governments, this same religion must be the shield of rulers. If people lose their religion, nothing remains to keep them living in society. They have no shield for their defense, no basis for their decisions, no foundation for their stability, and no form by which they exist in the world.[82]

This is why Vico repeatedly refers to his own work as "a rational civil theology of divine providence." At every stage of human development, people invent themselves by believing in religion, and they invent religion by believing in themselves.

Here we can see something of how modern belief became a creative principle. The sociologist Anthony Giddens has written that "no knowledge under conditions of modernity *is* knowledge in the 'old' sense, where 'to know' is to be certain." Instead, modern knowledge is constantly reconsidered in light of new evidence. In the social sciences, Giddens suggests, this produces "reflexivity": social knowledge reshapes society, which in turn reshapes social knowledge, so that a settled conclusion is neither possible nor desired. Thus, "the social sciences are actually more deeply implicated in modernity than is natural science . . . the chronic revision of social practices in the light of knowledge about those practices is part of the very tissue of modern institutions."[83] While it would be wrong to imagine Hobbes, Mandeville, and Vico as full participants in this thought-world, they were its prophets.

⟨⟩

One seemingly natural conclusion for this narrative would be Immanuel Kant. In fact, for reasons that will become clear, I do not think that Kant makes a satisfying endpoint at all. But it is worth taking a moment to consider what such a conclusion would look like, in order to emphasize by contrast how I think our story does end and what the stakes of that conclusion might be.

Kant, who produced his three critical *summae* in the 1780s, sought to reconcile empiricism with rationalism by arguing, in essence, that while the mind may not have innate ideas, it does have fundamental categories which make experience possible.[84] Kant granted Hume's argument that induction is irrational: we cannot reach general conclusions through the

mediation of our senses, which provide only local and particular data. But, Kant argued, knowledge of our mental architecture is not empirical, it is derived a priori from our own
internal "apperception" or self-consciousness: we do not perceive fundamental categories by experiencing the world but by
perceiving our minds experiencing the world. So, for instance,
Kant accepted Hume's argument that cause-and-effect was not
a valid inference from empirical observation. But, he argued,
causality is nonetheless objectively valid because we generate
it internally without mediation: it shapes our perception of the
world, rather than being shaped by that perception. Space and
time are likewise intuitions of our minds with which we construct our perception of reality, rather than concepts empirically generated by that perception: space and time are directly
entailed every time the mind thinks a thought. As Kant put
it, in terms that echoed Vico and the *verum factum*, "We can
cognize of things *a priori* only what we ourselves have put into
them."[85] The search for an authentic metaphysics, for Kant,
was thus an enquiry into ourselves. So Kant, the great theorist
of human autonomy, marks a milestone or horizon line beyond which the project of "belief in the human" becomes the
very heart of Western philosophy: transcendent operations of
thought are resuscitated, not by looking outward but by looking inward, in what Kant called "transcendental deduction."
Even God and religion are made real by the resources we bring
to discernment of them.

Kant also argued for an innate faculty of "judgment"
(*Urteil*), a middle term connecting empirical observation
to pure reason. Previous empiricist discussions of judgment
had focused on taste: particularities of experience make different people prefer different objects. Rationalists like the
authors of the Port Royal Logic, by contrast, saw judgment
more abstractly as a "representation of a relation between two

concepts."[86] Kant bridged these positions by suggesting that there is a transcendental component to judgment: we react positively to things that mirror our own minds, and insofar as this reaction is not the result of some private interest but the innate reason that shapes experience, that judgment is objectively valid. Kant's archetypal example is aesthetics. When we say an object is beautiful, we mean not only that it is beautiful to us, but that we believe it ought to be beautiful to everyone. Judgments, for Kant, are thus more than individual tastes; they are attempts by thinking subjects to universalize from individual experience by observing the categories of their own minds.[87] So here, again, if we were looking for an endpoint to our story, we would appear to have found one.

But the new philosophy represents only one outcome within a much broader array of novelties. While from one perspective Kant completed philosophy's reassessment of belief, from another perspective Kant broke philosophy and left it unable to speak to belief any longer. Kant's turn to a new metaphysics "solved" the problems in earlier systems by abandoning belief as a subjective response to the world and instead diving into the deep architecture of cognition. Thus, whatever its philosophical brilliance, post-Kantian philosophy would grow apart from the broader religious and cultural problem of belief, which remained focused on subjectivity. Kant understood judgment *not* as subjective but rather as a transcendental reflection of metaphysical reality. He thus opposed the whole thrust of modern belief in which *opinion*, traditionally the poor stepchild of epistemology, had emerged triumphant. Kant saw this rise of opinion and despised it. In his view, judgment was above the fray of taste and interest; hence, as critics of Enlightenment have noted, Kant could normatively project his own "reason" upon the world. But despite his best efforts, the judgment that came to define modern belief was not the Kantian faculty but rather something more mundane: the commensurability of different opinions, individual and inalienable, equally legitimate even if differently justified.

So instead of ending with Kant, let me suggest a different trajectory for our story in which belief proliferates in its newfound liberty. This trajectory might encompass not just rationalism but enthusiasm: the multitudinous unfolding of rival, self-authorizing evangelisms in modernity. It might equally encompass pantheism, occultism, and countless other beliefs which would not have been accounted beliefs in previous eras. In this view, there is a deep kinship between the Enlightenment project of rational inquiry and the anti-Enlightenment project of spiritual awakening. These two sides of modernity, however opposed, shared belief in the new belief, that deep well of human judgment that is the sovereign arbiter of every question. *Ex: Astrology, Tarot etc. Could be anti-Enlightenment.*

The avatar of this alternative trajectory was the Romantic poet, printer, painter, and mystic, William Blake. The only thing Blake hated as much as Enlightenment reason was Christian orthodoxy: for him they were partners in the soul-crushing, tyrannical project of limiting human freedom and forcing conformity to some monstrous, pre-ordained pattern. Blake insisted, by contrast, in a decidedly un-Kantian version of the transcendental, that "every thing possible to be believed is an image of truth."[88] The project of belief is a creative process, making things true by believing them, to release the deities that reside in the human heart:

> Then I ask: does a firm persuasion that a thing is so, make it so?
>
> He replied. All poets believe that it does, and in ages of imagination this firm persuasion removed mountains; but many are not capable of a firm persuasion of any thing.[89]

Virtue, for Blake, required this creative belief, remixing pre-existing ideas through the imagination to make new truths. Blake's belief is "reflexive," to borrow Giddens's terminology. It is by definition unfixed: "The man who never alters his opinion is like standing water, and breeds reptiles of the mind."[90] And so Blake was freed to invent his own mythology, derived from the raw materials of the Bible and pagan Europe but utterly idiosyncratic and autonomous. In his epic poem "Jerusalem," human reason tries to bind belief—"Vain foolish man! Wilt thou believe without experiment?"—but this "cold constrictive specter" is rebuffed by Los, the eternal prophet. Throughout Blake's mythical corpus, we find Urizen, the cruel god of rationality and tradition, locked in dialectical confrontation with Orc, god of passion and rebellion, breaker of the tablets of the law.[91]

Blake here stands for a broad swath of post-Enlightenment thinking that was enthusiastic, mystical, or anti-rationalist, but whose understanding of "belief" was utterly dependent upon the success of the Enlightenment project to redefine belief as individual sovereign freedom against the gathering forces of orthodoxy. So the endpoint of our story is not simply the emergence of rationalist belief, it is simultaneously the emergence of what we might call Romantic belief, the opinionative belief of genius. Harold Bloom called this the "faithless faith" of the Romantics; it operates, as J. R. Watson notes, "at a point where doctrine gives way to experience, where language is appropriated for new explorations, even for new formulations of a belief."[92] What marks this kind of modern belief, and makes it so different from what came before, is its resistance to external norms, its insistence that the individual is sovereign not only over what to believe but over the criteria of judgment.[93]

Western civilization thus entered the modern age of belief. Of course, figures like Vico and Blake were outliers rather than typical representatives of their worlds; change in the mind comes slowly when it comes at all. But they were visionaries of profound significance, framing a version of belief that was compatible with the release of infinite invention that characterizes modernity. We live today within the legacy of this innovation, this convergence between, on the one hand, belief as a point of contact with the divine, and on the other hand, belief as an act of human imagination.

Conclusion

BELIEF HAS A history; it changes over time. Thomas Kuhn famously borrowed the term "paradigm" to describe regimes of scientific principle and practice, while Michel Foucault adopted "episteme" to describe the intellectual conditions in which knowledge is made. This book has suggested that there are also "credulities": spaces or conditions of believing. A credulity is a framework of intellectual resources and assumptions that shapes religious knowledge and its relationship to other truth-claims. The term does not refer to a particular orthodoxy; on the contrary, I use the root *credo* ironically to challenge any account of belief that is limited to doctrines. Belief is not a fixed order of the human mind, it is not an empty vessel waiting to be filled with content; instead, changing intellectual conditions structure how the content of religion is known and experienced. Every era is credulous, but they are credulous in different ways.

Immanuel Kant identified belief as the category of truth-claim that is "subjectively sufficient, but objectively insufficient."[1] Without accepting his view, we can take from it the intuition that vulnerable reports or uncertain data—"the evidence of things not seen," to use a Christian vocabulary—may be interpreted using a variety of culturally specific resources, which render particular claims sufficient or insufficient for different purposes. A credulity is that matrix of interpretation. Thus, in part, a credulity delimits the legitimate conditions of religious knowledge, or what may normatively be counted as religious knowledge; but at the same time, by that act of limitation, it also describes the relationship between religion and other kinds of knowing. Things may be accepted, suspected, or inferred in many ways; as this book has shown, one culture's belief is another culture's doubt, one culture's knowledge is another culture's belief. How these epistemological categories are sorted—why certain kinds of claims seem *credible*—defines the credulity of a culture, which in turn shapes the character and function of religious knowledge in that culture.

Over the course of half a millennium in the Christian West, we have seen three separate credulities, which we may with some simplification call medieval, confessional, and modern. None of them were absolute—regimes of the mind are porous and contested, or else they would not change over time—but they were nonetheless profound. The cornerstone of the medieval credulity, amidst all its diversity, was the determination to reserve for Christianity a special epistemic prestige in the face of revived classical philosophy. Theologians asserted a category of belief based upon textual and institutional authority that transcended the limits of reason even while it relied upon reason. Subsequently, in the confessional credulity, this basic configuration remained intact; but with authority itself now shattered, the warring confessions of the Reformation pitilessly rationed belief, preserving the special epistemic status of Christianity only by shrinking the category and insisting that so much dubious religious speculation was not really belief at all. Then, finally, in the modern credulity, belief expanded again, not by returning to the medieval assumption of unitary authority, but by breaking down the partition wall that separated belief from opinion and knowledge, making sovereign judgment both the definition of belief and the foundation of the autonomous, critical subject. Belief thus flooded into modernity, at the cost of surrendering Christianity's privileged epistemic status. This is how the modern credulity in the West inaugurated a new age of belief even as it ended the age of faith.[2]

{⟨⟩}

To see this transition, it is useful to consider one last story, epitomizing the modern credulity a century after our main narrative ends. In the years after Charles Darwin tore natural history free from divine providence, a new organization called the Metaphysical Society met in London to debate the meaning, grounds, and legitimacy of religious belief in an age of scientific rationality.[3] Its membership was a veritable who's who of Britain's (male) elite: from politicians like William Gladstone and a very young Arthur Balfour; to the Anglican Archbishop of York and the Catholic Archbishop of Westminster; to scientists like Thomas Huxley; to the editor of the *Economist* Walter Bagehot; to the poet laureate Alfred Tennyson. Other luminaries who were not members of the Society, like Cardinal John Henry Newman (who refused to join), the English philosopher John Stuart Mill, and the American philosopher William James, read the Society's debates and responded to its provocations. In the spirit of open inquiry, the Society's Christian founders invited deists and atheists into their ranks—the word "agnostic" was even coined at the Metaphysical Society, when Thomas Huxley realized his position did not have a name.[4] The Society's monthly meetings, from 1869 to 1880, were politely Victorian, but tensions ran deep: at one point "Frederic Harrison declared that he considered a belief in miracles as the commencement of insanity," to which the Archbishop of Westminster replied "that he considered an incapacity to believe in the supernatural as a commencement of ossification of the brain."[5] It is therefore of enormous interest that, despite fundamental disagreement about so many things, the Society operated within a powerful consensus: a modern space of belief that would have been unrecognizable two centuries earlier.

Take, for example, "The Ethics of Belief" by the mathematician William Clifford, read to the Metaphysical Society on April 11, 1876 and then published in the *Contemporary Review*. Clifford was a Lockean who summarized his position with the blunt assertion that, "It is wrong always, everywhere, and for anyone, to believe anything upon insufficient evidence."[6] He insisted that the only rational way to believe things that go beyond our own personal experience is by "assuming that what we do not know is like what we do know." That is, we may add to our beliefs through an inductive process of extrapolation: Clifford's example is that the new science of spectroscopy has identified a chemical signature for hydrogen on earth, and the same chemical signature is found in the sun, therefore we may believe that the sun contains hydrogen.[7] But this model requires that nature is everywhere uniform; without the assumption of uniformity, we would have no rational basis to believe anything beyond our own sensory experience. And so, Clifford rejected revealed religion:

> No evidence, therefore, can justify us in believing the truth of a statement which is contrary to, or outside of, the uniformity of nature. If our experience is such that it cannot

be filled up consistently with uniformity, all we have a right
to conclude is that there is something wrong somewhere;
but the possibility of inference is taken away; we must rest
in our experience, and not go beyond it at all. If an event
really happened, which was not part of the uniformity of
nature, it would have two properties: no evidence could
give the right to believe it to any except those whose actual
experience it was; and no inference worthy of belief could
be founded upon it at all.[8]

Clifford's essay was written in part to answer the arguments
of Cardinal Newman, whose 1870 *Grammar of Assent* had rejected the Lockean argument that no belief should be held more
firmly than evidence dictates. We may understand that a proposition is more or less likely, Newman wrote, but to assent to it is
by definition to exceed that partial likelihood and declare that,
based upon incomplete evidence, we grant it to be so. Jurors
in courtrooms and doctors making diagnoses know perfectly
well that they might be wrong; but when they assent, they give
their full faith despite the possibility of error. Thus, we must
possess some instinct or intuition—Newman called it the "illative faculty"—that teaches us to grant assent without sufficient
rational cause. Newman did not argue that this illative faculty
was unique to religion; on the contrary, he modeled it on Newton's genius in making physical discoveries beyond what could
be seen, and Napoleon's genius as a tactical commander finding
victory where reason would have found only defeat.[9]

The need for supplements to reason in the formation of belief was a leitmotif throughout the life of the Metaphysical Society. So, for instance, Clifford's rationalist rebuttal of Newman
was answered by Richard Hutton, editor of the *Spectator*, in
an address entitled "On the Relation of Evidence to Conviction."
Hutton insisted that, while evidence is one legitimate ground

of conviction, to believe *only* upon evidence would be insane, like a "skeptical chicken" who, feeling a strong inclination to "chip the shell at the proper time for hatching," nonetheless rejects that inclination as "entirely destitute of good evidence" and therefore perishes.[10] Walter Bagehot likewise argued that "what we commonly term belief includes . . . both an intellectual and an emotional element." The laws of assent are the laws of evidence, but the laws of emotional conviction deserve equal weight. And while he denounced Cardinal Newman's attempts to authorize "stronger conviction than the evidence justifies," he nevertheless saw conviction itself as a necessary corrective to "dry minds" who must "refer to a notebook to know what they believe."[11]

In a very different kind of argument, the Catholic Archbishop of Westminster Henry Manning argued that *authority* must supplement reason, because reason demands that authority should be believed: "Authority is, therefore, not an imperious act substituting command for reason . . . but it is reason and evidence speaking by a legitimate voice. Authority and evidence are thereby identical and convertible. It is not authority that generates truth, but truth that generates authority."[12] In response to this and other Catholic provocations, the lawyer James Fitzjames Stephen argued that it is impossible to believe further than you yourself understand. He imagined assenting to two propositions: London is the capital of England, and *bahut gurm* is the capital of British India. Both are true, but if you do not know that *bahut gurm* means "very hot," then you are not really assenting to the proposition.[13] By contrast, the Catholic mathematician William Ward, editor of the *Dublin Review*, offered an elegant proof (*pace* David Hume) to reject the argument of Clifford and the empiricists. First, inductive knowledge is built upon the "rejection of all first premises except experienced facts." Second, the first premise of induction is "nature's uniformity." But, third, nature's uniformity cannot possibly be proved by experienced facts. Ergo, empiricism is irrational, and we must admit the possibility of beliefs that are not empirically grounded—including, ironically, empiricism itself.[14]

Much more could be said about the controversies of the Metaphysical Society, but I hope the point is clear. Here we have a spectrum of influential views, Catholic, Protestant, and atheist, engaged in debate over the nature of belief and how beliefs might be justified. They do not agree with one another, yet they are all clearly participants in the new thought-world I am calling "modern belief," taking as their foundation the notion that belief is a space of sovereign judgment: individual, propositional assent based upon whatever criteria the believer finds most convincing. Of course, they debate which grounds really are convincing; some stress empirical evidence, others stress intuition, or the weight of tradition, or the existential necessity of subsisting on incomplete evidence. But their different outputs are all equally belief, and while the justifications for them can be endlessly gainsaid, their belief-status cannot. The emergence of modern belief had made the Metaphysical Society possible; it also makes possible our own metaphysical society. This is the modern credulity.

Now, I certainly do not wish to argue that everyone in modern, Western society inhabits this magic circle: like any inside, modern belief undoubtedly creates an outside, and therein lies a new kind of exclusion. But this is a different problem than the one identified by Talal Asad, who showed how the category of "religion," by privileging inward faith, tacitly condemns religions with public aspirations. Our story ends not with the exclusion of the outward or political, but with the paradoxical exclusion of exclusivity. That is, modern belief leaves little or no room for claims that one kind of belief is qualitatively superior to another, a problem that mirrors the classic liberal conundrum of how to tolerate the intolerant.[15]

To be specific: in the meetings of the Metaphysical Society, several Roman Catholics insisted that belief properly adheres in obedience to authority. I take their positions generally to remain inside "modern belief," not only because they understood themselves to have individually judged obedience as correct, but also because they would not have denied belief-status to those who judged differently. But undoubtedly there were people in the nineteenth century, and there remain people today, who wish to police other people's beliefs, and who regard individual choice as a failure of belief while submission to authority constitutes belief itself. Such people are presumed to threaten the second-order consensus that makes belief-talk possible in a diverse society, and their positions are thus debarred—despite their cogent claims that this exclusion demonstrates their opponents' hypocrisy.

For another example: while "enthusiastic" Protestantism was not well represented in the Metaphysical Society, nonetheless direct, personal access to the Holy Spirit was a major theme of religious revival in the eighteenth and nineteenth centuries, as it remains today. Again, modern evangelicals generally subsist within "modern belief": they do not usually argue, like the evangelicals of the sixteenth century, that those who are not born again are atheists. Now, in fact, evangelicals today do sometimes hold versions of these positions; but unlike in the early modern period, they rarely use the category of "belief" to express them. They might describe outward Christians who lack spiritual gifts as lukewarm, or as hypocrites; but for them to call those outward Christians unbelievers or atheists sounds distinctly odd, precisely because belief has come to function as a more general category of judgment. In this sense, we might even say that evangelicals have ceded "belief" to secular society. Nonetheless, when modern evangelicals do suggest that those who believe other than they do lack the faculty of belief, or that only spiritual gifts make belief possible, they too are excluded from the modern credulity.

A harder group to categorize are those who hold the most militantly anti-rational views. Now, again, modern belief is not the same as "rational religion," as the debates of the Metaphysical Society demonstrate. There is plenty of room for what Kierkegaard called "leaps to faith," plenty of room for Friedrich Schleiermacher's contention that religion consists in "feeling" or "intuition," plenty of different sorts of inputs besides forensic evidence that might motivate sovereign judgment. But are there limits? I see no reason to omit from the modern credulity the vast numbers of modern Christians who believe, for instance, that dinosaur bones were planted under the ground at creation six thousand years ago to test our faith: modern belief is not about content or the alleged modernity of any particular viewpoint. However, it is easy to imagine a point where the denial of particular evidence might lead to denying evidentiary judgment altogether, a point where conversation ceases because one species of belief becomes radically incommensurate with others. At that point, indeed, modern belief begins to collapse.

So what does the emergence of the modern credulity tell us? There are, I think, three very different conclusions that might be drawn from this analysis. First, one could choose, in the manner of Michel Foucault, Talal Asad, Jean-François Lyotard, and other postmodern and postcolonial critics of the Enlightenment project, to see here a story of the hegemonic victory and naturalization of a peculiar kind of logic. That is, we could argue that the seventeenth century saw the birth of an aggressive new regime of believing, which has been sufficiently successful and normative in modernity that we have forgotten that it is historically contingent and shaped by power. Thus, we might use this story to denaturalize the present, and to critique scholarship that discounts, ignores, or belittles alternative ways of believing.

Second, in the manner of Christian and particularly Catholic theorists like Charles Taylor and Alasdair MacIntyre, we might see here a tragedy in which the flattening of belief onto opinion, and the marginalization of transcendent values and reliable authorities, has left a world where ethical claims are brittle and thin. In this version, the absence of any absolute standard or criteria to sort people's belief-claims has created what Brad Gregory calls "hyperpluralism," and what Charles Taylor calls an "immanent frame," a society without moral compass where people cannot agree on a direction because they do not agree on a destination.

The fact that these two interpretations are so starkly incompatible—after all, how can modern belief be both an ideological straightjacket and a pandemonium of relativism?—suggests that a third interpretation might be in order. In this view, the theological reaction within Christianity to exorcize belief of its demons produced something like the public sphere, overthrowing a confessional regime in which believing had become a privilege of the few, allowing genuine debate between rival belief-claims for the first time. This creation of a second-order consensus was the triumph, not of hegemonic and normative reason, but of subjective opinion. Enlightenment rationality did not devour the world in its ravenous maw, it was only a subset of the larger project to liberate human judgment. This outcome undoubtedly holds perils: the rights of subjects to formally equal beliefs on every topic from physics to philosophy, regardless of their ignorance; and the rights of subjects to sift and choose which facts to believe, even alternative facts that might seem irrational or poorly attested. But it also enables peace in a diverse society. In this model, belief has proliferated rather than waned in modernity. The cognitive space that used to frame religion now structures everything from political affiliation to consumer tastes to dietary habits, enveloping us in a rich atmosphere of private ethical judgment. Western subjects used to be incandescently religious, but believed only in one small corner of their lives; now religion is far less central, but Western subjects believe exhaustively, all the time, as instinctively as breathing.

It should be obvious that the third version is the one I believe. Nonetheless, because I "believe" it in the modern sense of the term, my judgment should not be taken as discounting the legitimacy of the others, which also contain a great deal of truth. Clearly the emergence of modern belief produced losers as well as winners, and in asymmetrical contact with non-Christian religions it has, ironically, become a weapon to restrict the meaning of belief once again. These consequences should not be denied or downplayed. Nonetheless, I believe that the evidence supports the notion that "modern belief" is the glue that prevents diverse societies from spiraling into chaos, a project I hope I can support without denying that it comes with costs. Of course, my sovereign judgment cannot prevent readers from forming alternative opinions. I will insist to them that my evidence is probative, and that in lieu of further evidence, they ought to believe with me. But if they choose to leap to faith in one of the other conclusions instead, all I can do is suggest that this book has shown that their procedure, as much as mine, is an outcome of modern belief, for which they should be thankful.

One final way to understand the distinctiveness of our own credulity, the modern age of belief, is to refer back to the ancient distinction between believing and believing *in*. According to

Augustine, belief *in* described a special condition which ought only to have God as its object: "What then is 'to believe *in* him?' By believing to love him, by believing to esteem highly, by believing to go into him and to be incorporated in his members." But in the modern world, *believing in* has been normalized and democratized, so that we believe *in* many things, promiscuously and freely. People today believe in the state and the nation, the law and the market, with little or no concern about the idolatry of loving, relying upon, and being incorporated into purely human categories, institutions, and movements. Believing *in* is now easy, and its objects are limitless.

The philosopher Slavoj Žižek briefly noticed this surprising configuration in *On Belief*, where he argued that believing and believing *in* now function in ways that would have scandalized the inventers of the distinction: just as we can have belief without believing *in*, so too we can believe *in* without belief in its traditional sense.[16] It is an ancient commonplace that propositional belief can subsist without binding commitment or trust: Hamlet might believe that the ghost is real without doing what the ghost's reality requires. But, much more surprisingly, it also appears possible to believe *in* something without *believing* it: to commit to what the ghost requires without requiring the ghost to be real.

The point is that, far from belief having declined, belief in Western society has proliferated, escaping the bounds that enclosed it in the past, colonizing neighboring epistemic categories, so that now belief is everywhere. Secularization has not segregated belief from the world, it has instead opened the world to belief, liberating a central category of Western civilization from the demands Christianity placed upon it. This observation helps to solve the riddle of how modernity displaced onto humanity so much cultural energy that used to be directed toward religion. The answer turns out to be: we believe.

CI   Teresa of Avila, "Moradas del castillo interior," in *Mística del Siglo XVI*, ed. Francisco Javier Díez de Revenga (Madrid, 1 volume with more expected, 2009–), vol. I

CP   Teresa of Avila, "Camino de Perfección," in *Mística del Siglo XVI*, vol. I

CR   *Corpus Reformatorum* (Leipzig, 101 vols., 1834–)

FB   Bernard Mandeville, *The Fable of the Bees: or, Private Vices, Publick Benefits* (London, 1714)

FB2   Bernard Mandeville, *The Fable of the Bees. Part II* (London, 1729)

INSTITUTES   John Calvin, *Institutes of the Christian Religion*, trans. Henry Beveridge (Grand Rapids, 1989). Checked against John Calvin, *Institutio Christianae Religionis* (Geneva, 1559).

JMEMS   *Journal of Medieval and Early Modern Studies*

JMH   *Journal of Modern History*

JR   *Jesuit Relations and Allied Documents*, ed. Reuben Thwaites (Cleveland, 73 vols., 1896–1901)

LV Teresa of Avila, "Libro de la vida," in *Mística del Siglo XVI*, vol. I

LW *Luther's Works*, ed. Jaroslav Pelikan et al. (St. Louis, 55 vols., 1955–86)

PL *Patrologia Latina* full text database, online at http://pld.chadwyck.com

PMS *The Papers of the Metaphysical Society, 1869–1880: A Critical Edition*, ed. Catherine Marshall, Bernard Lightman, and Richard England (Oxford, 3 vols., 2015)

RCC Teresa of Avila, "Las Relaciones o Cuentas de Conciencia," online at http://www.santateresadejesus.com/wp-content/uploads/Las-Relaciones.pdf

RCG *Registres du Consistoire de Genève au temps de Calvin*, ed. Thomas Lambert et al. (Geneva, 8 vols., 1996–2014)

SCJ *Sixteenth Century Journal*

ST Thomas Aquinas, *Summa Theologica*, online at http://www.logicmuseum.com/authors/aquinas/Summa-index.htm

TERESA *The Collected Works of St. Teresa of Avila*, trans. Kieran Kavanaugh and Otilio Rodriguez (Washington, D.C., 3 vols., 1980–85)

TRHS *Transactions of the Royal Historical Society*

WA *D. Martin Luthers Werke: Kritische Gesamtausgabe* [Weimarer Ausgabe] (Weimar, 120 vols., 1883–2009)

WRH   *The Folger Library Edition of the Works*
of Richard Hooker, ed. W. Speed Hill
(Cambridge, Mass., 7 vols. in 8, 1977–98)

WSJC   Kieran Kavanaugh and Otilio Rodridguez,
eds., *The Collected Works of St. John of the*
Cross (Washington, D.C., 1979)

NOTES

Introduction

1. A critical edition of the disputation, known as the *Twistreden*, is in Lienhard, Nelson, and Rott, eds., *Quellen*, pp. 156–231. I have used the English translation in Waite, ed., *The Anabaptist Writings of David Joris*. For the Strasbourg
Melchiorites, see Deppermann, *Melchior Hoffmann*, pp. 366ff.; for Joris's role
in the debate, see Waite, *David Joris and Dutch Anabaptism*, pp. 132–40.

2. *The Anabaptist Writings of David Joris*, p. 211. *Quellen*, p. 195: "Ten
eersten, of ghy mi geloouen wilt, zo wil ic v spreken."

3. *The Anabaptist Writings of David Joris*, pp. 196–97. *Quellen*, p. 178: "Alle
gelooue staet op waerheit vnde redelicheit. Daerom bewyst v voergeuen, zo wil-
len wi v geloouen." "Ghy weet immer, dattet kint zynder ouder niet en verstaet.
Hierom dat oordeel van desen, dat ic v spreken zoude, wie zal die geuen? Want
daer geen verstant van en is vnde niet gelooft en wert, hoe zal ic dan met v spreken? Daerom weet ic niet, hoe ict beginnen, v onderwisen mochte."

4. *The Anabaptist Writings of David Joris*, p. 206. *Quellen*, p. 190: "Wi
moeten van v met redelike bewisinge betuicht worden, oft anders is v zulcken
dicipul niet nut. Ooc zoude ghyt zelue niet begeeren, dat wi v zonder redelike
bewisinge geloofden, want dat en hadde doch geenen bestandt."

5. *The Anabaptist Writings of David Joris*, p. 210. *Quellen*, pp. 193–94:
"Wanneer ghy mi nu geloofden vnde v begeuen woudt, daerna tedoen, zoe mocht
ghy den Geest verstaen, zonder dat kont ghi mi niet verstaen. Doch hoe zoud ghy
mi verstaen, ghy en gelooft mi niet."

6. *The Anabaptist Writings of David Joris*, p. 215. *Quellen*, p. 199: "Zo ghy
mi niet anders hooren oft geloouen, dan al begripen wilt, vnde dat ghi die wy-
sheit hebt." "Off wt die woorden, datghi meer wysheits hebt: soudic daer wt geloouen? Dat waer mi een wonderlic geloof, zo wy zo souden geloouen, zo mosten
wy ooc andere voerheen geloof hebben alzo wt des Geestes driuinge, als wy geen
bewys en hadden."

7. http://news.gallup.com/poll/193271/americans-believe-god.aspx. When
given the option "not sure" instead of just "yes" or "no," the number saying yes
dropped from 89% to 79%.

8. Besides obviously being a legal term, in Western philosophy "judgment"
is often understood to be the act of mind that determines the relationship between two concepts or objects; it is noteworthy that, according to the *OED*, the
English word was first used to describe a religious belief only in 1609.

9. Many Christian theologians today also deny that religious doctrines are
primarily first-order truth-claims: they instead imagine doctrines as symbols of

existential orientations, or as rules to guide action. Yet when those theologians "believe" a doctrine, their affirmations bury any debate over the nature of propositional assent under their own sovereign judgment. See Lindbeck, *The Nature of Doctrine*, p. 16 and passim.

10. Bruno Latour argues that while moderns distinguish between belief in "fact-objects" and belief in "fairy-objects" in order to separate facts from fetishes, rationality from religion, nonetheless a distinctive feature of modernity is a practical elision between them: Latour, *On the Modern Cult of the Factish Gods*, p. 20 and ch. 1 passim.

11. Asad, *Genealogies of Religion*; Mahmood, *Politics of Piety*; Mahmood, "Religious Reason and Secular Affect: An Incommensurable Divide?," in Asad et al., *Is Critique Secular?*.

12. Hegel, *Elements*, §273.

13. Hegel, *Elements*, §124.

14. Hegel, *Elements*, §132.

15. Hegel, *Elements*, Preface.

16. Gregory, *The Unintended Reformation*. See also Taylor, *A Secular Age*; Gillespie, *The Theological Origins of Modernity*; MacIntyre, *After Virtue*. For a recent evangelical Protestant critique of the argument blaming Protestantism for modern pluralism and secularism, see Vanhoozer, *Biblical Authority*.

17. Here Gregory follows John Milbank and the "radical orthodoxy" school in modern Christian theology. See Milbank, *Theology and Social Theory*. More recently, Duns Scotus and univocity are the villains in Milbank, *Beyond the Secular Order*.

18. Koselleck, *Critique and Crisis*, p. 28.

19. Picciotto, "Implicit Faith and Reformations of Habit," p. 513.

20. Gregory, *Unintended Reformation*, p. 11.

21. I am by no means arguing that all believers in the modern West partake of modern belief. Nonetheless, my sense is that when people today accuse one another of failing to believe what they say they believe—for instance in accusations of hypocrisy—they are usually probing epistemic *content* (Do you *really* believe that? Surely your actions point to other beliefs instead). Only rarely do they dare to make categorical exclusions (What you have is not really belief. People like you do not believe, they have only lesser kinds of claims), because defining the category of belief in ways that exclude others is now fundamentally uncivil. An exception that proves the rule might be something like the Marxist concept of "false consciousness," which does indeed make categorical exclusions and is therefore a decidedly illiberal form of accusation.

22. Veyne, *Did the Greeks Believe in Their Myths?*, quotes on pp. 27 and 17.

23. Malcolm Ruel, "Christians as Believers," in his *Belief, Ritual*, first published in 1982, especially pp. 50–51. Ruel was in part responding to the important but much less satisfying history traced in Wilfred Cantwell Smith, *Belief and History*.

24. Ricoeur, 'La problématique de la croyance." in Parret, ed., *On Believing*.

25. Jean Wirth, "La naissance du concept de croyance (XIIe–XVIIe siècles)," *Bibliothèque d'Humanisme et Renaissance* 45, no.1 (1983): 7–58. And see the

response to Wirth in Frédéric Gabriel, "L'orthodoxie formulaire: subjectivité et normativité dans les commentaires au *Credo*," in Hummel, ed., *Doxa*.

26. Schreiner, *Are You Alone Wise?*.

27. Most, *Doubting Thomas*.

28. Justice, "Did the Middle Ages Believe in Their Miracles?"; Hoffmann, "Atheism as a Devotional Category." Other excellent works upon which the present study builds include: Hummel, ed., *Doxa*; Erdozain, *The Soul of Doubt*; Dixon, "William Perkins"; Arnold, *Belief and Unbelief*; Schmitt, "Du bon usage du 'credo'"; Lopez, "Belief"; Mukherji, "Trying, Knowing and Believing"; and McEachern, *Believing in Shakespeare*. See also the discussion of *conviction* in Labrousse, *Conscience et conviction*.

29. Shapin, *A Social History of Truth*; Green, *A Crisis of Truth*; Poovey, *A History of the Modern Fact*; Shapiro, *A Culture of Fact*; Clark, *Vanities of the Eye*; Muldrew, *The Economy of Obligation*; Groebner, *Who Are You?*.

30. The most influential example is Laqueur, *Making Sex*.

31. Herman Parret notes "the difficulty of identifying the problem of belief and believing, and the diversity of not as much solutions to the problem but rather the formulation of it," in Parret, ed., *On Believing*, pp. 1–2.

32. Cf. Michel de Certeau, who follows cultural anthropologists (see below) to suggest that *croire* is an embodied social construct, more akin to faithful performance of obligations than to epistemology: Michel de Certeau, "Une pratique sociale de la différence: croire," in *Faire Croire*, pp. 363–83.

33. See, e.g., Augustine, *De Trinitate*, 13.2.5, online at http://www.thelatin library.com/augustine/trin13.shtml: "Sed aliud sunt ea quae creduntur, aliud fides qua creduntur."

34. I owe this observation to Geoff Koziol. On faith outside of religion, I am particularly indebted to Albert Ascoli, "Worthy of Faith?"; and Ascoli's unpublished essay, "What's in a Word?: '*Fede*' and Its Doubles in the 16th Century."

35. A recent attempt to historicize faith, and sometimes its relationship to belief, is Hummel, ed., *Doxa*. The *locus classicus* for historicizing faith, locating the transition from Judaism to Christianity in the emergence of pistis from the Hebrew *emunah*, is Buber, *Two Types of Faith*. For Buber, pistis is very much an epistemological category, while emunah is a people's relationship to their God, and his theological project is to suggest the resources these alternative historical models of faith might provide for one another. A decidedly ahistorical discussion of faith, which perversely uses history to identify faith as universally and authentically separate from belief, is Smith, *Faith and Belief*. For the Roman and early Christian period, all of these have now been surpassed by Morgan, *Roman Faith and Christian Faith*.

36. On Plato and his successors on the unreliability of belief, see, e.g., Vogt, *Belief and Truth*.

37. Grimaldi, "A Note on the Pisteis"; William Grimaldi, "Appendix: The Role of the πίστεις in Aristotle's Methodology," in *Aristotle, Rhetoric I*, pp. 349–57; Arash Abizadeh, "The Passions of the Wise"; Swearingen, "Pistis, Expression, and Belief."

38. Kinneavy, *Greek Rhetorical Origins*, pp. 12–13 and 20–21. More generally, Kinneavy argues that the "intellectual element" of faith, belief *that* rather than belief *in*, was largely absent from the Old Testament and from Judaism before the Middle Ages (pp. 6–7). But see below.

39. Morgan, *Roman Faith and Christian Faith*.

40. Kinneavy, *Greek Rhetorical Origins*.

41. Marno, *Death Be Not Proud*, ch. 1. I am indebted to Marno for discussing these issues with me.

42. Russell and Lull, eds., *Martin Luther's Basic Theological Writings*, p. 327.

43. On the two Latin translations, see *Luther's Smaller and Larger Catechisms*, pp. 11–12; Flood, "The Book in Reformation Germany." Both Latin versions, and several German variants, are in WA 30.1, pp. 296–97 and p. 250.

44. Bentley, *Humanists and Holy Writ*, pp. 182–83.

45. I owe thanks to Kinch Hoekstra for discussing this and other linguistic issues with me.

46. Bellarmino, *Tertiae Controversiae*, p. 12. See also the final words of the Athanasian Creed, "This is the catholic faith [*fides*]; which except a man believe [*crediderit*] truly [*fideliter*] and firmly, he cannot be saved."

47. Mair, "Cultures of Belief," p. 452.

48. See Bell, *Ritual Theory*, relying on the foundational work of Pierre Bourdieu.

49. See, e.g., Pouillon, "Remarks on the Verb 'to Believe,'" first published in French in 1979; Malcolm Ruel, "Christians as Believers, " in his *Belief, Ritual and the Securing of Life*; special issue of *Social Analysis*, vol. 52, no.1 (2008), entitled *Against Belief?*; special issue of *Ethos: Journal of the Society for Psychological Anthropology* 40, no. 3 (2012), entitled *The Dynamics of Belief and Experience*; Springer, "Towards a Situation Theory"; Kirsch, "Restaging the Will to Believe"; Mair, "Cultures of Belief"; Bae, "Believing Selves." On specifically Christian anthropology, see, e.g., Keane, *Christian Moderns*; Smilde, *Reason to Believe*; and the comments on the religious commitments of anthropologists themselves in Larsen, *The Slain God*.

50. I hesitate to criticize works in another field, so I will only name a few of the finest works that fall victim to this trend even while trying valiantly to oppose it: Lindquist and Coleman, "Introduction: Against Belief?"; Mitchell and Mitchell, "For Belief"; Lindholm, "What Is Bread?"; Pouillon, "Remarks on the Verb 'To Believe.'"

51. One important exception is Malcolm Ruel, an anthropologist of Africa who wrote *en passant* a brilliant exposition of the history of Christian belief: Ruel, "Christians as believers." Another exception is Mair, "Cultures of Belief," p. 450, where he urges "an effort to describe with precision *historically specific modes or styles of belief,* in relation to their specific contexts." I would also point as positive models to Carlisle and Simon, "Believing Selves"; Kirsch, "Restaging the Will to Believe."

52. Asad, *Genealogies of Religion*, pp. 29 and 42. See also a slightly earlier version of the argument in Talal Asad, "Anthropological Conceptions of Religion."

53. Asad, *Genealogies of Religion*, pp. 45–46.

54. See Asad, "Free Speech, Blasphemy, and Secular Criticism," in Asad, Brown, Butler, and Mahmood, *Is Critique Secular?*, where he does acknowledge more fully the history of Christian belief, but where the *telos* of that history in Kant becomes the basis for an extended critique of belief's normalizing power.

55. The dated but still foundational work remains Price, *Belief.* Early and influential volumes of essays include Bogdan, ed., *Belief*; Parret, ed., *On Believing.* On intuitions and paradoxes in the philosophy of knowledge, see Wolgast, *Paradoxes of Knowledge.* My examples are chosen from epistemology, but belief is also important to ethics, the philosophy of language, and other subfields. See Nottelmann, ed., *New Essays on Belief*; and the wonderfully concise overview in the Stanford Encyclopedia of Philosophy: https://plato.stanford.edu/entries /belief/. On belief in the philosophy of action, see particularly Hunter, ed., *Belief and Agency.* One subfield where the philosophy of belief does make bluntly universalizing claims is the philosophy of mind, especially when it overlaps with cognitive science: see, e.g., Carruthers, *The Architecture of the Mind.*

56. The lottery paradox first appeared in Kyburg, *Probability*, and has spawned many more sophisticated versions. On justification, see, e.g., Swinburne, *Epistemic Justification*; Smith, *Between Probability and Certainty*; Audi, *Epistemology*; McCain, *Evidentialism.* A recent trend has turned away from justification and instead toward "reasons" for belief, suggesting that people might believe for more practical or ethical reasons rather than doxastic reliability: see, e.g., Reisner and Steglich-Petersen, eds., *Reasons for Belief*; McCormick, *Believing Against the Evidence.* In this vein also are studies of "acceptance": Cohen, "Belief and Acceptance"; Bratman, "Practical Reasoning"; Bouvier and Künstler, eds., *Croire ou accepter?.*

57. See Sheehan and Wahrman, *Invisible Hands.*

58. Byrne, *Probability and Opinion*, p. 68.

59. Nozick, *The Nature of Rationality*; Williams, "Deciding to Believe," in his *Problems of the Self*; Reisner, "Leaps of Knowledge," in Chen, ed., *The Aim of Belief.* And see Chen, ed., *The Aim of Belief*, passim. William James is here cited in the work of another voluntarist philosopher: Helm, *Belief Policies*, p. 100.

60. On Augustine's debt to stoic philosophy in this formulation, especially in his rejection of "voluntarism," see Frede, *A Free Will*, ch. 9.

61. Quoted in Green and Williams, "Introduction," in., *Moore's Paradox*, p. 7.

62. Stanford Encyclopedia of Philosophy online, entry for G. E. Moore, at: https://plato.stanford.edu/entries/moore/; Green and Williams, eds., *Moore's Paradox*; Engel, ed., *Believing and Acceptance.*

63. See the discussion of dissimulation in Sorin Alexandrescu, "Saying and (Dis)believing," in Parret, ed., *On Believing.* For a recent argument for why certain categories of belief-claims are irrational, see Pettigrew, *Accuracy.*

64. See Gibbons, *The Norm of Belief*, ch. 9, on Moore's paradox and nonstandard semantics.

65. I take as my model Euan Cameron's groundbreaking study *Enchanted Europe*, which analyzed "superstition" as an intellectual problem rather than a lived condition: Cameron, *Enchanted Europe*.

66. See, e.g., Plamper, *The History of Emotions*; Frevert, *Emotions in History*; Frevert et al., *Emotional Lexicons*; Menin, " 'Who Will Write the History of Tears?.' " The touchstone in this field is Reddy, *The Navigation of Feeling*. And of particular importance for my project is Karant-Nunn, *The Reformation of Feeling*. I owe thanks to Ute Frevert for discussing these issues with me.

67. A fascinating history of Jewish debates over the meaning of religious belief in the Middle Ages is Kellner, *Dogma*. On the importance of propositional or epistemic belief in the Muslim tradition, see the response to Asad and Mahmood in March, "Speech and the Sacred."

68. The literature on the epistemology of witchcraft, magic, and possession in early modern Europe is vast, but begin with Clark, *Thinking with Demons*; Sluhovsky, *Believe Not Every Spirit*.

69. Cf. Lilla, *The Stillborn God*; Taylor, *A Secular Age*; Gillespie, *The Theological Origins of Modernity*; Alasdair MacIntyre, *After Virtue*.

Chapter One: Medieval Varieties of Believing

1. *Mirk's Festial*, pp. 167–68. The manuscript reads "why God would be lieved," which I have modernized to "be believed," as it appears in the first printed edition in 1486.

2. Marrou, "Saint Augustin et l'ange," pp. 401–13. The story is perhaps based upon a stray reference, in an apocryphal letter from Cyril of Jerusalem to Augustine of Hippo, about the impossibility of pouring the sea into a *vasculo*, or small container.

3. Ahl, "Benozzo Gozzoli's Frescoes"; Gill, *Augustine*, p. 92.

4. De Voraigne, *Legenda Aurea*, pp. 276–77.

5. Frances Young writes that in the period of the creation of the Christian creeds, "the primary issue concerned the nature of God conceived as transcendent yet in relationship with the world": Young, *The Making of the Creeds*, p. 103. For a persuasive gendered reading of the gulf between God and creation in patristic theology, see Burrus, *"Begotten, Not Made."* See also Funkenstein, *Theology*, p. 49. As Samuel Robinson describes this dilemma, "God must be apart from the mutable, changing, created world—or else how is he an eternal, perfect, creating God? But he must also, at some level, participate in the temporal—or else whence creation? Or why bother with religion and the divine?": Robinson, "Flesh Redeemed."

6. The fundamental work is Colish, *The Mirror of Language*.

7. Augustine, *Predestination of the Saints*, ch. 5. "Ipsum credere, nihil aliud est, quam cum assensione cogitare."

8. Augustine, *Predestination of the Saints*, ch. 5: "cogitaverit esse credendum."

9. Augustine, *On the Spirit and the Letter*, ch. 54.

10. Ponitfex, ed., *St. Augustine: The Problem of Free Choice*, p. 79. Checked against *De Libero Arbitrio* 2.2.4-6, in http://www.augustinus.it/latino/libero _arbitrio/index2.htm: "Deinde iam credentibus dicit, Quaerite et invenietis: nam neque inventum dici potest, quod incognitum creditur; neque quisquam inveniendo Deo fit idoneus, nisi ante crediderit quod est postea cogniturus."

11. Augustine, Sermo 43.7-9, in *PL* 38, cols. 257-58. My translation.

12. Anselm, *Proslogium*, ch. 1, in *Works of St. Anselm*, trans. Sidney Norton Deane (1903), checked against: http://www.thelatinlibrary.com/anselmproslogion .html: "Non tento, Domine, penetrare altitudinem tuam, quia nullatenus comparo illi intellectum meum; sed desidero aliquatenus intelligere veritatem tuam, quam credit et amat cor meum. Neque enim quaero intelligere ut credam, sed credo ut intelligam."

13. Anselm, *De Incarnatione Verbi*, 1.i: pp. 267-70, trans. Hopkins, , checked against *D. Anselmi . . . Operum Omnium* (Cologne, 1612), vol. 3, p. 34.

14. Colish, *The Mirror of Language*, p. 59.

15. Greene, *Logical Fictions*, p. 110 and ch. 5 passim. See also Collish, *Mirror of Language*, ch. 2.

16. Richard of St. Victor, *On the Trinity*, I.1,. Checked against Richard de Saint-Victor, *De Trinitate*, pp. 86-87.

17. Richad of St. Victor, *On the Trinity*, I.4, checked against *De Trinitate*, pp. 89-90. I have kept Couser's translation of *probabiles* as "credible" rather than "probable," in recognition of the premodern meaning of probability, even though Couser translates *probabilia* as "probable" a few sentences later and notes that the expression "probable reasons" was derived from Richard's predecessor, Hugh of St. Victor.

18. On Anslem, see Colish, *Mirror of Language*, pp. 81-92.

19. John Tolan, *L'Europe latine*, pp. 121-24. My translations.

20. Tertullian, *De Carne Christi*, 5.4.

21. Lactantius, *The Divine Institutes*, 2.7. Checked against *PL* 6, col. 285B-286A: "Si credis, cur ergo rationem requiris, quae potest efficere ne credas? Si vero rationem requiris, et quaerendam putas, ergo non credis. Ideo enim quaeris, ut eam sequaris, cum inveneris."

22. See especially Pseudo-Dionysius, *On Divine Names*, ch. 7.

23. *Reading the Gospels with Gregory the Great*, ed. and trans. Bhattacharji, p. 92. Checked against *PL* 76, col. 1197C: "Sed sciendum nobis est quod divina operatio si ratione comprehenditur, non est admirabilis; nec fides habet meritum, cui humana ratio praebet experimentum."

24. Most, *Doubting Thomas*, p. 145.

25. This paragraph is drawn from Eileen Sweeney, "New Standards for Certainty: Early Receptions of Aristotle's Posterior Analytics," in Denery et al., eds., *Uncertain Knowledge*, pp. 37-62. See also Teske, "William of Auvergne on the Relation between Reason and Faith," in his *Studies*.

26. McGinn, *The Foundations of Mysticism*, p. xvii.

27. Suso, *The Exemplar*, pp. 70–71.

28. Justice, "Eucharistic Miracle."

29. Suso, *A Little Book of Eternal Wisdom*, pp. 77–79. Checked against Lehmann, ed., *Heinrich Seuses*, vol. 2, pp. 84–85.

30. Ruysbroeck, *The Adornment*, 1.21. Checked against *D. Ioannis Rvsbrochii*, p. 434.

31. From Balliol College MS 354, p. 340, cited online at http://www.dimev .net/record.php?recID=6709. The verse is sometimes attributed to Reginald Pecock, although there are many different versions. For another example, see Love, *Incipit Speculum*, sig.M6v, sometimes attributed to Bonaventura.

32. Bernard of Clairvaux, *Life and Works of St. Bernard*, vol. 2, pp. 871–72, Letter 338, to Cardinal Haimeric. See also vol. 2, pp. 565–66.

33. For Gerson, see, e.g., Gerson, *Early Works*, pp. 268–69. For Cusa, see, e.g., Cusa, Sermon 4 (Fides autem Catholica) in *Cusa's Early Sermons*, pp. 62–63; Sermon 189 (Qui manducat hunc panem) in vol. 3, pp. 284–85 of *Didactic Sermons*.

34. On medieval accounts of language as signs that cannot fully signify the divine, see Colish, *The Mirror of Language*.

35. There has been a recent surge of scholarship on medieval skepticism, especially by philosophers. See, e.g., Lagerlund, ed., *Rethinking the History of Skepticism*; for a more skeptical approach to medieval skepticism, see Perler, *Zweifel und Gewissheit*.

36. Byrne, *Probability and Opinion*, p. 54.

37. Byrne, *Probability and Opinion*, p. 68.

38. Peter Abelard famously argued that the trinity *was* available to reason even without revelation; but few concurred, and every theologian before the seventeenth century admitted at least some doctrines beyond or against reason.

39. *ST* IIb.2.1. "Knows or thinks by science" is an attempt by the translator to account for the technical meanings of words in scholastic theology: the Latin is simply "ea quae scit vel intelligit," words which imply deductive demonstration. See also *ST* I.1.8, where Aquinas argues that sacred doctrine is indeed susceptible to rational argument, which can prove things of God that were not previously known, as long as the discussants are believers.

40. Kempshall, *Rhetoric*, p. 420.

41. Coolman, *Knowing God*, p.127.

42. Mishtooni Bose, "Vernacular Opinions," in Denery et al., eds., *Uncertain Knowledge*, p. 252.

43. Colish, *The Mirror of Language*, p. 128.

44. On these issues see Evans, *Getting it Wrong*, especially part IV.

45. As Edmund Byrne put it, "The believer . . . might very well have a false opinion (*falsum aliquid aestimare*) about matters which require merely human conjecture, as for example with regard to the precise time of Christ's birth; but that he should have a false opinion about what is 'of faith' is impossible. In other words, within a carefully prescribed area, namely, that of the defined doctrines

of the Church, the believer shares in the knowledge of God himself and to just that extent is immune from error." Byrne, *Probability and Opinion*, p. 114.

46. Lactantius, *The Divine Institutes*, p. 417. See also further remarks on this subject on p. 568. For Cicero, see, e.g., Serjeantson, "Proof and Persuasion,", p. 147: "probabile inventum ad faciendam fidem."

47. Pasnau, "Medieval Social Epistemology"; Pasnau, *Theories of Cognition*, ch. 7. And see the wonderful collection, Denery et al., eds., *Uncertain Knowledge*, especially the contributions by Eileen Sweeney and Mishtooni Bose.

48. This paragraph is based upon Mishtooni Bose, "Vernacular Opinions."

49. Augustine, *De Utilitate Credendi*, 1.25.

50. Augustine, *De Utilitate Credendi*, 1.25. "Quod intellegimus igitur, debemus rationi: quod credimus, auctoritati: quod opinamur, errori." Giles of Rome attempted in the fourteenth century to frame this notion of belief as acceptance of authority in Aristotelian terms, arguing in a commentary on Artistotle's *Rhetoric* that we properly believe according to the character of the witness: see Rita Copeland, "Living with Uncertainty: Reactions to Aristotle's Rhetoric in the Later Middle Ages," in Denery et al., eds., *Uncertain Knowledge*, p. 126.

51. Augustine, *De Utilitate Credendi*, 1.26, 1.31. Checked against https://www.augustinus.it/latino/utilita_credere/index.htm.

52. Augustine, *Contra Epistolam Manichaei* 5.6 (*PL* 42:176).

53. Augustine, Sermo CXLIV, in *PL* 38:788. "Nam si fidem habet sine spe ac sine delectione, Christum esse credit, non in Christum credit. Qui ergo in Christum credit, credendo in Christum, venit in eum Christus, et quodam modo unitur in eum, et membrum in corpore eius efficitur. Quod fieri non potest, nisi et spes accedat et charitas."

54. Augustine, *Tractates on the Gospel of John*, tr. 29.6.: "Sed si creditis in eum, creditis ei: non autem continuo qui credit ei, credit in eum. Nam et daemones credebant ei, et non credebant in eum. Rursus etiam de Apostolis ipsius possumus dicere: Credimus Paulo; sed non: Credimus in Paulum: Credimus Petro; sed non: Credimus in Petrum. *Credenti* enim *in eum qui iustificat impium, deputatur fides eius ad iustitiam.* Quid est ergo credere in eum? Credendo amare, credendo diligere, credendo in eum ire, et eius membris incorporari."

55. Anselm, *Monologium* 76–78. "Satis itaque convenienter dici potest viva fides credere in id in quod credi debet, mortua vero fides credere tantum id quod credi debet."

56. Lombard, *Sentences*, vol. 3, 23: 3–4, pp. 97–99. Checked against *PL* 192: 805. The second category, "to believe in *a* God," is a loose translation of Lombard's *credere deum*, since Latin has no definite article. "To believe that there is God" might be a better translation, for Lombard describes it as "Credere quod ipse sit Deus, quod etiam mali faciunt." And see Aquinas, *ST* IIb.2.2.

57. *Le Mer des Hystoires*, fo. 20r: "Mais croire en dieu c'est famer et honorer en croyant qu'il est. Les bons et les mauvais indifferemment croyent dieu; mais il n'ya que les bons qui croyent en dieu, comme veult le maistre de senentces ou iiie livre en la distinction xxiii."

58. Hoffmann, *Die Lehre*, p. 123: "Credere implicite est credere in hoc universali, quicquid credit ecclesia, credere esse verum." See also the discussion of implicit faith in Schmitt, "Du bon usage du 'credo.'"

59. Van Engen, "Faith as a Concept of Order," p. 40.

60. Schmitt, "Du bon usage du 'credo.'"

61. Julian of Norwich, *Showing of Love*, ch. 33.

62. Mandeville, *Here begynneth a lytell treatyse*, pp. 107–8.

63. Ockham, *Dialogus*, I.3.10. "Dubitans autem de articulo aliquo speciali habet fidem firmam quod tota fides christiana est vera et certa. Habet etiam fidem firmam implicitam de eodem articulo de quo dubitat. Et ideo est catholicus licet de tali articulo non habeat fidem firmam explicitam." See also I.3.1.

64. McGrade, *The Political Thought of William of Ockham*, p. 49. See also Ritschl, *Fides implicita*; Hoffmann, *Die Lehre*; Reginald Schultes, *Fides Implicita*.

65. Augustine, *Tractates on the Gospel of John*, tr. 29.6. "Rursus etiam de Apostolis ipsius possumus dicere: Credimus Paulo; sed non: Credimus in Paulum: Credimus Petro; sed non: Credimus in Petrum."

66. Augustine, *Sermo 244*, in *PL* 39:2195: "Credite in Spiritum sanctum, credite sanctam Ecclesiam."

67. Rufinus, *A Commentary on the Apostles' Creed*, pp. 71–72. And see endnote 219 in this edition of Rufinus for other patristic examples of this argument, as well as for ancient authorities predating Augustine and Rufinus, like Tertullian, who seemed unembarrassed about believing *in* the Church.

68. Cited in Outlon, "The Apostles."

69. Cited in Lubac, *The Christian Faith*, pp. 164–65.

70. Chrysologus, *Sermo 62*, in *PL* 52:375: "In sanctam ecclesiam. Quia ecclesia in Christo, et in ecclesia Christus est; qui ergo ecclesiam fatetur, in ecclesiam se confessus est credidisse."

71. *PL* 23:167A and note.

72. *PL* 212:707D. "Credis in sanctam Ecclesiam, id est credis neminem posse salvari, nisi in unitate corporis Ecclesiae fideliter permanentem?"

73. *ST* IIb.1.9. See also Aquinas, *Scriptum Super Sententiis*, 3.25.q.1, art. 2, where he seems to think that Anselm has also used the preposition *in*.

74. Kroon, *We Believe in God and Christ*, p. 5.

75. See, e.g., Roye, *La Doctrinal de Sapience*, p. 4r. And in the English translation, the same formulation is used: *Thus Endeth the Doctrinal of Sapyence*, sig. A4r; and see Wood, *Conscience*, pp. 121–23, quoting the C Text of Piers Plowman, where Conscience says, "*credere in ecclesia*, in holy kyrke to bileue."

76. Van Engen, "Faith as a Concept of Order."

77. Augustine, Ep. 98 to Boniface, at https://www.ccel.org/ccel/schaff/npnf101 .pdf, checked against *PL* 33:364. "Nihil est autem aliud credere, quam fidem habere … Itaque parvulum, etsi nondum fides illa quae in credentium voluntate consistit, jam tamen ipsius fidei sacramentum fidelem facit. Nam sicut credere respondetur, ita etiam fidelis vocatur, non rem ipsa mente annuendo, sed ipsius

rei sacramentum percipiendo." The problem whether to translate *fides* as faith or belief is unusually acute in this passage.

78. Ivo of Chartres, *Panormia*, I.56.

79. Quoted in Van Engen, "Faith as a Concept of Order," p. 28. "Et sic pavuli credunt, quia habent fidem habitualem sicut dormiens visum."

80. Lombard, *Sentences* III.23.5, quoted in Hampson, *Christian Contradictions*, p. 30.

81. Watson, *Noble History of King Ponthus*, sig. L4r.

82. Voraigne, *Legenda Aurea*, p. 225r.

83. Henry Parker, *Dives et Pauper*, sig. P3r. See also sig.V1v for more examples.

84. Leo the Great, *Letters and Sermons*, pp. 208–9, 406.

85. See the Database of Latin Dictionaries, online at http://clt.brepolis.net /dld/pages/QuickSearch.aspx. Certainly there were contexts when *credentia* was used in a more fluid sense to mean the content of religious doctrine, whether true or false.

86. For this paragraph, see Tolan, *Saracens*. I owe thanks to Geoff Koziol for this reference.

87. Hyland, "John-Jerome of Prague," pp. 204–6.

88. *ST* IIb.2.2.

89. Abulafia, *Christians and Jews*; Klepper, *Insight of Unbelievers*, especially ch. 3; Cohen, *Friars and the Jews*.

90. See Moore, *Formation of a Persecuting Society*. See also Laursen and Nederman, eds., *Beyond the Persecuting Society*; Iogna-Prat, *Order and Exclusion*. I owe thanks to Maureen Miller for discussing these issues with me and directing me to relevant literature.

91. Reeves, "Teaching the Creed," p. 188.

92. See Arnold, *Belief and Unbelief*.

93. Augustine, *Eighty-Three Different Questions*, p. 83: "Question 48: On What Can Be Believed." Checked against *PL* 40, col. 31: "De Credibilibus: Credibiloum tria sunt genera. Alia sunt quae semper credentur, et nunquam intelliguntur: sicut est omnis historia, temporalia et humana gesta percurrens. Alia quae mox, ut creduntor, intelliguntur: sicut sunt omnes rationes humanae, vel de numeris, vel de quibuslibet disciplinis. Tertium, quae primo credentur, et postea intelliguntur: qualia sun tea quae de divinis rebus non possunt intelligi, nisi ab his qui mundo sunt corde; quod fit praeceptis servatis, quae de bene vivendo accipiuntur."

94. On the possibility of embodied belief, see, e.g., Sørensen and Rebay-Salisbury, eds., *Embodied Knowledge*; Lakoff and Johnson, *Philosophy in the Flesh*. On the relationship between the spiritual and the physical in the Middle Ages, see Bynum, *Christian Materiality*.

95. Mirk, *Liber Festivalis*, sig. N5r.

96. For an early version, see Quodvultdeus of Carthage, *The Creedal Homilies*, p. 69.

97. *Theologia Germanica*, p. 88, checked against *Theologia Deutsch*, pp. 100–101.

98. Aquinas, *Expositio in Symbolum Apostolorum*.

Chapter Two: The Reformation of Belief

1. *LW*, vol. 29, p. 235. *WA* 57, pp. 252–53: "'Credere Deum' adeo esse facile multis videtur, ut id et poetis et philosophis tribuerint . . . Verum talis fides humana est sicut et alia quaedam himinis cogitatio, ars, prudentia, somnium etc. Haec enim omnia, quam cito tentatio ingruit, mox ruunt."

2. See Hoffmann, "Atheism as a Devotional Category"; Erdozain, *The Soul of Doubt*; Schreiner, *Are You Alone Wise?*. And see Alec Ryrie's brilliant unpublished paper, "Faith, Doubt, and the Emergence of Atheism."

3. See Old, *Reading and Preaching of the Scriptures*, pp. 19–27.

4. *LW*, vol. 22, pp. 148–58. *WA* 46, p. 669. Note the similarity to John Calvin's later *duplex congitio Domini*, as brilliantly described in Pitkin, *What Pure Eyes Could See*. See also Dowey, "Influence of the Twofold Knowledge on Calvin's Theology," in his *Knowledge of God*.

5. *LW*, vol. 22, p. 364. *WA* 47, p. 88: "Dan er ist warhafftiger Gott nicht allein an seiner person, sonder auch, was sein ampt und werk anlanget." "Drumb ists recht essentialis definitio, das alhier von ihme gesaget wirdt: wer an ihnem gleubet, der hatt das ewige leben."

6. Luther, *Martin Luther's Basic Theological Writings*, p. 409. *WA* 7, p. 54.

7. *LW*, vol. 22, p. 358. *WA* 47, p. 83: "Den viel sagen mit dem munde: Ich bin ein Christ, aber im hertzen gleuben sie es nicht."

8. Susan Schreiner observes that for the reformers, uncertainty was "the natural state of the fallen human soul," while certainty, which is a prerequisite for belief, comes only from God: Schreiner, *Are You Alone Wise?*, p. 74.

9. Hamm, "Why Did 'Faith' Become for Luther the Central Concept of the Christian Life," in his *Reformation of Faith*, p. 166.

10. *Martin Luther's Basic Theological Writings*, p. 78. Checked against the forward to the Epistle to the Romans in the 1545 Luther Bible, *Biblia*.

11. *LW*, vol. 1, pp. 147–49. *WA* 42, pp.111–12. On this issue see Denery, *The Devil Wins*.

12. See Schreiner, *Are You Alone Wise?*

13. *LW*, Vol. 3, pp. 18–22. My emphasis. *WA* 42, pp. 561–63: "Et Deus cum promittit aliquid, hoc exigit, ut id credamus, hoc est, ut verum esse fide statuamus, nec dubitemus eventum responsurum promissioni."

14. *LW*, Vol. 3, pp. 21–22. *WA* 42, pp. 562–64.

15. Rupp and Watson, eds., *Luther and Erasmus*, p. 109. *WA* 18, p. 605: "Spiritus Sanctus non est Scepticus, nec dubia aut opiniones in cordibus nostris scripsit, sed assertiones ipsa vita et omni experientia certiores et firmiores."

16. *LW*, vol. 16, p. 82. *WA* 31.2, pp. 57–58: "Nam qui credunt deo, faciunt et repetunt veracem . . . et fiunt ipsi quoque veraces per fidem. Econtra Incredulis fallacia, infida, et incerta fiunt omnia."

17. *CR* 21, 163.

18. *CR* 21, 169.

19. *CR* 21, 171–72.

20. Ursinus, *Commentary of Dr. Zacharias*, pp. 139–40, and see p. 215. And see the Heidelberg Catechism itself, where belief is defined as not merely "Notitia" but also "certa fiducia, a spiritu sancto, per Evangelium in corde meo accensa, qua in Deo acquiesce, certo statuens, non solium aliis, sed mihi quoque remissionem peccatorum, aeternam iustitiam, et vitam donatum esse." Cited in Wandel, *Reading Catechisms*, pp. 77–78.

21. Calvin, *Institutes*, III.ii.2.

22. Here my argument corresponds closely to Pitkin, *What Pure Eyes Could See*, but while Pitkin sees this as a transition in Calvin's thought from fiducia to a kind of cognitio based in fiducia, to me the point is that authentic religious knowledge-claims have fiducia at their heart. It seems to me that we agree in substance while using different terminology for our different purposes.

23. *LW*, vol. 40 pp. 239–48. *WA* 26, pp. 154–61.

24. Foxe's preface to Rhegius, *An Instruccyon of Christen Fayth*, sig. A4r.

25. Ursinus, *Doctrinae Christianae Compendium*, p. 157: "Porro si fides est fiducia, ergo & notitia: utpote quam praesupponit. Oportet enim te primum novisse doctrinam antequam ei credas."

26. *CR* 21, 176. "Exercebis spiritum meditatione promisionum accurate, quod nisi e promissionibus cognosci neutiquam poterit Christus."

27. Wandel, *Reading Catechisms*, pp. 6–7.

28. Wandel, *Reading Catechisms*, p. 39.

29. *Credo*, p. 342.

30. Green, *Christian's ABC*.

31. This paragraph is gleaned from Pelikan, *Credo*, quotes on pp. 194 and 270–71.

32. Shagan and Shuger, eds., *Religion in Tudor England*, p. 560.

33. Fides historica was sometimes translated into English as "historical faith" and sometimes as "historical belief." See, for instance, two different Tudor translations of the runaway bestseller of the Italian Reformation, the *Beneficio di Cristo*, one of which translated the phrase as "historical faith" and the other as "historical belief": Babington, ed., *Benefit of Christ's Death*, from the Italian edition of 1543, pp. 30r-v. The 1548 English version of this passage is on pp. 131–32, for the 1580 version see *The Benefit that Christians Receiue by Iesus Christ Crucified*, sigs. D4v-D5r.

34. Fides historica in this positive sense was used, for instance, against the skeptic Philip Sidney, who mocked the historian "authorizing himself on the notable foundations of hearsay." Cited in Burke, "Two Crises of Historical Consciousness."

35. Within a very large literature, see, e.g., Grafton, *What Was History*; Grafton, *Forgers and Critics*; Popper, "An Ocean of Lies"; Kelley, "*Fides historiae*"; Kelley, *Foundations*; Ligota, "Annius of Viterbo and Historical Method,". My treatment of fides historica, both here and in chapter 5 below, has benefited from the constructive criticism of Tony Grafton.

36. Among Catholic writers, Gregory Martin, for instance, called fides historica an "heretical term, newly devised": *A discouerie of the manifold corruptions*, p. 193. For Catholic defenses of fides historica in Christianity, based upon the primacy of the intellect over the will in faith, see, e.g., Bellarmino, *Tertiae Controversiae*, pp. 12–16, 30, 77; Malderus, *In Primam Secundae*, pp. 584–85; Becanus, *Summa Theologiae Scholasticae*, pp. 283–85; Vasquez, *Commentarium*, pp. 506–11; Alvarez, *De Auxiliis Divinae Gratiae*, Disp. 49, pp. 341–53. I hope to write about this Catholic tradition elsewhere. Christian usage derives ultimately from Augustine: *De Vera Religione*, in *PL* 34, col.166, translated in Augustine, *Earlier Writings*, p. 275. But Augustine did not understand by historical faith what either humanists or Protestants would make of the term.

37. *The Loci Communes of Philip Melancthon*, pp. 174–75. See Römer, *Die Entwicklung*, p. 11. Heiko Oberman described this transformation as the replacement of *fides caritate formata* by *fides Christo formata*: faith formed by Christ. See Oberman, "'Iustitia Christi' and 'Iustitia Dei.'"

38. Calvin, *Institutes*, III, ii, 9–10. "Credunt certe plurimi Deum esse, Evangelicam historiam ac reliquas Scripturae partes versa esse arbitrantur (quale fere iudicium esse solet de iis quae vel olim gesta narrantur, vel ipsi praesentes spectavimus)." For a detailed review of the relationship between the intellect and the will in Calvin's understanding of faith, see Muller, "Fides and Cognitio," in his *The Unaccommodated Calvin*.

39. Vermigli, *In epistolam*, p. 539: "Sed requirimus assensum, non vulgarem, aut frigidum, qualis est illorum, qui ea, quae legunt in sacris literis, probare solent, humana persuasione, et probabili credulitate adducti, quemadmodum hodie Iudaei et Turcae multa nobiscum confitentur, et credunt: sed certum, et firmum, et efficacem, et ab afflatu Spiritus Sancti profectum." For another example, see *The Commentary of Dr. Zacharias Ursinus*, p. 114.

40. Rollock, *A Treatise of Gods Effectual Calling*, pp. 170–71.

41. Smith, *An Exposition of the Creed*, p. 17 and sig. A5v.

42. Walker, *The Key of Saving Knowledge*, pp. 82–3.

43. John Milton, *Areopagitica*, in St. John, ed., *The Prose Works of John Milton*, vol. 2, p. 85. I owe this reference to Vicky Kahn.

44. See the fascinating discussion in Hoekstra, "Hobbesian Equality," in Lloyd, ed., *Hobbes Today*. For Calvin's complex ruminations on this problem, see Pitkin, *What Pure Eyes Could See*, p. 29 and ch. 1 passim.

45. Bossy, *Christianity in the West*, passim but especially pp. 170–71.

46. For a description of the wide range of medieval Christian anthropology, from optimistic Ockhamists to pessimistic Augustinians, see Hamm, "From the Medieval 'Love of God' to the 'Faith' of Luther—A Contribution to the History of Penitence," in his *The Reformation of Faith*.

47. My translation from Ignatius's Spanish, "Debemos siempre tener para en todo acertar, que lo blanco que yo veo, creer que es negro, si la Iglesia hierárchica assí lo determina": Ignatius of Loyola, *Ejercicios Espirituales*, p. 172. Loyola's Spanish version was not published until 1615; the loose Latin translation ap-

proved by the pope in 1548, which circulated more widely, translated *"creer"* as *"pronunciare."* However, the extended Latin passage retained the notion of "believing" with the infallible Church: "quod oculis nostris apparet album, nigrum illa esse diffinierit, debemus itidem, quod nigrum sit, pronunciare. Indubitate namque credendum est: eundem esse Domini nostri Iesu Christi, et Ecclesiae orthodoxae, sponsae eius, spiritum, per quem gubernamur ac dirigimur ad salutem": Ignatius of Loyola, *Exercitia Spiritualia*, p. 139v.

48. This paragraph is gleaned from Gleason, *Gasparo Contarini*, especiallly ch. 4. Thanks to Ed Muir for bringing this book to my attention.

49. Du Perron, *Replique à la Response*, p. 44.

50. Bellarmino, *Catechismus*, p. 10: "D: Explica mihi verbotenus articulum primum, videlicet CREDO." "M: Tantundem est, ac si diceret: Credo firmiter, & indubitatè Omnia illa, quae his XII articulis comprehensa sunt, ideo quidem quod ipsemet Deus eos, Apostolos suos docuisset, Apostoli vero Ecclesiam, Ecclesia vero nobis eosdem tradidisset. Et quia impossibile est mentiri Deum, ideo credo mutlo firmius res illas, quam quas vel oculis videam, vel manibus contrectem."

51. Cited in Wandel, *Reading Catechisms*, pp. 76–77 (and an image of the Latin Text is on p. 42).

52. N.N. [Peter Talbot], *A Treatise of the Nature of Catholick Faith*, pp. 88–89. For a very similar discussion of the "rule of believing," see *Iudicium acatholicorum credenti* (1628) by the Jesuit leader of the Counter-Reformation in Bohemia, Valerianus Magni, discussed in Scholder, *Birth of Modern Critical Theology*, pp. 14–18.

53. Schreiner, *Are You Alone Wise?*, ch. 4.

54. Vigor, *Sermons Catholiques*, p. 38r. On Vigor's radicalism, see Diefendorf, *Beneath the Cross*; Larissa Taylor, "Dangerous Vocations: Preaching in France in the Late Middle Ages and Reformations," in Taylor, ed., *Preachers and People*.

55. Vigor, *Sermons Catholiques*, p. 39v: "Et quand tells ont esté enseignez ils n'ont pas demandé raison, mais simplement *Credo*."

56. Vigor, *Sermons Catholiques*, p. 41v.

57. Vigor, *Sermons Catholiques*, p.4 3v.

58. Vigor, *Sermons Catholiques*, p. 42v: "Bref, il nous fault croire en l'Eglise Catholique & adiouster foy sans douter aucunement de ce qu'elle nous proposera."

59. Vigor, *Sermons Catholiques*, p. 147v.

60. Vigor, *Sermons Catholiques*, p. 146r: "C'est ceste saincte Eglise qui luy dit qu'il faut croire en Iesus Christ."

61. Vigor, *Sermons Catholiques*, p. 148r: "Bref à tout les choses qui sont preches selon la foy & doctrine de ceste Eglise saincte & Catholique, i'y adiouste foy, & en general ie croy tout ce que l'Eglise croit, ce m'est assez d'estre ainsi bien fondé sur la foy de ceste Eglise, laquelle ne peut errer."

62. Lippomano, *Espositioni Volgari*, pp. 5r–6v.

63. *De Infidelitate et Tribus Eius Speciebus*, pp. 1–2, 17. "Et quoniam doctrina fidei nostrae, electione humana proprie non suscipitur, neque ingenio hominis invenitur."

64. Beauxamis, *De Fido et Symbolo*, pp. 77v and 80v–81r: "Credere vera esse quae loquitur, multi et mali possunt, qui quae credunt vera, non faciunt," and "Ex his manifestum est et Daemones, et Gentiles, Deum unum cognovisse, et credidisse. Veruntamen a nobis differunt, quod in eum quem noverant, non crediderunt: quia cum Deum cognovissent, non sicut Deum glorificaverunt. Et hoc maxima ignorantia est, cum Dei maiestatem, quem unum esse sciebant, alicui creatorum detulerit."

65. *Catechisme ou Instructions des Premiers Fondemens*, pp. 9–11. The text purports to be a translation of the famous catechism by the German Bishop of Merseburg, Michael Helding, but it is actually such a free translation as to be an original text. "Nous sommes transportez en luy par une amour & affection, pour prendre en bonne part tout ce qu'il nous commandera, ores que ce qu'il nous commande, ne soit beaucoup favorable à nos desirs & à nostre corrompu naturel."

66. *Catechism of the Council of Trent*.

67. Cardinal Cajetan, Tommaso De Vio, *Opuscula Omnia Thomae De Vio*, I.ii.21, p. 44: "pro ecclesia in terris, ut iungitur Spiritui sancto, ratione cuius dicimur credere in ecclesiam."

68. Martin, ed., *The New Testament of Jesus Christ*, p. 409.

69. Joanne Gibboni, *Disputatio Theologica de Sanctis*, sig. E4v, at no. 131. "Patres etiam antiqui ita legebant articulum fidei indifferenter, Credo in Ecclesiam Catholicam, vel credo Ecclesiam Catholicam."

70. Suarez, *Opus de Triplici Virtute Theologica*, I.ii.6, p. 18. "Sed vel tantum ad objectum creditum, ita ut credere in sanctam ecclesiam, nihil aliud sit quam credere illam esse unam et sanctam, vel ad summum, est credere illi, ut regulae infallibili fidei testificanti, et proponenti ex motione spiritus sancti."

71. See, e.g., Carboni, *Summae Summarum*, III.i, p. 26; Malderus, *De Virtutibus Theologicis*, pp. 84–85; Fassari, *Immaculata Deiparae Conceptio*, p. 138.

72. Hufton, "Every Tub on Its Own Bottom," p. 7; Moss and Wallace, *Rhetoric and Dialectic*, pp. 117–18; Schwickerath, *Jesuit Education*.

73. Wandel, *Reading Catechisms*, pp. 26–27. See also Walsham, "Wholesome Milk and Strong Meat"; Carter, *Creating Catholics*; Catto, "Les deux voies des catéchismes."

74. Quotations are from Franck, *280 Paradoxes or Wondrous Sayings*, checked against Franck, *Paradoxa*. The idea of a "radical Reformation" alongside its magisterial cousins was developed in Williams, *Radical Reformation*. For a recent review of the concept, see Heal and Kremers, eds., *Radicalism and Dissent*.

75. *280 Paradoxes*, p. 375; *Paradoxa*, p. 348.

76. *280 Paradoxes*, pp. 39–42; *Paradoxa*, pp. 40–43.

77. *280 Paradoxes*, pp. 48–49; *Paradoxa*, pp. 48–49.

78. *280 Paradoxes*, p. 354; *Paradoxa*, pp. 329–30.

79. *280 Paradoxes*, p. 372; *Paradoxa*, p. 348.

80. *280 Paradoxes*, p. 379; *Paradoxa*, p. 352. Franck here may have been influenced by Thomas Müntzer, on whose views of faith/belief see the insightful article: Scott, "Müntzer and the Mustard-Seed."

81. *280 Paradoxes*, p. 376; *Paradoxa*, p. 349. See similar views in Müntzer, "Through experiencing unbelief the elect leaves behind him all the counterfeit faith he has learnt, heard, or read from scripture; for he sees that an outward testimony cannot create inward reality": quoted in Schreiner, *Are You Alone Wise?*, p. 94.

82. *280 Paradoxes*, p. 375; *Paradoxa*, p. 348.

83. *De Fide* was first published posthumously in Latin on a secret press: Castellio, *Dialogi IIII*. On its publication and reputation, see Hudson, "An Identification." I have used here the English translation of 1679, Castellio, *Conference*, checked against the 1578 original. However, in the course of my research I also discovered the existence of a much earlier English translation by the prolific puritan translator Arthur Golding, who claimed in the preface not to have known the identity of the author: *A most excellent and profitable dialogue, of the powerfull iustifying faith shewing what it is to beleeue in God.*

84. Castellio, *Conference*, p. 61. *Dialogi IIII*, p. 291.

85. Castellio, *Conference*, p. 15. *Dialogi IIII*, p. 263.

86. Castellio, *Conference*, p. 19. *Dialogi IIII*, p. 266.

87. Castellio, *Conference*, p. 53. *Dialogi IIII*, p. 286.

88. Castellio, *Conference*, pp. 60–61. *Dialogi IIII*, pp. 290–91.

89. *Complete Writings of Menno*, p. 96. Checked against Simons, *Opera Omnia Theologica*, pp. 121–32 for *The New Birth* and pp. 1–70 for *The Foundation of Christian Doctrine*.

90. *The Complete Writings of Menno Simons*, p. 97.

91. *The Complete Writings of Menno Simons*, p. 124.

92. *The Complete Writings of Menno Simons*, p. 131.

93. Liechty, ed., *Early Anabaptist Spirituality*, p. 183. Checked against Müller, ed., *Glaubenszeugnisse oberdeutscher Taufgesinnter*, Vol. 2, pp. 175–238.

94. *Early Anabaptist Spirituality*, p. 150.

95. See Schreiner, *Are You Alone Wise?*, pp. 241–54.

96. As the Anabaptist Georg Knoblauch wrote in 1534, "Infant baptism is nothing" because infants "cannot believe" (*konnen nicht glawben*): Hill, *Baptism, Brotherhood*, pp. 120–23.

97. Febvre, *Problem of Unbelief in the Sixteenth Century*, conclusion and passim.

Chapter Three: The Invention of the Unbeliever

1. Gifford, *Countrie Divinitie*, pp. 6V–7rR.

2. Gifford, *Countrie Divinitie*, pp. 11v–12r.

3. Gifford, *Countrie Divinitie*, p. 15r.

4. Gifford, *Countrie Divinitie*, p. 61v.

5. Gifford, *Countrie Divinitie*, pp.79v–80r.

6. For early modern atheism before Spinoza, see, e.g., Febvre, *Problem of Unbelief in the Sixteenth Century*; Minois, *Histoire de l'athéisme*; Schröder,

Ursprünge des Atheismus; Barth, *Atheismus und Orthodoxie*; Kors, *Atheism in France*; Kors, *Naturalism and Unbelief in France*; Kors, *Epicureans and Atheists in France*; Sheppard, *Anti-Atheism in Early Modern England*; Buckley, *At the Origins of Modern Atheism*; Buckley, *Denying and Disclosing God*; Niewöhner and Pluta, eds., *Atheismus*; Hunter and Wooton, eds., *Atheism*; Erdozain, *The Soul of Doubt*; Norbrook, Harrison, and Hardie, eds. *Lucretius*; Wootton, "Lucien Febvre"; Wootton, *Paolo Sarpi*; Hunter, "The Problem of 'Atheism.'"

7. Plato, *Apology*, 26c. See David Sedley, "From the Pre-Socratics to the Hellenistic Age," in Bullivant and Ruse, eds., *Oxford Handbook of Atheism*, p. 139.

8. Drachmann, *Atheism*; Berlinerblau, "Jewish Atheism," in Bullivant and Ruse, eds., *Oxford Handbook of Atheism*.

9. Wilson, ed., *Encyclopedia of Ancient Greece*, p. 109.

10. *The Complete Sophocles*, ed. Burian and Shapiro, vol. 1, p. 299.

11. Kors, *Atheism in France*, p. 193.

12. Plutarch, *On Superstition*, 11.1.

13. Cicero, *De Natura Deorum*, 1.63 and 3.89: "Diagoras, ἄθεος qui dictus est," and "At Diagoras cum Samothracam venisset, ἄθεος ille qui dicitur."

14. See, e.g., Bibliothèque nationale de France MS Latin 17812, fo. 17v. I have looked in several Cicero incunabula, and several medieval mss from the BNF, and I have found none with Greek characters for *atheos*.

15. Augustine, *Answer to Petilian the Donatist*, 3.21.25. For the Latin see *PL* 43, col. 360: "Quid hic facit atheus Diagoras, qui esse Deum negavit, ut de illo videatur praedixisse propheta, Dixit stultus in corde suo, Non est Deus (Psal. XIII, 1)?"

16. Again, modern editions use Greek characters, and it is unclear what Lactantius intended. *PL* 7, col. 99A: "Diagoras, qui nullum esse omnino Deum diceret, ob eamque sententiam nominatus est ἄθεος." *PL* 6, col. 1083B: "Potest ergo existere perversus aliquis, qualis fuerit ἄθεος ille Theodorus."

17. *Arnobii Junioris Commentarii in Psalmos*, *PL* 53, col. 330B: "Titulum psalmi tertii hac una sententia explanamus. Persecutus est Absalon patrem, fronde a collo ligatur. Judas tradidit Dominum, et laqueo coarctatur: sicut historia passionem David praeteritam indicat, ita mysterium passionem Domini futuram annuntiat, in qua omnes cum negaverunt, dicentes: Non est salus ei in Deo ejus, sed si est ex Deo, liberet eum, cum irridentes illum, multis contumeliis conviciisque afficerent athei et pertinaces Judaei. Jesus autem voce sua ad Deum clamavit et exauditus est, ita ut mortem quasi soporem acciperet." For Erasmus, see sig. B2r of the 1522 edition: *Arnobii . . . in Omneis Psalmos Commentarii*.

18. *PL* 9, col.251b. "Impii athei.—Igitur secundum hoc propositum exemplum, impium discerni a peccatore non dubium est."

19. Arnobius of Sicca, *Seven Books against the Heathen*, 5.30. For the Latin, see *PL* 5, col. 1145A.

20. *PL* 190, col. 746c: "Stet in manu percutientis et vindicantis opprobria agminum Dei Israelis. Audisti atheum improperantem Domino, et manus tuas ad praelium et digitos ad bellum non aptasti?"

21. Robichaud, "Renaissance and Reformation," in Bullivant and Ruse, eds., *Oxford Handbook of Atheism*, p. 190.

22. Kusukawa, *Transformation of Natural Philosophy*, p. 128.

23. Knox, *An answer*, p. 73.

24. Elyot, *Dictionary of Syr Thomas Eliot Knyght*, sig. Hh2v. Other early adopters referred to the materialism of ancient epicureans: see, e.g., Arnould Bogaert, *A pronostication for diuers yeares*, sig. B5v.

25. Véron, *The ouerthrow*, p. 2v.

26. Tyndale, *Obedience of a Christen Man*, p. 7r.

27. Joye, *The subuersion of Moris false foundacion*, sig. A6r.

28. Mornay, *A woorke concerning the trewnesse of the Christian religion*, p. 355.

29. Froissart, *Here begynneth the thirde and fourthe boke*, pp. 269r and 30r.

30. Corro, *An epistle or godlie admonition*, p. 37v.

31. Osório, *An epistle of the reuerend father*, pp. 66r–v.

32. Viret, *Epistre envoyee aux fideles*, p. 131. "Car il n'y a pas grande différence entre les hypocrites, contempteurs et moqueurs de Dieu, et entre les blasphemateurs, qui pechent contre son sainct Esprit. Ilz sont Presque cousins germains, et voyons par experience, que de l'un de degrés l'on tombe en l'autre. Car plusieurs de ceux qui sont devenuz Atheistes et sans Dieu, qui ont eu premierement quelque congnoissance de verité, et puis maintenant la blasphement, sont descenduz en ces abysmes, par ces degrés."

33. Viret, *Dialogues*, p. 810: "Or par ces Epicuriens et Atheistes, I'entendz une nouvelle secte, qui commence ia fort à sespandre de toutes partz, par ceux mesmes, qui ont quelquefoys congneu la verité Evangelique, mais se sont retournez voutrer en la fange, comme les porceaux. Ie laisse à part, les anciens Epicuriens, et ceux de la court Romaine, qui Presque de tout temps, a faict profession de ceste Philosophie; et qui a pour le premier article de sa Foy, qu'il n'y a point de Dieu, sinon la ventre. Mais ie parle ici, d'une secte de nouveaux Epicuriens, qui on assez de cognoissance de verité, pour cognoistre les abuz du Pape, et pour se mocquer des idolatries et superstitions de l'Eglise Papale; mais ilz n'ont pas encore apprins à congnoistre vrayement Iesus Christ. Et pourtant qu'ilz ont abusé de celle cognoissance, qui leur avoit esté donnée, pour parvenir à plus grande congnoissance de Christ, et qu'ilz l'ont toute convertie en liberté charnelle, Dieu les a mis en sens reprouvé." I owe thanks to Tony Grafton for correcting my translation. For another, later example, see Viret, *Exposition*, sig. C5v.

34. Calvin, *Concerning Scandals*, pp. 62–63. For the French original: Calvin, *Des Scandales*, p. 92.

35. Billon, *Le Fort inexpugnable*, p. 220v.

36. Le Fèvre, *Iuste Complaincte*, p. 57: "pour nous faire vivre en bestes brutes, et nous faire tumber en atheism."

37. *Acta Concilii Tridentini*, sig. C8v. "Utinam non a religione ad superstitionem, a fide ad infidelitatem, a christo ad antichristum, quin a Deo ad Epicurum vel ad Pythagoram, velut prorsus unanimes declinassent, dicentes in corde impio, et in ore impudico: non est Deus."

38. *Les Actes de la Conference Tenue à Paris*, pp. 115r and 110v. For a similar example, see Villegagnon, *Responce par le Chevalier de Villegaignon*, p. 119.

39. Picart, *Les Sermons*, sig. A6r-v. "curiosité illicite" and "experimentons," leads "plus souvent en un Atheisme, oublians Dieu et son Eglise."

40. N.N. [Peter Talbot], *A Treatise of the Nature of the Catholick Faith*, pp. 83–89. Talbot was one of the very few early modern Catholics who appropriated the language of "historical faith" to hoist Protestants on their own petard.

41. See Höpfl, *Jesuit Political Thought*, pp. 107–9.

42. Lessius, *Rawleigh his Ghost*, pp. 5–6, checked against Lessius, *De Providentia Numinis*, p. 4.

43. Allen, *A Defense and Declaration of the Catholike Churchies Doctrine*, pp. 282–83.

44. Garasse, *Doctrine curieuse*, pp. 215–16.

45. Garasse, *Doctrine curieuse*, p. 216: "Les Huguenots croyent à demy en dieu, & vous n'y croyez point du tout."

46. Garasse, *Doctrine curieuse*, pp. 217–19: "Les heretiques ne renuoyent pas indifferemment tous les articles de foy: mais ils choisissent ce qui est a leur goust, pour en croire ce que bon leur semble."

47. Garasse, *Doctrine curieuse*, pp. 223–24.

48. Garasse, *Doctrine curieuse*, p. 235.

49. Garasse, *Doctrine curieuse*, p. 241: "Ainsi en est-il des artciles de nostre croyance, il est impossible d'en retrencher un sans arracher une plume de ses aisles."

50. Garasse, *Doctrine curieuse*, p. 237: "Luther estant par sa soigneuse diligence paruenu à l'Atheisme." See also p. 214, where Garasse writes that it took Luther ten years to reach the perfection of Atheism.

51. Garasse, *Doctrine curieuse*, p. 208: "La vraye liberté consiste en la simple & sage creance de tout ce que l'Eglise luy propose indifferemment & sans distinction."

52. Garasse, *Doctrine curieuse*, p. 210: "C'est estre philosophe non pas chrestien, vouloir sçauoir & non pas croire."

53. Anderton, *The Reformed Protestant*, sigs. B1v–B3r, sig. F1r for quote.

54. Anderton, *The Reformed Protestant*, sig. C1r.

55. Anderton, *The Reformed Protestant*, epistle sig. §2r-v.

56. Anderton, *The Reformed Protestant*, sig. D2r–D4v.

57. Anderton, *The Reformed Protestant*, sig. E1r-v.

58. Anderton, *The Reformed Protestant*, sig. E2r.

59. Parsons, *Christian Exercise*, pp. 410–12.

60. Parsons, *Christian Exercise*, p. 412.

61. Burne, *Disputation*, p. 188v. See also Broughton, *Resolution of Religion*, sig. F1r.

62. Gordon, *Calvin*, p. vii.

63. Calvin, *Institutes*, I.iii.1.

64. Calvin, *Institutes*, I.iv.1–2. Quoted from sig. A4v of 1561 English translation: Calvin, *Christian Religion*. To see the novelty of Calvin's position, compare

to the attempt by Anselm to resolve the same contradiction in his *Proslogion* 4, where he argues that even though *words signifying* God's nonexistence can be thought, those words cannot be understood with reference to the thing they signify, hence God's nonexistence is unthinkable. As Virginie Greene points out, one way to understand this argument is that the phrase "God is not" can be thought (*cogitare*) but not understood (*intelligere*): Greene, *Logical Fictions*, p. 113.

65. Rivius, *De Stultitia Mortalium*.

66. Rivius, *De Stultitia Mortalium*, pp. 2–3.

67. Rivius, *De Stultitia Mortalium*, p. 15: "Quid vero pontificii sacerdotes? Hi nimirum . . . a scelerato meretricis complexu properant ad altare." P. 18: "Nec vere (ut mentiuntur) credent, quantumuis licet inania sibi quaedem de fide somnia fingant."

68. Pierre Boquin, *Assertio Veteris*, pp. 75–76: "In instorum ecclesiae gubernatorum quibusdam superstitio cum ignoratione coelestis doctrine maiores vires indies acquirit, in aliis religionis verae contemptus augetur, in plerisque vel atheismus ver epicureismus palam regnant. Mores sunt longe corruptissimi, disciplina omnis, etiam illa cuius Pontifices sunt inventores et architecti, plane concidit."

69. Sutcliffe, *A briefe replie*, p. 106.

70. Perkins, *Golden Chain*, pp. 218–19, and see pp. 1013–14 for further doctrinal connections to atheism.

71. Marbury, *Sermon preached at Paules Crosse*, sig. D4r–v.

72. Discussed in Barth, *Atheismus und Orthodoxie*, pp. 78–82. Thanks to Erik Midelfort for alerting me to this important book.

73. As Barth noted, unbelief was necessarily complex because belief itself was complex. Barth, *Atheismus und Orthodoxie*, p. 84: "Offenbar was es den Zeitgenossen klar, dass der Glaube eine 'theoretische' und eine 'praktische' Seite hat: Entsprechend musste es sich beim Unglauben verhalten."

74. Young, *Drunkard's Character*, p. 558.

75. Younge, *Drunkard's Character*, p. 559.

76. Younge, *Drunkard's Character*, pp. 590–91.

77. Calvin, *Commentaries*, p. 419. For the Latin original, see *Joannis Calvini in Acta Apostolorum Commentarii*, p. 345: "Vocantur spiritualiter Dei cultores, qui nomen dederunt Deo Israel: illis solis tribuitur religio: ergo nihil aliis sit reliquum praeter ignominiam atheismi, utcunque in superstitionibus anxie se torqueant. Er merito: quicquid enim splendoris ostentent idololatrae, si excutiatur interior eorum affectus, nihil illic reperietur praeter horribilem Dei contemptum, merumque esse fucum patebit, quod se idolis blandiri simulant."

78. Israel, *Radical Enlightenment*; Israel, *Enlightenment Contested*. A powerful recent version is Kors, *Epicureans and Atheists*, especially ch. 4. For a subtle critique of the emphasis on atheism over other contemporaneous frameworks like "indifferentism," see Mulsow, *Enlightenment Underground*, ch. 7.

79. See, for instance, Isaiah Berlin: "The most dangerous enemy of the human race—the destroyer whose aim and function it is to sap the foundation

on which all societies rest—is the Protestant, the man who lifts his hands against the universal Church. Protestantism is the revolt of individual reason or faith, conscience against blind obedience, which is the sole base of all authority: hence it is *au fond* political rebellion." Berlin, *Crooked Timber*, p. 138.

80. Readers will immediately notice the affinity of my argument with Simpson, *Burning to Read*. But whereas Simpson sees Protestant Biblicism as the source of modern fundamentalism with all its violence, my own argument stresses that Catholics and Protestants adopted parallel projects; the Catholic version, insisting upon unitary authority over belief, should not be let off the hook so easily. I owe thanks to James Simpson for many stimulating conversations on this topic.

81. Raeff, "Well-Ordered Police State," at p. 1223.

82. Roper, *Holy Household*, p. 57.

83. Gorski, *Disciplinary Revolution*, pp. 63–64.

84. Todd, *Culture of Protestantism*.

85. Shagan, *Rule of Moderation*, pp. 65–68.

86. *RCG* IV, p. 68.

87. *RCG* IV, pp. 112–13. "c'estoit affaire de quelque riche home d'aller aux congregations et y demorer jusques à 10 heures et qu'il sroit bien meilleur qu'il travaillast pour norrir ses petis enfans, veu qu'il estoit povre."

88. *RCG* IV, p. 175.

89. *RCG* IV, pp. 23–24. "Il a prins son member honteux en la presence d'hommes, femes, et fillies à marier, l'a mis sur ung tranchoir, disant, 'N'est-il pas beau, le Redempteur?'" This was not his only outrage.

Chapter Four: The Unbearable Weight of Believing

1. On Spiera, see, e.g., Sheppard, *Anti-Atheism in Early Modern England*, ch. 5; Overall, "Exploitation of Francesco Spiera."

2. Gribaldi, *A Notable and Marvailous Epistle*, sigs. A6v–A7r. Checked against Gribaldi, *Epistola Clarissimi*.

3. Gribaldi, *A Notable and Marvailous Epistle*, sigs. B2v–B3v.

4. Gribaldi, *A Notable and Marvailous Epistle*, sigs. B4r–B5r.

5. Gribaldi, *A Notable and Marvailous Epistle*, sigs.C1r–C2r. Sig.B1v: "ut neque sperare, neque credere de divina in me gratia et misericordia possim."

6. Gribaldi, *A Notable and Marvailous Epistle*, sig. C4v.

7. I am indebted here to the seminal study by Susan Schreiner, *Are You Alone Wise?*.

8. Rhegius, *An Instruccyon of Christian Fayth*, sig. A5v. The original Latin is: "Nam qui de propicia Dei voluntate ac gratia dubitat, nec credit Deum propter Christum sibi esse propicium, nec ab eo sibi omnia peccata condonari, is vere pius non est, et in hac incredulitate non potest non dannari." Rhegius, *Doctrina Certissima*, sig. B1r–v.

9. Perkins, *Exposition*, p. 16.

10. *Institutes*, III.ii.4. "In cunctis semper mixta est fidei incredulitas."

11. See Pitkin, *What Pure Eyes Could See*, especially pp. 37–39.

12. Ryrie, *Being Protestant*, p. 3.

13. Bullinger, *Fiftie Godlie and Learned Sermons*, p. 41. Checked against Bullinger, *Sermonum Decades Quinque*.

14. Bullinger, *Fiftie Godlie and Learned Sermons*, p. 34.

15. Bullinger, *Fiftie Godlie and Learned Sermons*, p. 33. Bullinger, *Sermonum Decades Quinque*, p. 12: "Quod ea quæ ex uerbo dei credimus, firmissime & citra omnem ambiguitatem & dubitationem credimus, certita habere prorsus rem, ut habere credit fides."

16. Bullinger, *Fiftie Godlie and Learned Sermons*, p. 34.

17. Bullinger, *Fiftie Godlie and Learned Sermons*, p. 34.

18. Gerhard, *Gerhards Meditations*, pp. 281–82. Checked against Gerhard, *Quinquaginta Meditationes Sacrae*, sig. d1r in Meditation 45: "Fateor, O Domine Jesu, reatus me cum illis conjungit, sed reatus illius agnitio et salvifica tui cognitio ab illis me disjungit."

19. Bownd, *The Vnbeleefe of S. Thomas*, p. 18.

20. Shagan and Shuger, *Religion in Tudor England*, p. 572.

21. *Institutes*, III.ii.15.

22. Sedgwick, *The Humbled Sinner*, pp. 79–80.

23. Sedgwick, *The Humbled Sinner*, p. 79.

24. *Institutes*, III, ii, 17; III.ii.11.

25. *Institutes*, III.ii.11.

26. *Institutes*, III.ii.11.

27. *Institutes*, III.ii.12.

28. Greenham, *Propositions*, at #59. Here Greenham might have been reading Luther against the Anabaptists, *WA* 26, p. 155, where he described the uncertainty of belief/faith: "Denn es kompt, ia es gehet also zu mit dem glauben, des offt der, so da meinet, er glewbe, nichts uberall glewbe, und widderumb, der da meinet, er glewbe nichts, sondern verzweivele, am aller meisten glewbe."

29. Rhegius, *An Instruccyon*, sig. B3v: "Quare se probe exploret et in se respiciat quisque, ne seipsum seducat. Multi sunt qui opinantur se credere, cum tamen non credant." Rhegius, *Doctrina Certissima*, sig. B5r.

30. Bownd, *The Vnbeleefe of S. Thomas*, pp. 50–51.

31. That is, I have been unable to locate a source text except for the account of the Ten Commandments in Book III of Hyperius's *De Theologo*. If that is indeed the source, then it is hardly a translation at all.

32. Hyperius, *The True Tryall*, p. 2.

33. Hyperius, *The True Tryall*, p. 7.

34. Hyperius, *The True Tryall*, p. 34.

35. Hyperius, *The True Tryall*, pp. 34–35.

36. This psychic drama goes back to the beginning of the Reformation. Susan Karant-Nunn has noted division in the Lutheran ranks: Luther's own sermons tended to stress consolation, while the sermons of his followers Brenz,

Chemnitz, Spengenberg, and others stressed the losing battle against sin and urged listeners to identify with Christ's agony. The Reformed churches were starker, emphasizing that humans have "no good in them" and that penitence is only possible for the elect: Karant-Nunn, *The Reformation of Feeling*, pp. 97–98, 252.

37. I owe thanks to Patrick McGhee for bringing the Rogers diary to my attention and for allowing me to see his 2015 Cambridge Master's Thesis, "Unbelief and the Senses in Early Stuart Protestantism."

38. *Diary of Samuel Rogers*, pp. 163 and 144.

39. *Diary of Samuel Rogers*, p. 13.

40. *Diary of Samuel Rogers*, p. 70.

41. See, e.g., *Diary of Samuel Rogers*, pp. 64–65.

42. *Diary of Michael Wigglesworth*, p. 45.

43. *Diary of Michael Wigglesworth*, p. 49.

44. *Diary of Michael Wigglesworth*, pp. 52–53.

45. *Diary of Michael Wigglesworth*, p. 54.

46. *Diary of Michael Wigglesworth*, p. 94.

47. *Diary of Michael Wigglesworth*, p. 105.

48. *Diary of Michael Wigglesworth*, pp. 16 and 18.

49. *Diary of Michael Wigglesworth*, pp. 76–77.

50. *Diary of Michael Wigglesworth*, pp. 12–13.

51. *Diary of Samuel Sewall*, vol. I, pp. 10–11.

52. *Diary of Samuel Sewall*, vol. I, p. 47.

53. Allen, *A Narrative*, pp. 47–49, 53–54.

54. Allen, *A Narrative*, p. 14.

55. Allen, *A Narrative*, p. 64.

56. Although Hannah Allen could not have known it, Baxter had his own share of subjective unbelief, questioning "whether I were indeed a Christian or an infidel, and whether faith could consist with such doubts as I was conscious of." Baxter overcame that questioning by reading the works of Thomas Jackson, who will appear in chapter 5 below as one of the earliest promoters of the new, more open understanding of belief that emerged in the seventeenth century. See Baxter, *Reliquiae Baxterianae*, pp. 21–24. I owe this reference to Alec Ryrie.

57. Allen, *A Narrative*, p. 48.

58. Bunyan, *Grace Abounding*, p. 22. As Christopher Hill notes, Bunyan knew the life of Francesco Spiera and quoted often from an English account: see Hill, *Turbulent, Seditious and Factious People*, p. 185.

59. Bunyan, *Grace Abounding*, p. 25.

60. Bunyan, *Grace Abounding*, p. 26.

61. Bunyan, *Grace Abounding*, p. 51.

62. Bunyan, *Grace Abounding*, pp. 52–54.

63. Bunyan, *Grace Abounding*, pp. 74–75.

64. Bunyan, *Grace Abounding*, p. 84.

65. Bunyan, *Grace Abounding*, p. 92.

66. Bunyan, *Grace Abounding*, p. 94. See the illuminating reading of Bunyan in Conti, *Confessions of Faith*, ch. 5.

67. On Teresa's life and work, see, e.g., Weber, *Teresa of Avila*; Ahlgren, *Teresa of Avila*; Slade, *St. Teresa of Ávila*. On her broader context, see Bilinkoff, *The Avila of Saint Teresa*.

68. *Teresa*, I, p. 252. Checked against *LV* pp. 201–2: "Veìale en las manos un dardo de oro largo y al fin del hierro me parecìa tener un poco de fuego; este me parecìa metor por el corazón algunas veces y que me llegaba a las entrañas. Al sacarle me parecìa las llevaba consigo y me dejaba toda abrasada en amor grande de Dios. Era tan grande el dolor, que me hacìa dar aquellos quejidos y tan excesiva la suavidad que me pone este grandìsimo dolor, que no hay desear que se quite ni se contenta el alma con menos que Dios. No es dolor corporal, sino espiritual, aunque no deja de participar el cuerpo algo y aun harto. Es un requiebro tan suave que pasa entre el alma y Dios, que suplico yo a su bondad lo dé a gustar a quien pensare que miento."

69. *Teresa*, II, p. 385; *CI*, p. 576: "con razón no se cree."

70. *Teresa*, II, p. 372; *CI*, p. 564: "y querría, hermanas, que no penséis hacéis mal en no las dar crédito."

71. *Teresa*, I, p. 183; *CI*, p. 564: con razón.

72. *Teresa*, I, pp. 91 and 94; LV, p. 44: "mas creo no perderá quien humillándose, aunque sea fuerte, no lo crea de sí y creyere en esto a quien tiene experiencia."

73. *Teresa*, I, p. 273; *LV*, p. 222: "créanme, crean por amor del Señor a esta hormiguilla que el Señor quiere que hable."

74. *Teresa*, I, p. 182; *LV*, p. 134: "No hay quien lo crea si no ha pasado por ello."

75. On the question of authority in the Bernini sculpture, see Farmer, "'You Need but Go to Rome'"; Cuadro, "Iconografía"; Call, "Boxing Teresa."

76. Poska, *Women and Authority*, pp. 202–3.

77. Kamen, *Phoenix and the Flame*, p. 319 and ch. 6 passim.

78. Braga, *Historia*, p. 108: "Tratados or Orações, ou para melhor dizer Superstições que permittem a quem as fizer ou mandar fazer, que alcançarão o que pedirem, como privança, grande vingança de inimigos, vencimento de demandas, ou que escaparão de todo o perigo." See Burke, *Popular Culture*, p. 220.

79. Schwartz, *All Can Be Saved*.

80. Moore, *Formation of a Persecuting Society*, p. 68.

81. Brady, *German Histories*, p. 147.

82. More broadly, in an Aristotelian worldview, "experience" was not taken to refer to individual instances but to habitual occurrences; the transition to a form of experience that was "experimental" in a modern sense was central to the scientific revolution. See, e.g., Dear, *Discipline and Experience*.

83. On doctrinal discipline in the Counter-Reformation, see, e.g., Jean Delumeau, *Catholicism*; Bossy, *Christianity in the West*; Hsia, *World of Catholic Renewal*; Kamen, *The Phoenix and the Flame*; Ginzburg, *The Night Battles*.

84. Ginzburg, *The Cheese and the Worms*, pp. 2–12.

85. De Certeau, *The Mystic Fable*, pp. 255–56 and ch. 8 passim.

86. See, e.g., *Teresa*, II, p. 62; *Teresa*, II, p. 140; *Teresa*, I, pp. 229–30; *Teresa*, II, p. 430.

87. *Teresa*, II, p. 373. *CI*, p. 565.

88. *Teresa*, I, p.163. *LV*, p. 115: "y queda una certidumbre que en ninguna manera se puede dejar de creer."

89. *Teresa*, I, p. 227. *LV*, p. 178: "no me podía forzar a mí, aungue hacía cuanto podía por creerlo y desearlo, mas no era en mi mano." See also I, p. 348.

90. *Teresa*, I, p. 354. *LV*, p. 300: "A mí me pareció que siempre yo había creído esto y que todos los fieles lo creían."

91. *Teresa*, I, p. 218. *LV*, pp. 168–69: "siempre procura ir conforme a lo que tiene la Iglesia, preguntando a unos y a otros, como quien tiene ya hecho asiento fuerte en estas verdades, que no la moverían cuantas revelaciones pueda imaginar—aunque viese abiertos los cielos—un punto de lo que tiene la Iglesia."

92. *Teresa*, I, pp. 243–44. *LV*, p. 193. The original Spanish has "more than," not "rather than": "que sin duda yo lo creyera más que lo que había visto."

93. *Teresa*, I, pp. 243–44. *LV*, p. 193.

94. *Teresa*, I, p. 379. *RCC* 1.26: "aunque se junten cuantos letrados y santos hay en el mundo y me diesen todos los tormentos imaginables y yo quisiese creerlo, no me podrían hacer creer que esto es demonio, porque no puedo. Y cuando me quisieron poner en que lo creyese, temía viendo quién lo decía, y pensaba que ellos debían de decir verdad, y que yo, siendo la que era, debía de estar engañada; mas a la primera palabra o recogimiento o visión era deshecho todo lo que me habían dicho; yo no podía más y creía que era Dios." This is from 1560, in what is probably Teresa's earliest extant writing.

95. *Teresa*, I, p. 283. *LV*, pp. 231–32.

96. *Teresa*, I, p. 421. *RCC* 4a.10.

97. *Teresa*, I, pp. 285–87. *LV*, p. 235.

98. *Teresa*, II, pp. 338–89. *CI*, p. 531: "Siempre en cosas dificultosas, aunque me parece que lo entiendo y que digo berdad, voy coneste lenguaje de que me parece; porque si me engañare, estoy muy aparejada a creer lo que dijeren los que tienenletras muchas; porque aunque no hayan pasado por estas cosas, tienen un no sé qué grades letrados, que como Dios los tiene para luz de Iglesia, cuando es una verdad, dásela para que se admita Siempre en cosas dificultosas, aunque me parece que lo entiendo y que digo berdad, voy coneste lenguaje de que me parece; porque si me engañare, estoy muy aparejada a creer lo que dijeren los que tienenletras muchas; porque aunque no hayan pasado por estas cosas, tienen un no sé qué grades letrados, que como Dios los tiene para luz de Iglesia, cuando es una verdad, dásela para que se admita."

99. *Teresa*, II, p. 340. *CI*, p. 532: "que aunque un medio letrado de los que tengo dichos a quien preguntó cómo estaba Dios en nosotros (él lo sabía tan poco como ella antes que Dios se lo diese a entender) le dijo que no estaba más de por gracia, ella tenía ya tan fija la verdad, que no le creyó."

100. *Teresa*, II, p. 374. *CI*, p. 566.

101. For John of the Cross, see, e.g.: Thompson, *The Poet and the Mystic*; Tyler, *St. John of the Cross*; Kavanaugh, *John of the Cross*; Reynard, *Jean de la Croix*; Melquiades, *San Juan de la Cruz*; Baruzi, *Saint Jean de la Croix*; Payne, *St. John of the Cross*. Some of my discussion here and in chapter 5 is derived from Shagan, "Taking Belief Seriously?."

102. *WSJC*, p. 161. *Subida al Monte Carmelo*, 2.4.4. Citations to the Spanish original are from the *Obras Completas* consulted online at http://www.portal carmelitano.org/santos-carmelitas/juan-de-la-cruz/92-juan-de-la-cruz-obras -completas.html.

103. *WSJC*, p. 166. *Subida al Monte Carmelo*, 2.6.2.

104. *WSJC*, pp. 164–65.

105. This will be a controversial claim, as a great deal of scholarship on John is invested in the category of "mystical experience." But my argument is largely consonant with this scholarship, stressing that for John, achieving union was so unlike worldly experience that the difference between them became a wedge that performed much of his intellectual work. For a recent version, see, e.g., Carravilla Parra, *Razón Mística*, especially pp. 444–48. A contrasting view can be found in Gil, *La Experencia*.

106. *WSJC*, p. 180. *Subida al Monte Carmelo*, 2.11.2.

107. *WSJC*, p. 209. *Subida al Monte Carmelo*, 2.17.7.

108. *WSJC*, p. 280.

109. *WSJC*, p. 201.

110. *WSJC*, p. 204.

111. *WSJC*, p. 227. *Subida al Monte Carmelo*, 2.21.11.

112. *WSJC*, p. 243. *Subida al Monte Carmelo*, 2.24.8.

113. *WSJC*, p. 234. *Subida al Monte Carmelo*, 2.22.11.

114. *WSJC*, p. 248.

115. *WSJC*, p. 233.

116. *WSJC*, pp. 253–54. *Subida al Monte Carmelo*, 2.27.4.

117. *WSJC*, p. 160. *Subida al Monte Carmelo*, 2.4.4.

118. *WSJC*, p. 248. *Subida al Monte Carmelo*, 2.26.11.

119. *WSJC*, p. 179. *Subida al Monte Carmelo*, 2.10.4.

120. *WSJC*, p. 194, and see also pp. 500, 531. *Subida al Monte Carmelo*, 2.14.8–10.

121. *WSJC*, p. 195.

122. See the comments in Baldomero Jiménez Duque, "Experiencia y Teología," in Cardedal and Rodríguez, eds., *Actas del Congreso Internacional*, pp. 155–76.

Chapter Five: The Birth Pangs of Modern Belief

1. On the two paintings, see Lojkine, "Polemics as a World."

2. Livy, *History of Rome*, 5.48.

3. The literature on Montaigne is inexhaustible, but on the issue of authority, experience, and belief, see, e.g., Struever, *Theory as Practice*, ch. 7; Schreiner, *Are You Alone Wise?*, ch. 7; Thierry Ménissier, "L'autorité dans les *Essais* de Montaigne," 179–202; Ann Hartle, "Montaigne and Skepticism," in Langer, ed., *Cambridge Companion to Montaigne*, 183–206; Heitsch, *Practicing Reform*, ch. 5; Cavaillé, *Montaigne et l'experience*; Brahami, "Montaigne et la politique"; Quint, *Montaigne and the Quality of Mercy*, especially ch. 4. See also Shagan, "Taking Belief Seriously?."

4. Popkin, *History of Scepticism*, pp. 54–56.

5. Scholars who see Montaigne's fideism as merely strategic or disingenuous seem not to understand how very normal belief in authority was in the Catholic tradition. Somewhat more compelling is the notion of "conformist fideism," in which Montaigne's belief is mere acquiescence to authority rather than a philosophically rigorous construction that belief is beyond reason: see Penelhum, *God and Skepticism*.

6. Montaigne, *Complete Essays*, pp. 372–74. *Les Essais*, "Apologie de Raimond Sebond," p. 504. Citations of the French original are from the Villey-Saulnier edition, consulted online at "The Montaigne Project."

7. Montaigne, *Complete Essays*, p. 611. *Les Essais*, "Du Repentir," p. 805.

8. Montaigne, *Complete Essays*, p. 234. *Les Essais*, "De Prières," p. 323.

9. Montaigne, *Complete Essays*, p. 423. *Les Essais*, "Apologie de Raimond Sebond," p. 563.

10. Montaigne, *Complete Essays*, p. 322. *Les Essais*, "Apologie de Raimond Sebond," p. 442: "Les uns font accroire au monde qu'ils croyent ce qu'ils ne croyent pas. Les autres, en plus grand nombre, se le font accroire à eux mesmes, ne sçachants pas penetrer que c'est que croire."

11. Montaigne, *Complete Essays*, p. 229. *Les Essais*, "Des Prières," pp. 317–18.

12. Montaigne, *Complete Essays*, p. 612. *Les Essais*, "Du Repentir," p. 806.

13. Montaigne, *Complete Essays*, p. 375.

14. Montaigne, *Complete Essays*, pp. 386–87. *Les Essais*, "Apologie de Raimond Sebond," p. 520.

15. Montaigne, *Complete Essays*, p. 428. *Les Essais*, "Apologie de Raimond Sebond," p. 569.

16. Montaigne, *Complete Essays*, p. 229. *Les Essais*, "Des Prières," p. 318.

17. Montaigne, *Complete Essays*, p. 324. *Les Essais*, "Apologie de Raimond Sebond," p. 444.

18. Montaigne, *Complete Essays*, p. 402. *Les Essais*, "Apologie de Raimond Sebond," p. 539: "creances anciennes, par authorité et à credit, comme si c'estoit religion et loy."

19. Montaigne, *Complete Essays*, p. 499. *Les Essais*, "De la Praesumption," p. 658: "Cett'humeur libre de n'assubjectir aisément ma creance."

20. Montaigne, *Complete Essays*, p. 324.

21. Gatti, *Giordano Bruno*, p. 211. I would like to thank Ed Muir for bringing this work to my attention.

22. Cited in Gatti, *Renaissance Drama*, pp. 2–3. On Bruno's novel understanding of belief, see Sébastien Galland, "D'un usage raisonné de l'opinion: l'art de la doxa brunien," in Hummel, ed., *Doxa*.

23. The literature on Campanella is vast, but on the particular issue of belief, see, e.g., Headley, "Tommaso Campanella"; Headley, *Tommaso Campanella and the Transformation*; Giglioni, "Healing and Belief."

24. See Ernst, *Tommaso Campanella*, ch. 7.

25. Campanella, *Atheismus Triumphatus*, p. 1: "Ego intellectus humanus omnes examinavi Religiones in rerum universitate, et proprias et rationales, et improprias et naturales apud homines, et belluas et plantas, et apud Angelos, et stellas, et mundum, communi praeeunte ratione, sensatisque experimentis; ut meipsum certum redderem, atque alios, de fidei verae dogmatum credulitate." Campanella's masterpiece has never been translated into English.

26. A cogent interpretation of Campanella's apparent return to orthodoxy, usefully reviewing prior historiography, is Delumeau, *Le Mystère Campanella*, ch. 25, but Delumeau does not consider the possible radicalism of Campanella's path to orthodoxy through his own resources.

27. Campanella, *Atheismus Triumphatus*, pp. 2–5. As John Headley notes, Campanella thought it absurd to imagine that only Christians could be saved, and he imagined "religion" to be a faculty owed first to nature, then to reason, and only lastly to revelation: Headley, *Tommaso Campanella*, pp. 317–24.

28. Elsewhere, in his *Syntama de libris propriis*, Campanella wrote, "The great majority of men tend to believe everything when they are children; when they are adult, they believe nothing, so much so that they consider people who believe to be ignorant; once they arrive at the threshold of old age, they distinguish what we should believe from what we should not": Giglioni, "Healing and Belief," pp. 227–28.

29. Campanella, *Atheismus Triumphatus*, pp. 188–89.

30. See Blum, *Philosophy of Religion*, p. 141. Campanella may have been influenced by Peter of Cluny, who had argued in the twelfth century that Mohammed was not really a prophet because he did not predict the future: see Tolan, *Saracens*, ch. 5. As Tolan points out, the Muslim concept of *rasûl*, or prophet, does not refer to someone who predicts the future but to a messenger of God.

31. Campanella, *Atheismus Triumphatus*, p. 196. "Propositio omnis, aut vera est, aut falsa. Veritas et falsitas humanitus non cognoscuntur opinione, sed experimento omnium sensuum, nec ex revelation opinantium, sed testificantium." On the Renaissance understanding of testimony and the criteria for judgment, see Serjeantson, "Testimony and Proof"; Serjeantson, "Testimony." Crucial to Serjeantson's arguments about the scientific revolution is the separation of the evidence of testimony from the argument from authority.

32. On the historical development of this notion, see Ginzburg, "Clues: Roots of an Evidential Paradigm," in his *Myths, Emblems, Clues.*

33. Campanella, *Atheismus Triumphatus*, pp. 196–97.

34. Campanella, *Atheismus Triumphatus*, pp. 197–98.

35. See Grafton, *What Was History?*.

36. Campanella, *Atheismus Triumphatus*, p. 203.

37. Campanella, *Atheismus Triumphatus*, p. 189.

38. On Jesuit probabilism, the new standard work is Tutino, *Uncertainty*, which appeared just as this book was going to press. Tutino argues that Jesuit probabilism was a response to the radical insecurity of knowledge in early modern Europe: since it is impossible to know which position is genuinely more probable (*pace* David Hume), all probable positions may carry equal moral weight; although note that for the Jesuits, a "probable" position was one supported by authorities and following the dogma of the Church.

39. See Serjeantson, "Testimony and Proof." For a useful survey of the conceptions of proof and persuasion in different early modern disciplines, see Serjeantson, "Proof and Persuasion."

40. Drusius, *Observationum Libri XII*, p. 58: "Non assentior iis qui volunt aliud esse Deo credere, et in Deum, vel ob hoc quod Ebraei, quorum phrasis est, quae alias migrat leges latini sermonis, hoc discrimen non agnoscunt. Dicunt enim credere Deo, et in Deum indifferenter et pro eodem."

41. Drusius, *Observationum Libri XII*, pp. 59–60. And see also Drusius, *Miscellanea*, pp. 34–35 for further arguments along similar lines, including an attack on Rufinus's commentary on the Apostles' Creed.

42. Cited in Merkle, *Defending the Trinity*, p. 176 and ch. 5 passim. I owe this reference to Tony Grafton.

43. On Arminianism, see, e.g., Leeuwen, Stanglin, and Tolsma, eds., *Arminius, Arminianism, and Europe*; Stanglin, *Arminius on the Assurance of Salvation*; Stanglin and McCall, *Jacob Arminius*; Mulsow and Rohls, eds., *Socinianism and Arminianism*; Richard Muller, *God, Creation, and Providence in the Thought of Jacob Arminius*; Muller, "The Federal Motif." For Arminian theology in England, see Tyacke, *Anti-Calvinists*; Hughes, "The Problem of 'Calvinism.'"

44. Arminius, *The Works of James Arminius*, vol. 1, pp. 179–80. I quote here from the London edition, and elsewhere from the Auburn edition, which include different materials.

45. *WRH*, vol. 5, pp. 69–82. And for Travers's comments, see *WRH*, vol. 5, p. 200.

46. *WRH*, vol. 1, pp. 151–52 (*Lawes* 2.4.1).

47. Prynne, *Anti-Arminianisme*, p. 270.

48. Jackson, *Eternall Truth of Scriptures*, pp. 3–5, 19.

49. Jackson, *A Treatise*, pp. 1–2.

50. Jackson, *A Treatise*, p. 4.

51. Jackson, *A Treatise*, pp. 58–59.

52. Popper, *Walter Raleigh's History of the World*, pp. 3–4.

53. Within this vast historiography, see, e.g., Kelley, "*Historia Integra*"; Kelley, *Foundations*; Kelley, "Humanism and History"; Kelley, "The Theory of History"; Grafton, *Joseph Scaliger*; Grafton, *What Was History?*; Franklin, *Jean Bodin*; Backus, *Historical Method*. On the relationship between Baudouin and the Magdeburg Centuries, see Lyon, "Baudouin."

54. See, e.g., Chaunu, *Histoire et foi*; Laplanche, *L'évidence du Dieu chrétien*; Dulles, *A History of Apologetics*. Johann Albert Fabricius compiled several extensive bibliographies of Christian apologetics, grouped by subject matter and opponent, in his *Delectus*. Chapter 30, his most generic bibliography on "De veritate religionis christianae," begins with the works of Cusa and Ficino in the fifteenth century.

55. Chaunu, *Histoire et foi*, pp. 26–27.

56. Aquinas, *Summa contra Gentiles*, I.6.1 and I.6.3. This argument, that the historical victory of Christianity in its first two centuries is evidence of its veracity, would become central to all subsequent apologetics, but it would also be fodder for Enlightenment critics, who argued that by the same logic the defeat of Christianity by Islam in the seventh century was evidence of Christianity's corruption: see Pocock, *Barbarism and Religion, Volume Five*, pp. 106–7.

57. The work was printed in 1484 and then in many subsequent editions, none more important than the 1569 French translation by Montaigne which I cite here. *La theologie naturelle de Raymond Sebon*, ch. 211–13, pp. 239b–244b.

58. Vives, *De Veritate*, pp. 17–18.

59. Vives, *De Veritate*, p. 23.

60. Vives, *De Veritate*, pp. 159–61.

61. *Institutes*, 1.8. In the French 1541 edition, Calvin was still insisting more vehemently that in deciding whether the word of God is genuine, we cannot believe either our own judgment or the judgment of others: Calvin, *Institution de la Religion Chrestienne*, p. 21.

62. See the Elizabethan English translation: Philippe de Plessis Mornay, *A Woorke Concerning the Trewnesse of the Christian Religion*, e.g., pp. 435, 629.

63. Quotes are from Socinus, *An Argument for the Authority of Holy Scripture*, checked against Socinus, *De Sacrae Scripturae Auctoritate*. A parallel argument runs through part I of the Racovian Catechism, in which Socinus had a significant hand, first published in 1605, the year after his death: *The Racovian Catechism*, pp. 1–19. On Socinian revisions of apologetics and biblical criticism, see, e.g., Scholder, *Birth of Modern Critical Theology*; Mortimer, *Reason and Religion*; Lim, *Mystery Unveiled*.

64. As both Grafton and Popper have stressed, Bodin's "method" was not so innovative: he followed Annius of Viterbo in recommending that readers judge the credibility of historians by their fidelity to official sources (although he was careful to declaim against biased propaganda), and he used Annius's forged documents to make the claim: see Grafton, *What Was History?*; Popper, *Walter Raleigh's History of the World*.

65. *An Argument for the Authority of Holy Scripture*, pp. 122–23. *De Sacrae Scripturae Auctoritate*, p. 62.

66. *An Argument for the Authority of Holy Scripture*, pp. 126–27. *De Sacrae Scripturae Auctoritate*, p. 64. Socinus's original Latin does not use the word "evidence," he says only that one may "feel the truth of those things": "Cuius vi efficitur, ut quis veritatem sentiat earum rerum, quae de Iesu Nazareno narrant."

67. *An Argument for the Authority of Holy Scripture*, pp. 130–31. *De Sacrae Scripturae Auctoritate*, p. 66.

68. This paragraph is culled from arguments in *An Argument for the Authority of Holy Scripture*, pp. 125–28, 154–56. *De Sacrae Scripturae Auctoritate*, pp. 63–65, 79–80.

69. Mortimer, *Reason and Religion*, p. 237. Mortimer describes the developing link between Socinians and Arminians, particularly in terms of their views of human freedom.

70. See Muller, "Fides and Cognitio"; Muller, "The Priority of the Intellect." Cf. Stanglin, *Arminius on the Assurance of Salvation*, where Stanglin disagrees in part with Muller, Kendall, and others, but on issues too technical to affect the argument here.

71. *Works of James Arminius*, vol. 2, p. 109. Checked against Arminius, *Disputationes*, pp. 103–4.

72. *Works of James Arminius* (Auburn edition), vol. 2, p. 110. Checked against *Disputationes*, pp. 104–5: "Notitia est fidei antecedens prius enim conspicitur filius quam credatur in illum. Fiducia autem consequens: per fidem enim fiducia collocatur in Christum, et per eum in Deum . . . Instrumentum est Evangelium seu verbum fidei, continens sensum de Deo et Christo, quem Spiritus intellectui proponit et persuadet."

73. See the brilliant essay, to which I am deeply indebted: Kęstutis Daugirdas, "The Biblical Hermeneutics of Socinians and Remonstrants in the Seventeenth Century," in Leeuwen, Stanglin, and Tolsma, eds., *Arminius, Arminianism, and Europe*, pp. 89–114. See also Mortimer, *Reason and Religion*.

74. Jackson, *Eternall Truth of Scriptures*, pp. 11–13.

75. Jackson, *Iustifying faith*, p. 6.

76. Jackson, *Iustifying faith*, pp. 6–7. The "experiments" described here fit closely with Anthony Grafton's argument for the importance of physical evidence in the early modern *ars historica*: see Grafton, *What Was History?*.

77. Jackson, *Iustifying faith*, p. 10.

78. Jackson, *Iustifying faith*, p. 12. For Jackson's view of the will and the intellect in belief, see pp. 32–35.

79. See most recently Heering, *Hugo Grotius*. Grotius's debt to Socinus on the question of historical veracity is discussed in Henk Jan de Jonge, "Grotius' View of the Gospels and the Evangelists," in Nellen and Rabbie, eds., *Hugo Grotius Theologian*.

80. Grotius, *Truth of the Christian Religion*, p. 88.

81. Grotius, *Truth of the Christian Religion*, pp. 138–40.

82. Hacking, *Emergence of Probability*; Shapiro, *Probability and Certainty*; Shapin and Schaffer, *Leviathan and the Air-Pump*; Daston, *Classical Probability*; Shapin, *A Social History of Truth*; Poovey, *A History of the Modern Fact*. For the impact of this epistemological revolution on economics, see Wennerlind, *Casualties of Credit*.

83. A partial exception that deserves to be acknowledged is Shapiro, *Probability and Certainty*, which does indeed deal extensively with religion and ac-

knowledges the insufficiency of the knowledge/opinion dichotomy. I hope that the current work can be seen as extending the historical reach and significance of Shapiro's arguments. Following in Shapiro's footsteps, see also the comments about belief and probability in Sheppard, *Anti-Atheism in Early Modern England*, chs. 7–8.

84. See, e.g., Harrison, *Territories of Science and Religion*; Guakroger, *Emergence of a Scientific Culture*; Shapiro, *Probability and Certainty*. Attempts to link the scientific revolution to religious positions have tended to focus not on empiricist conceptions of belief but, contrariwise, on voluntarist, Augustinian, and millenarian theology: see, e.g., Merton, *Science, Technology and Society*; Webster, *The Great Instauration*; Harrison, *The Bible, Protestantism*; Harrison, *The Fall of Man*; John Henry, "Religion and the Scientific Revolution," in Harrison, ed., *Cambridge Companion to Science and Religion*. Guakroger, "Early Modern Idea of Scientific Doctrine," asserts the primacy of Christianity in the turn toward doctrinalism in the scientific revolution. A recent general overview of some of this ground is Steven Marrone, *A History of Science*.

85. On the Jesuits in Asia, see, e.g., Brockey, *Journey to the East*; Minamiki, *Chinese Rites Controversy*; Hsia, *Jesuit in the Forbidden City*. Paul Nelles, "Du savant au missionnaire," focuses in particular on the Jesuits' delineation of a concept of *fides* that could be distinguished from cultural mores and traditions.

86. On the Jesuits in Canada in the first half of the seventeenth century, see, e.g., Deslandres, *Croire et Faire Croire*; Leavelle, *Catholic Calumet*; Blackburn, *Harvest of Souls*; Lopenza, "Le Jeune Dreams of Moose"; Campbell, "Gender, Colonialism"; Ballériaux, "Adopted Children of God"; True, *Masters and Students*; Thomas Worcester, "A Defensive Discourse"; Friant, "Ils aiment bien leur chapelet." On explicit comparison to the Asian case, see Abé, *Jesuit Mission to New France*. On the religion of the Wyandot, see Trigger, *The Children of Aataentsic*.

87. All quotations are from the online version of *JR*, but I have checked the translations in the original printed edition and provided the original languages in the footnotes when useful. *JR* II, 7–11. "Enfin nous en sommes là encore, après plusieurs enquestes et travaux, à disputer s'ils ont aucune parolle qui corresponde droictement à ce mot *Credo*, je croy. Estimez un peu que c'est du reste du symbole et fondemens chrestiens."

88. This is the argument of Deslandres, *Croire et Faire Croire*, pp. 51–52 and part I passim.

89. *JR* III, 146–47; *JR* II, 86–87.

90. *JR* III, 144–45. "en faisant leurs anciens sacrifices, danses, & superstitions, ils alloyent à la saincte Communion, si l'on vouloit, mais c'estoit sans sçauoir ny *Credo*, ny *Confiteor*. Et au sortir de là, s'en alloyent enyurer, & chanter au Diable leurs sorceleries accoustumées."

91. With children it was a different story, and the Jesuits were willing to use very different tactics, for instance plying them with sugar in order to convince them to be baptized: see *JR* XIX, 166–67.

92. *JR* XIII, 120–21.

93. See, e.g., *JR* XXVI, 278: "les croyans (c'est icy le nom des Chrestiens)"; *JR* XXIX, 70: "dit-il, demeurer parmy les creans, c'est à dire parmy les Chrestiens de S. Ioseph"; and many other examples. Deslandres, *Croire et Faire Croire*, stresses that the slowness of conversion was due to the Jesuit demand for cultural conversion rather than syncretism; my own emphasis on interior and propositional belief may be viewed as compatible.

94. The classic work is Hodgen, *Early Anthropology*. See also, e.g., Strousma, *A New Science*; Pagden, *The Fall of Natural Man*; and the works of Sabine Mac-Cormack, especially her *Religion in the Andes*.

95. *JR* I, 286–87: "Esse tamen aliquod, velut in sublustri nocte, vident."

96. *JR* I, 260–61; *JR* III, 128–31.

97. *JR* XVII, 126–27.

98. *JR* XVI, 198–99: "Au reste la creance & les superstitions des Sauuages n'est pas bien profondement enracinée dans leur esprit; car comme toutes ces resueries ne sont fondeées que sur le mensonge, elles tombent d'elles mesmes, & se fondent, ou se dissipent aux rayons des veritez qu'on leur propose tres-côformes à la raison."

99. *JR* VI, 156.

100. *JR* III, 192–97.

101. Waddell, *Jesuit Science*.

102. *JR* I, 288–91.

103. *JR* VII, 129–33.

104. *JR* IX, 112–13.

105. *JR* VIII, 32–34. "Quand aux propositions que nous leur faisions de croire en Dieu, l'vn d'eux me dit vn iour. Si nous croyons en vostre Dieu, neigera-il? Il neigera, luy dis je. La neige sera-elle dure & profonde? Elle le sera. Trouuerõs nous des Orignaux? Vous en trouuerez. Les tuerons nous? Ouy; Car comme Dieu sçait tout, qu'il peut tout, & qu'il est tres bon, il ne manquera pas de vous assister."

106. *JR* X, 42–49.

107. On Jesuit science, see, e.g., Waddell, *Jesuit Science*; Prieto, *Missionary Scientists*; Hsia, *Sojourners in a Strange Land*; Harris, "Transposing the Merton Thesis."

108. *JR* VI, 176–77. Le Jeune evidently did not know that his Spanish predecessor in the Jesuit order, José de Acosta, had in 1590 proposed the existence of a land bridge from Asia to North America by which the indigenous peoples had reached their land.

109. *JR* VI, 176–81.

110. I owe knowledge of this to Edward Muir's unpublished paper on the *Incogniti*, "People Who Believe Nothing," which he sent to be read at the conference "Problems of Faith: Belief and Promise in Medieval and Early Modern Europe" at Berkeley in September 2013.

111. *JR* IX, 210–11.

112. *JR* X, 138–39.

113. *JR* X, 138–39. "Une plus curieuse recherche de la verité."

114. *JR* X, 132–33.

115. *JR* VIII, 14–15.

116. *JR* XV, 138–39. "Vne eclipse de Lune . . . nous donna icy vn grand credit pour faire approuuer ce que nous croyons. Car (leur disions nous) vous avez veu comme la Lune est eclypsée le mesme iour au mesme moment que nous auions predit. Au reste, nous n'eussios pas voulu mourir pour vous maintenir cette verité, come nous sommes prests de faire, pour vous maintenir que Dieu vous brûlera eternellement, si vous ne croyez en luy."

117. *JR* VII, 186–89.

118. Funkenstein, *Theology*, p. 346.

Chapter Six: Enlightened Belief

1. Descartes, *Discourse on Method and the Meditations*, p. 32. Checked against Descartes, *Discours de la Méthode*.

2. See Davies, *Descartes*, ch. 11.

3. Descartes, *Discourse on Method and the Meditations*, e.g., pp. 39, 53, 95.

4. On Descartes and belief, see, e.g., Davies, *Descartes*; Hatfield, "Reason, Nature, and God." On the disenchantment that Cartesianism evoked among his followers, see Ruler, "Minds, Forms, and Spirits." For Malebranche's elaboration of Descartes, arguing that the idea of an infinite God logically proceeds ideas of all finite things, see Kors, *Naturalism and Unbelief in France*, ch. 4.

5. Richard Serjeantson argues that the fields of rhetoric and dialectic opened space for subjective judgment in natural philosophy, while Barbara Shapiro argues that law served that function. My own argument is that religion was a leading rather than trailing indicator: Serjeantson, "Testimony and Proof"; Shapiro, *A Culture of Fact*.

6. See Marcia Colish, "Systematic Theology and Theological Renewal in the Twelfth Century," and Marcia Colish, "Authority and Interpretation in Scholastic Theology," both in her *Studies in Scholasticism*.

7. Israel, *Radical Enlightenment*, pp. 8–9.

8. Scholder, *Birth of Modern Critical Theology*, p. 111.

9. Jonathan Sheehan, "Suffering Job: Christianity Beyond Metaphysics," in *God in the Enlightenment*, ed. Bulman and Ingram, p. 197.

10. For general comments on the relationship between belief and knowledge in the early Enlightenment, see Pocock, *Barbarism and Religion, Volume Five*, pp. 99–109 and passim; Pitassi, *Entre croire et savoir*.

11. See Nadler, *Arnauld*, especially ch. 2 for a discussion of Arnauld's reception of Cartesianism. Arnauld was also, of course, a critic of the *Meditations*.

12. For the Jansenists' precocious attention to individual judgment and fact-finding, see an older literature including Jemolo, *Il Giansenismo*; Momigliano, "La formazione," first published in 1936, reproduced in his *Contributo alla Storia degli Studi Classici*. I am grateful to Tony Grafton for these references.

13. Arnauld and Nicole, *Logic*, p. 341, checked against Arnauld and Nicole, *La logique*. In this quotation, I have changed the translation of *creance* from "credence" to "belief," and I have corrected the Latin from *auctoritate* to *autoritati* [sic] as it appears in the original: *La logique*, pp. 355–56.

14. *Logic*, p. 346. *La logique*, p. 363. Serjeantson, "Testimony and Proof," p. 223 notes that a central breakthrough of *La logique* was to distinguish testimony from authority, as they had not been distinguished previously in the rhetorical and dialectical traditions.

15. *Logic*, pp. 342–43. *La logique*, pp. 357–58.

16. Farge, *Subversive Words*, p. 40.

17. Farge, *Subversive Words*, pp. 45–53, 36. See also Baker, "Public Opinion as Political Invention" in his *Inventing the French Revolution*. Jane Shaw has likewise shown that debates over miracles and the evidence for their occurrence were at the heart of the emergence of the public sphere in England: Shaw, *Miracles*.

18. Spinoza, *Theological-Political Treatise*, pp. 175–78. Checked against Spinoza, *Tractatus Theologico-Politicus*, p. 156.

19. See most recently Nadler, *A Book Forged in Hell*, and the 2013 colloquium in the *Journal of the History of Ideas*: Nadler, "Scripture and Truth"; Fraenkel, "Spinoza on Miracles"; Harvey, "Spinoza on Biblical Miracles." On Spinoza's rationalism, see Della Rocca, *Spinoza*, and the critique of that work in Garber, "Superheroes." See also Marrama, "Spinoza on Fictitious Ideas."

20. On Meyer, see Israel, *Radical Enlightenment*, pp. 200–205. On Hobbes, see Malcolm, "Hobbes and Spinoza," in his *Aspects of Hobbes*. I owe this reference to Tony Grafton.

21. Spinoza, *Theological-Political Treatise*, p. 151 and passim.

22. Spinoza, *Theological-Political Treatise*, p. 61. *Tractatus*, p. 47.

23. Spinoza, *Theological-Political Treatise*, pp. 77–78. *Tractatus*, p. 64. Cf. Sangiacomo, "Locke and Spinoza."

24. Wolff, *Logic*, pp. 190–91.

25. Toland, *Christianity not Mysterious*. On the striking modernity of Toland's view of belief, see Daniel, *John Toland*, e.g., pp. 21–22: "Men should believe only what they understand, he argued, only what is meaningful to them. He thus placed the authority of any belief, not in its intrinsic intelligibility or in the source of the doctrine, but in the believer himself."

26. Penelhum, *God and Skepticism*.

27. Pascal, *Great Shorter Works of Pascal*, pp. 128–29. I owe this reference to Jonathan Sheehan.

28. Pascal, *Pensées*, #230. Checked against the original French at https://www.ub.uni-freiburg.de/fileadmin/ub/referate/04/pascal/pensees.pdf. "Incompréhensible que Dieu soit et incompréhensible qu'il ne soit pas."

29. Pascal, *Pensées*, #233.

30. Pascal, *Pensées*, #430 and #229.

31. Pascal, *Pensées*, #233.

32. Pascal, *Pensées*, #260. "Tant s'en faut que d'avoir ouï dire une chose soit la règle de votre créance, que vous ne devez rien croire sans vous mettre en l'état comme si jamais vous ne l'aviez ouï. C'est le consentement de vous à vous-même et la voix constante de votre raison et non des autres qui vous doit faire croire."

33. In this section I am particularly indebted to the work of my colleague Barbara Shapiro and to many fruitful conversations with her.

34. Borghero, *La Certezza e la Storia*; Pocock, *Barbarism and Religion, Volume Two*, p. 22 and prelude passim. For a more sociological discussion of historical skepticism, linked to skepticism about news and the claims of governments, see Dooley, *Social History of Skepticism*.

35. Mulsow, *Enlightenment Underground*, pp. 88–89. Mulsow also emphasizes how much of the seventeenth-century debate over the historical verification of Christianity occurred in dialogue with Jews. See Völkel, *"Pyrrhonismus Historicus"*; Burke, *Social History of Knowledge*, ch. 9; Burke, "Two Crises of Historical Consciousness."

36. On the English case, see: Shapiro, *A Culture of Fact*; Shapiro, *Probability and Certainty*; Levine, "Matters of Fact"; Levine, "From Tradition to History"; van Leeuwen, *The Problem of Certainty*.

37. Chillingworth, *The Religion of Protestants*, pp. 35–37. See also Ward, *A Philosophicall Essay*, p 88: "Matters of fact being cleared, and the historical narrations being asserted to be true, the doctrinal parts will follow of their own accord." On Chillingworth's novel account of the difference between belief, knowledge, and opinion, see van Leeuwen, *Problem of Certainty*, pp. 20–21.

38. Barrow, *The Works of the Learned Isaac Barrow*, vol. 1, pp. 447–51. See Feingold, ed., *Before Newton*.

39. Mulsow and Rohls, eds., *Socinianism and Arminianism*, introduction.

40. Pocock, *Barbarism and Religion*, pp. 53, 56, and ch. 2 passim.

41. Locke, *Essay*, IV.15.3. Besides the Arminian tradition, another unacknowledged influence may be Hobbes, *Humane Nature*, ch. 6, which equates belief with probable opinion of a report, and defines conscience as "opinion of evidence" (p. 67).

42. Locke, *Essay*, IV.16.9–11.

43. Locke, *Essay*, IV.16.14 and IV.17.24. Although readers will note our disagreements about "opinion," I am deeply indebted to Nicholas Wolterstorff, *John Locke*.

44. Locke, *Reasonableness*, pp. 26–29.

45. Locke, *Reasonableness*, pp. 195–99.

46. Locke, *Reasonableness*, pp. 191–92. See Wallace, "Socinianism."

47. Of course, Enlightenment writers continued to attack "opinion," which kept its negative connotations; but they generally condemned poorly justified opinion rather than opinion itself. So, for instance, Keith Baker refers to the massive *Traité de l'opinion* (1735) by the Marquis de Saint Aubin as a compendium of conventional wisdom distinguishing knowledge from mere opinion (Baker, "Public Opinion as Political Invention," from his *Inventing the French*

Revolution, p. 175). But Saint Aubin declared that opposing sentiments should be carefully weighed and each opinion should be given "la degree de croïance qu'elle mérite": Gilbert-Charles Le Gendre, Marquis de Saint Aubin sur Loire, *Traité de l'opinion* (Paris, 6 vols., 1735), vol. 1, p. 2.

48. Here I respectfully depart from the sociopolitical explanation for the Anglican embrace of the new science in Jacob, *The Newtonians*.

49. On Boyle's experimentalism, especially in relation to religion and other kinds of truth-claims, see, e.g., Hunter, *Boyle*; Shapin, *A Social History of Truth*; Steffan Ducheyne, "The Status of Theory and Hypothesis," in Antsey, ed., *Oxford Handbook of British Philosophy*.

50. Boyle, *The Excellency of Theology*, pp. 142–43. Decades earlier, Campanella had described Galileo's *Starry Messenger* as "historical" because "it does not say why four planets move around Jupiter, or two around Saturn, but says that it was found to be so." Cited in Grafton, *What Was History?*, p .27.

51. Boyle, *Certain Physiological Essays*, p. 9.

52. Boyle, *The Christian Virtuoso*, pp. 62–65.

53. [Robert Boyle?], *Some considerations*, pp. 125–26.

54. My reading of Huet is based substantially on Shelford, "Thinking Geometrically"; and Shelford, *Transforming the Republic of Letters*. However, I think Shelford slightly misreads the Port Royal Logic and Huet's relationship to it when she asserts that "Huet collapsed the distinction Arnauld and Nicole made between things known through 'reasoning' and things known through 'authority.'" As we have seen, the *Logique* was itself already an attempt to collapse the dominant Counter-Reformation interpretation of this distinction.

55. On Huet's view of the Royal Society, see Van Leeuwen, *Problem of Certainty*, p. 145.

56. Shelford, "Thinking Geometrically," p. 611. Shelford's translation.

57. Shelford, "Thinking Geometrically," p. 614.

58. Huet, *Demonstratio Evangelica*, pp. 6–7.

59. Locke, *Essay*, III.iii.15.

60. Locke, *Essay*, IV.iii.18.

61. Locke, *Essay*, IV.vi.11.

62. Locke, *Essay*, IV.xii.10. Peter Antsey argues that Locke gradually changed his mind on this issue and, in contact with Newton's *Principia*, later embraced a form of demonstrative natural knowledge: Antsey, *John Locke and Natural Philosophy*.

63. Locke, *Essay* XIV, xv.5.

64. Cited in Baker, *Condorcet*, p. 92.

65. See, e.g., Hume, *Treatise*, p. 67 (1.3.7).

66. Hume, *Treatise*, p. 68 (1.3.7).

67. Hume, *Treatise*, p. 80 (1.3.9). "Here we must not be contented with saying, that the vividness of the idea produces the belief: we must maintain that they are individually the same."

68. Hume's successors like Immanuel Kant and John Stuart Mill, and most other major figures through Bertrand Russell, regarded him as inescapably skeptical. More recently, philosophers have tended to regard Hume as a positivist or a naturalist. For a discussion of this debate, see, e.g., Louis Loeb, "Inductive Inference in Hume's Philosophy," in Radcliffe, ed., *A Companion to Hume*; Meeker, *Hume's Radical Scepticism*.

69. Hume, *Enquiry*, p. 29 (5.1).

70. Hume, *Treatise*, p. 62 (1.3.6). On the induction problem, I am greatly indebted to Mary Poovey, *A History of the Modern Fact*.

71. Cited in Baker, *Condorcet*, p. 142.

72. Hume, *Enquiry*, 10.1.

73. Hume, *Enquiry*, p. 90 (10.1).

74. Hume, *Dialogues*, p. 79 (Dialogue VIII).

75. For changing views of probabilism, especially in scientific epistemology, see, e.g., Baker, *Condorcet*, ch. 3; Hacking, *Emergence of Probability*; Shapiro, *Probability and Certainty*; Daston, *Classical Probability*; Guicciardini, *Isaac Newton*; Poovey, *A History of the Modern Fact*.

76. Anthropologists have noticed this entanglement between post-Enlightenment science and religion. See, e.g,. Stroeken, "Believed Belief"; Good, *Medicine*; Bowie, *Anthropology of Religion*, pp. 244–45.

77. Online at http://edu.lva.virginia.gov/online_classroom/shaping_the_constitution/doc/religious_freedom.

78. See, e.g.. Harrison, *Territories of Science and Religion*; Quine, "Two Dogmas of Empiricism"; Quine, *From Stimulus to Science*; Quine, "Epistemology Naturalized."

79. See, e.g., Nadler, *Malebranche and Ideas*; Moreau, *Deux Cartesiens*.

80. For some wildly variant readings, see, e.g., Labrousse, *Pierre Bayle*; Labrousse, *Bayle*; Mori, *Bayle*; Popkin, *History of Scepticism*; and the judicious recent view in Lugt, *Bayle*.

81. Cited in Erdozain, *The Soul of Doubt*, p. 124.

82. Cited in Kors, *Naturalism and Unbelief in France*, p. 230. And on pp. 245–46, Kors notes how many rationalists, who desired religion to conform to reason, wrote bitter responses against Bayle.

83. Bayle, *Dictionaire*, vol. 3, p. 3153. "Personne ne doit être reçu à examiner s'il faut croire ce que Dieu ordonne de croire." All references to Bayle's dictionary are to the 1702 revised edition: Bayle, *Dictionaire Historique et Critique*. I have consulted the English version published in the 1730s, but its renderings are imprecise, so instead all Bayle translations are my own.

84. Bayle, *Dictionaire*, vol. 3, p. 3156.

85. Bayle, *Dictionaire*, vol. 3, p. 3158.

86. Bayle, *Dictionaire*, vol. 3, p. 3153.

87. Eusterschulte, "Bayle's *Dictionaire*," p. 309. See also the persuasive argument that for Bayle reason is not a source of objective truth but a critical function

to evaluate how persuasive beliefs are, in Irwin, "The Core Mysteries," especially ch. 4; and Irwin, "La foi et la croyance chez Pierre Bayle," in Hummel, ed., *Doxa*. My discussion of Bayle's unwillingness to deal with the first-order problem of whether revelation is divine corresponds well to Irwin's view of an epistemic "immunity" for faith on first-order questions.

88. Bayle, *Dictionaire*, vol. 1, p. 15.

89. Bayle, *Dictionaire*, vol. 1, pp. 16–17: "J'ai rassemblé dans les remarques un assez grand nombre de differens sentimens sur les choses qui concernent Abel. C'est avoir rassemblé bien des mensenges, et bien des fautes. Or comme c'est le but et l'esprit de ce Dictionaire, le Lector ne doit point donner son jugement sur ce ramas, sans ce souvenir de ce but. Et cela soit dit une foit pour toutes."

90. Bayle, *Dictionaire*, vol. 1, pp. 74–75. On the "science" of Adam, see Harrison, *The Fall of Man*; Picciotto, *Labors of Innocence*.

91. I paraphrase Arlette Farge, *Subversive Words*, pp. 85–88, who makes this argument more broadly about the space of public skepticism in the eighteenth century.

92. Locke, *Essay*, IV.16.10.

93. "John Craige," in the *Oxford Dictionary of National Biography*.

94. Craige, *Mathematical Principles*, pp. 53–54. Checked against Craige, *Theologiae Christianae Principia Mathematica*, preface pp. vi–vii.

95. *Mathematical Principles*, p. 60.

96. *Mathematical Principles*, p. 65.

97. *Mathematical Principles*, p. 70. In January 1697, the Edinburgh University student Thomas Aikenhead had been executed for blasphemy; among his crimes was the claim that no later than 1800 Christianity "will be utterly extirpate." Given Craige's strong links to Edinburgh, it is an intriguing possibility that Aikenhead's timetable for incredulity might have been a context for Craige's work. See Michael Hunter, "Aikenhead the Atheist," in his *Science and the Shape of Orthodoxy*, p. 312.

98. Mencken, *Herrn Joh. Burckhardt Menckens zwey Reden von der Charlatanerie*, p. 194.

99. *Mathematical Principles*, introduction, pp. 3–5. The "Clerk" to whom Pope referred may have been Samuel Clarke, but the decay of moral evidence clearly referred to Craige.

100. Labrussel, *Traité*, p. 27. Another figure who briefly treated Craige as impious was the English high church Anglican Francis Atterbury in "A Representation of the Present State of Religion Among us," in *Quadriennium*, vol. 1, p. 333.

101. [George Hooper], "A Calculation."

102. *Dictionnaire historique*, vol. 8, pp. 53–54.

103. Houtteville, *La religion Chrétienne*, p. 337.

104. Houtteville, *La religion Chrétienne*, pp. 338–39: "J'appelle *impression*, l'étonnement, le plaisir, la peine, et les autres passions, compagnes assiduës d'un fait important. J'appelle conviction, l'évidence, ou l'acquiescement à l'évidence

des raisons qui décident que ce fait est. J'avouë que l'impression diminuë pro-portionellement à la distance des tems ou des lieux . . . Mais ce qui est vrai de l'impression, ne l'est pas de la conviction. La preuve d'un fait subsiste la même invariablement." Houtteville also argued that the certitude of Christianity had actually increased rather than diminishing, because of the ever-increasing num-ber of witnesses to its truth.

105. Bayle, *Dictionaire*, vol. 3, pp. 3157–58. Bayle, whether intentionally or not, misread Craige as arguing that Christ would return *before* the year 3150 rather than after.

106. *Encyclopedia of Diderot and d'Alembert*. And see the discussion in Baker, *Condorcet*, pp. 155–94, on the broader extension of the science of probabilities to the social sciences.

107. See Sheehan, *Enlightenment Bible*. And more broadly on rationalist historical arguments both for and against scriptural authority, see Pocock, *Barbarism and Religion, Volume Five*, ch. 10 and passim.

108. Diderot, "Believe," in *Encyclopedia of Diderot and d'Alembert*.

109. For Bernard, see Kors, *Naturalism and Unbelief in France*, p. 12. For Bayle, see, e.g., the entries in his *Dictionaire* on Mathias Knuzen and on Spinoza.

Chapter Seven: Belief in the Human

1. Hume, *Treatise*, p. 85 (1.3.10).

2. Coleridge, *Biographia Literaria*, vol. 2, ch. 14.

3. This discussion of Coleridge was written independently of the wonderful discussion in McEachern, *Believing in Shakespeare*, which I was privileged to read in draft.

4. Sheehan and Wahrman, *Invisible Hands*. See also Funkenstein, *Theology*, p. 204 on "invisible hand" theories: "From Vico to Marx, they envision the subject of human history—human society—as capable of generating all of its in-stitutions, beliefs, and achievements of itself . . . The 'finger of God' disappeared from the course of human events."

5. See Kahn, *Wayward Contracts*.

6. Bell, *Cult of the Nation*, p. 26.

7. See, e.g., Fox, Porter, and Wolker, eds., *Inventing Human Science*; Gus-dorf, *Les sciences humaines*; Vidal, *Sciences of the Soul*; Hunt, Jacob, and Mijn-hardt, *The Book that Changed Europe*.

8. Foucault, *The Order of Things*. See also Cunningham, "Getting the Game Right"; Baker, *Condorcet*, preface.

9. Porter, "Medical Science and Human Science in the Enlightenment," in Fox et al., eds., *Inventing Human Science*, p. 68.

10. Cited in Christopher Fox, "Introduction: How to Prepare a Noble Savage: The Spectacle of Human Science," in Fox et al., eds., *Inventing Human Science*, p. 1.

11. Hume, *Treatise*, p. 4 (Introduction, para. 4).

12. Vidal, *The Sciences of the Soul*, p. 1, citing Gabriel Mingard's article in Fortunato Bartolomeo de Felice (ed.), *Encyclopédie, ou Dictionnaire universal raisonné des connoissances humaines*.

13. Pope, *Essay on Man*, II.i. In subsequent editions, the second line was changed to the better known "The proper study of mankind is man."

14. Ferguson, *Essay*, p. 12.

15. See Subha Mukherji, "Trying, Knowing and Believing."

16. See, e.g., Snook, "The Beautifying Part of Physic"; Lanoë, *La Pudre et le fard*.

17. *Troisieme Centurie*, pp. 29–32. For the rehabilitation of artificial beauty in England, see, e.g., *A discourse of auxiliary beauty. Or artificiall hansomenesse. In point of conscience between two ladies* (London, 1656), attributed to both John Gauden (unlikely) and John Taylor (very possible).

18. Stevin, *Disme*, sig.C1r-v.

19. Willsford, *Willfords Arithmetick*, p. 1.

20. Willsford, *Willfords Arithmetick*, pp. 287 and 299.

21. Wingate, *Arithmetique Made Easie*, pp. 151–52.

22. Bobynet, *L'Horographie Ingenieuse*, p. 4.

23. I would like to thank Caitlin Rosenthal for bringing imaginary accounts to my attention.

24. Monteage, *Debtor*, sig. I3v.

25. Alexander Malcolm, *New Treatise*, esp. pp. 121–25.

26. Hobbes, *Leviathan*, p. 19.

27. On the metaphysics behind this claim, see Marrama, "Spinoza on Fictitious Ideas": "According to Spinoza, true ideas of nonexistent things need not be regarded as fictitious ideas," they are instead reorganizations of present knowledge of actually existent things.

28. Spinoza, *Theological-Political Treatise*, pp. 20 and 32. Checked against Spinoza, *Tractatus*. Silverthorne's and Israel's translation has Isaiah seeing Seraphim with seven wings; but Isaiah 6:2 has "six wings" and Spinoza's Latin is *senis*, presumably intended as a form of *senio* rather than *senex* or *septem*, so I have changed their translation.

29. Spinoza, *Theological-Political Treatise*, ch. 2 passim.

30. Spinoza, *Theological-Political Treatise*, p. 93. Spinoza, *Tractatus*, pp. 78–79. I have twice here changed Silverthorne's and Israel's translation: they had "apparitions" for *repraesentationes* and "beliefs" for *opinionibus*.

31. Spinoza, *Theological-Political Treatise*, ch. 7 passim. See LeBuffe, "The Doctrine of the Two Kingdoms."

32. Massimo Mazzotti describes how the Enlightenment ideal of analysis—reducing real things in the social or natural world to the generalized abstractions of algebra—interposed a kind of fictionality in which it was essential to believe, requiring provisional or contextual rather than absolute knowledge. See Mazzotti, *Mathematics at the Barricades* (forthcoming). I am grateful to Professor Mazzotti for sharing his work with me prior to publication.

33. René Descartes, *Discours de la Méthode*, p. 380 in the essay "la geometrie."

34. See, e.g., Mancosu, *Philosophy of Mathematics*; Guicciardini, *Isaac Newton*.

35. See, e.g., Heinemann, "Truths of Reason and Truths of Fact." For Herbert of Cherbury's distinction between *veritas rei* and *veritas apparentiae*, among other kinds of truths, see his *De Veritate*.

36. Leibniz, *Mathematische Schriften*, vol. 5, p. 357. "Verum enim vero tenacior est varietatis suae pulcherrimae Natura rerum, aeternarum varietatum parens, vel potius Divina Mens, quam ut omnia sub unum genus compingi patiatur. Itaque elegans et mirabile effugium reperit in illo Analyseos miraculo, idealis mundi monstro, pene inter Ens et non-Ens Amphibio, quod radicem imaginariam appellamus." I would like to thank Massimo Mazzotti and Maureen Miller for helping me to decode the various possibilities in this passage.

37. McClenon, "A Contribution of Leibniz."

38. See, e.g., *Mathematische Schriften*, vol. 4, p. 110.

39. Samuel Levey, "Archimedes," p. 128.

40. Leibniz, *Philosophical Papers and Letters*, vol. 2, pp. 543–44.

41. See also Leibniz's remarks in his 1693 *Matheseos Universalis*, reproduced in *Mathematische Schriften*, vol. v7, p. v73. Ex irrationalibus oriuntur quantitates impossibiles seu imaginariae, quarum mira est natura, et tamen non contemnenda utilitas; etsi enim ipsae per se aliquid impossibile significent, tamen non tantum ostendunt fontem impossibilitatis, et quomodo quaestio corrigi potuerit, ne esset impossibilis, sed etiam interventu ipsarum exprimi possunt quantitates reales.

42. *The Works of Dugald Stewart in Seven Volumes* vol. 7, pp. 30–31.

43. Locke, *Two Treatises of Government, Second Treatise*, ch. 5.

44. Evrigenis, *Images of Anarchy*, p. 1.

45. See, e.g., Benjamin Straumann, "Ancient Caesarian Lawyers"; Kingsbury and Straumann, "The State of Nature."

46. Grotius, *Freedom of the Seas*, ch. 5, checked against the Latin in the same edition. A parallel discussion, with much of the same language, is in *De jure praedae*, ch. 12.

47. Hobbes, *Leviathan*, ch. 13, pp. 88–90.

48. Evrigenis, *Images of Anarchy*, p. 161 and prologue passim.

49. Hobbes, *Leviathan*, ch. 17, p. 120.

50. Wolker, "Anthropology and Conjectural History in the Enlightenment," in Fox et al., eds., *Inventing Human Science*, pp. 36–37. As Martin Mulsow notes, Pufendorf and more overtly his followers Nikolaus Gundling and Christian Thomasius argued that the Fall of man had impaired the will but not the intellect. So, in this tradition, the act of theorizing intellectually about the state of nature was itself proof about the state of nature: Mulsow, *Enlightenment Underground*, pp. 212–13.

51. Pufendorf, *Of the Law of Nature and Nations*, pp. 102–3.

52. Rousseau, *Discourses*, p. 132. Checked against Rousseau, *Discours*.

53. Rousseau, *Discourses*, p. 157.

54. Hobbes, *Leviathan*, pp. 9–10. And see Hobbes, *Leviathan*, p. 111: "A person, is he, whose words or actions are considered, either as his own, or as representing the words or actions of an other man, or of any other thing to whom they are attributed, whether truly or by fiction." See Skinner, "Hobbes and the Purely Artificial Person of the State," in his *Visions of Politics*.

55. Hobbes, *Leviathan*, p. 94.

56. Hobbes, *Leviathan*, pp. 96, 100–101.

57. Hobbes, *Leviathan*, p. 99.

58. Hobbes, *Leviathan*, p. 97.

59. As Jürgen Habermas noted in his classic essay on the public sphere, Hobbes took a "momentous step" when he identified conscience with opinion: "Hobbes defined a 'chain of opinions' that extended from faith to judgment. In the sphere of 'opinion' he reduced all acts of believing, judgment, and opining to the same level. Even 'conscience' was 'nothing else but a man's settled judgment and opinion.'" Habermas, *Structural Transformation*, p. 90.

60. See Mulsow, *Enlightenment Underground*, pp. 144–49.

61. *FB*, preface, sig. A4v.

62. *FB2*, p. 382. On the Epicurean roots of this secular providence, see Hundert, *Enlightenment's Fable*, ch. 1.

63. *FB2*, p. 385.

64. *FB2*, pp. 386–87.

65. *FB2*, p. 207.

66. *FB2*, pp. 207–8.

67. *FB2*, pp. 203–6. On the influence of Mandeville's view that man is artificer of his own nature, see M. M. Goldsmith, "Regulating Anew."

68. *FB*, pp. 139–40. See Daniel, "Myth and Rationality."

69. *FB*, p. 30.

70. *FB*, pp. 179, 50–51. And see Mandeville, *Enquiry*, where Mandeville stresses how honor culture is deeply anti-Christian. On Mandeville and honor, see Hundert, *Enlightenment's Fable*, ch. 2.

71. *FB*, pp. 50–51, 206–7.

72. *FB*, pp. 181–93.

73. *FB*, pp. 194–96.

74. *FB2*, p. 248.

75. *FB*, pp. 202–3. This argument is specifically attributed to Pierre Bayle.

76. As David Marshall notes in "The Current State of Vico Scholarship," the fact that Mark Lilla interprets Vico as a Counter-Enlightenment thinker and Jonathan Israel interprets Vico as a radical Enlightenment thinker should give us cause for concern. I would hope that my focus here on the capacity of a novel conception of belief to bridge between rationalism and some of its critics might help to resolve this tension. On Vico, see Lilla, *G.B. Vico*; Israel, *Radical Enlightenment*, pp. 664–70; Remaud, *Les Archives de l'Humanité*; Chabot, *Giambattista Vico*; on Vico and Romanticism, see Berlin, *Vico and Herder*.

77. Vico, *New Science*, pp. 119–20. Checked against Giambattista Vico, *Princìpi de scienza nuova* (1744), in *Opere*, vol. I, pp. 541–42: "perché l'avevano fatto gli uomini, ne potevano conseguire la scienza gli uomini."

78. Vico, *New Science*, p. 144. Vico, *Opere*, vol. I, pp. 569–70: "ch'essi immaginavano le cagioni delle cose . . . essere dèi."

79. Vico, *New Science*, pp. 145–49. Vico, *Opere*, vol. I, pp. 573–75. Frank Manuel writes that for Vico, the first human invention was the idea of a god, and "in the same frightful process curiosity was aroused, the mind was opened to reason, religion and civilization were born together": Manuel, *The Eighteenth Century Confronts the Gods*, p. 155.

80. Vico, *New Science*, p. 154. See Schaeffer, "From Natural Religion to Natural Law in Vico."

81. Funkenstein, *Theology and the Scientific Imagination*, p. 280, and see another lovely version on p. 328.

82. Vico, *New Science*, pp. 489–90. Vico, *Opere*, vol. I, p. 970.

83. Giddens, *Consequences of Modernity*, ch. 1. I owe this reference to Victoria Kahn.

84. My brief discussion here of Kant will satisfy no philosophers, but I am nonetheless indebted to: Guyer, ed., *Cambridge Companion to Kant*; Caygill, *Art of Judgment*; Guyer, *Kant and the Claims of Taste*; Wood, *Kant's Moral Religion*; Allison, *Kant's Transcendental Idealism*.

85. Kant, *Critique of Pure Reason*, p. 111. This quotation is from Kant's preface to the second edition.

86. For the history of the philosophical category of judgment, see Caygill, *Art of Judgment*. Caygill distinguishes not only between rationalist and empiricist views but between views based on civil society, as in England, and views based on the cameralist police state, as in Germany.

87. Schneewind, *Invention of Autonomy*.

88. *Complete Poetry and Prose of William Blake*, p. 37 (The Marriage of Heaven and Hell, Plate 8).

89. *Complete Poetry and Prose of William Blake*, p. 39 (The Marriage of Heaven and Hell, Plate 12).

90. *Complete Poetry and Prose of William Blake*, p. 42 (The Marriage of Heaven and Hell, Plate 20). On Blake's opposition to empiricism, see Quinney, *William Blake*, especially ch. 1.

91. For other important examples of "believing" in Blake's corpus, see "The Everlasting Gospel" and "You don't believe I won't attempt to make ye."

92. Bloom, *Visionary Company*, p. 1; Watson, "Wordsworth and the Credo," in Jasper, ed., *Interpretation of Belief*, p. 159 and p. 174: "He [Wordsworth] knew the truth because, being a god-poet, he knew what the truth was. His credo was a belief in himself."

93. See the comments of Gillespie, *Theological Origins of Modernity*, p. 2: "To be modern is to be self-liberating and self-making, and thus not merely to be

in history and tradition, but to *make* history . . . Being modern at its core is thus something titanic, something Promethean. But what could possibly justify such an astonishing, such a hubristic claim?" The answer, I have tried to suggest, is that belief in the human was a kind of jailbreak from a confessional regime so restrictive that it left most people unable to believe at all.

Conclusion

1. See, e.g., Dario Perinetti, "Ways to Certainty," in Aaron Garrett, ed., *Routledge Companion to Eighteenth-Century Philosophy*; Yvonne Sherwood, "The Problem of 'Belief,'" in Carling, ed., *Social Equality of Religion or Belief.*

2. Here I am in dialogue with Robert Bellah, who argued that in modernity, "It is no longer possible to divide mankind into believers and non-believers. All believe something." But Bellah meant by this claim that secularization had been overstated and that "religion, as that symbolic form through which man comes to terms with the antinomies of his being, has not declined, indeed, cannot decline unless man's nature ceases to be problematic to him." Bellah, *Beyond Belief*, pp. 227–28. I am also interested in Jean-Claude Guillebaud's contention that in modernity, science, religion, politics, and other forms of conviction constitute related belief systems, but that history has "vaccinated" modern people against particular beliefs while encouraging others: Guillebaud, *La force de conviction.*

3. See Marshall, Lightman, and England, eds., *Papers of the Metaphysical Society*; McCarthy, ed., *Ethics of Belief Debate*; Madigan, *W.K. Clifford*; Brown, *Metaphysical Society*. The "ethics of belief" debate at the heart of the Metaphysical Society continues in contemporary philosophy, organized under the heading of "evidentialism": see, e.g., Dougherty, ed., *Evidentialism*; Booth, *Islamic Philosophy*; Dole and Chignell, eds., *God and the Ethics of Belief*; McCormick, *Believing against the Evidence.*

4. *PMS*, vol. I, p. 3.

5. *PMS*, vol. II, p. 327.

6. I quote here from the published version: *Ethics of Belief Debate*, p. 24.

7. *Ethics of Belief Debate*, p. 34.

8. *Ethics of Belief Debate*, p. 36.

9. *Ethics of Belief Debate*, p. 94.

10. *Ethics of Belief Debate*, p. 113.

11. *PMS*, vol. I, pp. 198–99.

12. *PMS*, vol. I, p. 370.

13. *PMS*, vol. II, p.239–40.

14. *Ethics of Belief Debate*, pp. 119–27.

15. On the problem of tolerating intolerance, see: Bejan, *Mere Civility*; Kaplan, *Divided by Faith.*

16. Žižek, *On Belief*, pp. 109–10, with reference to the work of the French philosopher Octave Mannoni.

BIBLIOGRAPHY

Note: all online sources, listed here and in the notes, were last accessed on December 12, 2017.

Primary Sources

Acta Concilii Tridentini. Paris, 1546.

Les Actes de la Conference Tenue à Paris es Moys de Iuillet et Aoust, 1566. Paris, 1568.

Allen, Hannah. *A Narrative of God's Gracious Dealings.* London, 1683.

Allen, William. *A Defense and Declaration of the Catholike Churchies Doctrine, Touching Purgatory, and Prayers for the Soules Departed.* Antwerp, 1565.

Alvarez, Didacus. *De Auxiliis Divinae Gratiae.* Rome, 1610.

Anderton, Lawrence. *The Reformed Protestant, Tending Directly to Atheisme.* Cologne?, 1621.

Anselm of Canterbury. *D. Anselmi . . . Operum Omnium.* Cologne, 1612.

Anselm of Canterbury. *De Incarnatione Verbi.* Translated by Jasper Hopkins and Herbert Richardson. Online at http://jasper-hopkins.info.

Anselm of Canterbury. *Monologium.* Translated by Sidney Norton Deane. Online in Latin and English at http://www.logicmuseum.com/authors/anselm/mo nologion/anselmmonologion.htm.

Anselm of Canterbury. *Proslogium.* Online at http://www.thelatinlibrary.com /anselmproslogion.html.

Anselm of Canterbury. *Works of St. Anselm.* Translated by Sidney Norton Deane. Chicago, 1903.

Aquinas, Thomas. *Scriptum Super Sententiis.* Online at http://www.corpustho misticum.org/snp3023.html.

Aquinas, Thomas. *Expositio in Symbolum Apostolorum.* Translated by Joseph Collins. Online at http://dhspriory.org/thomas/Creed.htm.

Aquinas, Thomas. *Summa contra Gentiles.* Translated by Anton Pegis et al. Online at http://dhspriory.org/thomas/ContraGentiles1.htm.

Aquinas, Thomas. *Summa Theologica.* Translated by the Fathers of the English Dominican Province. Online in Latin and English at http://www.logicmuseum .com/authors/aquinas/Summa-index.htm.

Arminius, Jacobus. *The Works of James Arminius.* Edited and translated by James Nichols. London, 3 vols., 1825–1875.

Arminius, Jacobus. *The Works of James Arminius.* Edited and translated by James Nichols. Auburn, 3 vols., 1853.

Arminius, Jacobus. *Disputationes . . . Publicae et Privatae.* Leiden, 1614.

Arnauld Antoine and Pierre Nicole. *La logique ou l'art de penser*. Paris, 1662.

Arnauld, Antoine and Pierre Nicole. *Logic, or the Art of Thinking: Being the Port-Royal Logic*. Translated by Thomas Baynes. Edinburgh, 1850.

Arnobius of Sicca. *Seven Books against the Heathen*. Translated by Hamilton Bryce and Hugh Campbell. Online at http://www.newadvent.org/fathers /06315.htm.

Arnobius the Younger. *Arnobii . . . in Omneis Psalmos Commentarii*. Basel, 1522.

Augustine of Hippo, *Eighty-Three Different Questions*. Edited and translated by David Mosher. Washington, DC, 1982.

Augustine of Hippo. *Answer to Petilian the Donatist*. Translated by J. R. King. Online at http://www.newadvent.org/fathers/1409.htm.

Augustine of Hippo. *De Libero Arbitrio*. Online at http://www.augustinus.it /latino/libero_arbitrio.

Augustine of Hippo. *De Trinitate*. Online at http://www.thelatinlibrary.com/augustine /trin13.shtml.

Augustine of Hippo. *De Utilitate Credendi*. Translated by C. L. Cornish. Online at http://www.newadvent.org/fathers/1306.htm; in Latin at https://www .augustinus.it/latino/utilita_credere/index.htm.

Augustine of Hippo. *Earlier Writings*. Edited by J.H.S. Burleigh. Louisville, 1953.

Augustine of Hippo. *On the Spirit and the Letter*. Translated by Peter Holmes and Robert Wallis; revised by Benjamin Wafield. Online at http://www.newadvent .org/fathers/1502.htm; in Latin at http://www.augustinus.it/latino/spirito _lettera/index.htm.

Augustine of Hippo. *Predestination of the Saints*. Translated by Peter Holmes and Robert Wallis; revised by Benjamin Wafield. Online at http://www.newadvent .org/fathers/15121.htm; in Latin at http://www.augustinus.it/latino/predesti nazione_santi/index.htm.

Augustine of Hippo. *St. Augustine: The Problem of Free Choice*. Edited by Dom Mark Ponitfex. London, 1955.

Augustine of Hippo. *Tractates on the Gospel of John*. Translated by John Gibb. Online at http://www.newadvent.org/fathers/1701029.htm; in Latin at http://www.augustinus.it/latino/commento_vsg/index2.htm.

Barrow, Isaac. *The Works of the Learned Isaac Barrow*. London, 3 vols., 1683–87.

Baxter, Richard. *Reliquiae Baxterianae*. London, 1696.

Bayle, Pierre. *Dictionaire Historique et Critique*. Rotterdam, 3 vols., 1702.

Beauxamis, Thomas. *De Fido et Symbolo*. Paris, 1573.

Becanus, Martin. *Summa Theologiae Scholasticae*. N.p., 1614.

Bellarmino, Roberto. *Tertiae Controversiae Generalis, Controversia Secunda Principalis. Quae Est De Justificatione*. Ingolstadt, 1598.

Bellarmino, Roberto. *Catechismus, seu: explication doctrinae Christianae*. Prague, 1747.

The Benefit of Christ's Death: Probably Written by Aonio Paleario: Reprinted in Fac-simile. Edited by Churchill Babington. London, 1855.

The Benefit that Christians Receiue by Iesus Christ Crucified. London, 1580.

Bernard of Clairvaux. *Life and Works of St. Bernard.* Edited and translated by John Mabillon and Samuel Eales. Second edition. London, 2 vols., 1912.

Billon, François de. *Le Fort inexpugnable de l'honneur du sexe feminine.* Paris, 1555.

Blake, William. *The Complete Poetry and Prose of William Blake.* Newly revised edition. Edited by David Erdman. New York, 1988.

Bobynet, Pierre. *L'Horographie Ingenieuse.* Paris, 1647.

Bogaert, Arnould. *A pronostication for diuers yeares.* London, 1553.

Boquin, Pierre. *Assertio Veteris ac Veri Christianisimi.* Lyon, 1576.

Bownd, Nicholas. *The Vnbeleefe of S. Thomas the Apostle.* Cambridge, 1608.

Boyle, Robert. *Certain Physiological Essays.* London, 1669.

Boyle, Robert. *The Excellency of Theology Compar'd with Natural Philosophy.* London, 1674.

[Boyle, Robert?]. *Some considerations about the reconcileableness of reason and religion by T.E., a lay-man ; to which is annex'd by the publisher, a discourse of Mr. Boyle, about the possibility of the resurrection.* London, 1675.

Boyle, Robert. *The Christian Virtuoso.* London, 1690.

Braga, Theophilo. *Historia da Poesia Popular Portugueza.* Lisbon, 1902.

Broughton, Richard. *The First Part of the Resolution of Religion.* London, 1603.

Bullinger, Heinrich. *Sermonum Decades quinque, de potissimis Christianæ religionis capitibus, in tres tomos digestæ.* Zurich, 1557.

Bullinger, Heinrich. *Fiftie Godlie and Learned Sermons.* London, 1577.

Bunyan, John. *Grace Abounding to the Chief of Sinners.* London, 1666.

Burne, Nicol. *The Disputation Concerning the Controuersit Headdis of Religion.* Paris, 1581.

Cajetan, Cardinal, Tommaso De Vio. *Opuscula Omnia Thomae De Vio Caietani Cardinalis.* Lyons, 1575.

Calvin, John. *Institution de la Religion Chrestienne.* Geneva, 1541.

Calvin, John. *Des scandales.* Geneva, 1551.

Calvin, John. *Institutio Christianae Religionis.* Geneva, 1559.

Calvin, John. *The Institution of Christian Religion.* Translated by Thomas Norton. London, 1561.

Calvin, John. *Commentaries of M. Iohn Calvin upon the Actes of the Apostles.* London, 1585.

Calvin, John. *Concerning Scandals.* Translated by John Fraser. Grand Rapids, 1978.

Calvin, John. *Joannis Calvini in Acta Apostolorum Commentarii.* Edited by A. Tholuck. Berlin, 1833.

Calvin, John. *Institutes of the Christian Religion.* Translated by Henry Beveridge. Grand Rapids, 1989.

Campanella, Tomasso. *Atheismus Triumphatus.* Paris, 1636.

Carboni, Ludovico. *Summae Summarum Casuum Conscientiae.* Venice, 1606.

Castellio, Sebastian. *Dialogi IIII.* Basel, 1578.

Castellio, Sebastian. *A most excellent and profitable dialogue, of the powerfull iustifying faith shewing what it is to beleeue in God.* Translated by Arthur Golding. London, 1610.

Castellio, Sebastian. *A Conference on Faith*. London, 1679.

Catechism of the Council of Trent. Translated by J. Donovan. Online at https://archive.org/details/thecatechismofth00donouoft.

Catechisme ou Instructions des Premiers Fondemens de la Religion Chrestienne. Paris, 1575.

Chillingworth, William. *The Religion of Protestants*. Oxford, 1638.

Cicero. *De Natura Deorum*. Translated by H. Rackham. Online in Latin and English at http://www.loebclassics.com/view/marcus_tullius_cicero-de_natura_deorum/1933/pb_LCL268.3.xml?rskey=bclMaU&result=9.

Coleridge, Samuel Taylor. *Biographia Literaria*. London, 2 vols., 1817.

Corpus Reformatorum. Leipzig, 101 vols., 1834–.

Corro, Antonio del. *An epistle or godlie admonition, of a learned minister of the Gospel of our sauiour Christ sent to the pastoures of the Flemish Church in Antwerp*. Translated by Geffray Fenton. London, 1569.

Craige, John. *Theologiae Christianae Principia Mathematica*. London, 1699.

Craige, John. *John Craige's Mathematical Principles of Christian Theology*. Edited and translated by Richard Nash. Carbondale, 1991.

Cusa, Nicholas of. *Cusa's Didactic Sermons*. Translated by Jasper Hopkins. Online at http://jasper-hopkins.info.

Cusa, Nicholas of. *Cusa's Early Sermons*. Translated by Jasper Hopkins. Online at http://jasper-hopkins.info.

De Infidelitate et Tribus Eius Speciebus. Dillingen, 1591.

Descartes, René. *Discours de la Méthode*. Leiden, 1637.

Descartes, René. *Discourse on Method and the Meditations*. Translated by F. E. Sutcliffe. New York, 1968.

Dictionnaire historique, critique et bibliographique. Paris, 30 vols., 1821.

A Discourse of Auxiliary Beauty. Or Artificiall Hansomenesse. In Point of Conscience between Two Ladies. London, 1656.

Drusius, Johannes. *Observationum Libri XII*. Antwerp, 1584.

Drusius, Johannes. *Miscellanea Locutionum Sacrarum*. Franeker, 1586.

Du Perron, Jacques Davy. *Replique à la Response du Serenissime Roy de la grand' Bretagne*. Paris, 1622.

Early Anabaptist Spirituality: Selected Writing. Edited by Daniel Liechty. New York, 1994.

Elyot, Thomas. *The Dictionary of Syr Thomas Eliot Knyght*. London, 1538.

The Encyclopedia of Diderot and d'Alembert Collaborative Translation Project. Online at https://quod.lib.umich.edu/d/did/.

Fabricius, Johann Albert. *Delectus Argumentorum et Syllabus Scriptorum*. Hamburg, 1725.

Fassari, Vincenti. *Immaculata Deiparae Conceptio Theologicae Commissa Trutinae*. Lyons, 1666.

Ferguson, Adam. *An Essay on the History of Civil Society*. Edited by Fania Oz-Salzberger. Cambridge, 1995.

Franck, Sebastian. *Paradoxa*. Edited by Siegfried Wollgast. Berlin, 1966.

Franck, Sebastian. *280 Paradoxes or Wondrous Sayings*. Translated by Edward Furcha. Lewiston, New York, 1986.

Froissart, Jean. *Here begynneth the thirde and fourthe boke of sir Iohn Froissart of the cronycles*. Translated by Jean Bourchier. London, 1525.

Garasse, François. *La doctrine curieuse des beaux esprits de ce temps*. Paris, 1623.

Gerhard, Johann. *Quinquaginta Meditationes Sacrae*. Jena, 1607.

Gerhard, Johann. *Gerhards Meditations*. Translated by Ralph Winterton. Cambridge, 1638.

Gerson, Jean. *Early Works*. Translated by Brian McGuire. New York, 1998.

Gibboni, Joanne. *Disputatio Theologica de Sanctis*. Trier, 1584.

Gifford, George. *A briefe discourse of certaine points of the religion which is among the common sort of Christians, which may bee termed the countrie diuinitie*. London, 1581.

Greenham, Richard. *Propositions Containing Answers to Certaine Demaunds*. Edinburgh, 1597.

Gregory the Great. *Reading the Gospels with Gregory the Great: Homilies on the Gospels, 21–26*. Edited and translated by Santha Bhattacharji. Petersham, Mass., 2001.

Gribaldi, Matteo. *Epistola Clarissimi Doctoris Mathaei Gribaldi, in Gymnasio Patauino,Legaum professoris, de tremendo diuini iudicii exemplo super eum, qui hominum metu pulsus, Christum & cognitam ueritatem abnegate*. Basel, 1549.

Gribaldi, Matteo. *A Notable and Marvailous Epistle of the Famous Doctor Mathewe Gribalde*. Translated by Edward Aglionby. Worcester, 1550.

Grotius, Hugo. *The Truth of the Christian Religion*. London, 1719.

Grotius, Hugo. *The Freedom of the Seas*. Translated by Ralph van Deman Magoffin. New York, 1916.

Herbert, Edward, First Baron Herbert of Cherbury. *De Veritate*. Translated by Meyrick Carré. Bristol, 1937.

Hobbes, Thomas. *Humane Nature*. London, 1650.

Hobbes, Thomas. *Leviathan*. Revised student edition. Edited by Richard Tuck. Cambridge, 1996.

Hooker, Richard. *The Folger Library Edition of the Works of Richard Hooker*. Edited by W. Speed Hill. Cambridge, Mass., 7 vols. in 8, 1977–98.

Hooper, George. "A Calculation of the Credibility of Human Testimony." *Philosophical Transactions of the Royal Society* 21 (1699): pp. 359–65.

Houtteville, François. *La religion Chrétienne prouvée par les faits*. Paris, 1722.

Huet, Pierre Daniel. *Demonstratio Evangelica*. Paris, 1679.

Hume, David. *Dialogues and Natural History of Religion*. Edited by J.C.A. Gaskin. Oxford, 1993.

Hume, David. *An Enquiry Concerning Human Understanding*. Edited by Eric Steinberg. Second edition. Indianapolis, 1993.

Hume, David. *A Treatise of Human Nature*. Edited by David Norton and Mary Norton. Oxford, 2001.

Hyperius, Andreas. *The True Tryall and Examination of a Mans Owne Selfe.* Translated by Thomas Newton. London, 1587.

Ivo of Chartres. *Panormia.* Online at https://ivo-of-chartres.github.io/panormia /pan_1.pdf.

Jackson, Thomas. *The Eternall Truth of Scriptures.* London, 1613.

Jackson, Thomas. *Iustifying faith, or The faith by which the just do liue.* London, 1615.

Jackson, Thomas. *A Treatise Containing the Originall of Vnbeliefe.* London, 1625.

Jefferson, Thomas. "Act for Establishing Religious Freedom." Online at http://edu .lva.virginia.gov/online_classroom/shaping_the_constitution/doc/religious _freedom.

John of the Cross. *The Collected Works of St. John of the Cross.* Edited by Kieran Kavanaugh and Otilio Rodridguez. Washington, D.C., 1979.

John of the Cross. *Obras Completas.* Online at http://www.portalcarmelitano .org/santos-carmelitas/juan-de-la-cruz/92-juan-de-la-cruz-obras-completas .html.

Joris, David. *The Anabaptist Writings of David Joris, 1535–1543.* Edited by Gary Waite. Waterloo, 1994.

Joye, George. *The subuersion of Moris false foundacion.* Antwerp, 1534.

Julian of Norwich. *Showing of Love.* Translated by Julia Holloway. Online at http://www.umilta.net/love2.html.

Kant, Immanuel. *Critique of Pure Reason.* Translated and edited by Paul Guyer and Allen Wood. Cambridge, 1998.

Knox, John. *An answer to a great nomber of blasphemous cauillations written by an Anabaptist.* Geneva, 1560.

Labrussel, Ignace de. *Traité des abus de la critique en matière de religion.* Paris, 1710.

Lactantius. *The Divine Institutes.* Translated by William Fletcher. Online at http://www.newadvent.org/fathers/07012.htm.

Lambert, Thomas et al., eds. *Registres du Consistoire de Genève au temps de Calvin.* 8 vols., Geneva, 1996–2014.

Le Gendre, Gilbert-Charles, Marquis de Saint Aubin sur Loire. *Traité de l'opinion.* 6 vols., Paris, 1735.

Leibniz, G. W. *Philosophical Papers and Letters.* Edited and translated by Leroy Loemker. 2 vols., Chicago, 1956.

Leibniz, G. W. *Mathematische Schriften.* Edited by C. I. Gerhardt. 7 vols., Hildesheim, 1971.

Le Mer des Hystoires. Lyon, 1491.

Leo the Great. *Letters and Sermons.* Translated by Charles Feltoe. Online at http://www.ccel.org/ccel/schaff/npnf212.

Lessius, Leonard. *De Providentia Numinis et Animi Immortalitate.* Antwerp, 1617.

Lessius, Leonard. *Rawleigh his Ghost.* Saint-Omer, 1631.

Lienhard, Marc, Stephen Nelson, and Hans Georg Rott, eds. *Quellen zur Geschichte der Taufer.* Vol. 15, Elsass III, Stadt Strassburg 1536–1542. Gutersloh, 1986.

Lippomano, Luigi. *Espositioni Volgari Del Reverendissimo Monsignor Luigi Lippomano, Vescouo di Verona, sopra il Simbolo Apostolico*. Vinegia, 1568.

Livy. *History of Rome*. Translated by B. O. Foster. Online in Latin and English at https://www.loebclassics.com/browse?t1=author.livy.

Locke, John. *An Essay Concerning Human Understanding*. London, 1689.

Locke, John. *The Reasonableness of Christianity as Delivered in the Scriptures*. London, 1695.

Locke, John. *Two Treatises of Government*. Edited by Peter Laslett. Cambridge, 1988.

Lombard, Peter. *The Sentences*. Translated by Giulio Silano. 4 vols., Toronto, 2007–10.

Love, Nicholas. *Incipit Speculum Vite Cristi*. Westminster, 1494.

Loyola, Ignatius of. *Ejercicios Espirituales de S. Ignacio de Loyola . . . en su texto original*. Madrid, 1833.

Loyola, Ignatius of. *Exercitia Spiritualia*. Vienna, 1563.

Luther, Martin. *Biblia. Das ist: Die gantze Heilige Schrifft*. Wittenberg, 1545. Online at https://catalog.hathitrust.org/Record/100206895.

Luther, Martin. *D. Martin Luthers Werke: Kritische Gesamtausgabe* [Weimarer Ausgabe]. 120 vols., Weimar, 1883–2009.

Luther, Martin. *Luther's Smaller and Larger Catechisms, Together with an Historical Introduction*. Second edition. Newmarket, 1855.

Luther, Martin. *Luther's Works*. Edited by Jaroslav Pelikan et al. 55 vols., St. Louis, 1955–86.

Luther, Martin. *Martin Luther's Basic Theological Writings*. Edited by William Russell and Timothy Lull. Third edition. Minneapolis, 2012.

McCarthy, Gerald, ed. *The Ethics of Belief Debate*. Atlanta, 1986.

Malcolm, Alexander. *A New Treatise of Arithmetick and Book-Keeping*. Edinburgh, 1718.

Malderus, Johannes. *De Virtutibus Theologicis et Iustitia et Religione Commentaria ad Secundum Secudnae D. Thomae*. Antwerp, 1616.

Malderus, Johannes. *In Primam Secundae D. Thomae Commentaria*. Antwerp, 1623.

Mandeville, John. *Here begynneth a lytell treatyse or booke named Johan Mau[n] deuyll knight*. Westminster, 1499.

Mandeville, Bernard. *The Fable of the Bees: or, Private Vices, Publick Benefits*. London, 1714.

Mandeville, Bernard. *The Fable of the Bees. Part II*. London, 1729.

Mandeville, Bernard. *An Enquiry into the Origins of Honour*. London, 1732.

Marbury, Francis. *A sermon preached at Paules Crosse the 13. of Iune. 1602*. London, 1602.

Marshall, Catherine, Bernard Lightman, and Richard England, eds. *The Papers of the Metaphysical Society, 1869–1880: A Critical Edition*. 3 vols., Oxford, 2015.

Martin, Gregory. *A discouerie of the manifold corruptions of the Holy Scriptures by the heretikes of our daies*. Rhemes, 1582.

Martin, Gregory. *The New Testament of Jesus Christ, translated faithfully into English*. Translated by Gregory Martin et al. Reims, 1582.

Melanchthon, Philip. *The Loci Communes of Philip Melanchthon*. Translated by Charles Leander Hill. Eugene, 2007.

Mencken, Johannes. *Herrn Joh. Burckhardt Menckens zwey Reden von der Charlatanerie*. Leipzig, 1716.

Le Mer des Hystoires. Lyon, 1491.

Milton, John. *The Prose Works of John Milton*. Edited by J. A. St. John. 5 vols., London, 1877–88.

Mirk, John. *Liber Festivalis*. Oxford, 1486.

Mirk, John. *Mirk's Festial: A Collection of Homilies by Johannes Mirkus*. Edited by Theodor Erbe. London, 1905.

Montaigne, Michel de. *The Complete Essays of Montaigne*. Edited and translated by Donald Frame. Palo Alto, 1958.

Montaigne, Michel de. "The Montaigne Project." Online at http://www.lib.uchi cago.edu/efts/ARTFL/projects/montaigne/.

Monteage, Stephen. *Debtor and Creditor Made Easy*. London, 1675.

Mornay, Philippe du Plessis. *A woorke concerning the trewnesse of the Christian religion, written in French: against atheists, Epicures, Paynims, Iewes, Mahumetists, and other infidels*. Translated by Philip Sidney and Arthur Golding. London, 1587.

Müller, Lydia, ed. *Glaubenszeugnisse oberdeutscher Taufgesinnter*. 2 vols., Leipzig and Heidelberg, 1938 and 1967.

Ockham, William of. *Dialogus*. Translated by John Kilcullen and John Scott. Online at http://www.britac.ac.uk/pubs/dialogus/.

Osório, Jerónimo. *An epistle of the reuerend father in God Hieronymus Osorius Bishop of Arcoburge in Portugale, to the most excellent Princesse Elizabeth*. Translated by Richard Shacklock. Antwerp, 1565.

Parker, Henry. *Dives et Pauper*. Westminster, 1496.

Parsons, Robert. *The First Book of the Christian Exercise*. Rouen, 1582.

Pascal, Blaise. *Great Shorter Works of Pascal*. Translated by Émile Cailliet and John Blankenagel. Philadelphia, 1948.

Pascal, Blaise. *Penséss*. Translated by W. F. Trotter. New York, 1958.

Pascal, Blaise. *Pensées*. Online at https://www.ub.uni-freiburg.de/fileadmin/ub /referate/04/pascal/pensees.pdf.

Patrologia Latina. Full text database. Online at http://pld.chadwyck.com.

Perkins, William. *An Exposition of the Symbole or Creed of the Apostles*. London, 1595.

Perkins, William. *A Golden Chain: or, the Description of Theologie*. Cambridge, 1600.

Picart, François le. *Les Sermons et Instructions Chrestiennes pour Tous les Dimenches*. Paris, 1566.

Plato. *Apology*. Translated by Chris Emlyn-Jones and William Preddy. Online in English and Greek at https://www.loebclassics.com/browse?t1=author.plato .the.philosopher.

Plutarch. *On Superstition*. Translated by F. C. Babbitt. Online at http://penelope
.uchicago.edu/Thayer/E/Roman/Texts/Plutarch/Moralia/De_superstitione*
.html.

Pope, Alexander. *Essay on Man. In Epistles to a Friend. Epistle II*. London, 1733.

Prynne, William. *Anti-Arminianisme. Or The Church of Englands old antithesis
to new Arminianisme*. London, 1630.

Pseudo-Dionysius. *On Divine Names*. Translated by John Parker. Online at
https://en.wikisource.org/wiki/Dionysius_the_Areopagite,_Works/On
_Divine_Names.

Pufendorf, Samuel. *Of the Law of Nature and Nations*. Translated by Basil Ken-
nett. London, 1729.

Quadriennium Annae Postremum; or the Political State of Great Britain. Second
edition. 8 vols., London, 1718–19.

Quodvultdeus of Carthage. *The Creedal Homilies*. Translated by Thomas Macy
Finn. New York, 2004.

Rhegius, Urbanus. *Doctrina Certissima et Consolatio Solidissima*. Frankfurt, 1545.

Rhegius, Urbanus. *An Instruccyon of Christen Fayth*. London, 1548.

Rivius, Johann. *De Stultitia Mortalium*. Basel, 1547.

Rogers, Samuel. *The Diary of Samuel Rogers, 1634–1638*. Edited by Tom Webster
and Kenneth Shipps. Church of England Record Society, vol. 11. Woodbridge,
2004.

Rollock, Robert. *A Treatise of Gods Effectual Calling*. London, 1603.

Rousseau, Jean-Jacques. *Discours sur l'origine et les fondements de l'inégalité*. Online at https://eet.pixel-online.org/files/etranslation/original/Rousseau%20
JJ%20Discours%20sur.pdf.

Rousseau, Jean-Jacques. *The Discourses and Other Early Political Writings*. Edited and translated by Victor Gourevitch. Cambridge, 1997.

Roye, Guy de. *La Doctrinal de Sapience*. Geneva, 1480.

Roye, Guy de. *Thus Endeth the Doctrinal of Sapyence*. Westminster, 1489.

Rufinus. *A Commentary on the Apostles' Creed*. Edited by J.N.D. Kelly. Westminster, Md., 1955.

Rupp, E. Gordon and Philip Watson, eds. *Luther and Erasmus: Free Will and
Salvation*. Louisville, 1969.

Ruysbroeck, John of. *The Adornment of the Spiritual Marriage*. Translated by
C. A. Wynschenk Dom. Online at https://www.ccel.org/ccel/ruysbroeck
/adornment.html.

Ruysbroeck, John of. *D. Ioannis Rvsbrochi i . . . Opera Omnia*. Cologne, 1609.

St. Victor, Richard of. *De Trinitate*. Edited by Jean Ribaillier. Paris, 1958.

St. Victor, Richard of. *On the Trinity*. Translated by Jonathan Couser. Online at
http://pvspade.com/Logic/docs/StVictor.pdf.

Sebond, Raymond. *La theologie naturelle de Raymond Sebon*. Translated by
Michel de Montaigne. Paris, 1569.

Sedgwick, Obadiah. *The Humbled Sinner Resolved What He Should Do to Be
Saved*. London, 1657.

Sewall, Samuel. *Diary of Samuel Sewall*. Collections of the Massachusetts Historical Society, series 5, vols. 5–7. 3 vols., Boston, 1878–82.

Shagan, Ethan and Debora Shuger, eds. *Religion in Tudor England: An Anthology of Primary Sources*. Waco, 2016.

Simons, Menno. *Opera Omnia Theologica*. Amsterdam, 1681.

Simons, Menno. *The Complete Writings of Menno Simons c.1496–1561*. Translated by Leonard Verduin; edited by J. C. Wenger. Scottsdale, Pa., 1956.

Smith, John. *An Exposition of the Creed*. London, 1632.

Socinus, Faustus. *De Sacrae Scripturae Auctoritate*. Raków, 1611.

Socinus, Faustus. *An Argument for the Authority of Holy Scripture*. London, 1731.

Socinus, Faustus et al. *The Racovian Catechism*. Translated by Thomas Rees. London, 1818.

Sophocles. *The Complete Sophocles*. Edited by Peter Burian and Alan Shapiro. 2 vols., Oxford, 2010–11.

Spinoza, Baruch. *Tractatus Theologico-Politicus*. Hamburg [*vere* Amsterdam], 1670.

Spinoza, Baruch. *Theological-Political Treatise*. Translated by Michael Silverthorne and Jonathan Israel. Cambridge, 2007.

Stevin, Simon. *Disme: The art of Tenths or Decimall Arithmetike*. Translated by Robert Norton. London, 1608.

Stewart, Dugald. *The Works of Dugald Stewart in Seven Volumes*. 7 vols., Cambridge, 1829.

Suarez, Francisco. *Opus de Triplici Virtute Theologica*. Lyons, 1621.

Suso, Henry. *Heinrich Seuses Deutsche Schriften*. Edited by Walter Lehmann. Jena, 1922.

Suso, Henry. *The Exemplar, with Two German Sermons*. Translated and edited by Frank Tobin. Mahwah, N.J., 1989.

Suso, Henry. *A Little Book of Eternal Wisdom*. Online at http://www.ccel.org/ccel/suso/wisdom.html.

Sutcliffe, Matthew. *A briefe replie to a certaine odious and slanderous libel*. London, 1600.

Talbot, Peter [pseud. N.N.]. *A Treatise of the Nature of Catholick Faith*. Rouen, 1657.

Teresa of Avila. *The Collected Works of St. Teresa of Avila*. Edited by Kieran Kavanaugh and Otilio Rodriguez. 3 vols., Washington, D.C., 1980–85.

Teresa of Avila. *Mística del Siglo XVI*. Edited by Francisco Javier Díez de Revenga. Madrid, 1 volume with more expected, 2009–.

Teresa of Avila. *Las Relaciones o Cuentas de Conciencia*. Online at http://www.santateresadejesus.com/wp-content/uploads/Las-Relaciones.pdf.

Tertullian. *De Carne Christi*. Translated by Peter Holmes. Online at http://www.newadvent.org/fathers/0315.htm; in Latin at http://www.thelatinlibrary.com/tertullian/tertullian.carne.shtml.

Theologia Deutsch. Edited by Franz Pfeiffer. Stuttgart, 1851.

Theologia Germanica. Translated by Susanna Winkworth. Online at http://www.ccel.org/ccel/anonymous/theologia.html.

Thwaites, Reuben, ed. *Jesuit Relations and Allied Documents*. 73 vols., Cleveland, 1896–1901. Partially available online at http://moses.creighton.edu/kripke /jesuitrelations/.

Toland, John. *Christianity not Mysterious*. London, 1696.

Troisieme Centurie des Questions Traictees aux Conferences du Bureau d'Adresse. Paris, 1639.

Tyndale, William. *The Obedience of a Christen Man*. Antwerp, 1528.

Ursinus, Zacharias. *Doctrinae Christianae Compendium*. Geneva, 1584.

Ursinus, Zacharias. *The Commentary of Dr. Zacharias Ursinus on the Heidelberg Catechism*. Translated by G. W. Williard. Columbus, 1852.

Vasquez, Gabriel. *Commentarium, ac Disputationum in Primam Secundae Sancti Thomae*. Lyon, 1631.

Vermigli, Peter Martyr. *In epistolam s. Pauli apostoli ad romanos, d. Petri Martyris Vermilii*. Heidelberg, 1612.

Véron, John. *The ouerthrow of the iustification of workes and of the vain doctrin of the merits of men*. London, 1561.

Vico, Giambattista. *Opere*. Edited by Andrea Battistini. 2 vols., Milan, 1990.

Vico, Giambattista. *New Science*. Translated by David Marsh. New York, 2000.

Vigor, Simon. *Sermons Catholiques sur le Symbole des Apostres*. Paris, 1585.

Villegagnon, Nicolas Durand de. *Responce par le Chevalier de Villegaignon aux Remonstrances faictes à la Rpyne mere du Roy*. Paris, 1561.

Viret, Pierre. *Epistre envoyee aux fideles conversans entre les Chrstiens Papistiques*. Geneva, 1543.

Viret, Pierre. *Dialogues du desordre qui est a present au monde*. Geneva, 1545.

Viret, Pierre. *Exposition de la doctrine de la foy chrestienne*. Geneva, 1564.

Vives, Juan Luis. *De Veritate Fidei Christianae Libri Quinque*. Lyon, 1551.

Voraigne, Jacobus de. *Legenda Aurea*. London, 1483.

Walker, George. *The Key of Saving Knowledge*. London, 1641.

Ward, Seth. *A Philosophicall Essay*. Oxford, 1652.

Watson, Henry. *The Noble History of King Ponthus*. London, 1511.

Wigglesworth, Michael. *The Diary of Michael Wigglesworth, 1653–1657: The Conscience of a Puritan*. Edited by Edmund Morgan. Gloucester, Mass., 1970.

Willsford, Thomas. *Willfords Arithmetick, Naturall, and Artificiall*. London, 1656.

Wingate, Edmund. *Arithmetique Made Easie*. London, 1630.

Wolff, Christian. *Logic, or Rational Thoughts on the Powers of the Human Understanding*. London, 1770.

Young, Richard [R. Iunius]. *The Drunkard's Character*. London, 1638.

Secondary Sources

Abé, Takao. *The Jesuit Mission to New France: A New Interpretation in the Light of Earlier Jesuit Experience in Japan*. Leiden, 2011.

Abizadeh, Arash. "The Passions of the Wise: Phronêsis, Rhetoric, and Aristotle's Passionate Practical Deliberation." *Review of Metaphysics* 56, no. 2 (December 2002): 267–96.

Abulafia, Anna. *Christians and Jews in the Twelfth-Century Renaissance.* London, 1995.

Against Belief? A special issue of *Social Analysis* 52, no. 1 (2008).

Ahl, Diane Cole. "Benozzo Gozzoli's Frescoes of the Life of Saint Augustine in San Gimignano: Their Meaning in Context." *Artibus et Historiae* 7, no. 13 (1986): 35–53.

Ahlgren, Gillian. *Teresa of Avila and the Politics of Sanctity.* Ithaca, 1996.

Alexandrescu, Sorin. "Saying and (Dis)believing." In Herman Parret, ed. *On Believing: Epistemological and Semiotic Approaches / De la croyance: approches épistémologiques et sémiotiques.* Berlin, 1983.

Allison, Henry. *Kant's Transcendental Idealism: An Interpretation and Defense.* New Haven, 1983.

Antsey, Peter. *John Locke and Natural Philosophy.* Oxford, 2011.

Antsey, Peter, ed. *The Oxford Handbook of British Philosophy in the Seventeenth Century.* Oxford, 2013.

Arnold, John. *Belief and Unbelief in Medieval Europe.* London, 2005.

Asad, Talal. "Anthropological Conceptions of Religion: Reflections on Geertz." *Man.* New series 18, no. 2 (1983): 237–59.

Asad, Talal. *Genealogies of Religion: Discipline and Reasons of Power in Christianity and Islam.* Baltimore, 1993.

Asad, Talal, Wendy Brown, Judith Butler, and Saba Mahmood. *Is Critique Secular? Blasphemy, Injury, and Free Speech.* Berkeley, 2009.

Ascoli, Albert. "Worthy of Faith? Authors and Readers in Early Modernity." In *The Renaissance World.* Edited by John Martin. New York, 2007.

Audi, Robert. *Epistemology: A Contemporary Introduction to the Theory of Knowledge.* Second edition. New York, 2009.

Backus, Irena. *Historical Method and Confessional Identity in the Era of the Reformation.* Leiden, 2003.

Bae, Bosco. "Believing Selves and Cognitive Dissonance: Connecting Individual and Society via Belief." *Religions* 7, no. 7 (2016): 86.

Baker, Keith. *Condorcet: From Natural Philosophy to Social Mathematics.* Chicago, 1975.

Baker, Keith. *Inventing the French Revolution: Essays on French Political Culture in the Eighteenth Century.* Cambridge, 1990.

Ballériaux, Catherine. "'Adopted Children of God': Native and Jesuit Identities in New France, c. 1630–1690." *French History & Civilization* 5 (2014): 102–11.

Barth, Hans-Martin. *Atheismus und Orthodoxie: Analysen und Modelle christliche Apologetik im 17. Jahrhundert.* Göttingen, 1971.

Baruzi, Jean. *Saint Jean de la Croix et le problème de l'expérience mystique.* Paris, 1924.

Bejan, Teresa. *Mere Civility: Disagreement and the Limits of Toleration.* Cambridge, Mass., 2017.

Bell, Catherine. *Ritual Theory, Ritual Practice.* Oxford, 1992.

Bell, David. *The Cult of the Nation in France: Inventing Nationalism, 1680–1800.* Cambridge, Mass., 2001.

Bellah, Robert. *Beyond Belief: Essays on Religion in a Post-Traditionalist World.* Berkeley, 1970.

Bentley, Jerry. *Humanists and Holy Writ: New Testament Scholarship in the Renaissance.* Princeton, 1983.

Berlin, Isaiah. *Vico and Herder: Two Studies in the History of Ideas.* New York, 1976.

Berlin, Isaiah. *The Crooked Timber of Humanity: Chapters in the History of Ideas.* Princeton, 2013.

Bilinkoff, Jodi. *The Avila of Saint Teresa: Religious Reform in a Sixteenth-Century City.* Ithaca, 1990.

Blackburn, Carole. *Harvest of Souls: The Jesuit Missions and Colonialism in North America, 1632–1650.* Montreal, 2000.

Bloom, Harold. *The Visionary Company.* Revised edition. Ithaca, 1971.

Blum, Paul. *Philosophy of Religion in the Renaissance.* Farnham, 2010.

Bogdan, Radu, ed. *Belief: Form, Content, Function.* Oxford, 1986.

Booth, Anthony. *Islamic Philosophy and the Ethics of Belief.* London, 2016.

Borghero, Carlo. *La Certezza e la Storia: Cartesianesimo, Pirronismo e Conoscenza Storica.* Milan, 1983.

Bossy, John. *Christianity in the West, 1400–1700.* Oxford, 1985.

Bouvier, Alban and Raphaël Künstler, eds. *Croire ou accepter? Analyses conceptuelles et études de cas.* Paris, 2016.

Bowie, Fiona. *The Anthropology of Religion.* Oxford, 2000.

Brady, Thomas. *German Histories in the Age of Reformations, 1400–1650.* Cambridge, 2009.

Brahami, Frédéric. "Montaigne et la politique." *Bulletin de la société des amis de Montaigne.* 8th series, no. 33–34 (2004): 15–37.

Bratman, Michael. "Practical Reasoning and Acceptance in a Context." *Mind* 101, no. 410 (1992): 1–15.

Brockey, Liam. *Journey to the East: The Jesuit Mission to China, 1579–1724.* Cambridge, Mass., 2009.

Brown, Alan. *The Metaphysical Society: Victorian Minds in Crisis, 1869–1880.* New York, 1947.

Buber, Martin. *Two Types of Faith.* Translated by Norman Goldhawk. New York, 1951.

Buckley, Michael. *At the Origins of Modern Atheism.* New Haven, 1987.

Buckley, Michael. *Denying and Disclosing God: The Ambiguous Progress of Modern Atheism.* New Haven, 2004.

Bullivant, Stephen and Michael Ruse, eds. *The Oxford Handbook of Atheism.* Oxford, 2013.

Bulman, William and Robert Ingram, eds. *God in the Enlightenment*. Oxford, 2016.

Burke, Peter. *Popular Culture in Early Modern Europe*. New York, 1978.

Burke, Peter. "Two Crises of Historical Consciousness." *Storia della Storiografia* 33 (1998): 3–16.

Burke, Peter. *A Social History of Knowledge from Gutenberg to Diderot*. Cambridge, 2000.

Burrus, Virginia. *"Begotten, Not Made": Conceiving Manhood in Late Antiquity*. Stanford, 2000.

Bynum, Caroline Walker. *Christian Materiality: An Essay on Religion in Late Medieval Europe*. New York, 2011.

Byrne, Edmund. *Probability and Opinion: A Study in the Medieval Presuppositions of Post-Medieval Theories of Probability*. The Hague, 1968.

Call, Michael. "Boxing Teresa: The Counter-Reformation and Bernini's Cornaro Chapel." *Woman's Art Journal* 18, no. 1 (1997): 34–9.

Cameron, Euan. *Enchanted Europe: Superstition, Reason, and Religion, 1250–1750*. Oxford, 2010.

Campbell, Mary Baine. "Gender, Colonialism, and the Queerness of Dreams: Seventeenth-Century Dreamwork." *JMEMS* 44, no. 1 (2014): 187–213.

Cardedal, Olegario González de and José Vicente Rodríguez Rodríguez, eds. *Actas del Congreso Internacional Sanjuanista*. Valladolid, 1993.

Carling, Alan, ed. *The Social Equality of Religion or Belief*. Basingstoke, 2016.

Carlisle, Steven and Gregory Simon. "Believing Selves: Negotiating Social and Psychological Experiences of Belief." *Ethos: Journal of the Society for Psychological Anthropology* 40, no. 3 (2012): 221–36.

Carravilla Parra, María Jesús. *Razón Mística: Aproximación Filosófica a la Obra de San Juan de la Cruz*. Madrid, 2002.

Carruthers, Peter. *The Architecture of the Mind: Massive Modularity and the Flexibility of Thought*. Oxford, 2006.

Carter, Karen. *Creating Catholics: Catechism and Primary Education in Early Modern France*. Notre Dame, 2011.

Catto, Michela. "Les deux voies des catéchismes: les controverses et l'endoctrinement." In Gigliola Fragnito and Alain Tallon, eds. *Hétérodoxies croisées: Catholicismes pluriel entre France et Italie, XVIe–XVIIe siècles*. Rome, 2015.

Cavaillé, Christian. *Montaigne et l'experience*. Paris, 2012.

Caygill, Howard. *Art of Judgment*. Oxford, 1989.

Chabot, Jacques. *Giambattista Vico: La Raison du Mythe*. Aix-en-Provence, 2005.

Chaunu, Pierre. *Histoire et foi: deux mille ans de plaidoyer pour la foi*. Paris, 1980.

Chen, Timothy, ed. *The Aim of Belief*. Oxford, 2013.

Clark, Stuart. *Thinking with Demons: The Idea of Witchcraft in Early Modern Europe*. Oxford, 1997.

Clark, Stuart. *Vanities of the Eye: Vision in Early Modern European Culture*. Oxford, 2007.

Cohen, Jeremy. *Friars and the Jews: The Evolution of Medieval Anti-Judaism*. Ithaca, 1982.

Cohen, L. Jonathan. "Belief and Acceptance." *Mind* 98, no. 391 (1989): 367–89.

Colish, Marcia. *The Mirror of Language: A Study in the Medieval Theory of Knowledge*. Revised edition. Lincoln, Nebraska, 1983.

Colish, Marcia. *Studies in Scholasticism*. Aldershot, 2006.

Conti, Brooke. *Confessions of Faith in Early Modern England*. Philadelphia, 2014.

Coolman, Boyd. *Knowing God by Experience: The Spiritual Senses in the Theology of William of Auxerre*. Washington, D.C., 2004.

Cuadro, Fernando Moreno. "Iconografía de los testigos de los procesos teresianos. A propósito de Adrian Collaert y la escenografía de la capilla Cornaro." *Archivo Español de Arte* 87, no. 345 (2014): 29–44.

Cunningham, Andrew. "Getting the Game Right: Some Plain Words on the Identity and Invention of Science." *Studies in History and Philosophy of Science* 19 (1988): 365–89.

Daniel, Stephen. *John Toland: His Methods, Manners, and Mind*. Kingston, 1984.

Daniel, Stephen. "Myth and Rationality in Mandeville." *Journal of the History of Ideas* 47, no. 4 (October 1986): 595–611.

Daston, Lorraine. *Classical Probability in the Enlightenment*. Princeton, 1988.

Davies, Richard. *Descartes: Belief, Scepticism and Virtue*. London, 2001.

Dear, Peter. *Discipline and Experience: The Mathematical Way in the Scientific Revolution*. Chicago, 1995.

De Certeau, Michel. "Une pratique sociale de la différence: croire." In *Faire Croire: Modalités de la diffusion et de la réception des messages religieux du XIIe au XVe siècles, Publications de l'École française de Rome* 51, no. 1 (1981): 363–83.

De Certeau, Michel. *The Mystic Fable, Volume 1: The Sixteenth and Seventeenth Centuries*. Translated by Michael Smith. Chicago, 1992.

Della Rocca, Michael. *Spinoza*. London, 2008.

Delumeau, Jean. *Catholicism between Luther and Voltaire: A New View of the Counter-Reformation*. London, 1977.

Delumeau, Jean. *Le Mystère Campanella*. Paris, 2008.

Denery, Dallas. *The Devil Wins: A History of Lying from the Garden of Eden to the Enlightenment*. Princeton, 2015.

Denery, Dallas, Kantik Ghosh, and Nicolette Zeeman, eds. *Uncertain Knowledge: Scepticism, Relativism, and Doubt in the Middle Ages*. Turnhout, Belgium, 2014.

Deppermann, Klaus. *Melchior Hoffmanm: Social Unrest and Apocalyptic Visions in the Age of Reformation*. Trans. Malcolm Wren. Edinburgh, 1987.

Deslandres, Dominique. *Croire et Faire Croire: Les Missions Françaises au XVIIe Siècle*. Paris, 2003.

Diefendorf, Barbara. *Beneath the Cross: Catholics and Huguenots in Sixteenth-Century Paris*. New York, 1991.

Dixon, Leif. "William Perkins, 'Atheisme,' and the Crises of England's Long Reformation." *Journal of British Studies* 50, no. 4 (2011): 790–812.

Dole, Andrew and Andrew Chignell, eds. *God and the Ethics of Belief: New Essays in Philosophy of Religion*. Cambridge, 2005.

Dooley, Brendan. *The Social History of Skepticism: Experience and Doubt in Early Modern Culture*. Baltimore, 1999.

Dougherty, Trent ed. *Evidentialism and Its Discontents*. Oxford, 2011.

Dowey, Edward. *The Knowledge of God in Calvin's Theology*. Expanded edition. Grand Rapids, 1994.

Drachmann, A. B. *Atheism in Pagan Antiquity*. London, 1922.

Dulles, Avery. *A History of Apologetics*. New York, 1971.

Dynamics of Belief and Experience. A special issue of *Ethos: Journal of the Society for Psychological Anthropology* 40, no. 3 (2012).

Engel, Pascal, ed. *Believing and Acceptance*. Dordrecht, 2000.

Erdozain, Dominic. *The Soul of Doubt: The Religious Roots of Unbelief from Luther to Marx*. New York, 2016.

Ernst, Germana. *Tommaso Campanella: The Book and the Body of Nature*. Translated by David Marshall. Dordrecht, 2010.

Eusterschulte, Anne. "Pierre Bayle's *Dictionaire historique et critique*: Historical Criticism and Impartiality of Judgment." In Kathryn Murphy and Anita Traninger, eds. *The Emergence of Impartiality*. Leiden, 2014.

Evans, G. R. *Getting It Wrong: The Medieval Epistemology of Error*. Leiden, 1998.

Evrigenis, Ioannis. *Images of Anarchy: The Rhetoric and Science in Hobbes's State of Nature*. Cambridge, 2014.

Farge, Arlette. *Subversive Words: Public Opinion in Eighteenth-Century France*. Translated by Rosemary Morris. University Park, Penn., 1995.

Farmer, Julia. "'You Need but Go to Rome': Teresa of Avila and the Text/Image Power Play." *Women's Studies* 42 (2013): 390–407.

Febvre, Lucien. *The Problem of Unbelief in the Sixteenth Century: The Religion of Rabelais*. Translated by Beatrice Gottlieb. Cambridge, Mass., 1982.

Feingold, Mordechai, ed. *Before Newton: The Life and Times of Isaac Barrow*. Cambridge, 1990.

Flood, John. "The Book in Reformation Germany." In Jean-François Gilmont, ed. *The Reformation and the Book*. Translated by Karin Maag. Aldershot, 1998.

Foucault, Michel. *The Order of Things: An Archaeology of the Human Sciences*. New York, 1994.

Fox, Christopher, Roy Porter, and Robert Wolker, eds. *Inventing Human Science: Eighteenth-Century Domains*. Berkeley, 1995.

Fraenkel, Carlos. "Spinoza on Miracles and the Truth of the Bible." *Journal of the History of Ideas* 74, no. 4 (2013): 643–58.

Franklin, Julian. *Jean Bodin and the Sixteenth-Century Revolution in the Methodology of Law and History*. Westport, 1977.

Frede, Michael. *A Free Will: Origins of the Notion in Ancient Thought*. Edited by A. A. Long. Berkeley, 2011.

Frevert, Ute. *Emotions in History: Lost and Found*. Budapest, 2011.

Frevert, Ute, et al. *Emotional Lexicons: Continuity and Change in the Vocabulary of Feeling 1700–2000*. Oxford, 2014.

Friant, Emmanuelle. "'Ils aiment bien leur chapelet': le discours jésuite sur la transmission du religieux aux Hurons par l'objet d piété (1634–1649)." *Etudes d'Histoire Religieuse* 77 (2011): 7–20.

Funkenstein, Amos. *Theology and the Scientific Imagination from the Middle Ages to the Seventeenth Century*. Princeton, 1986.

Garber, Daniel. "Superheroes in the History of Philosophy: Spinoza, Super-Rationalist." *Journal of the History of Philosophy* 53, no. 3 (2015): 507–21.

Garrett, Aaron, ed. *The Routledge Companion to Eighteenth-Century Philosophy*. Abingdon, 2014.

Gatti, Hilary. *The Renaissance Drama of Knowledge*. London, 1989.

Gatti, Hilary. *Giordano Bruno and Renaissance Science*. Ithaca, 1999.

Gibbons, John. *The Norm of Belief*. Oxford, 2013.

Giddens, Anthony. *The Consequences of Modernity*. Stanford, 1990.

Giglioni, Guido. "Healing and Belief in Tommaso Campanella's Philosophy." *Intellectual History Review* 17, no. 3 (2007): 225–38.

Gil, Carlos Andrés. *La experiencia poética y la experiencia mística en la poesía de San Juan de la Cruz*. Potomac, 2004.

Gill, Meredith. *Augustine in the Italian Renaissance: Art and Philosophy from Petrarch to Michelangelo*. Cambridge, 2005.

Gillespie, Michael. *The Theological Origins of Modernity*. Chicago, 2008.

Ginzburg, Carlo. *The Night Battles: Witchcraft and Agrarian Cults in the Sixteenth and Seventeenth Centuries*. Translated by John and Anne Tedeschi. Baltimore, 1983.

Ginzburg, Carlo. *Myths, Emblems, Clues*. Translated by John and Anne Tedeschi. London, 1990.

Ginzburg, Carlo. *The Cheese and the Worms: The Cosmos of a Sixteenth-Century Miller*. Translated by John and Anne Tedeschi. Baltimore, 1991.

Gleason, Elizabeth. *Gasparo Contarini: Venice, Rome, and Reform*. Berkeley, 1993.

Goldsmith, M. M. "Regulating Anew the Moral and Political Sentiments of Mankind: Bernard Mandeville and the Scottish Enlightenment." *Journal of the History of Ideas* 49, no. 4 (1988), 587–606.

Good, Byron. *Medicine, Rationality, and Experience: An Anthropological Perspective*. Cambridge, 1994.

Gordon, Bruce. *Calvin*. New Haven, 2009.

Gorski, Philip. *The Disciplinary Revolution: Calvinism and the Rise of the State in Early Modern Europe*. Chicago, 2003.

Grafton, Anthony. *Joseph Scaliger: A Study in the History of Classical Scholarship*. Oxford, 2 vols., 1983–93.

Grafton, Anthony. *Forgers and Critics: Creativity and Duplicity in Western Scholarship*. Princeton, 1990.

Grafton, Anthony. *What Was History? The Art of History in Early Modern Europe*. Cambridge, 2007.

Green, Ian. *The Christian's ABC: Catechisms and Catechizing in England c.1530–1740.* New York, 1996.

Green, Mitchell and John Williams, eds. *Moore's Paradox: New Essays on Belief, Rationality, and the First Person.* Oxford, 2007.

Green, Richard. *A Crisis of Truth: Literature and Law in Ricardian England.* Philadelphia, 1999.

Greene, Virginie. *Logical Fictions in Medieval Literature and Philosophy.* Cambridge, 2014.

Gregory, Brad. *The Unintended Reformation: How a Religious Revolution Secularized Society.* Cambridge, Mass., 2012.

Grimaldi, William M. "A Note on the Pisteis in Aristotle's *Rhetoric*, 1354–1356." *American Journal of Philology* 78 (1957): 188–92.

Grimaldi, William. *Aristotle, Rhetoric I: A Commentary.* New York, 1980.

Groebner, Valentin. *Who Are You? Identification, Deception, and Surveillance in Early Modern Europe.* Translated by Mark Kyburz and John Peck. New York, 2007.

Guakroger, Stephen. *The Emergence of a Scientific Culture: Science and the Shaping of Modernity 1210–1685.* Oxford, 2006.

Guakroger, Stephen. "The Early Modern Idea of Scientific Doctrine and Its Early Christian Origins." *JMEMS* 44, no. 1 (2014): 95–112.

Guicciardini, Niccolò. *Isaac Newton on Mathematical Certainty and Method.* Cambridge, Mass., 2009.

Guillebaud, Jean-Claude. *La force de conviction: à quoi pouvons-nous croire?* Paris, 2005.

Gusdorf, Georges. *Les sciences humaines et la pensée occidentale.* Paris, 13 vols., 1966–88.

Guyer, Paul, ed. *The Cambridge Companion to Kant.* Cambridge, 1992.

Guyer, Paul. *Kant and the Claims of Taste.* Second edition. Cambridge, 1997.

Habermas, Jürgen. *The Structural Transformation of the Public Sphere: An Inquiry into a Category of Bourgeois Society.* Translated by Thomas Burger with Frederick Lawrence. Cambridge, Mass., 1991.

Hacking, Ian. *The Emergence of Probability: A Philosophical Study of Early Ideas about Probability, Induction and Statistical Inference.* London, 1975.

Hamm, Berndt. *The Reformation of Faith in the Context of Late Medieval Theology and Piety.* Edited by Robert Bast. Leiden, 2004.

Hampson, Daphne. *Christian Contradictions: The Structures of Lutheran and Catholic Thought.* Cambridge, 2001.

Harris, Steven. "Transposing the Merton Thesis: Apostolic Spirituality and the Establishment of the Jesuit Scientific Tradition." *Science in Context* 3, no. 1 (1989): 29–65.

Harrison, Peter. *The Bible, Protestantism, and the Rise of Natural Science.* Cambridge, 1998.

Harrison, Peter. *The Fall of Man and the Foundations of Science.* Cambridge, 2007.

Harrison, Peter, ed. *The Cambridge Companion to Science and Religion.* Cambridge, 2010.

Harrison, Peter. *The Territories of Science and Religion.* Chicago, 2015.

Harvey, Warren Zev. "Spinoza on Biblical Miracles." *Journal of the History of Ideas* 74, no. 4 (2013): 659–675.

Hatfield, Gary. "Reason, Nature, and God in Descartes." *Science in Context* 3, no. 1 (1989): 175–201.

Headley, John. "Tommaso Campanella and the End of the Renaissance." *Journal of Medieval and Renaissance Studies* 20, no. 2 (1990): 157–74.

Headley, John. *Tommaso Campanella and the Transformation of the World.* Princeton, 1997.

Heal, Bridget and Anorthe Kremers, eds. *Radicalism and Dissent in the World of Protestant Reform.* Göttingen, 2017.

Heering, J. P. *Hugo Grotius as Apologist for the Christian Religion: A Study of His Work "De veritate religionis christianae" (1640).* Leiden, 2004.

Hegel, G.W.F. *Elements of the Philosophy of Right.* Edited by Allen Wood. Translated by H. B. Nisbet. Cambridge, 1991.

Heinemann, F. H. "Truths of Reason and Truths of Fact." *Philosophical Review* 57, no. 5 (1948): 458–80.

Heitsch, Dorothea. *Practicing Reform in Montaigne's "Essais."* Leiden, 2000.

Helm, Paul. *Belief Policies.* Cambridge, 1994.

Hill, Christopher. *A Turbulent, Seditious and Factious People: John Bunyan and His Church.* London, 1988.

Hill, Kat. *Baptism, Brotherhood, and Belief in Reformation Germany: Anabaptism and Lutheranism, 1525–1585.* Oxford, 2015.

Hodgen, Margaret. *Early Anthropology in the Sixteenth and Seventeenth Centuries.* Philadelphia, 1964.

Hoekstra, Kinch. "Hobbesian Equality." In S. A. Lloyd, ed. *Hobbes Today: Insights for the 21st Century.* Cambridge, 2012.

Hoffmann, Georg. *Die Lehre von der Fides Implicita innerhalb der Katholischen Kirche.* Leipzig, 1903.

Hoffmann, George. "Atheism as a Devotional Category." *Republic of Letters* 1, no. 2 (2010): 44–55.

Höpfl, Harro. *Jesuit Political Thought: The Society of Jesus and the State, c.1540–1630.* Cambridge, 2004.

Hsia, Florence. *Sojourners in a Strange Land: Jesuits and the Scientific Missions in Late Imperial China.* Chicago, 2009.

Hsia, Ronnie Po-Chia. *The World of Catholic Renewal.* Cambridge, 1998.

Hsia, Ronnie Po-Chia. *A Jesuit in the Forbidden City: Matteo Ricci 1552–1610.* Oxford, 2010.

Hudson, Elizabeth. "An Identification of a Controversial English Publication of Castellio's 'De fide.'" *Harvard Theological Review* 69, no. 1/2 (1976): 197–206.

Hufton, Olwen. "Every Tub on Its Own Bottom: Funding a Jesuit College in Early Modern Europe." In John O'Malley et al., eds. *The Jesuits II: Cultures, Sciences, and the Arts, 1540–1773.* Toronto, 2006.

Hughes, Sean. "The Problem of 'Calvinism': English Theologies of Predestination, c.1580–1630." In Susan Wabuda and Caroline Litzenberger, eds. *Belief and*

Practice in Reformation England: A Tribute to Patrick Collinson from his Students. Aldershot, 1998.

Hummel, Pascale, ed. *Doxa: etudes sur les forms et la construction de la croyance*. Paris, 2010.

Hundert, E. J. *The Enlightenment's Fable: Bernard Mandeville and the Discovery of Society*. Cambridge, 1994.

Hunt, Lynn, Margaret Jacob, and Wijnand Mijnhardt. *The Book that Changed Europe: Picart and Bernard's Religious Ceremonies of the World*. Cambridge, Mass., 2010.

Hunter, David, ed. *Belief and Agency*. Calgary, 2009.

Hunter, Michael. "The Problem of 'Atheism' in Early Modern England." *TRHS*, 5th series, 35 (1985): 135–57.

Hunter, Michael. *Science and the Shape of Orthodoxy: Intellectual Change in Late Seventeenth-Century Britain*. Woodbridge, 1995.

Hunter, Michael. *Boyle: Between God and Science*. New Haven, 2009.

Hunter, Michael and David Wooton, eds. *Atheism from the Reformation to the Enlightenment*. Oxford, 1992.

Hyland, William. "John-Jerome of Prague and the Religion of the Saracens." In John Tolan, ed. *Medieval Christian Perceptions of Islam*. New York, 1996.

Iogna-Prat, Dominique. *Order and Exclusion: Cluny and Christendom Face Heresy, Judaism, and Islam (1000–1150)*. Translated by Graham Edwards. Ithaca, 2012.

Irwin, Kristen. "The Core Mysteries: Pierre Bayle's Philosophical Fideism." University of California, San Diego, Ph.D. Dissertation, 2010.

Israel, Jonathan. *Radical Enlightenment: Philosophy and the Making of Modernity 1650–1750*. Oxford, 2001.

Israel, Jonathan. *Enlightenment Contested: Philosophy, Modernity, and the Emancipation of Man, 1670–1752*. Oxford, 2006.

Jacob, Margaret. *The Newtonians and the English Revolution 1689–1720*. Ithaca, 1976.

Jasper, David, ed. *The Interpretation of Belief: Coleridge, Schleiermacher and Romanticism*. Basingstoke, 1986.

Jemolo, Arturo. *Il giansenismo in Italia prima della rivoluzione*. Bari, 1928.

Justice, Steven. "Did the Middle Ages Believe in Their Miracles?" *Representations* 103 (2008): 1–29.

Justice, Steven. "Eucharistic Miracle and Eucharistic Doubt." *JMEMS* 42, no. 2 (2012): 307–32.

Kahn, Victoria. *Wayward Contracts: The Crisis of Political Obligation in England, 1640–1674*. Princeton, 2004.

Kamen, Henry. *The Phoenix and the Flame: Catalonia and the Counter Reformation*. New Haven, 1993.

Kaplan, Benjamin. *Divided by Faith: Religious Conflict and the Practice of Toleration in Early Modern Europe*. Cambridge, Mass., 2007.

Karant-Nunn, Susan. *The Reformation of Feeling: Shaping the Religious Emotions in Early Modern Germany*. Oxford, 2010.

Kavanaugh, Kieran. *John of the Cross: Doctor of Light and Love*. London, 2000.

Keane, Webb. *Christian Moderns: Freedom and Fetish in the Mission Encounter*. Berkeley, 2007.

Kelley, Donald. "*Historia Integra*: François Baudouin and His Conception of History." *Journal of the History of Ideas* 25 (1964): 35–57.

Kelley, Donald. "*Fides historiae*: Charles Dumoulin and the Gallican View of History." *Traditio* 22 (1966): 347–402.

Kelley, Donald. *Foundations of Modern Historical Scholarship: Language, Law, and History in the French Renaissance*. New York, 1970.

Kelley, Donald. "Humanism and History." In Albert Rabil, ed. *Renaissance Humanism*. Philadelphia, 1988.

Kelley, Donald. "The Theory of History." In Charles Schmitt and Quentin Skinner, eds. *The Cambridge History of Renaissance Philosophy*. Cambridge, 1988.

Kellner, Menachem. *Dogma in Medieval Jewish Thought: From Maimonides to Abravanel*. Oxford, 1986.

Kempshall, Matthew. *Rhetoric and the Writing of History, 400–1500*. Manchester, 2011.

Kingsbury, Benedict and Benjamin Straumann. "The State of Nature and Commercial Sociability in Early Modern International Legal Thought." *Grotiana* 21 (2010): 22–43.

Kinneavy, James. *Greek Rhetorical Origins of Christian Faith*. New York, 1987.

Kirsch, Thomas. "Restaging the Will to Believe: Religious Pluralism, Anti-Syncretism, and the Problem of Belief." *American Anthropologist* 106, no. 4 (2004): 699–709.

Klepper, Deeana. *The Insight of Unbelievers: Nicholas of Lyra and Christian Reading of Jewish Text in the Later Middle Ages*. Philadelphia, 2008.

Kors, Alan. *Atheism in France, 1650–1729, Volume I: The Orthodox Sources of Disbelief*. Princeton, 1990.

Kors, Alan. *Epicureans and Atheists in France, 1650–1729*. Cambridge, 2016.

Kors, Alan. *Naturalism and Unbelief in France, 1650–1729*. Cambridge, 2016.

Koselleck, Reinhart. *Critique and Crisis: Enlightenment and the Pathogenesis of Modern Society*. Cambridge, Mass., 1988.

Kroon, Marijn de. *We Believe in God and Christ. Not in the Church: The Influence of Wessel Gansfort on Martin Bucer*. Translated by Maria Sherwood Smith. Louisville, 2009.

Kusukawa, Sachiko. *The Transformation of Natural Philosophy: The Case of Philip Melanchthon*. Cambridge, 1995.

Kyburg, Henry. *Probability and the Logic of Rational Belief*. Middletown, 1961.

Labrousse, Elizabeth. *Pierre Bayle*. La Haye, 2 vols., 1963–64.

Labrousse, Elizabeth. *Bayle*. Translated by Denys Potts. Oxford, 1983.

Labrousse, Elizabeth. *Conscience et conviction: études sur le XVIIe siècle*. Paris, 1996.

Lagerlund, Henrik, ed. *Rethinking the History of Skepticism: The Missing Medieval Background*. Leiden, 2010.

Lakoff, George and Mark Johnson. *Philosophy in the Flesh: The Embodied Mind and Its Challenge to Western Thought.* New York, 1999.

Langer, Ullrich, ed. *The Cambridge Companion to Montaigne.* Cambridge, 2005.

Lanoë, Catherine. *La Pudre et le fard: une historie des cosmétiques de la Renaissance aux Lumières.* Seyssel, 2008.

Laplanche, François. *L'évidence du Dieu chrétien: religion, culture et société dans l'apologétique protestante de la France classique, 1576–1670.* Strasbourg, 1983.

Laqueur, Thomas. *Making Sex: Body and Gender from the Greeks to Freud.* Cambridge, Mass., 1990.

Larsen, Timothy. *The Slain God: Anthropologists and the Christian Faith.* Oxford, 2014.

Latour, Bruno. *On the Modern Cult of the Factish Gods.* Durham, 2010.

Laursen, John and Cary Nederman, eds. *Beyond the Persecuting Society: Religious Toleration before the Enlightenment.* Philadelphia, 1998.

Leavelle, Trace. *The Catholic Calumet: Colonial Conversions in French and Indian North America.* Philadelphia, 2012.

LeBuffe, Michael. "The Doctrine of the Two Kingdoms: Miracles, Monotheism, and Reason in Spinoza." *British Journal for the History of Philosophy* 23, no. 2 (2015): 318–32.

Leeuwen, Henry van. *The Problem of Certainty in English Thought 1630–1690.* The Hague, 1963.

Leeuwen, Marius van, Keith Stanglin, and Marijke Tolsma, eds. *Arminius, Arminianism, and Europe: Jacobus Arminius (1559/60–1609).* Leiden, 2009.

Jacques le Fèvre, *Iuste complaincte de l'Eglise Catholique et Romaine, sur la confession et protestation des simulez fideles.* Paris, 1562.

Levey, Samuel. "Archimedes, Infinitesimals, and the Law of Continuity: On Leibniz's Fictionalism." In Ursula Goldenbaum and Douglas Jesseph, eds. *Infinitesimal Differences: Controversies between Leibniz and his Contemporaries.* Berlin, 2008.

Levine, Joseph. "From Tradition to History: Chillingworth to Gibbon." In Anthony Grafton and J.H.M. Salmon, eds. *Historians and Idealogues: Essays in Honor of Donald R. Kelley.* Rochester, 2001.

Levine, Joseph. "Matters of Fact in the English Revolution." *Journal of the History of Ideas* 64, no. 2 (2003): 317–35.

Ligota, Christopher. "Annius of Viterbo and Historical Method." *Journal of the Warburg and Courtauld Institutes* 50 (1987): 44–56.

Lilla, Mark. *G. B. Vico: The Making of an Anti-Modern.* Cambridge, Mass., 1993.

Lilla, Mark. *The Stillborn God: Religion, Politics, and the Modern West.* New York, 2007.

Lim, Paul. *Mystery Unveiled: The Crisis of the Trinity in Early Modern England.* Oxford, 2012.

Lindbeck, George. *The Nature of Doctrine: Religion and Theology in a Postliberal Age.* Louisville, 1984.

Lindholm, Charles. "What Is Bread? The Anthropology of Belief." *Ethos: Journal of the Society for Psychological Anthropology* 40, no. 3 (2012): 342–57.

Lindquist, Galina and Simon Coleman. "Introduction: Against Belief?" *Social Analysis* 52, no. 1 (2008): 1–18.

Lojkine, Stéphane. "Polemics as a World." Unpublished lecture at Tel Aviv University. Online at http://utpictura18.univ-montp3.fr/Dispositifs/Polemics.php.

Lopenza, Drew. "Le Jeune Dreams of Moose." *Early American Studies* 13, no. 1 (2015): 3–37.

Lopez, Donald. "Belief." In *Critical Terms for Religious Studies*. Edited by Mark Taylor. Chicago, 1998.

Lubac, Henri de. *The Christian Faith: An Essay on the Structure of the Apostles' Creed*. Translated by Richard Arnandez. San Francisco, 1969.

Lugt, Mara van der. *Bayle, Jurieu, and the Dictionaire Historique et Critique*. Oxford, 2016.

Lyon, Gregory. "Baudouin, Flacius, and the Plan for the Magdeburg Centuries." *Journal of the History of Ideas* 64, no. 2 (2003): 253–72.

MacCormack, Sabine. *Religion in the Andes: Vision and Imagination in Early Colonial Peru*. Princeton, 1991.

MacIntyre, Alasdair. *After Virtue: A Study in Moral Theory*. Third edition. Notre Dame, 2007.

Madigan, Timothy. *W. K. Clifford and "The Ethics of Belief."* Newcastle, 2009.

Mahmood, Saba. *Politics of Piety: The Islamic Revival and the Feminist Subject*. Princeton, 2005.

Mair, Jonathan. "Cultures of Belief." *Anthropological Theory* 12, no. 4 (2013): 448–66.

Malcolm, Noel. *Aspects of Hobbes*. Oxford, 2002.

Mancosu, Paolo. *Philosophy of Mathematics and Mathematical Practice in the Seventeenth Century*. Oxford, 1996.

Manuel, Frank. *The Eighteenth Century Confronts the Gods*. Cambridge, Mass., 1959.

March, Andrew. "Speech and the Sacred: Does the Defense of Free Speech Rest on a Mistake about Religion?" *Political Theory* 40, no. 3 (2012): 319–46.

Marno, David. *Death Be Not Proud: The Art of Holy Attention*. Chicago, 2016.

Marrama, Oberto. "Spinoza on Fictitious Ideas and Possible Entities." *European Legacy* 21, no. 4 (2016): 359–72.

Marrone, Steven. *A History of Science, Magic and Belief: From Medieval to Early Modern Europe*. London, 2015.

Marrou, Henri-Irénée. "Saint Augustin et l'ange. Une légende medieval." In his *Christiana tempora: Mélanges d'histoire, d'archéologie, d'épigraphie et de patristique*. Rome, 1978.

Marshall David. "The Current State of Vico Scholarship." *Journal of the History of Ideas* 72, no. 1 (2011): 141–60.

McCain, Kevin. *Evidentialism and Epistemic Justification*. New York, 2014.

McClenon, R. B. "A Contribution of Leibniz to the History of Complex Numbers." *American Mathematical Monthly* 30 (1930): 369–74.

McCormick, Miriam. *Believing Against the Evidence: Agency and the Ethics of Belief*. New York, 2015.

McEachern, Claire. *Believing in Shakespeare: Studies in Longing.* Cambridge, 2018.

McGhee, Patrick. "Unbelief and the Senses in Early Stuart Protestantism." Cambridge University M.A. Thesis, 2015.

McGinn, Bernard. *The Foundations of Mysticism.* New York, 1991.

McGrade, Arthur. *The Political Thought of William of Ockham: Personal and Institutional Principles.* London, 1974.

Meeker, Kevin. *Hume's Radical Scepticism and the Fate of Naturalized Epistemology.* Basingstoke, 2013.

Melquiades, Andrés. *San Juan de la Cruz: Maestro de la espiritualidad.* Madrid, 1996.

Menin, Marco. "'Who Will Write the History of Tears?' History of Ideas and History of Emotions from Eighteenth-Century France to the Present." *History of European Ideas* 40, no. 4 (2014): 516–32.

Ménissier, Thierry. "L'autorité dans les *Essais* de Montaigne: nature et limite de la relation d'obéissance." In Pierre Magnard and Thierry Gontier, eds. *Montaigne.* Paris, 2010.

Merkle, Benjamin. *Defending the Trinity in the Reformed Palatinate: The Elohistae.* Oxford, 2015.

Merton, Robert. *Science, Technology and Society in Seventeenth-Century England.* New York, 1970.

Milbank, John. *Theology and Social Theory: Beyond Secular Reason.* Oxford, 1990.

Milbank, John. *Beyond the Secular Order: The Representation of Being and the Representation of People.* Oxford, 2014.

Minamiki, George. *The Chinese Rites Controversy: From Its Beginning to Modern Times.* Chicago, 1985.

Minois, Georges. *Histoire de l'athéisme: les incroyants dans le monde occidental des origines à nos jours.* Paris, 1998.

Mitchell, Jon and Hildi Mitchell. "For Belief: Embodiment and Immanence in Catholicism and Mormonism." *Social Analysis* 52, no. 1 (2008): 79–94.

Momigliano, Arnaldo. "La formazione della moderna storiografia sull'impero romano." In his *Contributo alla Storia degli Studi Classici.* Rome, 1979.

Moore, R. I. *The Formation of a Persecuting Society.* Malden, Mass., 1987.

Moreau, Denis. *Deux Cartesiens: la polemique entre Antoine Arnauld et Nicolas Malebranche.* Paris, 1999.

Morgan, Teresa. *Roman Faith and Christian Faith: Pistis and Fides in the Early Roman Empire and Early Churches.* Oxford, 2015.

Mori, Gianluca. *Bayle: Philosophe.* Paris, 1999.

Mortimer, Sarah. *Reason and Religion in the English Revolution: The Challenge of Socinianism.* Cambridge, 2010.

Moss, Jean Dietz and William Wallace. *Rhetoric and Dialectic in the Time of Galileo.* Washington, D.C., 2003.

Most, Glenn. *Doubting Thomas.* Cambridge, Mass., 2005.

Mukherji, Subha. "Trying, Knowing and Believing: Epistemic Plots and the Poetics of Doubt." In Yota Batsaki, Subha Mukherji, and Jan-Melissa Schramm, eds. *Fictions of Knowledge: Fact, Evidence, Doubt*. New York, 2012.

Muldrew, Craig. *The Economy of Obligation: The Culture of Credit and Social Relations in Early Modern England*. New York, 1998.

Muller, Richard. "The Federal Motif in Seventeenth-Century Arminian Theology." *Dutch Review of Church History* 62, no. 1 (1982): 102–22.

Muller, Richard. "Fides and Cognitio in Relation to the Problem of Intellect and Will in the Theology of John Calvin." *Calvin Theological Journal* 25, no. 2 (1990): 207–24.

Muller, Richard. *God, Creation, and Providence in the Thought of Jacob Arminius*. Grand Rapids, 1991.

Muller, Richard. "The Priority of the Intellect in the Soteriology of Jacob Arminius." *Westminster Theological Journal* 55, no. 1 (1993): 55–72.

Muller, Richard. *The Unaccommodated Calvin: Studies in the Foundation of a Theological Tradition*. Oxford, 2002.

Mulsow, Martin. *Enlightenment Underground: Radical Germany, 1680–1720*. Translated by H. C. Erik Midelfort. Charlottesville, 2015.

Mulsow, Martin and Jan Rohls, eds. *Socinianism and Arminianism: Antitrinitarianism, Calvinists and Cultural Exchange in Seventeenth-Century Europe*. Leiden, 2005.

Nadler, Steven. *Arnauld and the Cartesian Philosophy of Ideas*. Manchester, 1989.

Nadler, Steven. *Malebranche and Ideas*. Stanford, 1992.

Nadler, Steven. *A Book Forged in Hell: Spinoza's Scandalous Treatise and the Birth of the Secular Age*. Princeton, 2011.

Nadler, Steven. "Scripture and Truth: A Problem in Spinoza's 'Tractatus Theologico-Politicus.'" *Journal of the History of Ideas* 74, no. 4 (2013): 623–42.

Needham, Rodney. *Belief, Language, and Experience*. Chicago, 1972.

Nellen, Henk and Edwin Rabbie, eds. *Hugo Grotius Theologian: Essays in Honour of G.H.M. Posthumus Meyjes*. Leiden, 1994.

Nelles, Paul. "Du savant au missionnaire: la doctrine, les moeurs et l'écriture de l'histoire chez les jésuites." *Dix-Septième Siècle* 59, no. 4 (2007): 669–89.

Niewöhner, Friedrich and Olaf Pluta, eds. *Atheismus im Mittelalter und in der Renaissance*. Wiesbaden, 1999.

Norbrook, David, Stephen Harrison, and Philip Hardie, eds. *Lucretius and the Early Modern*. Oxford, 2016.

Nottelmann, Nikolaj, ed. *New Essays on Belief: Constitution, Content, and Structure*. Basingstoke, 2013.

Nozick, Robert. *The Nature of Rationality*. Princeton, 1993.

Oberman, Heiko. "'Iustitia Christi' and 'Iustitia Dei': Luther and the Scholastic Doctrine of Justification." *Harvard Theological Review* 59, no. 1 (1966): 1–26.

Old, Hughes Oliphant. *The Reading and Preaching of the Scriptures in the Worship of the Christian Church, vol. 4: The Age of the Reformation*. Grand Rapids, 2002.

Outlon, J.E.L. "The Apostles' Creed and Belief Concerning the Church." *Journal of Theological Studies* (1938): 239–43.

Overall, M. A. "The Exploitation of Francesco Spiera." *SCJ* 26, no. 3 (1995): 619–37.

Pagden, Anthony. *The Fall of Natural Man: The American Indian and the Origins of Comparative Ethnology*. Cambridge, 1986.

Parret, Herman, ed. *On Believing: Epistemological and Semiotic Approaches / De la croyance: approches épistémologiques et sémiotiques*. Berlin, 1983.

Pasnau, Robert. *Theories of Cognition in the Later Middle Ages*. Cambridge, 1997.

Pasnau, Robert. "Medieval Social Epistemology: *Scientia* for Mere Mortals." *Episteme* 7, no. 1 (2010): 23–41.

Payne, Steven. *St. John of the Cross and the Cognitive Value of Mysticism*. Dordrecht, 1990.

Pelikan, Jaroslav. *Credo: Historical and Theological Guide to Creeds and Confessions of Faith in the Christian Tradition*. New Haven, 2003.

Penelhum, Terence. *God and Skepticism: A Study in Skepticism and Fideism*. Boston, 1983.

Perler, Dominik. *Zweifel und Gewissheit: Skeptische Debatten im Mittelalter*. Frankfurt, 2006.

Pettigrew, Richard. *Accuracy and the Laws of Credence*. Oxford, 2016.

Picciotto, Joanna. *Labors of Innocence in Early Modern England*. Cambridge, Mass., 2010.

Picciotto, Joanna. "Implicit Faith and Reformations of Habit." *JMEMS* 46, no. 3 (2016): 513–43.

Pitassi, Maria-Cristina. *Entre croire et savoir: le problème de la méthode critique chez Jean Le Clerc*. Leiden, 1987.

Pitkin, Barbara. *What Pure Eyes Could See: Calvin's Doctrine of Faith in Its Exegetical Context*. Oxford, 1999.

Plamper, Jan. *The History of Emotions: An Introduction*. Translated by Keith Tribe. Oxford, 2015.

Pocock, J.G.A. *Barbarism and Religion, Volume One: The Enlightenments of Edward Gibbon, 1737–1764*. Cambridge, 1999.

Pocock, J.G.A. *Barbarism and Religion, Volume Two: Narratives of Civil Government*. Cambridge, 1999.

Pocock, J.G.A. *Barbarism and Religion, Volume Five: Religion: The First Triumph*. Cambridge, 2010.

Poovey, Mary. *A History of the Modern Fact: Problems of Knowledge in the Sciences of Wealth and Society*. Chicago, 1998.

Popkin, Richard. *The History of Scepticism from Savonarola to Bayle*. Oxford, 2003.

Popper, Nicholas. "An Ocean of Lies: The Problem of Historical Evidence in the Sixteenth Century." *Huntington Library Quarterly* 74, no. 3 (2011): 375–400.

Popper, Nicholas. *Walter Raleigh's History of the World and the Historical Culture of the Late Renaissance*. Chicago, 2012.

Poska, Allyson. *Women and Authority in Early Modern Spain*. Oxford, 2005.

Pouillon, Jean. "Remarks on the Verb 'to Believe.'" Translated by John Leavitt. *HAU: Journal of Ethnographic Theory* 6, no. 3 (2016): 485–92. First published in French in 1979.

Price, H. H. *Belief: The Gifford Lectures Delivered at the University of Aberdeen in 1960*. New York, 1969.

Prieto, Andrés. *Missionary Scientists: Jesuit Science in Spanish South America, 1570–1810*. Nashville, 2011.

Quine, W. V. "Two Dogmas of Empiricism." *Philosophical Review* 60 (1951): 20–43.

Quine, W. V. "Epistemology Naturalized." In his *Ontological Relativity and Other Essays*. New York, 1969.

Quine, W. V. *From Stimulus to Science*. Cambridge, Mass., 1995.

Quinney, Laura. *William Blake on Self and Soul*. Cambridge, Mass., 2009.

Quint, David. *Montaigne and the Quality of Mercy: Ethical and Political Themes in the "Essais."* Princeton, 1998.

Radcliffe, Elizabeth, ed. *A Companion to Hume*. Malden, Mass., 2008.

Raeff, Marc. "The Well-Ordered Police State and the Development of Modernity in Seventeenth- and Eighteenth-Century Europe: An Attempt at a Comparative Approach." *American Historical Review* 80, no. 5 (1975): 1221–43.

Reddy, William. *The Navigation of Feeling: A Framework for the History of Emotions*. Cambridge, 2001.

Reeves, Andrew. "Teaching the Creed and Articles of Faith in England: Lateran IV to *Ignorantia Sacerdotum*." University of Toronto Ph.D. Dissertation, 2009.

Reisner, Andrew and Asbjørn Steglich-Petersen, eds. *Reasons for Belief*. Cambridge, 2011.

Remaud, Olivier. *Les archives de l'humanité: essai sur la philosophie de Vico*. Paris, 2004.

Reynard, Elisabeth. *Jean de la Croix, fou de Dieu*. Paris, 1999.

Ricoeur, Paul. "La problématique de la croyance: opinion, assentiment, foi." In Herman Parret, ed. *On Believing: Epistemological and Semiotic Approaches / De la croyance: approches épistémologiques et sémiotiques*. . Berlin, 1983.

Ritschl, Albrecht. *Fides Implicita: Eine Untersuchung über Köhlerglauben, Wissen und Glauben*. Bonn, 1890.

Robinson, Samuel. "Flesh Redeemed: Religious Materialism in Early Enlightenment Britain, 1640–1715." University of California, Berkeley Ph.D. dissertation, 2017.

Römer, Heinrich. *Die Entwicklung des Glaubensbegriffes bei Melanchthon nach dessen dogmatischen Schriften*. Bonn, 1902.

Roper, Lyndal. *The Holy Household: Women and Morals in Reformation Augsburg*. Oxford, 1989.

Ruel, Malcolm. *Belief, Ritual and the Securing of Life*. Leiden, 1997.

Ruler, Han van. "Minds, Forms, and Spirits: The Nature of Cartesian Disenchantment." *Journal of the History of Ideas* 61, no. 3 (2000): 381–95.

Russell, William and Timothy Lull, eds. *Martin Luther's Basic Theological Writings*, third edition. Minneapolis, 2012.

Ryrie, Alec. *Being Protestant in Reformation Britain*. Oxford, 2013.

Sangiacomo, Andrea. "Locke and Spinoza on the Epistemic and Motivational Weaknesses of Reason: The Reasonableness of Christianity and the Theological-Political Treatise." *Intellectual History Review* 26, no. 4 (2016): 477–95.

Schaeffer, John. "From Natural Religion to Natural Law in Vico: Rhetoric, Poetic, and Vico's Imaginative Universals." *Rhetorica* 15, no. 1 (1997): 41–51.

Schmitt, J. C. "Du bon usage du 'credo.'" In *Faire croire: modalités de la diffusion et de la réception des messages religieux du XIIe au XVe siècles, Publications de l'École française de Rome* 51, no. 1 (1981): 337–61.

Schneewind, J. B. *The Invention of Autonomy: A History of Modern Moral Philosophy*. Cambridge, 1998.

Scholder, Klaus. *The Birth of Modern Critical Theology: Origins and Problems of Biblical Criticism in the Seventeenth Century*. Translated by John Bowden. Philadelphia, 1990.

Schreiner, Susan. *Are You Alone Wise? The Search for Certainty in the Early Modern Era*. Oxford, 2011.

Schröder, Winfried. *Ursprünge des Atheismus: Untersuchungen zur Metaphysik- und Religionskritik des 17. und 18. Jahrhunderts*. Stuttgart, 1998.

Schultes, Reginald. *Fides Implicita: Geschichte der Lehre von der Fides Implicita und Explicita in der Katholischen Theologie*. Regensburg, 1920.

Schwartz, Stuart. *All Can Be Saved: Religious Tolerance and Salvation in the Iberian Atlantic World*. New Haven, 2009.

Schwickerath, Robert. *Jesuit Education*. St. Louis, 1903.

Scott, Tom. "Müntzer and the Mustard-Seed: A Parable as Paradox?" In his *The Early Reformation in Germany: Between Secular Impact and Radical Vision*. Farnham, 2013.

Serjeantson, Richard. "Testimony and Proof in Early Modern England." *Studies in the History and Philosophy of Science* 30, no. 2 (1999): 195–236.

Serjeantson, Richard. "Testimony: The Artless Proof." In Sylvia Adamson, Gavin Alexander, and Katrin Ettenhuber, eds. *Renaissance Figures of Speech*. Cambridge, 2007.

Serjeantson, Richard. "Proof and Persuasion." In *The Cambridge History of Science, Volume 3: Early Modern Science*. Edited by Katherine Park and Lorraine Daston. Cambridge, 2008.

Shagan, Ethan. *The Rule of Moderation: Violence, Religion and the Politics of Restraint in Early Modern England*. Cambridge, 2011.

Shagan, Ethan. "Taking Belief Seriously? An Early Modern Catholic Perspective." In Mark Jurdjevic and Rolf Strøm-Olsen, eds. *Rituals of Politics and Culture in Early Modern Europe: Essays in Honour of Edward Muir*. Toronto, 2016.

Shapin, Steven. *A Social History of Truth: Civility and Science in Seventeenth-Century England*. Chicago, 1994.

Shapin, Steven and Simon Schaffer. *Leviathan and the Air-Pump: Hobbes, Boyle, and the Experimental Life*. Princeton, 1985.

Shapiro, Barbara. *Probability and Certainty in Seventeenth-Century England: A Study in the Relationships between Natural Science, Religion, History, Law, and Literature*. Princeton, 1983.

Shapiro, Barbara. *A Culture of Fact: England, 1550–1720*. Ithaca, 2000.

Shaw, Jane. *Miracles in Enlightenment England*. New Haven, 2006.

Sheehan, Jonathan. *The Enlightenment Bible: Translation, Scholarship, Culture*. Princeton, 2005.

Sheehan, Jonathan and Dror Wahrman. *Invisible Hands: Self-Organization and the Eighteenth Century*. Chicago, 2015.

Shelford, April. "Thinking Geometrically in Pierre-Daniel Huet's *Demonstratio Evangelica* (1679)." *Journal of the History of Ideas* 63, no. 4 (2002): 599–617.

Shelford, April. *Transforming the Republic of Letters: Pierre-Daniel Huet and European Intellectual Life, 1650–1720*. Rochester, 2007.

Sheppard, Kenneth. *Anti-Atheism in Early Modern England 1580–1720*. Leiden, 2015.

Simpson, James. *Burning to Read: English Fundamentalism and Its Reformation Opponents*. Cambridge, Mass., 2007.

Skinner, Quentin. *Visions of Politics: Volume 3, Hobbes and Civil Science*. Cambridge, 2002.

Slade, Carole. *St. Teresa of Ávila: Author of a Heroic Life*. Berkeley, 1995.

Sluhovsky, Moshe. *Believe Not Every Spirit: Possession, Mysticism, and Discernment in Early Modern Catholicism*. Chicago, 2007.

Smilde, David. *Reason to Believe: Cultural Agency in Latin American Evangelicalism*. Berkeley, 2007.

Smith, Martin. *Between Probability and Certainty: What Justifies Belief*. Oxford, 2016.

Smith, Wilfred Cantwell. *Belief and History*. Charlottesville, 1977.

Smith, Wilfred Cantwell. *Faith and Belief*. Princeton, 1979.

Snook, Edith. "'The Beautifying Part of Physic': Women's Cosmetic Practices in Early Modern England." *Journal of Women's History* 20, no. 3 (2008): 10–33.

Sørensen, M.L.S. and Katharina Rebay-Salisbury, eds. *Embodied Knowledge: Historical Perspectives on Belief and Technology*. Oxford, 2013.

Springer, Martin. "Towards a Situation Theory of Belief." *Journal of the Anthropological Society of Oxford* 27 (1996): 217–34.

Stanglin, Keith. *Arminius on the Assurance of Salvation: The Context, Roots, and Shape of the Leiden Debate, 1603–1609*. Leiden, 2007.

Stanglin, Keith and Thomas McCall. *Jacob Arminius: Theologian of Grace*. Oxford, 2012.

Straumann, Benjamin. "'Ancient Caesarian Lawyers' in a State of Nature: Roman Tradition and Natural Rights in Hugo Grotius's *De iure praedae*." *Political Theory* 34, no. 3 (2006): 328–50.

Stroeken, Koen. "Believed Belief: Science/Religion versus Sukuma Magic." *Social Analysis* 52, no. 1 (2008): 144–65.

Strousma, Guy. *A New Science: The Discovery of Religion in the Age of Reason.* Cambridge, Mass., 2010.

Struever, Nancy. *Theory as Practice: Ethical Inquiry in the Renaissance.* Chicago, 1992.

Swearingen, C. Jan. "Pistis, Expression, and Belief: Prolegomenon for a Feminist Rhetoric of Motives." In Stephen White, Neil Nakadate, and Roger Cherry, eds. *A Rhetoric of Doing: Essays on Written Discourse in Honor of James L. Kinneavy.* Carbondale, 1992.

Swinburne, Richard. *Epistemic Justification.* Oxford, 2001.

Taylor, Charles. *A Secular Age.* Cambridge, Mass., 2007.

Taylor, Larissa, ed. *Preachers and People in the Reformations and Early Modern Period.* Leiden, 2001.

Teske, Roland. *Studies in the Philosophy of William of Auvergne.* Milwaukee, 2006.

Thompson, Colin. *The Poet and the Mystic: A Study of the 'Cántico espiritual' of San Juan de la Cruz.* Oxford, 1977.

Todd, Margo. *The Culture of Protestantism in Early Modern Scotland.* New Haven, 2002.

Tolan, John. *Saracens: Islam in the Medieval European Imagination.* New York, 2002.

Tolan, John. *L'Europe latine et le monde arabe au Moyen Âge.* Rennes, 2009.

Trigger, Bruce. *The Children of Aataentsic: A History of the Huron People to 1660.* Kingston, 1976.

True, Micah. *Masters and Students: Jesuit Mission Ethnography in Seventeenth-Century New France.* Montreal, 2015.

Tutino, Stefania. *Uncertainty in Post-Reformation Catholicism: A History of Probabilism.* Oxford, 2018.

Tyacke, Nicholas. *Anti-Calvinists: The Rise of English Arminianism, c.1590–1640.* Oxford, 1987.

Tyler, Peter. *St. John of the Cross.* New York, 2010.

Van Engen, John. "Faith as a Concept of Order in Medieval Christendom." In Thomas Kselman, ed. *Belief in History.* Notre Dame, 1991.

Vanhoozer, Kevin. *Biblical Authority after Babel: Retrieving the Solas in the Spirit of Mere Protestant Christianity.* Grand Rapids, 2016.

Veyne, Paul. *Did the Greeks Believe in Their Myths? An Essay on the Constitutive Imagination.* Translated by Paula Wissing. Chicago, 1988.

Vidal, Fernando. *The Sciences of the Soul: The Early Modern Origins of Psychology.* Translated by Saskia Brown. Chicago, 2011.

Vogt, Katja. *Belief and Truth: A Skeptic Reading of Plato.* Oxford, 2012.

Völkel, Markus. *"Pyrrhonismus Historicus" und "Fides Historica": Die Entwicklung der Deutschen Historischen Methodologie unter dem Gesichtspunkt der Historischen Skepsis.* Frankfurt, 1987.

Waddell, Mark. *Jesuit Science and the End of Nature's Secrets.* Farnham, 2015.

Waite, Gary. *David Joris and Dutch Anabaptism.* Waterloo, 1990.

Waite, Gary, ed. *The Anabaptist Writings of David Joris, 1535–1543*. Waterloo, 1994.

Wallace, Dewey. "Socinianism, Justification by Faith, and the Sources of John Locke's 'The Reasonableness of Christianity.'" *Journal of the History of Ideas* 45, no. 1 (1984): 49–66.

Walsham, Alexandra. "Wholesome Milk and Strong Meat: Peter Canisius's Catechisms and the Conversion of Protestant Britain." *British Catholic History* 32 (2015): 293–314.

Wandel, Lee Palmer. *Reading Catechisms, Teaching Religion*. Leiden, 2016.

Weber, Alison. *Teresa of Avila and the Rhetoric of Femininity*. Princeton, 1990.

Webster, Charles. *The Great Instauration*. London, 1975.

Wennerlind, Carl. *Casualties of Credit: The English Financial Revolution, 1620–1720*. Cambridge, Mass., 2011.

Williams, Bernard. *Problems of the Self*. Cambridge, 1973.

Williams, George. *The Radical Reformation*. Philadelphia, 1962.

Wilson, Nigel, ed. *Encyclopedia of Ancient Greece*. New York, 2006.

Wirth, Jean. "La naissance du concept de croyance (XIIe–XVIIe siècles)." *Bibliothèque d'Humanisme et Renaissance* 45, no. 1 (1983): 7–58.

Wolgast, Elizabeth. *Paradoxes of Knowledge*. Ithaca, 1977.

Wolterstorff, Nicholas. *John Locke and the Ethics of Belief*. Cambridge, 1996.

Wood, Allen. *Kant's Moral Religion*. Ithaca, 1970.

Wood, Sarah. *Conscience and the Composition of Piers Plowman*. Oxford, 2012.

Wootton, David. *Paolo Sarpi: Between Renaissance and Enlightenment*. Cambridge, 1983.

Wootton, David. "Lucien Febvre and the Problem of Unbelief in the Early Modern Period." *Journal of Modern History* 60 (1988): 695–730.

Worcester, Thomas. "A Defensive Discourse: Jesuits on Disease in Seventeenth-Century New France." *French Colonial History* 6 (2005): 1–15.

Younge, Frances. *The Making of the Creeds*. London, 1991.

Žižek, Slavoj. *On Belief*. London, 2001.

A NOTE ON THE TYPE

THIS BOOK has been composed in Miller, a Scotch Roman typeface designed by Matthew Carter and first released by Font Bureau in 1997. It resembles Monticello, the typeface developed for The Papers of Thomas Jefferson in the 1940s by C. H. Griffith and P. J. Conkwright and reinterpreted in digital form by Carter in 2003.

Pleasant Jefferson ("P. J.") Conkwright (1905–1986) was Typographer at Princeton University Press from 1939 to 1970. He was an acclaimed book designer and AIGA Medalist.

The ornament used throughout this book was designed by Pierre Simon Fournier (1712–1768) and was a favorite of Conkwright's, used in his design of the *Princeton University Library Chronicle*.

CPSIA information can be obtained
at www.ICGtesting.com
Printed in the USA
JSHW042100210421
13760JS00001B/3